Part of the Land,

A History
of the Yukon Indians

Part of the Water

Catharine McClellan

with Lucie Birckel, Robert Bringhurst, James A. Fall,
Carol McCarthy *and* Janice R. Sheppard

Douglas & McIntyre
Vancouver/Toronto

Douglas & McIntyre Ltd.
1615 Venables Street
Vancouver, British Columbia
V5L 2H1

Published with assistance from the
Council for Yukon Indians and the
Yukon Department of Education.

Designed by Robert Bringhurst. The
text is set in Meridien roman and italic
and the sidenotes in Frutiger. These
typefaces were designed by Adrian
Frutiger, Paris. The titling face is
Cartier, designed in Toronto by Carl
Dair. The book was set into type by The
Typeworks, Vancouver, and printed by
Everbest Printing, Hong Kong.

Several of the photographs appear
here courtesy of the Yukon Archives,
Whitehorse; the Yukon Government;
the Canadian Museum of Civilization,
Ottawa; the Alaska Historical Library,
Juneau; the Field Museum of Natural
History, Chicago; Frederica de Laguna;
Dorothy Rainier Libby, and John T.
Hitchcock. Most of the photos not
credited to other sources were taken
by Catharine McClellan.

The photo on the first page of this
book shows a drum from Teslin Lake,
made before 1911, and the photo on
the last page a pair of moccasins, also
from Teslin Lake, made before 1912.
These and the broken bone beamer
(drawknife) shown on page 2 are now
in the Canadian Museum of Civilization
(National Museums of Canada), Ottawa
(see page 119).

Canadian Cataloguing in Publication Data:

McClellan, Catharine, 1921–
    Part of the land, part of the water

    Includes index.
    ISBN 0-88894-553-1

1. Indians of North America – Yukon
    Territory.
2. Tlingit Indians.
3. Athapascan Indians.
4. Yukon Territory – Description and
    travel.
I. Birckel, Lucie.
II. Title.

E78.Y8M22 1987   971.9'100497
C87-091220-8

Contents

LIST OF MAPS

This book is the joint effort of the Council for Yukon Indians, the Yukon Department of Education, three anthropologists, one poet, and many Yukon Indian people. It is a history of the Yukon Indian people, written for and to a large extent told by Yukon Indian people themselves. For that very reason, it should be of value to many other readers as well. The book can be used in school classes or read at home.

Daniel Tlen, former head of the Council for Yukon Indians, and Paul Birckel, the Council's Executive Director, first planned the book in 1976 and asked for my help with the project. So in the summer of 1977, two Yukon Indians (Lucy Birckel and Carol McCarthy), two University of Wisconsin graduate students in anthropology (James Fall and Janice Sheppard) and I travelled through the Yukon asking the native people what they wanted to contribute to the book. In each community a contact person for the Council for Yukon Indians helped explain the project. Whatever the local Indians wanted to say was taped or written down, and if possible, pictures were taken of the narrators and of the village or fish camp where they were living. In this way we collected many stories of Yukon Indian life as it was in the past and as it is in the present.

These accounts usually tell about something that somebody had seen, done or heard about, and people often added their thoughts about the value of different experiences in their own lives or experiences retold from the lives of their ancestors. Sometimes they pointed out how these experiences could be guides for others.

One of these accounts was given by Virginia Smarch, a Yukon Indian woman from Teslin, who tells her story in Chapter Twelve. Virginia talked about how the oldtimers knew the habits of the land animals and the fish and how the people moved about the country with the seasons and "did not make a mess of it." Then she said, "That's why I don't hesitate to say an old native person is part of the land, part of the water. . . . "

That phrase, "part of the land, part of the water," says a lot about how the Indian people have felt about the Yukon and about themselves. It says a lot about how they have adapted to their world and a lot about their values. So it became the title for this book.

I have tried to organize the book so you can either read it straight through or skip around in it. Still there is a sequence to the chapters, for the book is about how the Indians have responded to a changing

Preface

world. It is about how some things have changed very slowly while others have sometimes changed suddenly and fast.

The first chapter consists of stories that show how the lives of the hunters and fishermen who have lived in the Yukon since the Ice Age have changed during this time. The second chapter reviews some facts about the present Yukon landscape and its inhabitants — both the animals and the people. Chapter Three describes important changes in the climate, the landscape, and the ways people lived in the Yukon from the Ice Age until about 1800 AD. It tells how these changes are understood by "outside" scientists such as geologists and archaeologists. Chapter Four tells of the arrival, in the 1800s, of white people in the Yukon.

Chapter Five summarizes some important events in the recent history of Yukon Indians. It explains how and why the Council for Yukon Indians, the Yukon Native Brotherhood and other modern Indian organizations were formed. In Chapter Six there is a short discussion of the different languages used by Yukon Indians and how these languages have been used both by natives and by linguists as a basis for distinguishing different groups of native people. This chapter also discusses the systems which have recently been developed so that Yukon Indian languages can be written down.

In the old days everything had to be passed along orally, for there was no way of writing memories down. People learned about their past by listening to what the elders told them about it. Chapters Seven to Twelve are a link to this old way of learning history. They are based on the spoken accounts which we collected from Yukon Indians in 1977.

When these oral accounts were translated into writing, some peoples' stories were reordered and condensed, and sometimes other information was added from published ethnographies or from field notes made long before 1977. These chapters do include many of the exact words that people spoke to us in 1977, but it would be impossible to put all of the taped material from that year between the covers of a single book.

The chapter closest to spoken history is Chapter Twelve, which is made up almost wholly of representative accounts from the communities we visited.

It is those accounts and the earlier summaries that make this book truly the work of the Yukon Indians. I hope all Yukon natives will consider it to be their own and be proud of it. I hope too that all newcomers to the Yukon, as well as armchair travellers in other places, will be interested in learning from this book about those who were in the Yukon first. And I hope that both native and non-native readers of the book will understand each other better because of it.

Catharine McClellan
1987

1

The Changing Ways of Yukon Hunters and Fishers

AUTUMN ON THE EDGE OF OLD CROW FLATS, 25,000 YEARS AGO

The day is windy and raw. The low rays of the afternoon sun that touch only the tops of the bare brown hills on either side of the valley give little warmth. Six men crouch in the tall grass watching a herd of mammoths downwind from them move along the valley floor. For three days the men have followed the herd at a distance. Now they have closed in on the huge creatures whose thick woolly coats are matted with mud and whose large tusks curve outward and upward. One animal, a young male, lags behind the others, browsing contentedly on the coarse, high grass.

Suddenly the leader of the hunting party raises his left arm. All of the men jump up together to surround the straggler, and several men hurl their spears at his soft underbelly. Two of the spears drive home. Roaring with pain, the wounded mammoth wheels to charge his tormentors while the rest of the herd thunders away down the valley.

One of the hunters stands his ground, confident in his power because the sharp bone tip of his spear has been treated by a dream doctor. The man looks very small up close to his quarry, but the thrust of his spear into the mammoth's forequarters makes the animal stumble. This gives another man the chance to thrust with his spear. The animal stumbles again and falls. The other hunters move in at once to finish the kill.

Their luck has been good. They have followed the herd only a short time and have managed to corner a single animal instead of several, which might have made the kill much more difficult and risky.

As soon as the animal is dead, the hunters gather around the carcass to share a ritual taste of fresh blood and a morsel of fat from the tip of the heart. While the older men butcher the steaming hill of flesh, a boy of fifteen, just learning to hunt big game, starts back up the valley to tell the old people, women and children in camp of their good fortune.

The camp will move up to feast off the kill and will stay there beside it perhaps a month, since it is late enough in the season that meat will freeze quickly. For days the children have been sucking the last bones of a giant beaver, which is all the nourishment that re-

3

mains in the earlier camp. But the boy messenger never reaches his people. On the way he is killed by a short-faced bear, whom the boy surprises on the brow of a hill, where the bear has brought down a caribou. The boy's friends and relatives never learn what has become of him, but after a few days a woman from the camp finds the hunters and guides the people to the kill.

LATE WINTER ON A BRANCH OF THE PORCUPINE RIVER, 11,000 YEARS AGO

It is bitterly cold. Although the snow blows about on the arctic tundra, it is rarely deep enough, except for occasional big drifts, to cover the tallest of the stunted willows. Travel is not easy for the hunters. Their feet often break through the sharp crust and drop with a thud through the dry snow between hummocks of frozen grass. To keep a steady pace is impossible.

Six families are camped in the shelter of some small poplar and spruce that have managed to grow in a sunny, south-facing spot along a branch of a river which later will be called the Porcupine. Not far from here, men hunted mammoth 15,000 years earlier. Nowadays hunters hardly ever see mammoths; they seem, in fact, to be disappearing.

Again the people are hungry. The older ones look tired and very thin, and they do not talk much. The young children and babies cry easily. It is hard to keep warm, even though everybody wears shirts and pants made of caribou or elk hide. Some have parkas made of hare pelts which have been cut into strips and woven. Each adult has a heavy robe of bison hide too, but only a tiny willow-twig fire burns in the big brush-and-skin shelter where four of the families live. The two smaller shelters nearby are unheated, since so few trees grow in the country. Hands and feet ache with the cold. There is only a single tundra hare to feed everybody. The river and lakes are frozen too deep for spearing fish.

Suddenly a howl comes from one of the dogs that has been left in camp. Five hunters are approaching, who have been gone for almost a week. Each has on his back a net hunting bag full of dark, rich bison meat. The men have been lucky enough to creep close to a sleeping bison cow, and with their sharp, bone-pointed darts have been able to kill her.

Bison meat is rare at this season of the year. In summer, everybody in camp can help to drive a herd over a cliff or up a narrow canyon by setting fires in the grass and then running and shouting behind to scare the animals. The dogs help in the drive too. Bison that break their bones as they fall over the cliff, or bunch up at the head of a canyon, can be quite easily killed by the hunters. In winter it is not so easy. The hunters had to follow the herd on foot for many miles before they had a chance to make this kill, but it was a specially good one. Butchering the cow, the hunters found an unborn calf in her — just the kind of food to give to the two wise but nearly toothless older men on whose knowledge the welfare of the group depends.

The old men and the women gather just enough dry willow twigs to set ablaze the few cakes of dried bison dung they have been hoarding for a cooking fire. One man puts meat, fat and snow into the bison's paunch, while one of the women brings out her store of dried berries to add to the mixture. Tying the bag-like paunch closed with rawhide, they hang it from a pole, so that it twists over the low flame. Ladles of musk-ox and bison horn are brought out: one for each person to eat the bison stew.

Later, as the ladles are filled, the old men caution the children to take just small sips of the broth. If they eat too much too quickly, they will be sick, for they have been without food for four days.

The women and young men build up the fire again with the last of the bison chips and a little willow brush so they can roast big chunks of juicy meat. The shelter warms with the sound of well-fed voices. When the meal has ended, the hunters recount just how they got the bison. Then the older men tell of earlier hunts in which they or their fathers took part. Darkness has long since fallen. Finally the oldest man begins a favorite story about a hero whose father-in-law sent him to get the sinews of a giant bison. It is a long and exciting adventure, but the younger children are soon fast asleep. After a while even the adults begin to doze, but two or three listen carefully, one of them silently repeating some of the old man's words. Eleven thousand years later, the story will still be told in the Yukon, passed down by word of mouth from one group of people to another through all those years.

When the story ends, the old man and his few listeners settle into their sleeping furs. No sound breaks the silence of the tundra except the distant howling of wolves.

SPRING AT KLO-KUT, 1000 YEARS AGO

Far away, in the eastern part of North America and Greenland, the first meetings between native Inuit and the European Norsemen are about to take place. But here in a village on the banks of the Porcupine River, the ancestors of the present-day Loucheux Indians are eagerly preparing for the northbound caribou migration. Almost 800 years will pass before *their* descendants first meet white men!

The Yukon country now looks quite different from the way it did 24,000 or 10,000 years earlier. Much of what was then glacial ice, arctic tundra, grass or shrubs is now covered with spruce, birch, cottonwood and willow. There is still tundra in the mountains, especially in the Brooks Range, and on the coastal plain beyond, and the huge herds of caribou that winter in the forests farther south move north each spring to the arctic slope for calving and summer browsing. At any hour now the villagers expect to see the first caribou arrive, even though the ice on the river broke up only last week.

The men have mended all the birchbark canoes and are ready to launch them at the caribou ford as soon as the animals appear. Men, women and children wait along the bank to drive back into the water any caribou that succeed in crossing the river.

A doe appears on the opposite bank, then another, and another. Soon hundreds of caribou crowd the far shore and more press from behind. After some hesitation, the first arrivals start to swim toward the shore where the people are waiting. When the animals are well out in the river, the men emerge from hiding and launch their canoes into the midst of the swimming herd. They paddle their light craft right up onto the animals' backs. As the mass of caribou and canoes swirls about in the water, the hunters strike at the closely packed animals again and again with their antler-tipped spears. They kill many, and the water turns pink and rose with caribou blood. Some of the dying animals are carried downriver by the current, but in less than an hour the people have recovered hundreds of carcasses close to the camp, where all can enjoy the fresh meat. Most of the flesh will be dried, to last until summer fishing begins.

In late summer and early autumn, the people will kill even more caribou by driving them into huge corrals built where the low hills and flatlands meet. They will use spears, as they have today in the canoes, but they will also set snares in the brush fences of the corral to choke the animals, and will shoot others with arrows. Working with others, a family can store up enough dried meat to last most of the winter, both for themselves and their guests. During the darkest days of the year, they will not have to leave camp to hunt at all. Instead, they can play games and tell stories and think about the spring hunt, which today once again has been successful. The long days of summer are ahead, and no one is hungry.

JULY AT NESKATAHIN, 1825 AD

"It is already the moon of New Fur on the Game," the old woman tells her granddaughter, who is helping her to turn over the fish. More than a hundred fine sockeye salmon that have been split from head to tail cover the long poles of her fish rack. The fish have dried in the sun for several days, skin side up, and now it is time to turn them flesh side up for further drying.

The old woman's hands ache and her arms are tired from all her work. Early every morning for more than two weeks she has cleaned and split the fish her husband has gaffed out of the heart of the rectangular wooden fish trap. He is the boss of this trap, which is set beside two others; together they completely block the shallow stream that divides the large plank houses of Neskatahin village from the little cluster of tiny raised houses that hold the ashes of the dead. The salmon are swimming up to a small lake to spawn, but a brush fence diverts them into the fish traps.

"It's a beautiful knife, grandmother," says the girl, stroking the polished wooden handle and the blade shaped like a half moon. The old woman's husband hammered that blade from a copper nugget he got from a White River Indian in exchange for a plug of trade tobacco.

"Even with such a good knife, the fish make a big job," says the old woman. After gutting, beheading and splitting each fish, she has made a special slash on one side. It looks like a crow's foot, with the three toes. Because she belongs to the Crow side of the local people, she has chosen this way to mark the fish she cuts. When the dried fish are folded together and baled, fifty to a bundle, for storage or trade, she will know which bundles are hers.

After cutting the fish, the grandmother washes her hands and knife in the cold stream. She cleans the roe that she has saved in a little side pool, so it too can be dried. The discarded heads and entrails she dumps into a bark basket full of water. Later she will heat the mixture by dropping several hot stones into it, and she will feed the soup to the hunting dogs. She has already thrown some of the offal back in the stream. The rest clings to the stalks and leaves of fireweed on which she has been cutting the fish. That too she now sends floating down the stream.

When all the fish are dry, the old woman will have enough to see her family through the worst of the winter and to feed any unexpected guests. It makes her happy to think that already she has filled half her storehouse.

With her granddaughter she rests now on the grassy bank near the fish rack. They can hear the murmuring of other women and girls working their fish nearby, the shrieks of the younger children launching toy rafts in a little slough, and the occasional chatter of men repairing their equipment for the late summer hunt. A tiny yellow warbler makes soft chirping sounds in the nearby brush, and several white gulls are screeching at each other over a morsel of fish-gut caught on the edge of the stream. The warm sun draws out the scent of the willows and cottonwoods, making the little girl sleepy. She drops her head onto her grandmother's lap and dreams that when the Tlingit traders next come to Neskatahin, a handsome young man will give her a big brass kettle for the skin of a single gopher that she has snared. Then she, in turn, will give the kettle to her grandmother, who has taken care of her since her mother died. Her grandmother could show the kettle off and use it to feast everybody in the village. After all, her grandfather is the headman and the best hunter in the group. By late summer, when people begin to tire of fish, he will be bringing in delicious, fat groundhogs, sheep and caribou meat. She knows two names for the next month — August in English. They are, When the Game Gets Fat, and When Its Fur Begins to Whiten.

Of course, the powerful Tlingit traders would never really sell a brass kettle so cheaply. Even her grandfather has not been able to afford such a luxury. But he is hoping to collect enough fox and beaver skins so he can pile them as high as a muzzle loader standing upright. That is what the Tlingit charge for such a gun.

The girl's grandmother, meanwhile, has been thinking of

whether it is too late in the day to start work on a big moose skin she has saved in its rawhide state since last fall. Her husband needs a new shirt and moccasins, as do some of the grandchildren. Her granddaughter sighs, waking and still thinking of the kettle.

"You've helped me a lot today, granddaughter," says the old woman. "Go find your younger sister and cousins. I'll tell you all about what happened when two sisters made a wish about some stars. Then we'll put that big skin to soak so we can have plenty of tanned hide. This summer I'll show you how to sew moccasins for your brother. You are old enough to do that now."

The girl smiles and jumps up. Nothing could be better than a good story from her grandmother. She runs to find the other children.

AUTUMN NEAR FRANCES LAKE, 1840 AD

The wind is cool today, and the highest peaks have been newly dusted with snow during the night. The noon sun brings out the deep reds of the buckbrush marching up the high slopes to meet the bare grey scree and snow. Golden patches of birch and cottonwood are scattered in the dark green spruce forest of the mountain flanks and valleys. Little lakes and a winding river glint far below.

The racks are heavy with singed and split groundhogs and strips of drying sheep meat, and the women have already stored much fully dried meat and many big bags of grease and berries on the tripod caches by the brush shelters of the mountain camp.

Katesta, the headman of the camp, is enjoying the sun as he braids a caribou snare. Autumn, he says, is the best time of the year. Soon more families will come together from all directions to hunt the woodland caribou that usually congregate nearby in late fall. If the caribou hunt is as successful as the groundhog and sheep hunt has been, everybody will have plenty of meat and skins for the winter.

Today nobody is hunting. When Katesta asked during his regular morning speech concerning the welfare of the camp, each family head announced that he had enough fresh and dried meat. There is no need to snare any more sheep or to set any more snares or dead-falls for groundhogs. The rest of the animals should be left for seed. If people take only what they can use, the animal spirit-owners will not be offended, and they will offer their bodies to be killed another time.

Coming upriver, Katesta and his people saw many signs of beaver, but they left the animals alone, so that next winter they might have prime pelts for their trading partners from Teslin Lake. Early every summer now, the Teslin Indians come over the divide to a place near Watson Lake. They bring valuable Russian goods — tea and tobacco, metal knives and glass beads — which they themselves get from Coast Tlingit relatives who come up the Taku River. Of course the Teslin people always want as many marten and fox skins as they can get, in addition to the beaver pelts. They know that the Frances River marten have choice fur and that the Russians like marten and fox best. Besides, beaver skins are heavy to carry.

But the Teslin people charge very dearly for the white men's goods, so some Frances River Indians have begun to take their furs south to Dease Lake instead. There they sell them to local Indians or to Indian traders from still farther south, who later barter them at a huge fair held on the upper Stikine River, across the divide. Every year many Coast Tlingit, and sometimes a few Russians, come there from salt water to dry salmon and to trade with the interior people. The Frances River and Dease Lake Indians themselves rarely go that far. It is a dangerous trip, and they have heard that the followers of the powerful Tlingit Chief Shakes, if angered, just take away the furs of the inland people and give nothing in return.

Other Frances River Indians prefer to trade with their relatives down the Liard River or with Mountain Indians of the Beaver River. These people can get trade goods at Fort Simpson, the Hudson's Bay Post miles to the east, where the Liard empties into the Mackenzie River. There is also a small outpost called Fort Halkett in the Sekani country, at the mouth of the Smith River, a branch of the Liard nearer to Watson Lake, but that outpost is usually not well supplied. Often nobody is there at all, and the Indians who wait for the trader run short of food because they neglect their hunting and fishing.

Suddenly a volley of musket fire shatters the still air and echoes back from the surrounding mountains. Everybody in Katesta's camp is startled, though not everyone is alarmed. Some know that the shots probably announce the arrival of another family whose campfire smoke one of the groundhog hunters saw a few days earlier. But others think a thunderbird may have landed near camp, and they are frightened. Some have never heard gunshots, and others have heard them only rarely. They may soon hear more, since it is becoming the custom of the country for friends to announce their arrival in this noisy way.

By late afternoon, not one but three new families have arrived. One large family, led by a man named Nokagah, has come up the Frances River and actually belongs to the same band as Katesta. The other two families have crossed the pass from the Pelly River. Katesta's oldest daughter is married to their headman, Tucumasta. The members of Tucumasta's band speak a little differently from Katesta's people, but they can understand each other well enough.

Everybody wants to hear how people have fared since they last met — who has been sick or has died, who has been married, who has new children. First, however, the arriving families must be helped with setting up their brush camps, and after the chores are done, they must be well fed. Only then do the adults settle down around the fire by the headman's brush house for a real exchange of news. The young children, who have been taking up old friendships or shyly making new ones, leave off their play and slowly drift into the group. They snuggle up to their parents and grandparents and soon fall asleep. The older children have helped with fetching water and firewood and feeding the pack dogs brought by the newcomers. Now they listen quietly as the adults talk.

The headman of each of the new groups has astounding things to tell, for each has discovered that white traders are reaching more deeply into the country. According to Nokagah, one of these traders is a Hudson's Bay Company man by the name of Campbell, who has already been in various parts of the Liard River country during the past five or six years. Last winter, Nokagah himself saw Campbell at Fort Halkett, and all the Frances River Indians know that Campbell spent the winter before that at Dease Lake, after first going down to the Stikine River trade fair and meeting Shakes. Everybody says that Campbell is a brave man, but that he and his men would still have starved to death if some Mountain Indians had not brought them food. Even so, they say, the white men had to eat their snowshoe lacings and parchment window before they left. Campbell's interpreter, Francis Hoole, had told Katesta about it.

Nokagah says that this summer, shortly after Katesta and his people headed up the Frances River, Campbell followed, bringing seven men. Just like the Indians ahead of him, Campbell fished for trout on the way upstream, but he and his party also killed and ate some of the beaver and moose. They went far beyond Simpson Lake, which another white man visited a few years earlier. When they got to Frances Lake they built a strange-looking house on the island at the head of the west arm. Then they explored Finlayson's River and Finlayson's Lake and even went over to the headwaters of the Pelly River. Nokagah says he found their traces repeatedly as he and his family came up the Frances and crossed to their hunting grounds northwest of Finlayson Lake.

Tucumasta, the headman of the family from Pelly River, has strange stories too, about Russian traders pushing their way up the Yukon River. No one here in the mountain camp knows much about these Russians. Tucumasta has his news from Indians farther down the Pelly River. They had met White River Indians who had been trading with people from the Upper Tanana, and the Upper Tanana Indians had heard about the Russians from Loucheux who had been trading on the Yukon River. Another story has come from these Loucheux also, that the Hudson's Bay traders from the Mackenzie now have a trading post up the Peel River, near the Rat.

The elders in the mountain camp talk of these things for some time. What will it mean, they ask, if Campbell comes right into their own hunting grounds with guns and powder and tobacco and beads? If he came to Frances Lake again, everyone could trap enough to buy the guns without having to deal through other Indian intermediaries or to make long journeys to the white traders far away in hostile territory. And what would it mean if the Russians came up the Yukon River as far as the mouth of the Pelly? Or if the Hudson's Bay traders moved farther up the Peel? The people fall silent as they think about this. They are not sure whether it would be good to have the white strangers here in their own country. Perhaps they should drive the white men out. On the other hand, they are eager to have their guns, metal knives, tobacco and beads. The elders think that their people's way of life may soon change greatly.

WINTER ON THE FORT SELKIRK – AISHIHIK TRAIL, 1889 AD

It is nearly fifty years later, in the depth of February, near the head of Aishihik Lake. Four Aishihik families are returning on snowshoes to their winter trapping camp, after visiting the trader at Fort Selkirk. In exchange for red and silver fox, lynx and beaver furs, tanned caribou and moose hides, and some half-dried caribou meat, they received two rifles, some shells, some powder for their old flintlock, metal traps for fox and beaver, two iron files, a pair of scissors, lengths of calico, beads, a harmonica, tea, sugar, tobacco, and a little flour.

One young man and his partner are eager to test the power of the new rifles, and they borrow one from the headman, their uncle. Armed with the new rifle, an old flintlock musket, a bow and a quiver of arrows – in case the firearms should fail – they move off ahead of the others.

On their light snowshoes the young men run easily through the snowy spruce forest and across a more open valley where the willow twigs are just starting to turn deep red.

One of the hunters sees the splayed tracks of a big moose. He tests their freshness, probing the snow with a long stick. The tracks are still soft, and the young men decide that the moose probably passed by within the last hour. Before setting out to stalk it, they study the lay of the land in relation to the light northwest breeze that is blowing. Their fathers and uncles have been instructing them on such points since they first began to hunt.

The older men themselves had little instruction from their elders in the habits of moose. Fifty years ago these animals were rarely seen, and the people mostly hunted caribou and sheep. Now there are many moose, and caribou are becoming scarcer. Some say they have dropped in numbers because the white prospectors, who have recently come up the Yukon River as far as Fort Selkirk or over the passes from the coast, have caused many forest fires. The new growth that follows the fires makes good moose browse, but spoils the lichens for caribou. Others say the shift in numbers of moose and caribou began before the whites arrived and has something to do with the anger of Animal Mother. In any case, the white men are bringing other changes to the country. They are strange people, but some of them seem to be good fellows, like little Doctor Dawson, who is tireless on the trail in spite of his hunched back. He looks at rocks through his magnifying glass and tries to learn the Indian names for rivers and mountains wherever he goes.

There is a new trading post now at Fort Selkirk. Campbell, the first white man to come into the upper Yukon River country, had one there thirty or forty years ago, but Chilkat Tlingit traders destroyed his post a few years after he built it. Campbell never returned to the country after that – although his spirit came back to a baby at Tatlmain Lake, people say. After that there were no more stores along the upper Yukon River until a white man named McQuesten built the one called Fort Reliance, near the mouth of the Klondike River. Forty Mile, built a little further down river, has now become a bigger place, but both are in Han Indian country. The Aishihik Indians were glad when McQuesten and another white man named Harper put a third store at Stewart River two or three years ago, but it did not last either. Now the Aishihik people hope that the new store Harper opened just a few months ago back at Fort Selkirk will do better. Nearby are the ruined chimneys from Campbell's old buildings.

The Aishihik Indians like Harper but are not quite sure about his Indian wife from way down the Yukon River. Her language sounds strange, and it is rumored that she has a lot of spirit power. It is convenient, though, not to have to travel far to get white men's trade goods. The Tlingit traders from the coast still bring up only what they want to, no matter what their trading partners ask for, and they never let any Yukon natives — even those who are their relatives by marriage and can speak Tlingit — buy goods directly from Healy's Store at Dyea on the coast, nor from the American ships that come to Haines.

But the young men have learned their hunting lessons well, in spite of such changes. Keeping downwind, they move quietly in a series of arcs that cut in at points on the straight line they believe the moose to be travelling. On the fourth inward turn the hunters are rewarded. They see the large animal just getting to its feet in the copse of willows where it has been resting. The older of the two raises the new rifle and fires, and the fatally wounded moose at once drops heavily.

Both partners run up to the fallen animal, astonished to find it already dead. First they punch out its eyeballs, as their fathers have taught them. This allows the moose's spirit to escape, and saves it from seeing what happens to its dead body. Next the young hunters slit the throat and chest to remove the windpipe and heart. They cut off the tip of the heart and hang up all these pieces for the camp robbers — the Canada jays who gather at the kill even more quickly than do the ravens. The young men tell each other there would no longer be any need to carry their bows and arrows or old muskets, if only they could both have new rifles. They hope they can trap enough furs during the rest of the winter so that each can buy such a rifle at Fort Selkirk in the spring. They forget that they will need to trade for bullets too.

Since they know that the rest of the party will soon be passing nearby, the young hunters go to intercept them. Although it means adjusting loads, they want one of the wooden toboggans on which to put the meat, and two or three dogs to pull it. This is much better than having to drag the meat along by hand on a drag made of caribou leg skins. That is what their parents did before the white traders brought wooden sleds and toboggans from the Mackenzie River posts and showed the Yukon Indians how to harness dogs to pull them.

Now everyone in the party is eager to get back to the snug winter trapping cabins on Isaac Creek. There is plenty of meat for everyone, and there will be time to enjoy the other treasures from the store. The headman has a new harmonica in his pocket. He is happy, thinking of all the singing and dancing that the next few weeks will bring while the people eat the moose meat and enjoy all the tobacco, tea and flour.

What more could he want? He does not know that within a few years gold will be discovered in such quantity near Fort Reliance that thousands of white men will come into his country. He does not know that in their crazy search for gold, the newcomers will break up the coastal Tlingit blockade forever as they scramble over the mountain passes or puff their way noisily up the Yukon River in sternwheelers. He does not know that within a few years, along with his dogs, he will own animals he has never yet seen, called horses — and that these, like the new rifles, will change his people's patterns of hunting. He does not know that he will be given a new name, Chief Isaac of Aishihik.

EARLY SPRING ON KLUANE LAKE, 1975 AD

It is late March and already the days are getting longer and the sun warmer. A man, his nephew, and the nephew's wife are heading out to spend the weekend at a trapping cabin across the lake from their village. They travel on a skidoo, pulling an old toboggan behind. The uncle thinks about how people used to cross the lake with good dog teams and toboggans. The dog teams did not break down as skidoos sometimes do, nor did people have to buy expensive oil and gas for them. But the man does not mention how much time he and his father and mother and brothers and sisters used to spend catching and drying fish for the dogs as well as for their own winter food. He only comments to the others that perhaps the noise of skidoo and trail bike motors is one reason that moose and other animals have become so hard to find in the bush. Not everybody agrees with this point of view. His nephew thinks that the game does not mind the sound of motors, even those of trucks and airplanes, so long as they are run steadily without too many stops and starts or changes in speed.

Very early the next morning the two men set out from the trapping cabin travelling silently, on snowshoes. About four miles from the cabin they find the tracks of a pack of nine wolves following a female moose. She seems to have made her way out of the deep snow of the valley and up onto the ridge. In the end, the wolves will probably get her, for she is heavy with calf and will need to come down to the valley again to browse on the willow shoots. The wolves do not give up easily. They can travel on top of the light snow crust, wear her out, corner and hamstring her, and then easily bring her down.

The men themselves succeed only in shooting two spruce hens. There is, however, a prime lynx in one of their traps. This is good luck because the trapline is very short. Lynx now bring $100 a pelt, a much better price than in the 1960s.

During the course of the day, the silence of the bush is shattered several times by the noise of two low-flying helicopters taking supplies to an oil-pumping station. When the wind is right the men can also hear the faint sound of the heavy trucks shifting gears on the Alaska Highway, climbing the foothills along the opposite shore of the lake. The older man thinks again about how the animals must dislike the noise. The younger man thinks about how soon he will be able to buy a pickup truck of his own.

While the men are out hunting, the woman runs the fish net she and her husband set last fall under the ice near the cabin. It is a hard job to do alone. First she must chop out the ice around the upright poles to which the opposite ends of the net are anchored. Even though the lake ice has grown dark as it begins to soften under the spring sun, it takes about twenty minutes to chop through to open water at each end of the net. Daytime temperatures may still fall below freezing, and the nights are colder. About six centimeters of new ice have formed around the anchor poles since she ran the net two weeks ago. The woman must chop out this new ice very carefully so as not to damage the poles by mistake, and she must make the holes of open water around each of them large enough to work the net easily. When she has done this, she reaches into the water and releases an end of the net from one of the anchor poles, and ties a line to it.

The line is longer than the net itself, and she stretches it way out along the ice beyond the pole, since there will be nobody to hold it. Then she walks to the far anchor pole, unties that end of the net and begins to pull the net up through the hole, laying it in folds on the ice beside her where it begins to freeze almost at once in the open air. As she pulls the net, she reaches into the water and carefully removes the five whitefish and the single lake trout caught in the mesh by their gills.

In spite of the cold, she does this with her bare hands. When she was a tiny girl her mother rubbed both of her hands on a beaver skin and said a kind of spell, which she believed would help her daughter to have warm hands even in the coldest weather. The woman too thinks this magic must have helped, for she has been running fish nets this way ever since she was young. The white traders and prospectors taught her grandparents how to do it and sold them twine to make the nets. Before that the Yukon Indians had always speared lake fish under the ice in winter.

Before she began running the net, the woman had put a pail of water to heat on a small fire made of kindling that she had carried out onto the ice in her pack sack. Now she thaws out the frozen net piled up on the ice by pouring the warm water on it. This makes it easy to push the net back through the opening in the ice. Then she reties one end of the net to its anchor pole. Using the line she had earlier attached to the opposite end of the net, she pulls the entire net taut again under the ice, retying the far end to the second anchor pole. She releases and coils up the haul line, for if she leaves it by the pole, it will freeze hard in the open air and become useless. Each time she runs the net she must bring out the line and take it home again.

Such a small catch of fish for all this work is disappointing. In the late fall after the net is first set, she often gets thirty or forty fish, but now the net has become slimy and it has a few holes in it. On these short weekend trips, she does not find time to wash and mend it often enough, for that can take all day and it involves resetting the net as well. She is too tired to start on the job now.

Later the woman chops down a little green spruce on the hill behind the cabin so she can put out some snares for rabbits. She hangs the wire snares from dry poles that she lays above the openings in the spruce boughs along the trails the rabbits have already made, and she adds more green spruce near the snares as bait. Then she goes further along the hillside and sets other wire loops on the ends of poles which she leans vertically against several big spruce trunks. These smaller snares are for tree squirrels, whose skins bring fifty cents apiece.

Next morning the woman finds two rabbits and six squirrels in the snares, but at this season the rabbits are poor, without much fat. Some already have a bluish tint to their flesh instead of a rich red.

Late on Sunday afternoon the group returns to the village. They want to go to evening mass, and the two men have jobs on the Alaska Highway for which they must be ready early Monday morning. The squirrel skins, lynx pelt and whitefish are the only things of material value that the party brings back to Burwash. They have eaten the two rabbits the woman caught, as well as the lake trout. But the chance to be in the bush has had value of a different kind. It has given all three of the adults renewed ties with their *keyi* — their country. The nephew and his wife talk about how they will take their oldest son and daughter with them next time instead of leaving them with their grandparents. The parents will make the children come, even if they protest that they would rather go to a curling tournament or a movie at Haines Junction. It will be good to have their help in running the nets, setting snares and getting firewood, and the boy and girl can learn more about how to live well in the bush. The older people agree that the young people ought to know that, as well as how to read, do arithmetic and play cards.

A CONFERENCE ROOM IN WHITEHORSE,
WINTER 1980 AD

It is the morning of 12 December 1980. The place is a room in an office building in downtown Whitehorse. It is a plain room, containing a very large table encircled with chairs. This morning the chairs are occupied by negotiating teams representing the Government of Canada, the Yukon Territorial Government, and the Council for Yukon

Indians. For the past two weeks the Yukon Indians have been bargaining here on their land claims, and the session is now drawing to a close.

On many occasions the mood around the table has been tense, even angry, but today the atmosphere is notably different. There is a feeling of accomplishment, of satisfaction, circulating in the room. The chief federal negotiator has before him a document which he scans, then signs. The papers are passed to a Tutchone Indian elder, Elijah Smith, who began the Yukon land-claims movement several years earlier and who is vice-chairman of the Council for Yukon Indians. He also signs the document, witnessing the federal signature. Next it is signed and witnessed by representatives of the territorial government. Then it is passed along the table for the final signature. Dave Joe, lawyer, member of the Champagne/Aishihik Indian Band and chief negotiator for the Indians, signs his name as well. The process is now complete.

The document, which has now been casually dropped into a briefcase, ratifies four major land-claim agreements. The agreements have to do specifically with hunting, fishing, trapping, and land-use planning. When the final, overall land-claim settlement is achieved, these agreements will define and establish many of the legal rights, roles and responsibilities of Yukon Indians within the ancestral homeland in which they have hunted, trapped and fished for so long.

In a few minutes the room will be empty, but first, some unfinished business has to be dealt with. The three negotiators must agree on a time and place for their next session as well as the issues that will be discussed. With this done, the three negotiating teams gather their materials and leave. They have much work to do in preparation for the next round of negotiations. The special knowledge and skills needed by Yukon hunters so they can live good lives have changed still further. It is no longer just a matter of knowing animal behavior and having good weapons and cooperative friends and relatives. Now the headmen must know about territorial and national government behavior as well.

2

The Yukon as It is Now: Landscape, Animals, People

Perhaps none of the events recounted in Chapter One happened exactly as they have been described. We have eye-witness accounts only for the last one. Yet any one of them could have taken place, to judge from the traces of past human activity that have been found in the Yukon, and from historical documents, the stories Yukon Indian elders tell of how their grandparents lived, and from the way Yukon Indians live today. Taken all together, these different sources give us a good idea of the history of Yukon Indians, particularly in the last 200 years. Much must still be discovered, and some things will never be known, but we know enough to try to put much of the story together.

People have lived in what is now called the Yukon for perhaps 30,000 years. During that long period both the climate and the landscape have changed. The weather was sometimes much colder than it is now, sometimes warmer. For at least half of the last 30,000 years, instead of being covered by forests, most of the land was mossy or grassy tundra, surrounded on the east and south by glaciers and on the north by the frozen ocean. Trees grew only in sheltered river valleys, when they grew at all.

The lakes too have changed in number, location, and shape. Rivers once flowed in places where there are none today, and salmon once spawned where they do no longer. Many of the animals that the early peoples hunted were unlike those they hunt today; some were much larger and fiercer than modern grizzly bears. Some of the earlier people themselves may also have been different from those who now live in the Yukon. Some of the earlier groups probably moved on to other places long ago or disappeared without leaving any descendants in the Yukon.

Chapter Three will describe in more detail the major changes in the landscape of the past and discuss more fully what is known of the people who lived in the Yukon up until the first contact with whites in the late eighteenth century. Here in Chapter Two, our subject is the present: the main features of Yukon landscape, climate and vegetation; the more important animals; the different groups of Indians and non-Indians who live in the Yukon today.

Richardson Mountains (Yukon Government photo)

THE LANDSCAPE

Topography*

The Yukon Territory covers about 200,000 square kilometers in the northwest corner of Canada. Most of the Yukon is high country separated from the Pacific coast by the still higher Coast Mountains. In fact, the Yukon is a part of the Canadian Cordillera, which is the huge complex of mountain and plateau country including the Rocky Mountains and the Coast Mountains. This cordillera runs north from the United States, through British Columbia and into the Yukon, then curves northwest into Alaska.

The Coast Mountains block much of the moisture and warmth that the Pacific Ocean currents and winds bring to southeastern Alaska. When the seawinds hit the south and west faces of the Coast Mountains, the moisture that the winds carry falls as rain or snow. So Skagway and Haines, on the Alaskan coast, are much wetter than Whitehorse or Dawson, on the inland side of the mountains.

Besides keeping the moist, warm air of the Pacific coast out of the Yukon, the Coast Mountains have in the past made it hard for Yukon and coast people to travel into one another's country. There are only three good passes from the coast into the Yukon—the Chilkat, the Chilkoot, and White Pass. For thousands of years, people have used one or another of these three routes to get from the tall, thick forests and beaches of the Pacific shore with its rich marine life into the high Yukon interior with its big game and fur-bearing animals. Two other passes at the head of the Taku River in British Columbia also lead into the Yukon by way of Atlin and Teslin lakes.

In addition to the Coast Mountains, the Yukon has other major mountain ranges. The Richardson and Selwyn ranges in the northeast and east are part of the Rocky Mountain system. Keele Peak at the head of the Hess River in the Selwyns reaches almost 3000 meters in height, but most other peaks in this area are around 2000 meters or less. The Ogilvie Mountains in the northwestern part of the territory are again not so high – generally under 2000 meters – but the North Fork Pass of the Ogilvies leads to an impressive mountain and plateau section of the northern Yukon.

In the south-central Yukon, the northern Cassiar and the Pelly mountains also have peaks over 2000 meters, but the Saint Elias Range, along the Yukon/Alaska border in the southwest, has the highest peaks of all. Fifteen of these peaks are over 5700 meters in height. Other lower mountain ranges also crisscross the territory.

Other prominent features of Yukon topography include the Shakwak and Tintina trenches. These are wide depressions between mountain ranges. The first runs northwest/southeast between the base of the St Elias and the Ruby ranges. Some of the Haines Highway and the Alaska Highway north of Haines Junction follow the Shakwak Trench. The wider and longer Tintina Trench runs more or less parallel to it but lies farther east, between the Pelly Mountains on the one side and the Selwyns and Ogilvies on the other. It is the

* The word *topography* is made from two Greek words – *topos*, which means place, and *graphein*, which means to draw or describe. Topography means the shape of the earth's surface, or a description of it. A topographical map is a map which shows not merely the names of places but the lay of the land – hills and valleys, forests and glaciers and gravel beds and the drainage patterns of rivers.

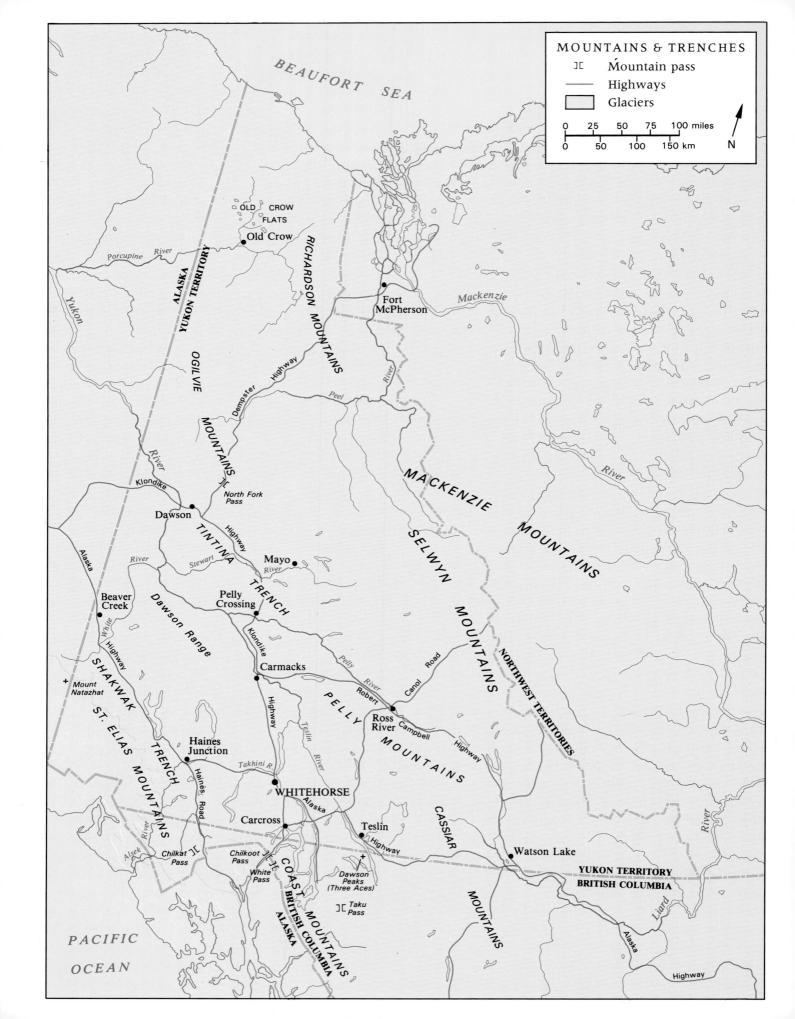

BEAUFORT SEA

OLD CROW FLATS
Old Crow

Porcupine River

ALASKA
YUKON TERRITORY

RICHARDSON MOUNTAINS

Fort McPherson

Mackenzie

OGILVIE MOUNTAINS

Dempster Highway

Peel River

Yukon River

Klondike

North Fork Pass

Dawson

Highway

TINTINA TRENCH

Stewart River

Mayo

River

MACKENZIE

SELWYN MOUNTAINS

MOUNTAINS

Beaver Creek

Pelly Crossing

Dawson Range

Klondike

Mount Natazhat

White River

Carmacks

Pelly River

Robert

Canol Road

NORTHWEST TERRITORIES

SHAKWAK TRENCH

Highway

Highway

Teslin River

PELLY MOUNTAINS

Ross River

Campbell

Highway

ST. ELIAS MOUNTAINS

Haines Junction

Takhini R.

WHITEHORSE

Alaska

CASSIAR

Alsek River

Haines Road

Carcross

Teslin

Highway

Chilkat Pass

Chilkoot Pass

White Pass

COAST MOUNTAINS

BRITISH COLUMBIA
ALASKA

Dawson Peaks (Three Aces)

Taku Pass

MOUNTAINS

Watson Lake

YUKON TERRITORY
BRITISH COLUMBIA

Liard

River

Alaska Highway

PACIFIC OCEAN

MOUNTAINS & TRENCHES
Mountain pass
Highways
Glaciers

0 25 50 75 100 miles
0 50 100 150 km
N

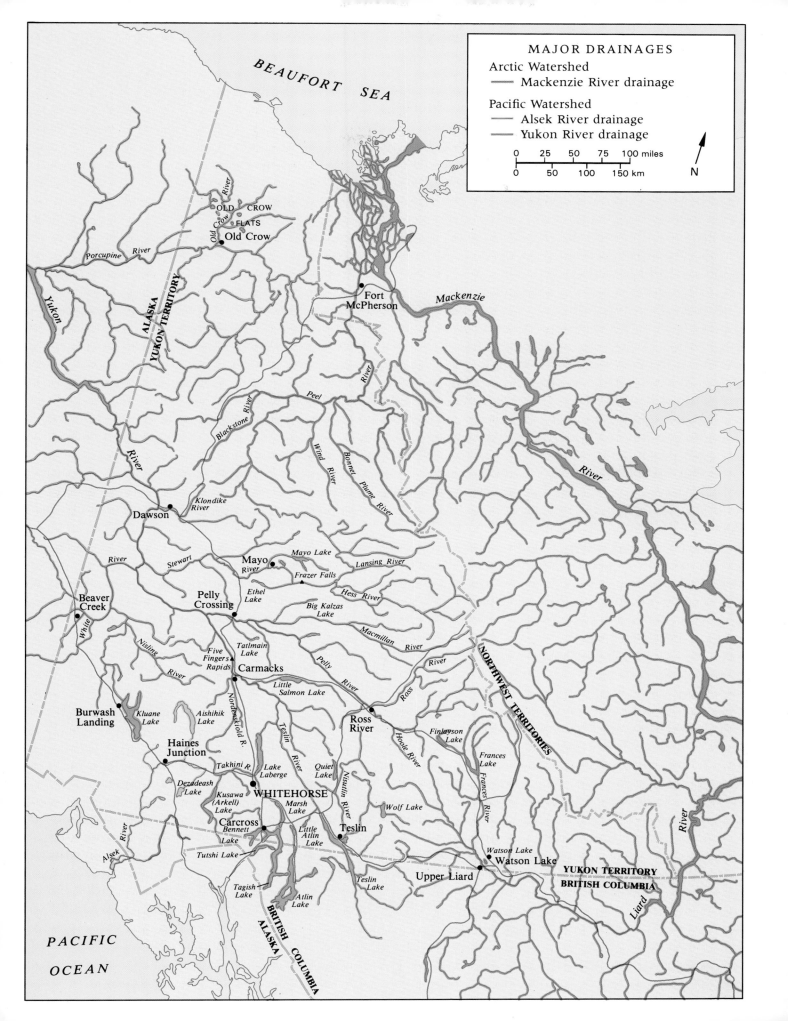

BEAUFORT SEA

MAJOR DRAINAGES
Arctic Watershed
—— Mackenzie River drainage
Pacific Watershed
—— Alsek River drainage
—— Yukon River drainage

0   25   50   75   100 miles
0   50   100   150 km

N

Porcupine   River
Old Crow River
OLD   CROW
FLATS
Old Crow

Yukon

ALASKA
YUKON TERRITORY

Fort
McPherson

Mackenzie

River

Peel

Blackstone River
Wind River
Bonnet Plume River

River

Klondike River
Dawson

Stewart
River

Mayo
River
Mayo Lake
Frazer Falls
Lansing River

Ethel Lake
Hess River

Pelly
Crossing
Big Kalzas Lake

Beaver
Creek

White

Macmillan River

River

NORTHWEST TERRITORIES

Nisling River
Tatlmain Lake
Five Fingers Rapids
Carmacks
Pelly River
Ross River

Kluane Lake
Aishihik Lake
Nordenskiold R.
Little Salmon Lake

Burwash
Landing

Ross River
Hoole River
Finlayson Lake
Frances Lake

Haines
Junction
Takhini R.
Teslin River
Quiet Lake
Nisutlin River
Wolf Lake

Frances River

Dezadeash Lake
Lake Laberge
WHITEHORSE
Kusawa (Arkell) Lake
Marsh Lake

Carcross
Bennett Lake
Little Atlin Lake
Teslin

Tutshi Lake
Alsek River

Tagish Lake
Atlin Lake
Teslin Lake

Watson Lake
Watson Lake

Upper Liard
YUKON TERRITORY
BRITISH COLUMBIA

Liard River

PACIFIC

OCEAN

BRITISH COLUMBIA
ALASKA

Ogilvie Mountains (Yukon Government photo)

valley through which the Pelly River runs, and it now also carries the western end of the Campbell Highway and northern end of the Klondike Highway. Yet another major feature of Yukon topography, at the extreme north of the territory, is the coastal plain that gradually slopes from the Richardson and British mountains down to the Arctic Ocean.

Many minerals, such as silver, gold, copper, lead and asbestos, have been found in the mountains of the Yukon, and much gold in the stream gravels. The Indians of earlier times were not interested in the gold nor in most of the other minerals that are mined today, but they did prize the copper nuggets from the White Mountains in the northern St Elias Range. They also valued the red and yellow ochres, or colored earths, from which they made paints, and the black, glass-like rock, called obsidian, as well as the smooth grey flint from which they made knives, arrow points and skin scrapers. Native placenames often tell of the presence of copper, ochres and other minerals traditionally valued in the Yukon. For example, the knob-like mountain at Pine Lake Campground, near Haines Junction, has a Southern Tutchone name meaning Red Paint Mountain, and to the west of the old Aishihik Road is Flint Mountain.

The topography of the Yukon also includes many rivers, and the canyons and valleys they form. Like mountain passes, valleys are

22

Peaks in the St Elias Range (Yukon Government photo)

routes by which animals and people can move from one area to another. But where the currents are swift, or when the ice is forming or breaking up, rivers can also be dangerous barriers to travel. The drainage basins of rivers, with their headwaters surrounded by mountains, often make naturally defined living areas for human groups.

The Yukon has four major river systems. The largest is that of the territory's largest river, the Yukon River, which flows over 3000 kilometers from Atlin, Teslin, Tagish and Bennett lakes in British Columbia and the southern Yukon, through the Yukon Territory to Alaska, where it finally drains into the Bering Sea. It has several major tributaries, including the Porcupine, White, Klondike, Stewart, Pelly, and Teslin rivers. Parts of these rivers, especially near their headwaters, flow swiftly through steep canyons, but other sections meander slowly through miles of flat, swampy country. For instance, Hoole Canyon on the upper Pelly River looks very different indeed from the low-lying Old Crow Flats with their many scattered lakes. The Old Crow River is a northern tributary of the Porcupine, which in its turn is a tributary of the Yukon River.

The Peel River, in the northeastern Yukon, is separated from the Yukon River drainage system by the Ogilvie and Selwyn mountains. Fed by its many branches in both the Yukon and Northwest Territo-

The North Slope (Yukon Government photo)

ries, the Peel flows northeastward into the Mackenzie River in the Northwest Territories, and the Mackenzie then empties into the Arctic Ocean.

Much of the southeastern Yukon Territory is drained by the Liard River system. The Liard in turn flows into the upper Mackenzie River, so that its waters eventually mingle with those of the Peel before entering the Arctic Ocean.

The fourth river system is in the southwestern portion of the Yukon. Here the Alsek River originates in the icefields of the St Elias Mountains, then cuts through the Coast Mountains directly to the Pacific Ocean.

Lakes are another noticeable feature of the Yukon landscape. In the southern Yukon are many large ones, such as Kluane, Aishihik, Dezadeash, Kusawa, Laberge, Bennett, Tagish, Marsh, and Teslin lakes. There are others of considerable size – including Little Salmon, Tatlmain, Big Kalsas, Ethel, Mayo, Frances, and Finlayson lakes – in the central Yukon, and countless smaller ones are scattered throughout the territory. The bigger lakes are often rough and can be dangerous for boat travel, but they can make for easy winter travel by snowshoe, toboggan, sled or skidoo.

Climate   Lake Kusawa

A very close relationship exists between landscape and climate. The climate of a place is affected both by the location of that place on the surface of the earth and by the local topography. There would not be many glaciers in the St Elias Mountains, nor any arctic tundra on the north slope, if the Yukon Territory were at the equator. But since it lies north of 60° N latitude and the Coast Mountains cut it off from the warm Pacific winds, most of the Yukon has what is called a sub-arctic climate. The temperatures average above 10° C for no more than four months of the year, and fewer than 120 days a year are frost-free. On the northernmost coastal strip of the Yukon, the climate is classified as arctic. There, temperatures even in the warmest months average less than 10° C.

Another feature of the Yukon's climate is that the temperatures run to extremes. Snag, near Beaver Creek at the western Yukon border, is famous for having the lowest official temperature ever recorded at a human settlement in North America, − 64° C. Yet in the summer at the same place a thermometer may reach near +27° C. At Dawson it may drop well below − 50° C in January but rise to +35° C in July. Simply put, Yukon summers are quite warm and Yukon winters are very cold.

25

Blueberry, stoneberry and lichen in the southern Yukon (Yukon Government photo)

The relative dryness of the Yukon, however, lasts all year around. There is more precipitation in winter than summer, but still the snow averages only 50 to 75 centimeters in depth. Much more snow than that falls in many parts of southern Canada. In the Yukon too, of course, more snow falls in some places than in others — much more in the St Elias Mountains, for example, than at Whitehorse or Dawson.

There is more daylight in some places than others as well, but this is easier to predict than the depth of the snow. North of the Arctic Circle, which is at 66°30' — north of Dawson but south of Old Crow — the sun does not dip below the horizon at all on the summer solstice, June 21, and the days are very long just before and after that date. By December, however, the days become very short. North of the Arctic Circle on December 21, the winter solstice, even if it is a clear day, you cannot see the sun itself. Only its glow is visible on the southern horizon. Farther south in the Yukon, though the sun does not shine for a full 24 hours even on June 21, the days are still very long in June and July and the nights very short. South of the Arctic Circle, if the country is flat and the weather is clear, the sun can also be seen, for at least a few minutes, even on December 21. But in many places the mountains block out all direct sunlight at that time of year.

Vegetation

Trees, shrubs, low flowering plants, grasses, mosses and lichens make up the Yukon vegetation. Their growth is determined in part by all the factors we have been discussing — drainage, precipitation, temperature, amounts of darkness and daylight — and also by altitude. What grows well in a valley cannot always survive on a mountain top.

Most of the valleys, hills and lower mountain slopes of the Yukon are now covered by boreal* forest. The most common kinds of trees in boreal forests are evergreens — spruce, pine and fir. These trees have needle-like leaves that are green year round. Other common trees of the boreal forest are birch, poplar and aspen. These deciduous trees turn brilliant yellows and reds in autumn and then lose their leaves until the following spring. The many kinds of willows that grow on the river banks and other low-lying areas, the alders, and the dwarf birch shrubs or buckbrush of the mountain heights, are also deciduous. The tamaracks or larches found in parts of the northern and eastern Yukon look like evergreens in summer, but they turn gold in autumn and drop their needles. They are deciduous trees too.

All the principal Yukon evergreens — fir, larch, black spruce, white spruce and lodgepole pine — resemble one another in many ways and seem to have a common ancestry. Botanists express this relationship by saying that all these trees belong to the pine *family*. Poplar, aspen and the willows all resemble one another too; they are all members of the willow family. Birch and alder belong to the birch

*Boreal comes from the Greek word for north, and boreal forests are the sort that grow in the north: open forests containing the kinds of trees that can live in the thin soil of subarctic climates.

27

Poplar in autumn (Yukon Government photo)

Young flowers of the lodgepole pine (Yukon Government photo)

Pine Family
Subalpine fir *Abies lasiocarpa*
Larch (Tamarack) *Larix laricina*
Lodgepole pine *Pinus contorta*
Black spruce *Picea mariana*
White spruce *Picea glauca*

Willow Family
Aspen *Populus tremuloides*
Poplar (Cottonwood) *Populus
    balsamifera*
Bebb willow *Salix bebbiana*
Bog willow *Salix pyrifolia*
Feltleaf willow *Salix alaxensis*
Littletree willow *Salix arbusculoides*
Sandbar willow *Salix exigua*
Yellow willow *Salix lasiandra*
Scouler willow *Salix scoulerana*

Birch Family
Mountain alder *Alnus tenuifolia*
Speckled alder *Alnus rugosa*
Sitka alder *Alnus sinuata*
White birch *Betula papyrifera*

Rose Family
Saskatoon *Amelanchier alnifolia*
Mountain-ash *Sorbus scopulina*

Dogwood Family
Red-osier *Cornus stolonifera*

family. Each of these families includes other members in other parts of the world — other types of pine, poplar, or birch which share the same ancestry but have not adapted to the climate of the Yukon.

The differences among these families of trees are not always obvious at first glance — like the differences among different groups of people — but they can be quite striking. All members of the willow family, for example, have separate male and female trees. Male flowers grow on one tree and female flowers on another. Where there is only one tree, the species cannot reproduce. All the other families of trees and shrubs in the Yukon bear male and female flowers on the same tree. Some of them — like mountain-ash and saskatoon, which belong to the rose family — not only have male and female parts on the same shrub; they have them right in the same flower. Each of these families, and each individual species, has developed its own traditional strategies for living in the land.

Mosses, lichens, grasses, berry bushes and other low-growing plants cover the forest floor beneath the trees. Some of the same kinds of lichens, mosses and berries also grow on the treeless stretches of alpine tundra above the timberline and on the North Slope. The in-between areas or transition zones, where there are only a few scattered trees, have many kinds of grasses too.

Tundra vegetation is found where the climate is very cold and the soil just beneath the surface is frozen year round. Even though the surface soil may melt a little in summer, trees cannot grow easily because of the cold, the wind, and the difficulty of putting their roots through the frozen soil below. The line where the trees stop growing is also more or less the line where subarctic temperatures give way to arctic temperatures.

Frozen soil, or permafrost, also occurs under parts of the boreal forest, causing the tree roots to spread out horizontally, close to the earth's surface, instead of anchoring the trees deep into the soil. In heavy winds or snow storms the trees easily fall over, and these windfalls often hinder the travel of people and other animals.

The tundra and forest lichens make good food for the caribou if the snow does not become too deep or crusted for them to graze, and berries are eaten by both animals and humans. Some of the most common berries are blueberries, mossberries, stoneberries and low-bush cranberries. Other plant foods that humans eat are wild onions, wild rhubarb, bear root or "Indian sweet potatoes," and some kinds of mushrooms. A number of these plants grow in the grassy natural meadows that here and there break up the forest cover, or in the sodden marshes that also dot parts of the landscape.

This is a brief and very generalized description of Yukon vegetation. The trees, lichens, mosses, grasses and other plants vary from place to place within the boreal forest, the tundra, meadows and swampland. For example, it is hard to find a big birch tree in the southern Yukon forest, while lodgepole pines are rare in the forests farther north. Wild onions grow plentifully on some grassy river terraces but not on others. Blueberries are common in the high Coast Mountains, cranberries in the northern Yukon. Because altitude, the lay of the land, local climate and forest fires affect the vegetation, the plant cover can be quite varied even within a small area. It can also change drastically over the years.

A detailed knowledge of vegetation has always been essential for Yukon Indians living a traditional way of life. The trees and plants have provided not only some of their foods, but also the materials for making houses and tools, and the fuel for fire. Beyond that, the animals have always depended on the vegetation, either directly or indirectly, and the people themselves on the animals.

THE ANIMALS

Animals of the subarctic area are different from those of southern Canada in three important ways. To begin with, the number of different kinds, or species, is not as great as in southern Canada. Second, the animals are usually larger than those of the same species farther south, and third, their population cycles generally differ from those of southern animals. In the Yukon, most species of mammals go through fairly regular population cycles of from five to ten years. Because the cycles of different species may overlap each other but are not all of the same length, hunting and trapping may be excellent in some years, but in other years several important species may all be scarce at the same time. It was the cyclical nature of the game and some of the fish populations that sometimes caused the Yukon Indians of the past to starve or forced them to travel out of their accustomed hunting areas. The cycles are often quite localized, so that there might be plenty of hares in one valley and none at all in a valley fifty kilometers away.

Caribou and Moose

Some Yukon animals are hunted primarily for their meat, others primarily for their fur. A few provide good meat as well as good hides or fur. One important large game animal in the Yukon is the caribou, whose meat and skins are both valued. Like moose, caribou are members of the deer family, but unlike moose, they range throughout much of the arctic and subarctic region of the world. In Europe and Asia, where they have been domesticated, they are called reindeer. Caribou can be found almost everywhere in the Yukon, but recently their numbers have dropped drastically, probably because of disturbances of their habitat by road building and other human activities. At Carcross, which is a shortened form of Caribou Crossing, no caribou have been seen crossing the river since the early 1900s.

Full-grown caribou generally range in size from 90 to 160 kilograms, bulls being larger than the cows. They eat lichen and other plants that grow in the arctic and mountain tundra and in the spruce forests, but sometimes they visit the low country to browse on grasses, sedges and willows. They are very good at pawing up plant foods, which they can smell under the snow wherever they are.

PROMINENT YUKON MAMMALS

There are many species of shrews, voles and mice in the Yukon, one species of bat, and one primate: the human, *Homo sapiens*. The other native mammals widely found in the territory are these:

Deer Family
Moose *Alces alces*
Mountain goat *Oreamnos americanus*
Mountain sheep *Ovis dalli*
Caribou *Rangifer tarandus*

Cat family
Lynx *Lynx lynx*

Weasel Family
Wolverine *Gulo gulo*
Otter *Lontra canadensis*
Marten *Martes americana*
Ermine *Mustela erminea*
Weasel *Mustela nivalis*
Mink *Mustela vison*

Bear Family
Black bear *Ursus americanus*
Grizzly bear *Ursus arctos*

Dog Family
Arctic fox *Alopex lagopus*
Coyote *Canis latrans*
Wolf *Canis lupus*
Red fox *Vulpes vulpes*

Porcupine Family
Porcupine *Erithizon dorsatum*

Mouse family
Muskrat *Ondatra zibethicus*

Beaver family
Beaver *Castor canadensis*

Squirrel family
Chipmunk *Eutamias minimus*
Flying squirrel *Glaucomys sabrinus*
Hoary marmot *Marmota caligata*
Groundhog (Lowland
  marmot) *Marmota monax*
Gopher (Arctic ground
  squirrel) *Spermophilus parryii*
Red squirrel *Tamiasciurus hudsonicus*

Rabbit family
Rabbit (Snowshoe hare) *Lepus
  americanus*

Pika Family
Pika *Ochotona princeps*

Members of the Porcupine caribou herd, in winter and summer (Yukon Government photos)

Caribou are herd animals, but the sizes of the herds vary with the season and habitat. Until recently, there were two large herds of barren-ground caribou in the Yukon. Each of the two came together to bear young in the early summer, then separated into smaller bands in the fall. One of these large herds, the Porcupine Herd of the northern Yukon, still exists. Its members winter in groups in the Ogilvie Mountains, the Eagle Plain, and the Richardson Mountains. In spring, the herd gathers on its slow journey to the northwest, crossing the Porcupine River in late April near Old Crow and arriving at the calving grounds in the arctic tundra of the northern Yukon and Alaska in late May or early June. Here the calves are dropped, and the herd remains together until late August, when it begins to migrate south to the wintering range. Rutting or mating occurs in mid-October in the mountains. In the 1970s, this herd numbered about 110,000 animals, but it was probably larger in the past.

The second major caribou herd in the Yukon Territory is called the Forty Mile or Dawson Herd. It once ranged over the west-central and southwestern portions of the territory and parts of Alaska. This herd may have been larger than the Porcupine Herd, but overhunting has drastically reduced its numbers. The great migrations of the past no longer occur. During the nineteenth century, caribou from this herd are said to have wintered as far southeast as Atlin in British Columbia, and in the early twentieth century the herd still migrated in the autumn to the headwaters of the White River and to the Whitehorse area. For summer calving, it concentrated in the area around Dawson and the Forty Mile River. Today, far fewer caribou are found there. They live now in smaller bands and do not move about very much.

Lesser numbers of mountain or woodland caribou occur throughout the rest of the Yukon Territory. They behave much like the remnants of the Forty Mile Herd. These animals, which are as a rule somewhat larger than barren-ground caribou, do not form large groups or make long migrations. They spend most of the year in small bands of about twenty animals, moving between the mountains and lower country with the seasons. They will, however, often congregate in larger groups during the rutting season, in September and October.

The moose is the largest member of the deer family, with large males weighing over 800 kilograms. These animals are found now in all but the northernmost portions of the Yukon. They provide a great deal of meat and also large skins for tanning. Moose seem to be fairly recent in much of their Yukon range, having gradually moved north from British Columbia between about 1875 and 1900. At that time caribou were becoming scarce, and this replacement of caribou by moose may be part of a much older natural cycle. It is possible too that moose numbers suddenly increased in the Yukon because careless white prospectors caused an increase in forest fires, and burned-over areas make good moose browse. The numbers of moose fluctuate in any case, whether or not there are forest fires, evidently because variations in snowfall also affect the vegetation on which the animals depend.

The feeding habits of moose change with the seasons. In the spring and summer, moose prefer leaves, bark, woody plants, and the aquatic plants growing in ponds and lakes. In the winter, they browse on willow, birch, fir and other trees. Moose like places with a wide variety of foods. Ideal country for moose would be a flat area near rivers, with forests broken by swamps, lakes and meadows, but with mountains nearby that have sheltered canyons and some open parkland with clumps of trees.

Unlike caribou, moose tend to live either singly or in pairs of a mother and her calf. They do not make long, seasonal migrations but remain within a limited area. During the rutting season, in September and October, however, moose may temporarily form small groups, and in winter up to three or four animals may concentrate in a small area. This is known as "yarding."

Caribou can be driven by hunters and will usually remain bunched together. Moose, on the other hand, are easily excited and will quickly leave an area by their separate ways if disturbed. These differences in behavior mean that the Yukon Indians had to think of quite different ways to capture these two important game animals.

Mountain Sheep and Mountain Goats

Two other large herbivorous (plant-eating) animals that have been important game for the Yukon Indian people are mountain sheep and mountain goats. Their meat is excellent, and very warm clothing can be made from their skins.

Male sheep weigh up to 90 kilograms; females are slightly smaller. These animals eat grasses and sedges, willows and other plants. They roam in the mountain ranges of the Yukon from the Richardson Mountains of the north to the most southerly chains. Mountain sheep live in bands of up to fifty or a hundred animals, but usually fewer, and the rams and ewes often separate into two herds in summer. Although they are mountain dwellers, sheep also cross valleys to get to salt licks and to reach new mountain pastures, especially in the spring and autumn.

Mountain goats, like sheep, eat grass, shrubs, moss and lichen, but they live higher up in the mountains than the sheep. They are also slightly smaller than sheep. The females (nannies) and the kids form into groups in summer, while the males (billies) remain alone or associate loosely with each other. The mountain goat range within the Yukon is quite limited, however, including only the St Elias and Coast Mountains and some of the mountainous areas near the headwaters of the Pelly and Liard Rivers.

Black Bears and Grizzlies

Two kinds of bears are common in the Yukon — the black bear and its larger cousin the grizzly bear. A few polar bears also sometimes wander along the Arctic coast. Males of all species of bear generally travel alone, but a female and her cubs may stay together for two years or more, until the sow (the mother) starts a new family. All adult bears are large and can be very dangerous to humans. Not all Yukon Indians will hunt or eat bears today, and it seems that this was true in the past as well.

Black bears average from 90 to 135 kilograms in weight. They live in the forest and on grassy hillsides and eat both plants and animals. The most important foods of black bears include berries, leaves, carrion (dead animals), and small mammals and birds. Bears spend most of the spring and summer getting fat for the winter. In October, the black bears den up in crevices, under stumps, or beneath piles of brush, where they enter a deep sleep for the winter. Between mid-January and early February, young are born and begin to nurse, but even then the mothers remain drowsy. When black bears leave their dens in late March and April they are hungry, and this is when they are most dangerous to humans.

Grizzly bears, though usually brown, are sometimes quite blond, and they are larger than black bears, weighing up to 360 kilograms. The grizzly bears' habits and diet are much like those of black bears, but grizzlies like to live at the edge of the timber in the mountains, where they can dig for ground squirrels. Like black bears, grizzlies den up in November and sleep until the spring.

Rodents* and Hares

There are more rodents than any other kind of mammal in the Yukon, as there are in the world as a whole. Beaver, muskrat, chipmunks, squirrels, flying squirrels, lemmings, mice, voles, groundhogs, gophers and porcupines are all rodents. Yukon Indians have long depended on several important species of rodents for both food and fur.

*Rodent comes from the Latin word *rodens*, which means gnawing. All rodents have two pairs of large front teeth, the incisors, which are set apart from their other teeth and shaped like chisels. The upper incisors continue to grow throughout the animal's lifetime.

The largest rodent now living in the Yukon is the beaver, with powerful teeth, a broad, flat tail, and rich brown fur. Beavers, particularly their tails, are very good to eat, and their fur has been in demand by white traders since the seventeenth century. The Yukon Indians themselves have also long prized it. Beavers generally weigh from 13 to 36 kilograms. They prefer wooded waterways — lakes and streams below timberline, where they feed on the wood and bark of trees, especially aspen and willow. They may build their lodges and dams from the trunks and small branches of trees they have chewed down, or dig lodges in the river banks. Beavers are always active, keeping their constructions in good repair.

The muskrat is a smaller rodent than the beaver, weighing between 800 and 1600 grams, and it breeds rapidly. Hunted both for their meat and for their skins, muskrats live in marshes, ponds, lakes and streams, especially those with plenty of cattails and pond weeds for their food. Muskrats den in the mud or make nests of reeds, staying under the ice until late spring.

Ground squirrels — or gophers, as they are often called in the

Gopher (Yukon Government photo)

*Outside the Yukon, a distinction is generally made between rabbits and hares. Hares look much like rabbits, but their young are born well-developed and active, with fur already covering their bodies. The young of rabbits are born naked and must be nursed and protected by their mothers for some time before they can function alone. If we follow these definitions, we must say there are no rabbits in the Yukon, only hares. But in the Yukon, many people prefer to call the hares rabbits. Here, either word can mean only one animal: the only long-eared, rabbit-like creature in the Yukon.

Yukon — are also rodents that are good to eat. A big one may weigh a kilogram. These animals live in open parkland, mountain meadows or tundra. They eat seeds, berries and roots, and they dig burrows to protect themselves from their numerous predators. Their larger cousins the marmots or groundhogs live in burrows above the timberline and were once a major food for Indians of the eastern Yukon. Both ground squirrels and marmots (gophers and groundhogs) also provided furs for the robes and clothing of Yukon Indians in the past.

Another small rodent common in the Yukon Territory is the red squirrel. In summer these squirrels live in trees, eating nuts, seeds, berries, birds' eggs and the seeds from pine and spruce cones. In winter they burrow under piles of pine cones, but if the weather is not too cold, they come out to climb the trees again. Few people ever eat them, but in recent times they have been snared and their pelts sold to fur buyers.

The porcupines, with their long, sharp quills, are rodents unlike any others. They feed on bark, leaves and birds, they are solitary and are active in all seasons. Although they are good climbers, they are slow and awkward on the ground. A person alone in the bush has a good chance of catching one, even without a snare or weapons. A fat porcupine weighs about nine kilograms.

The varying hare — often called a rabbit* in the Yukon — is not a rodent but resembles the rodents in several ways. Hares live in willow thickets along streams and where there is plenty of young spruce to eat. They are called varying hares because their fur changes from brown in summer to white in winter. Another of their names is snowshoe hare, because their hind feet are very large and broad, like snowshoes. A varying hare weighs about 1.5 kilograms when full grown. They eat herbs, shrubs and twigs, and they are rapid breeders. Their numbers rise and fall slightly over a cycle of about two years, but varying hares become particularly abundant about

Black bear tracks near the Tatshenshini River (Yukon Government photo)

every ten years, and then almost disappear for several seasons. In earlier times, when people could not find hares to eat they sometimes starved.

Fur Bearers

There is another group of animals which Yukon people traditionally did not depend on for food, though they have used their pelts for clothing and blankets or have traded them to other Indians or to Inuit and more recently to whites. These animals usually feed on other animals rather than on grasses or other vegetation, and they are active year round.

The marten is an agile tree-dweller that eats mainly squirrels, which it catches in the trees. It will also hunt on the ground. Martens are often found in the same area as wolverines. Their skins have always been highly valued, and some of the best marten pelts come from the Yukon.

Yukon foxes, which are quite common, also have pelts of very fine quality compared to those from many other parts of Canada. A fox may be red, cross, silver, black, grey or white in color. Cross foxes are partly red, with black cross-like patches on their shoulders. In the early part of this century a fine black or silver fox might be worth $2000. White foxes, whose coats are greyish in summer, white in winter, are usually found only on the Arctic coast. Foxes live both in the forest and on the tundra, and though they make winter dens, they do not hibernate. They live on mice and other small animals.

Wolves too are numerous in the Yukon, and some of them are large, weighing up to 45 kilograms. Their coats range from white and cream to black, but most often they are grey. Usually wolves hunt in packs which may number over thirty animals. They live in both wooded and open country. Coyotes, the wolves' smaller cousins,

Johnny Joe's granddaughter with trapped beaver, Marsh Lake, 1982

moved into the Yukon only in this century but are now widespread. Sometimes you may see them raiding garbage cans in downtown Whitehorse. Traditional Yukon Indians did not often hunt wolves, but recently they have killed both wolves and coyotes for the market value of their pelts.

The lynx, a large member of the cat family, weighing from five to more than fifteen kilograms, lives in wooded swampy areas. Because its major food is the hare, which it hunts year round, the lynx population rises and falls with the population cycle of its prey. It has very fine fur, and some people relish the meat as well.

Wolverines are large members of the weasel family, weighing up to fifteen kilograms or more. They are strong, wide-ranging and solitary animals, and they live both in the forests and on open tundra. They eat small mammals, birds and carrion, and can be very destructive on a trapline. Some Yukon Indians call the cream-colored markings on the wolverine's back his packsack.

Otter and mink, also members of the weasel family, generally live in ponds and streams. They eat fish, frogs and birds. Mink are more common in the Yukon than otters. Both animals are highly valued for their fur, but they are eaten only when people are starving.

Birds

The birds of the Yukon can be divided into two main groups: the migratory species that fly north to spend the spring and summer in the Yukon and then fly back south in the fall, and the species that live in the territory year round. Most migratory birds arrive in April or May. They live in marshes, lakes, and flat regions as well as in the forests, building their nests and raising their young. Among the most common migratory birds are waterfowl such as ducks, loons, swans

38

Frozen lynx thawing in Geoffrey Sheldon's cabin, Teslin, 1951

and geese. These large birds have long been important food for Yukon Indians.

Grouse and ptarmigan are ground-dwelling species that live year round in the Yukon. They too are good game birds.

Predatory and carrion-eating birds such as ravens*, eagles, owls and hawks also live in the Yukon year round. The Indians have not traditionally eaten them, but they hunted them to get the spines of the feathers for making snares and the feathers themselves both for arrows and for ritual purposes.

Fish

Fish, especially salmon and whitefish, are another important food source for humans in the Yukon.

Salmon begin their lives in small freshwater streams and lakes, then swim long distances to the salt water of the Pacific Ocean or Bering Sea where they grow to maturity. When they are ready to spawn, which means to lay and fertilize their eggs, they begin their long return journey from the ocean to the waters in which they were born. Here they spawn and then die.

Salmon runs occur in two of the four main Yukon drainage basins: those of the Yukon River and the Alsek. In Whitehorse, where there is a fish ladder, you can see a detailed map showing where the different species of salmon go to spawn, and in late summer you can see the salmon themselves going up the ladder over the hydroelectric dam.

Both king (chinook) salmon and dog (chum) salmon travel up the Yukon River from the Bering Sea. The king salmon, which runs in July and August, can weigh up to 23 kilograms, while the dog salmon, which arrive in September, are smaller. Because these fish must travel so far to reach their spawning grounds, many of them

* The situation with crows and ravens is much like that with hares and rabbits. The large, curious, omnivorous black birds found all over the Yukon are also found in many parts of the south, and there they are always called ravens, to distinguish them from their much smaller cousins called crows. By these definitions, there are no crows in the Yukon, only ravens. But in the Yukon, many people call the ravens crows.

Albert Isaac with goshawk caught in a snare, Aishihik, 1963

are thin and poor by the time they are caught by humans high up the Yukon River system. However, they are still fat and good along the lower Nisling and the Stewart, Pelly, Little Salmon and Big Salmon rivers. Yukon Indians used to have fish camps for salmon on the McClintock and Nisutlin Rivers too.

The salmon in the Alsek River have a much shorter trip from the ocean. Here there are four species of salmon: the king (chinook), the dog (chum), the sockeye, and the silver (coho) salmon. Sockeyes are the most numerous species in the Alsek drainage.

Salmon do not reach all of the upper limits of the Yukon and Alsek river systems. For example, they do not go beyond Fraser Falls on the Stewart River, nor do they reach Aishihik Lake.

Except for some chum salmon in the Peel River, no salmon come into the Yukon Territory through tributaries of the Mackenzie. But the Peel and Liard rivers do have heavy runs of whitefish, inconnu, river trout, cisco (often called freshwater herring) and loche (often called ling cod). Trout, whitefish and loche are also found in most other Yukon streams. Grayling, suckers and jackfish (northern pike) are common too. In many Yukon lakes, trout, whitefish, jackfish, grayling, inconnu and loche can be caught both summer and winter.

Trout are very close relatives of the salmon. Grayling is a more distant member of the same family. Whitefish, inconnu and cisco belong to a group called the coregonins, and they are members of the salmon family too. Loche, which spawn in midwinter under the ice, belong to the cod family. Pike and suckers both belong to families of their own.

THE PEOPLE

The Yukon Indians

In 1976 about 20,000 people were recorded living in the Yukon, and by 1981 the number had increased to more than 23,000. About 6000 of these were native people as counted by the Council for Yukon Indians. This includes what are called both status and non-status Indians. In the Yukon there are now roughly equal numbers of each.

The federal government, through the Department of Indian and Northern Affairs, makes a distinction between status and non-status Indians, and the difference between these two is discussed in this book in Chapter Five. Here it is enough to say simply that status Indians are those whom the Department of Indian and Northern Affairs includes on its official band lists. But in this book, generally no distinction is made between status and non-status Indians. This book is about the Yukon Indian heritage and culture, which are common to all.

Before 1839 the entire population of the Yukon was native Indian, except for a few Inuvialuit (Western Eskimo) along the Arctic coast. All the Inuvialuit settlements are now gone from the Yukon, and Inuvialuit culture is not discussed in this book except for a brief note at the end of this chapter. Thousands of white people have

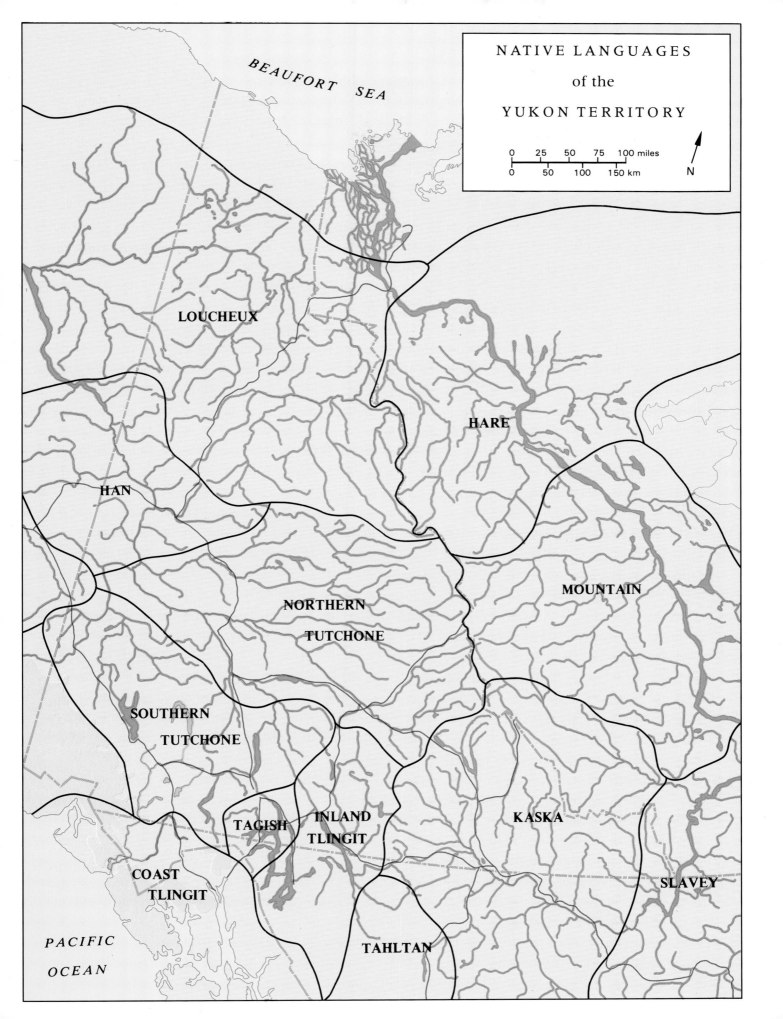

NATIVE LANGUAGES
of the
YUKON TERRITORY

0   25   50   75   100 miles
0   50   100   150 km

N

BEAUFORT SEA

PACIFIC OCEAN

LOUCHEUX

HAN

HARE

MOUNTAIN

NORTHERN
TUTCHONE

SOUTHERN
TUTCHONE

TAGISH

INLAND
TLINGIT

KASKA

SLAVEY

COAST
TLINGIT

TAHLTAN

come to the Yukon in the last 150 years, but since this is a book about the Yukon Indians, whites in the Yukon are discussed only in their relationship to the Indian people.

In 1980 the Department of Northern Affairs and the Council for Yukon Indians recognized twelve formal bands of Yukon Indians. These were: Old Crow, Dawson, Mayo, Carmacks, Fort Selkirk– Pelly Crossing, Ross River, Whitehorse, Kluane, Champagne– Aishihik, Carcross, Teslin, and Watson Lake–Liard. This list represents a slight reorganization of earlier lists of bands set up for administrative purposes by the Canadian government or by the Indians themselves. The number of bands recognized has varied from time to time, and the names have also sometimes changed. In 1984, there was a further change, when the Whitehorse Band altered its name to Kwänlin Dun (Southern Tutchone for "People of the Rapids").

The band names now in use all refer to the towns or areas where most of the band members live. But we know that the Yukon Indians were once hunters who moved from place to place with the seasons instead of living in these towns. Do all the Indians in each of these present-day towns live exactly the same way and speak the same language? It turns out they do not. They have a great deal in common, but different groups of present-day Yukon Indians do have different customs and languages, developed and enriched over centuries of traditional life on the land. For this reason modern scholars — ethnographers* and linguists — often use names for Yukon Indians which are different from the official band names used by the government and by Indian organizations.

Ethnographers and linguists have placed the Yukon Indians into seven groups on the basis of their languages and, to some extent, of their cultures. These seven groups are Loucheux (sometimes called Kutchin), Han, Northern Tutchone, Southern Tutchone, Kaska, Tagish, and Tlingit. The native languages of members of the first five groups are slightly different from each other, but all belong to one great language family called Athapaskan. The original Tagish language too was Athapaskan, but present-day Tagish Indians speak a dialect of Tlingit, which does not belong to the Athapaskan language family. (Yukon Indian languages are discussed in more detail in Chapter Six.)

The map on page 41 shows the location of these linguistic groups at about the time of the gold rush of 1898. If the map were drawn to show where the ancestors of these groups had been living a hundred years earlier, it would look a little different. The Kaska-speaking Indians would probably not be as far down the Pelly River, nor the Tlingit speakers as far up the Nisutlin.

A map drawn today to locate the descendants of those 1898 Indians would also look different. For example, modern Whitehorse is located in an area where there was formerly a Southern Tutchone settlement. The incoming whites built Whitehorse into an urban centre after 1898, and as the town has grown it has attracted Indians from all over the Yukon. In Whitehorse one now finds Indians who speak several different languages. People move about, and their cul-

* The word *ethnographer* comes from the Greek words *ethnos*, which means people, and *graphein*, which means to write or describe. Ethnographers are people who study and write about the ways of life of different people throughout the world. *Linguists* are those who study the languages used by different people and explore the similarities and differences between them.

tures and languages change, sometimes slowly, sometimes fast. This means that in order to understand the Yukon Indians and their cultures, we must look at their past as well as their present. In later chapters of this book, we will do just that.

What happened to the Yukon Inuvialuit?

At present there are no Inuvialuit – or western Arctic Inuit – settlements in the Yukon. Alaskan and Canadian Eskimo groups certainly passed back and forth along the Arctic coast of the Yukon for many centuries, and until recently some of them hunted on the north slope and along the Arctic shore. It seems, however, that the Inuvialuit population of the Yukon was always very small. In 1890, when white whalers began to use Herschel Island, off the coast of the Yukon, as a storage and wintering centre, about 400 or 500 Inuvialuit gathered there. Others lived on small islands along the coast, from Demarcation Point to Shingle Point. In the nineteenth century too, the great Porcupine caribou herd still visited the coast each summer, attracting Inuit from east and west. By about 1920, however, because of disease and other disruptions brought in by the white whalers and traders, many Inuvialuit had died and the rest had left the Yukon. All remaining Inuvialuit settlements are in the Northwest Territories.

THE TWELVE CURRENT
YUKON INDIAN BANDS

Old Crow
Dawson
Mayo
Carmacks
Fort Selkirk– Pelly Crossing
Ross River
Kwänlin Dun
Kluane
Champagne-Aishihik
Carcross
Teslin
Watson Lake– Liard

THE SEVEN YUKON
INDIAN LANGUAGES

Athapaskan family:
    Loucheux
    Han
    Northern Tutchone
    Southern Tutchone
    Kaska
    Tagish
Tlingit family:
    Tlingit

3

The Earth and Her Memories: Geology and Archaeology in the Yukon

THE ICE AGE AND THE BERING LAND BRIDGE

What did the landscape look like when the first hunters wandered into the Yukon long ago? For help with this question, we may turn to modern scientists, although they themselves do not know all the answers.

Geology* is the study of the nature and history of the earth itself. Geologists look at the locations of different kinds of rocks; they study pebbles or clay which were once in the beds of rivers and lakes; they inspect the rocks in mountains and valleys for signs of glacial action and for old volcanic ash, different kinds of minerals, or other traces of past geological activity. All of this helps them to reconstruct past landscapes.

Geologists work with other scholars who are interested in ancient animals and plants and how they were affected by changing climates. The fossil bones of ancient animals are studied by paleontologists* and the remains of ancient plants by paleobotanists*. Some paleobotanists specialize in studying ancient pollens. Pollen is like fine dust, but it is usually well preserved in layers of soil laid down in earlier times by wind or water. Paleobotanists count the amounts and kinds of pollen in older soils to see whether they contain more grass or more tree pollens. Grasses can grow in very cold tundra-like conditions, but trees such as spruce and poplar grow only when there are warm summers. Soil which is built up in cold weather may have a lot of grass pollen in it, while that formed in warmer times may contain more tree pollen. Analysis of the kinds of pollen in sample layers of old soil shows how climates have changed over thousands of years.

Working with all these clues – from rocks, soils, animals and plants – geologists and other scientists have divided the earth's past into four great eras, which they subdivide further into periods and epochs or ages of different lengths. Here we discuss only the last two ages or subdivisions of the Cenozoic era – the era of recent life. These ages are called the Pleistocene and the Holocene. The first humans appeared in the Pleistocene age, probably in Africa.

In everyday terms, the Pleistocene is often called the Ice Age and the Holocene is referred to as Recent time. Recent in this sense means during the last 10,000 to 12,000 years. During the Ice Age, which began about 3,000,000 years ago, the climate of the northern

Precambrian Era	origin of earth to 570,000,000 years ago	The Precambrian covers the first four billion years or so of the earth's life. During this period were formed the land, the sea, the air and the first plants and animals.
Paleozoic Era	570,000,000 to 225,000,000 years ago	First fishes, amphibians, reptiles and conifers.
Mesozoic Era	225,000,000 to 70,000,000 years ago	Appearance of the dinosaurs, then the first mammals, birds and flowering plants, then the extinction of the dinosaurs.
Cenozoic Era	70,000,000 years ago to present	Rise of the modern mammals and flowering plants. Then, about two million years ago, the first humans. Since the appearance of humans, geologists say, there have been four major glaciations. These are the Nebraskan (about 1.5 million years ago), the Kansan (one million years ago), the Illinois (300,000 years ago) and the Wisconsin (from about 50,000 to 10,000 years ago).

part of the world got very cold at least four times — far colder than it ever gets today. Each time it grew so cold, great ice sheets spread out over much of the land in North America, Europe and Asia, and each of these ice sheets lasted for thousands of years. When it snowed, the snow froze to the ice sheets. Not much ice melted, even in summer, so very little water ran down the rivers into the oceans, and the oceans and seas became very shallow.

Between the very cold periods, however, the climate warmed up again for a few thousand years. Every time it warmed up, the ice sheets melted and the oceans rose again, because more water flowed into them.

The cold periods of the Ice Age are called glacials, and the periods when the climate became warmer are called interglacials. The climate is warm now, but geologists do not know how long it will stay that way. Some think that we may be living in another interglacial period like the earlier ones, and that more glaciations will occur in the future.

In North America, the last glacial stage of the Pleistocene or Ice Age is called the Wisconsin period. It began about 50,000 years ago and ended about 10,000 years ago.

During the Wisconsin glacial period people probably began to live for the first time in North America. They came here from northeast Asia. Though they may not have been aware of it, they had left the Old World for the New.

Scientists do not yet all agree on how early in the Wisconsin period these human beings first arrived. They are pretty sure, however, that whenever it was, they did not have to use boats. During the Wisconsin glacial a huge land bridge joined Siberia to Alaska. So much water had frozen up in Wisconsin ice sheets that the water level in the Bering Sea and Bering Strait dropped drastically. The sea-

Palaios means old, and *botanê* is the Greek word for plant. *Paleobotany* is the branch of science concerned with the plants of earlier times.

bottom became land, and people could walk from Siberia to Alaska and the Yukon.

Most geologists think that the land bridge remained high and dry throughout the Wisconsin glacial, even though there was some warming in the middle of the period. But at the end of the Wisconsin glacial, about 10,000 years ago, the climate became so warm that almost all of the giant glaciers in the world melted. The oceans rose to their present levels, and the waters of the Bering Sea and Bering Strait as we know them today once again divided Siberia and Alaska.

Beringia is the geologists' name for the former land bridge and the parts of Siberia, Alaska and the Yukon that it connected. Beringia stretched several thousand miles north and south of where the Bering Strait is today.

Beringia itself was never covered by ice in the Wisconsin glacial period. It was a vast tundra with no trees, rather like the present North Slope of Alaska and the Yukon. Low birches and willows, mosses and lichens, grasses and herbs probably grew on it. This would have made good browse for great woolly mammoths, bison, musk ox, caribou, wild horses, camels and other Ice Age animals. Early hunters could have followed the big game on foot from Siberia (Western Beringia) right into the Yukon (Eastern Beringia).

What happened when Wisconsin hunters reached Eastern Beringia? Did they keep travelling right across the mountains, moving out of what is now the Yukon into the Northwest Territories and onto the great plains in Alberta and Manitoba? A number of scientists think that is what happened. Others say that it would not have been possible.

Disagreement on this point stems from uncertainty about when and how the edges of two huge ice sheets were joined together during the Wisconsin glacial, or whether they were ever joined at all. In each of the four major glacial periods of the Ice Age, one huge ice sheet, called the Laurentide, spread out from Hudson Bay, while another ice sheet, called the Cordilleran, spread out from the North American Cordillera. If the edges of these two big ice sheets touched each other during the Wisconsin period, the ice would have blocked any travel east and south of the Yukon. Any animals or people who had crossed from Siberia into North America would all have had to stay in Beringia. They would have been living in what is sometimes called the Beringian Refugium — a place of refuge from all the surrounding ice.

If, however, the two big ice sheets did *not* touch each other during the Wisconsin glacial, or if they only did so during parts of the period, then the early hunters could have moved out of the Yukon along an ice-free corridor and continued south.

So far nobody has proven whether or not there really was such a Wisconsin Corridor. Everybody agrees, however, that by about 10,000 years ago the Laurentide ice sheet had almost disappeared, and the only Cordilleran glaciers left were in the high mountains and on the North Pacific coast. Animals and humans could then have travelled east and south. About this time, however, many Ice Age

46

animals such as the mammoths, wild horses and camels that had been living in Beringia died out. In some places they had already disappeared a few thousand years earlier.

Why did the animals die out? Perhaps it was because of a change in vegetation. There was probably not enough arctic forage left for the Ice Age animals to eat. Because the weather had grown warmer, much of the open grassland and tundra was gradually changing to forests more like those in the Yukon today. Another idea is that the big animals disappeared, not because they ran out of food, but because human hunters had killed too many of them and not enough were left to reproduce. There is no strong archaeological evidence for such overkill by ancient hunters in Yukon, but there is definite evidence that human hunters were here in the territory at the end of the Wisconsin glacial stage.

ICE AGE ARCHAEOLOGY* IN THE YUKON

Archaeologists are people in the present who study peoples of the distant past. An archaeologist is often somewhat like a hunter trying to track down an animal that passed by so long ago that its trail has almost been wiped out. The hunter asks: "How long ago did the animal go past? Which way did it go? Where did it stop to rest? What kind of animal was it?" In the same way, the archaeologist asks: "How long ago did the first people come to the Yukon? Where did they camp? What was their culture like?"

When any group of people makes the same kind of things and shares the same language, ideas and behavior, this group is said to have the same culture. Archaeologists cannot retrieve vanished languages, but they can sometimes dig up the material part — the artifacts of ancient cultures. An artifact is any material object made by humans. It could be of bone, stone, metal or some other substance. It could be a weapon, an ornament, a tool. The ideas and behavior of past peoples remain clearest in written records or in human memory. An archaeologist trying to describe an ancient culture often has only some artifacts and — if he is lucky — some remains of the food that a group of people left behind. He has to guess about the rest of their culture.

When archaeologists do find traces of human culture, they usually talk with geologists who might help them understand the age and nature of the gravels, caves or other places where the artifacts have been discovered. To help determine the purpose of old tools and weapons, archaeologists also try to find out if anybody has used similar artifacts in more recent times. They ask the old people in the country if they know where their ancestors used to stay, and how they made a living. Yukon Indian elders have important things to tell archaeologists, though of course the field investigations are essential too.

Archaeologists do not always agree on how to date or interpret their finds, especially those that seem to be very old. Often they have little evidence to go on. If they find traces of human activity in undis-

*Archaios is a Greek word meaning old or early. Archaeology is the study of the old ones — that is, the study of earlier cultures.

47

turbed levels of earth on top of one another, like cake layers, they know that the things in the bottom levels are older than those on top. However, unless they can associate each layer with a dated geological or other natural or historical event, they have no way of knowing the precise age of the things in it. There could be long gaps between the time when people lived at one level and the time when the next level of human occupation was formed. If the site cannot be dated geologically, archaeologists have to guess the date by analyzing the style or kinds of artifacts in it, or by using some other method.

Every archaeologist hopes to discover ancient camp sites with lots of tools and weapons in them, as well as the bones of animals or the seeds of berries that the people were eating. But often the archaeologist finds only broken bits of knives or spear points, or just chips of the stone from which such tools may have been made. People usually take their good things with them when they break camp.

Even if the people had left all of their belongings in their camps, archaeologists still could not possibly find everything that the families actually were using every day. Stone artifacts last for thousands of years, but conditions have to be just right for bone and antler to be preserved for that long. Only in very special cases do wood, bark, fur, hide or sinew survive for more than a century.

Yet another problem in finding out about past Yukon cultures is that the Yukon is a big country and not many archaeologists have worked in it. So far, they have found only a few sites where people lived at different times in the past. When more archaeologists are at work in the Yukon looking for them, more old living places will be found, but no matter how many archaeologists there are, they can never find *all* of the old camps. Water, frost and ice have destroyed many of them, and things that once were in the camps have now been rolled about in river beds, mixed by frost heaves, or pushed about by ice and other natural forces. When the artifacts are discovered, they may be far from where the people who made and used them once lived. It is hard to tell which ones belong together and whether they are of the same age.

Nor are ice and water the only agents that spoil archaeological sites. Animals may disturb them, and people sometimes thoughtlessly disturb them too. They push the earth about with bulldozers when they are making roads, or they tear down sandy hillsides racing their motorcycles or other vehicles. The artifacts and associated bones of food animals are crushed and scattered. Some precious clues to the Yukon's past have already been lost through such actions.

For all these reasons, there is still a great deal of guesswork about when and how people used to live in the Yukon and who they were, especially in the earliest times. Archaeologists are still finding, interpreting, and then reinterpreting new materials. Parts of this chapter will certainly have to be corrected or added to within a few years.

Anybody might be lucky enough to add to the archaeological record by finding a place used by people long ago but now abandoned.

It might be an old brush house or a broken-down part of a brush fence once used for surrounding caribou. It might be a collapsed log cabin, or an old tree with roots entwined around a stone adze lost long ago. At the oldest sites there may be just a few stone chips or broken animal bones or an ancient river terrace. If you discover an archaeological site, you ought not to disturb it or take anything away. You should try to note how large the place is, how to get there, and what kinds of artifacts are visible. If possible, the location of the place should be marked on a map. The discovery should always be reported to the Director of the Yukon Department of Heritage and Cultural Resources in Whitehorse or to the Council for Yukon Indians, who will notify the Department.

Possible Archaeological Finds from the Early Period:
30,000 to 25,000 Years Ago

What may be the earliest traces of human activity in the Yukon Territory are some battered pieces of fossil bones, antler and teeth — possibly once used as tools — and the cracked bones of animals that the toolmakers may have eaten. Many of the bones, antlers, and teeth come from kinds of animals that no longer live anywhere on earth. So far, most of these finds are from the Old Crow River valley, but a few possible early bone artifacts have also been found near Dawson and along the Stewart River. All of these possible artifacts and food bones were found mixed in with many naturally cracked bones of different kinds of animals of the Wisconsin glacial.

We call these *possible* artifacts because it is often hard to tell a naturally cracked stone or bone from one that a human has cut or cracked for a special purpose. This is particularly true of very simple tools. A cobblestone that someone has deliberately split to make a skin scraper may look almost the same as one split by the frost or by knocking against other stones in a stream bed. A piece of bone used by a human as a temporary cutting or scraping tool may look like one cracked by a wolf or by the jostling of river gravels. For these reasons archaeologists do not all agree on whether the old bones from near Old Crow or elsewhere really are artifacts.

One tool that everybody is quite certain about is a caribou-bone flesher or punch used to take the meat off an animal hide. Peter Lord, a Loucheux Indian, found the flesher near Old Crow in 1966. It is made of a fossil caribou leg bone, and has little notches at the working end. In fact, it looks very much like the moose or caribou bone fleshers with which some Yukon Indian women still work their skins. Only a human with a definite purpose in mind could have split the bone and cut the notches in the end.

When was the flesher made? And when were the other possible artifacts from the Old Crow area made? One big difficulty in dating them has been that neither the flesher nor any of the other possible tools or bones in question were actually found in places where they were first used or deposited. All of them had been washed out of their original sites and then rolled along in silty river beds at some

The Old Crow flesher, 26 cm long, now dated at only about 1000 years old (Canadian Museum of Civilization)

time in the past. These objects show up now in the banks of the Old Crow River or on gravel terraces of former lakes and streams in the area. Careful study of the gravel layers suggests that many must date from about 25,000 years ago. Some may be older, some younger. But even the most accurate dating of the gravel layers cannot absolutely date the materials in them, since these may have come from other places.

Fortunately there is another way to date old bone and other organic material. This is the radiocarbon or carbon-14 method of dating, developed by atomic physicists. It can be used to find the age of material such as bone, wood or charcoal, so long as it is not older than about 40,000 years. The method depends on measuring the amount of carbon-14 (C^{14}) that has been lost since the death of the animal or plant from which the material comes.

The C^{14} dating system has been in use since the 1950s and has been improved over the years, but dates obtained by this method are still not always reliable. It is possible, for example, that an artifact will be contaminated by more recent living matter, which may be hard to detect and may spoil the dating. And C^{14} dating will not work for inorganic materials such as stone.

When the flesher from the Old Crow gravels was first discovered, scientists dated it at about 27,000 years old. In 1985, using newer techniques, they estimated that it was only about a thousand years old. New tests have given the same date for three pieces of antler found near Old Crow that look like they may have been tools. Some other fragments of bone and antler that come from the same area but look less like known human artifacts are still dated between 30,000 and 25,000 years old. From this evidence, we still cannot be sure whether or not human hunters were living in the Yukon in mid-Wisconsin times.

Yukon People at the End of the Ice Age

Big Ice Age animals remained plentiful in the Yukon after 25,000 years ago, but this was a period of very harsh conditions. The southern Yukon was covered by thick glacial ice, and the northern part was a wide, cold, windswept plain where only mosses, lichens, grasses and other low plants grew. Large glacial lakes filled the Old Crow valley. Human beings might well have found it impossible to survive in the Yukon then, even if they had been here earlier.

After a few thousand years of these harsh conditions, the climate began to warm up a bit, some of the ice melted, and the level of the water in the Bering Sea rose. Dwarf birch began to grow in the northern Yukon. From this period, scientists have found unmistakable signs of human activity in the area, though the record is still sparse and hard to interpret.

The best signs of people in the northern Yukon at this period come from Bluefish Caves, on the Bluefish River, south of Old Crow. In these caves archaeologists have found a pounding stone and a few stone chips. These chips look as if they were knocked off flint cores from which the people were making tools, or as if they had broken off the tools themselves. Along with the stone chips, investigators found the bones of animals that the people in Bluefish Caves were probably eating – some mammoth, wild horse, bison, caribou, moose, musk ox and mountain sheep. They also found two bone tools probably used for fleshing hides. All these finds have been dated by older C^{14} methods to between 17,000 and 12,000 years ago.

There may or may not have been an ice-free corridor south out of the Yukon during the middle of the Wisconsin glacial period – that is, around 30,000 to 25,000 years ago. But toward the end of the Wisconsin period – after 15,000 years ago – humans could probably have travelled south out of the Yukon into other parts of North America. There is even some evidence that people began to live along the Cordillera in the Yukon, British Columbia and Alberta during this time. A number of stone spear points, leaf-shaped stone knives, a few fluted points and other stone implements have been found scattered through the region, and some archaeologists date these artifacts from between 15,000 and 10,000 years ago. Taken together, these artifacts represent what some archaeologists call the Cordilleran Tradition. Perhaps the most likely Cordilleran sites in the Yukon are along Flint Creek, a few miles from the Arctic coast. Another possible site is near Kluane Lake.

Few of the Cordilleran tools are very distinctive, but they are unlike anything in the Bluefish Caves. Perhaps the Cordilleran artifacts will prove to have been made by several different groups living at different times. It is also possible that the Cordilleran toolmakers moved north from what is now the United States into Alberta and British Columbia and on into the Yukon. Still another possibility is that the Cordilleran Tradition was introduced into the Yukon by hunters who had earlier been living in interior Alaska. To solve the problem, we must discover many more well-dated sites and more distinctively Cordilleran tools.

Leaf-shaped point from Little Arm, Kluane Lake, about 7.5 cm long (Canadian Museum of Civilization)

THE MICROBLADE MAKERS: 10,000 TO 4500 YEARS AGO

By 10,000 years ago the Ice Age had ended, and the era we call the Holocene or Recent had begun. Many large Ice Age animals, like the woolly mammoth, had disappeared, but there were still plenty of bison, which could eat the tall grasses that continued to cover parts of Alaska and the Yukon. Caribou also survived, and there were more of them than ever before.

It is pretty certain that at the end of the Ice Age a new group of hunters was moving from Eastern Siberia across the shrinking land bridge into Alaska and on into the Yukon. They brought with them a distinctive kind of artifact: a tiny, specially shaped stone flake called a microblade. A well-made microblade is long compared to its width. It has two perfectly straight, sharp edges and is of even width and thickness. A typical microblade is about 7 x 40 x 2.5 millimeters, or one-quarter inch wide, one and a half inches long and very thin. The

Typical northern microblades
(Canadian Museum of Civilization)

closest modern thing to a microblade is an injector razor blade, made of steel, but the ancient craftsmen produced their microblades one at a time, by hand, out of stone. Making such tools requires great skill.

What did people do with microblades? When mounted in a handle, a microblade might have been used for delicate tasks such as cutting babiche, cutting out patterns for skin clothing, fine carving of bone or wood, or even for surgery. Mounted in grooves along the sides of bone and antler arrow points, microblades formed keen cutting edges that would have been useful for killing animals. At first, the points with microblade inserts were probably fastened to long, spear-like darts which were cast with the aid of a spear thrower. Inuit and some Coast Tlingit hunters used spear throwers with their harpoon darts until almost modern times. Microblade points may also have been used with arrows. We do not know when bows and arrows first appeared in the Yukon, but it may have been while microblades were still being made.

The study of microblades helps archaeologists to trace the history of northern peoples, because not every early group of hunters had microblades. The specially prepared blocks or cores of stone from which they are struck off seem to have appeared earlier in northern Asia. The oldest microblades yet found in North America come from central Alaska, and they appear to be nearly 11,000 years old. Evidently the people who were making them continued to spread eastward.

The early Yukon sites with microblades are hard to date, but by about 8000 years ago the record becomes clearer, especially in the southwestern part of the territory. At Canyon Creek, where the Alaska Highway now crosses the Aishihik River, is an old camp which once overlooked the grasslands covering what had earlier been the bottom of glacial Lake Champagne. The Canyon Creek site is layered, and in its lowest levels archaeologists found two broken stone spearheads, some other stone flakes, some microblades, and some large bison bones. The ancient hunters who left these things must have found the place a good spot from which to search the landscape for the large bison or other game out in the grasslands. In much later times, during this century, the Southern Tutchone Indians built several of their grave houses high up on this bluff as if it were still a special place. You can stand there now and look across miles of forests and meadows stretching to the mountains in the southeast.

The microblades and other flaked stone tools in the early Canyon Creek level belong to what archaeologists call the Little Arm Culture, because these kinds of artifacts were first found along the Little Arm (Brooks Arm) of Kluane Lake. Similar stone tool kits have now been located in other places in the Yukon — for example, near Otter Falls on the Aishihik Road. This does not mean that Little Arm people lived wherever microblades are found. Other early hunters also knew how to make microblades, but the rest of their tools were often different from those found at Little Arm and Canyon Creek.

Microblades were made in the Yukon for a long time — from about 10,000 years ago to about 4500 years ago — and there is much yet to learn about the people who made them. Unfortunately, most of the microblades discovered in the Yukon have come from scattered surface finds, which means they come with very few additional clues.

Whoever they were, the Yukon hunters of this period had to adapt to the changing conditions that followed the end of the Ice Age. At first, they could go on hunting the bison and other animals of the open tundra, but as time went on, the spruce forests spread and people had to learn to hunt the animals of the mountains, hills and valleys — mountain sheep, mountain goats, woodland caribou, moose and smaller mammals such as marmots. Perhaps as they travelled east and south, the makers of microblades also met and mixed with other bands of hunters. It looks as though the people of the microblade cultures continued to learn new ways of doing things. Perhaps they developed all the new ideas themselves, but it seems more likely that they borrowed some of these new ideas from people of other cultures whom they met through trade, marriage or war. Perhaps they also taught other groups how to make microblades, for these handsome tools are very widespread in northwestern North America.

Microblade cores. The upper one comes from King Lake, in the northern Yukon, and the lower one from Little Arm. The cores are about 4 cm high. (Canadian Museum of Civilization)

THE NOTCHED-POINT HUNTERS: 4500 TO 100 YEARS AGO

The Taye Lake Culture: 4500 to 1300 Years Ago

What happened next? Sometime about 5000 or 4500 years ago, most of the Yukon hunters stopped making microblades. Especially in the southwestern Yukon, a new kind of stone point with a notch on each side became common, marking the beginning of a new archaeological tradition.

The notches in these stone points are located near the base, so that the points could easily be tied onto the ends of wooden shafts to make spears. Some notched points with crooked edges might have been used as knives. And along with the appearance of these notched points come many other changes. For the first time, the old camp sites of this period have stone chopping tools and stone sinkers for fish nets. Other tools, such as skin scrapers, exhibit new forms. In fact there are so many changes in the stone artifacts of the southern Yukon at this period, and the changes are so great, that it seems likely an entirely new people had arrived in the country.

Since the notched points and other new-style artifacts were first found around Taye Lake (part of the Mendenhall River system, north of the Alaska Highway between Champagne and Whitehorse), the people who made these tools have come to be known as the Taye Lake people. Archaeologists later found other sites containing notched points and other tools and weapons very much like those at

Notched points. The upper one, from Black Fox Ridge in the northern Yukon, is about 3 cm long, and the lower one, from Aishihik (Taye Lake Culture), is about 8 cm long. (Canadian Museum of Civilization)

Taye Lake. Some were in other parts of the Yukon, others in neighboring Alaska and the Northwest Territories. The people who made these artifacts were either very closely related or else they visited each other so much that they ended up copying each other's tools. Altogether, these notched-point cultures constitute what archaeologists call the Northern Archaic Tradition. The Taye Lake Culture is the southern Yukon phase of this tradition.

The oldest sites of the Northern Archaic Tradition are probably 6000 or 7000 years old, and they occur in northern Alaska. Because of this, some scholars think that the Taye Lake people came into the Yukon from the northwest. Others believe that they may have come from south and east of the Yukon. Wherever they came from, when they got to the Yukon these newcomers appear to have mixed in some places with people who were still making microblades.

The people of the Taye Lake Culture were probably ancestors of the Athapaskan-speaking Indians who still live in the southern Yukon. It is rarely possible to know what language was spoken by the makers of any set of really old artifacts. Microblades and notched points keep those secrets to themselves; they do not talk. But there is one strong reason for thinking that the Taye Lake people may have chatted to each other in Athapaskan languages. The reason is that the archaeological record of the Northern Archaic Tradition shows so much continuity with the cultures of modern Athapaskan speakers. The overall style of the Northern Archaic artifacts and associated patterns of living seems to have persisted from the beginning of Taye Lake times right up to the time when the first whites arrived and found most of the Yukon natives speaking Athapaskan languages. So it seems a good guess that the Northern Archaic hunters and fishers spoke Athapaskan languages too.

It is unlikely, however, that every single Northern Archaic band that once lived in the Yukon has left modern descendants. Some small groups must have prospered and grown in numbers until there were so many people that it was hard to get enough game to feed everybody. Then these bands would have divided. Some of the people would have moved to new hunting grounds while others stayed behind. Other bands may have had such hard times that all the people died off, or the few who still lived joined up with neighbors.

By about 3000 years ago both the new people making notched points and any remaining makers of microblades were once more facing major geological changes, and they had to adjust their ways of living to meet the new conditions. First, the climate grew very cold again. This was not a real Ice Age glacial, but the glaciers in the St Elias Mountains did become very large. They pushed out huge piles of gravel into the valleys below, blocking up rivers and making new lakes. Around present-day Champagne and Haines Junction several big lakes formed and then disappeared. These geological changes caused great shifts in peoples' hunting and fishing patterns, their paths of travel and choice of places to live.

Then, about 1900 years ago, a volcano in the St Elias Mountains erupted. It spread a thin layer of ash all over the country around the northern part of Kluane Lake. Roughly 600 years later, around 700 AD, there was a much bigger volcanic eruption. This tremendous explosion scattered several inches of volcanic ash over the southwestern part of the Yukon. The white ash deposits are easy to see now in the road cuts along the Alaska Highway between Champagne and Burwash Landing or on the road to Dawson, especially near Carmacks. Both of these eruptions must surely have frightened the people living in the area. Perhaps the second explosion even caused some of the Taye Lake people to move south toward the southwestern United States, where many Athapaskan-speaking Indians live today.

The Aishihik Culture: 1300 to 200 Years Ago

The successors to the Taye Lake people in the southwestern Yukon are represented by the people who left behind the artifacts of the Aishihik Culture, a later phase of the Northern Archaic Tradition. The Aishihik Culture takes its name from a site near the old village of Aishihik, where such tools were first found.

Many of the stone and bone tools used by people of the Aishihik Culture were like those of the Taye Lake Culture, but certain kinds of tools became more popular. For example, the Aishihik people used many more stone wedges for splitting wood than did the Taye Lake people, although the wedges themselves look just about the same. Certain kinds of stone knives and thick stone scrapers which were perhaps used for working wood and bone are also more plentiful in Aishihik Culture sites.

What seems to be really new and important in the Aishihik technology is the introduction of bows and arrows and of copper. It is quite certain that Aishihik people regularly used bows and arrows. Their notched stone points are usually smaller than the Taye Lake points, which were probably for spears. Other small stone points with narrow stems come from Aishihik sites. These too look like arrowheads, and so do the long, thin Aishihik points hammered from native copper. The hunters may have had antler arrowheads too, but if so, these have decayed.

The large bifacial blade, above, from the southern Yukon, is about 13 cm long. Below, on the same scale, is a native copper point from the Little Arm site (but not from the Little Arm Culture, which occurred much earlier). The copper point is 6 cm long. (Both from the Canadian Museum of Civilization)

Having bows and arrows must have made hunting easier. An arrow can go a greater distance than a spear, even one propelled with the help of a spear thrower, and a man on foot can easily carry more arrows than spears with him. The new weapon would have been a welcome addition to the hunter's kit, although Aishihik people probably continued to spear swimming and snared caribou, as well as bears and fish.

The use of copper marks a major technological change. People of both the Taye Lake and Aishihik cultures lived close to the White River country where they could get copper nuggets, but only those of the Aishihik culture and the nearby Alaskan Indians seem to have used this valuable material.

Modern Yukon Indians say that their ancestors heated the raw copper, dipped it into cold water, and then hammered it into shape. There is no evidence that they knew how to smelt and pour it into a mould, but even so, copper had a great advantage over stone or bone. It could quite easily be worked into a fine, thin cutting edge or other delicate shape, and if a copper artifact broke it could often be repaired. Nineteenth-century Yukon Indians valued copper highly, and the people of the Aishihik Culture must have done so too.

In addition to making arrowheads, Aishihik people hammered out thin bars of copper, pointed at each end, which they probably covered with fish skin and dangled in the water at the end of a line. When a fish tried to swallow the bait, the double-pointed bar, called a gorge, stuck in the fish's throat. Oldtime Yukon Indians remember using gorges of the same type, but they usually made them of bone or antler rather than copper. Aishihik Culture fishermen probably had gorges of these materials too.

Other copper items that have turned up in Aishihik Culture sites are awls and danglers. Awls are pointed tools for making holes in wood or bark or skin. Some Yukon women still use steel awls to punch holes through which they push sinew thread when they are sewing moccasins or other items of tanned skin. Danglers are small pieces of copper, hammered thin, and rolled into a cone shape. Aishihik Culture women probably knotted danglers onto the fringes of shirts or trousers. Of course, the clothes from the Aishihik period have not lasted, but in museums there are several nineteenth-century skin shirts that have such copper danglers, beaver toenails, or beads strung on the fringes of the yokes.

When he was a boy, Albert Isaac, a Southern Tutchone from Aishihik, learned a story from the Copper Chief who lived near Beaver Creek. It is a story well known to many Yukon Indians. It tells how, long ago, an Indian had both an iron pick and a copper pick. Using the picks, he climbed up the steep icewall high on a mountain known as *Nat'ayat* (Mt Natazhat), but when he got there, he could not climb back down. The steps he had chipped out with his picks had melted into smooth ice. So the man just sat there until he finally turned into rock. Before he died he threw his iron pick down towards the salt water. It is said that is why the Indians there had iron. But he threw his copper pick towards the Interior, saying, "Be copper on this side!" That is why the Yukon Indians have copper. Oldtimers said you could still see the man turned to rock up in the glacier.

The Aishihik Culture lasted from right after the second big volcanic eruption of about 700 AD until about 1800 AD. During this time the landscape and climate continued to change. In the early part of the period, spruce and other forest trees began to spread over parts of the country that had still been grassland in Taye Lake times. In the southwestern Yukon, forests grew up in much the same places where they are today. Perhaps the Aishihik people used more wedges than the Taye Lake people simply because there were more trees. Soon, however — between 1400 and 1800 AD — the climate of Yukon cooled again. Glaciers in the St Elias Mountains once more spread out, pushing gravel about, and making ice-dammed lakes. The last of these lakes did not finally dry up until the end of the nineteenth century. The biggest one was Lake Alsek, around present-day Haines Junction. Archaeologists found part of an old wooden paddle on a gravel bank which was once the beach of this lake. The paddle may date from the Aishihik Culture.

The memory of these lakes may also be preserved in another story told by Southern Tutchone Indians about a bald-headed Indian doctor from near Kloo Lake. It is said that he once grew so angry when teased about his bald head that he caused the flood that made the lakes. Annie Nicholas of Haines Junction mentions the flood in a story she tells in Chapter Twelve of this book.

Jimmy Kane, another Southern Tutchone Indian, who grew up in the late nineteenth century and lived around Dalton Post, Klukshu and Champagne, could remember when there were still no trees on the old Lake Alsek bottom near Haines Junction. He said you could see the women hunting gophers (ground squirrels) in the wide grassy meadows between Haines Junction and Bear Creek. Maggie Jim of Haines Junction described these meadows too. Now the trees grow thickly there, for the forest came back when the climate warmed up.

More than forty old camps of the Aishihik Culture have been found in the southwestern Yukon — at Aishihik Lake itself, Annie Lake, Riverdale North in Whitehorse, and elsewhere. At some of them the people were probably fishing; at others they were hunting caribou or moose or mountain sheep. It is almost certain that the Indians who were doing these things were the ancestors of living Yukon Indians.

The Bennett Lake Culture: 200 to about 100 Years Ago

The Bennett Lake phase of the Northern Archaic Tradition brings us up to the present century. So far, only a few Bennett Lake sites have been thoroughly studied, although quite a number of them are known. Besides the one on Bennett Lake that gave the culture its name, there are sites at Neskatahin on the Alsek River, at Aishihik Lake, Taye Lake, Annie Lake, and Little Atlin Lake. Clusters of old log cabins mark each of these places. During the Bennett Lake period, which was from 200 to about 100 years ago, Yukon Indians began to live for at least part of the year in settlements of permanent log houses.

The stone, bone, antler and copper artifacts in Bennett Lake sites are almost exactly like those of the Aishihik Culture, and the camps or villages themselves are located in just about the same area in the southwestern Yukon and nearby British Columbia. How then do archaeologists distinguish a Bennett Lake site from an earlier Aishihik site? The big difference is that Bennett Lake sites always have some white men's trade goods along with the stone, bone and copper artifacts. Iron or steel axes, saws, chisels, knives, and traps, brass and iron kettles, scissors, metal spoons, guns, glass beads — both large

New Dalton Post, 1949

and small — all become common, and these items were not manufactured by the Indians themselves. All Bennett Lake sites show that the Yukon Indians had made contact with the incoming whites.

Indians and whites interacted during this period in many different ways. The archaeology shows that they did not just exchange artifacts; they also learned each other's customs and ideas. For example, in a Bennett Lake site at Old Aishihik village there was a girl's drinking tube which is probably made of a swan bone. At first sight, the tube looks like it might have come from the earlier Aishihik Culture, but scratched on its side is the name "Jenny." Indians living near where the drinking tube was found in 1963 thought that the name had been cut into it with a pen knife by the first person from their band who had learned to read and write. Some of the elders remembered him well. In about 1892, as a young boy, he had gone to an Anglican mission school at Fort Selkirk. When he returned to Aishihik a few years later, his friends and relatives often asked him to carve their names on the things they owned. The Indians remembered Jenny too.

From the same site came two nice bone tools for skinning small animals. One is broken, but their elongated shapes and notched ends are reminiscent of the thousand-year-old bone flesher from Old Crow found by Peter Lord. These tools are smaller, though, and each

Camp near Champagne, on the Dalton Trail, 1898 (Yukon Archives)

has a design incised on it with a metal implement. Aishihik Indians of the 1960s saw in one of these designs a giant woodworm — a creature that the Coast Tlingit say was raised long ago by a girl at Kluk-wan. Aishihik people of Bennett Lake times probably learned the story from the Coast Tlingit with whom they used to trade.

The Bennett Lake Culture, then, brings us right up to the beginning of the twentieth century. The archaeological remains in Bennett Lake sites reflect the story of how the southern Yukon Indians first began to get white men's trade goods from other Indians, especially the Coast Tlingit, and then from the whites themselves as they came into the country. In studying the Bennett Lake Culture we have both written documents and the memories of Indian elders to help fill out details of the archaeological record. Our knowledge of Yukon Indian life becomes much more complete than for the earlier periods, as later chapters of this book will show.

Above: A bone spear point from the Old Crow area, about 18 cm long, and a bone point from Klo-kut, about 5 cm long. *Below:* Adze head from the northern Yukon, about 19 cm long. (Canadian Museum of Civilization)

PEOPLE IN THE NORTHERN, CENTRAL AND EASTERN YUKON AFTER THE ICE AGE

Prehistoric Cultures of the Northern Yukon: 1200 to 100 Years Ago

The archaeological record for the southwestern Yukon after the Ice Age is far from perfect, but it is better than that for the rest of the territory. We still do not know who left the scattered microblades found in the northern Yukon, and we do not have a clear picture of the Cordilleran Tradition. Notched points and other artifacts from the Northern Archaic Tradition have also been found at several sites in the Porcupine River drainage. For the later archaeology of the northern Yukon, scholars often just use the terms prehistoric and historic. The prehistoric period is everything before 1900 AD, and the historic period is everything after.

At Klo-kut, just above Old Crow, on the Porcupine River, archaeologists have found material going back to about 800 AD and continuing up to the early historic period. It seems probable that a single group of Loucheux Indians and their descendants camped at Klo-kut during this time. The name Klo-kut comes from the Loucheux words *Tl'oo k'at,* meaning grassy place. This is what Old Crow people still call that spot, and the archaeology of Klo-kut shows that people waited there each spring for the caribou to come, just as Old Crow people wait today.

There is evidence that in earlier prehistoric times the Klo-kut people used more birchbark than they did later. They may have been making birchbark baskets for cooking and storage, and they may have had birchbark canoes. The Klo-kut people also manufactured fine arrow points, awls, fleshers and other articles of bone and antler. An example is the beautiful carved bone fish from Klo-kut, now in the Canadian Museum of Civilization in Ottawa. The fish, which looks like a grayling, was probably used as a lure.

It is interesting that some of the Klo-kut artifacts are very much like those made by prehistoric Inupiat (Alaska Eskimo) of the Kobuk River, Alaska, just west of the homeland of the modern Loucheux Indians. But other things from Klo-kut — stone arrowheads, scrapers and other tools — look more like those from the Aishihik and Bennett Lake cultures of the southwestern Yukon. We cannot be absolutely sure, then, that the earliest people to live at Klo-kut really were Loucheux Indians, but it seems very likely.

About the late prehistoric and historic occupants of Klo-kut, there can be no doubt. Older people of Old Crow remember that Klo-kut was one of their parents' or grandparents' villages, and they tell some exciting stories about it. One such tale is about a giant who once killed many of the Indians living there. He kept pulling out the arrows the Indians shot into his body, because they tickled him and made him laugh. Then he burned up the arrow shafts in the fire. Two warriors finally tracked down the giant and his two brothers and killed them all.

There are other archaeological sites near Old Crow — at Rat Indian Creek and Old Chief Creek, for example — and it seems that ancestors of modern Loucheux Indians were living there as well.

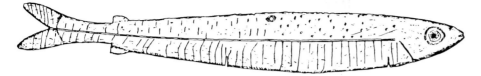

The Archaeology of the Central and Eastern Yukon

The parts of the Yukon that archaeologists know least about are the large central and eastern areas where modern Han, Northern Tutchone, Kaska and Inland Tlingit now live. In 1977 archaeologists from the Heritage Resource Department and the Council for Yukon Indians began to follow up the scanty archaeological investigations that had earlier been made along the Pelly River and some of the roads in the area, but the overall history of the region has not yet been worked out.

It was mentioned earlier that some of the scattered bones from gravels near Dawson and in the Stewart River valley look like the very oldest presumed tools from near Old Crow, but so far only *possible* artifacts have been found, and they have not been dated precisely.

Excavations also show that people with microblades once lived near Moosehide, just downriver from Dawson City. Other artifacts from Moosehide look much like those from Klo-kut. They may have been made by ancestors of either the Han or the Loucheux.

The early Northern Archaic Tradition is represented by Taye Lake sites on the lower Pelly River, but other stone points from Pelly Farms and nearby are harder to place in any Yukon archaeological tradition. Some might possibly be linked to early cultures of the Great Plains.

Artifacts from both the Aishihik Culture and the historic period have been found at Fort Selkirk, and also at Diamain Lake, just north of Granite Canyon on the Pelly River. This lake was fished by Robert Campbell, the fur trader who founded the original Fort Selkirk, as well as by ancestors of the modern Northern Tutchone who fish there still.

Farther up the Pelly River a number of excavated or surface sites have also yielded artifacts in the Northern Archaic style. Some may date from the early period, but quite a few are late prehistoric and historic. Near where the Macmillan meets the Pelly River, archaeologists have found stone points matching those from the upper level of Klo-kut. These could have been made by ancestors of the Northern Tutchone, the Kaska, or of some other group of Indians.

Tools such as stone adzes and thin stone scrapers found at the foot of Teslin Lake, on the Teslin River opposite the mouth of Squanga Creek, and at a few other places where the Inland Tlingit now live, seem to belong to the Aishihik Culture. Some of this mate-

Bone fish from Klo-kut, about 16 cm long, now in the Canadian Museum of Civilization

Below: Native copper point from the Rat Indian Creek site, northern Yukon, about 1.5 cm wide and 5.5 cm long (Canadian Museum of Civilization, photo by Raymond Le Blanc)

Barbed bone point from Rat Indian Creek, actual size (Canadian Museum of Civilization, photo by Raymond Le Blanc)

rial is probably related to that recently excavated in Tagish Indian country at Little Atlin, Tarfu, and Annie lakes.

Farther east, where the Frances River and Liard River Kaska now live, the archaeological picture is even less clear. Although some quick surveys have been made along the Alaska Highway and on the shores of some of the rivers and lakes, only a scattering of stone artifacts has been collected. There is one important site on the Alaska Highway, but it is quite far east and south of the Yukon/British Columbia border, near the Toad River Roadhouse. Called the Callison Site, it is important because the various notched points and stone scrapers found there are like those of the Taye Lake Culture in the southwestern Yukon. A few other sites in British Columbia and the Northwest Territories probably also belong to the Northern Archaic Tradition. The people who made them could have been ancestors of some of the Kaska Indians who live in the Yukon today, or of the Sekani, or of the Slavey Indians of British Columbia and the Northwest Territories.

YUKON ARCHAEOLOGY SUMMED UP

Despite the great need for more archaeological work and the uncertainty about the nature and dates of the finds already made, the story of the human past in the Yukon is slowly emerging. Throughout, it shows groups of hunting peoples with different technologies successfully adapting to a challenging series of climates and landscapes. It begins with the possibility that Ice Age hunters were living on the tundra of the northern Yukon as long ago as 25,000 years ago and more certainly by 15,000 years ago. It continues up to the time when the grandparents and parents of modern Yukon natives hunted and fished in an almost wholly forested land. The story is about a remarkable achievement. No matter what the changes in the climate and landscape over a very long period of time, small groups of people were always smart enough to figure out ways of making a living from the land and the water in what is now the modern Yukon.

We do not know the languages spoken by the varied peoples who left their traces behind. It seems likely that all these people spoke Indian languages — but not necessarily Athapaskan languages, especially in the early times. Only the Aishihik and Bennett Lake cultures of the southern and western Yukon, and the late prehistoric cultures of the northern Yukon, seem firmly linked with the languages of Yukon Indians today. By the late eighteenth century, however, the Yukon Indian past begins to take on detail and certainty. In quite a few areas it can be reconstructed not only from archaeological remains, but also from historical documents and the memories of living people.

4

THE EARLY EXPLORERS AND FUR TRADERS

Archaeological sites show that a few European trade items such as beads, tobacco, iron knives and so on, began to reach the Yukon by the end of the eighteenth century: that is, in the late 1700s. At first these goods were brought in by Tlingit Indians from the Pacific coast, or by Athapaskan Indians from the Mackenzie River side of the mountains, from down the Yukon River, or from the Copper River in Alaska. Some things came also from the Inuvialuit on the Arctic coast. All of those people were nearer to the Russian, English and American traders than were the Yukon Indians. They acted as middlemen who passed along white men's goods to their Yukon Indian trading partners, long before the white traders themselves ever came into the Yukon.

Alexander Mackenzie, the Scottish explorer and fur trader, was perhaps the first white person actually to meet any Yukon Indians and to write about them. When he was exploring the mouth of the Mackenzie River in 1789, he met some Loucheux who told him about the country to the west and about a great river, which was probably the Yukon. Some of those Loucheux may have been visitors to the Mackenzie Valley from the Porcupine River or the Peel River.

The British explorer John Franklin, and the fur traders Thomas Simpson and Peter Dease, who were looking for a passage along the Arctic coast in the 1820s and 1830s, also met Loucheux Indians. Then, because of Mackenzie's and others' reports that the people who lived along the great western river had much fine fur, the Hudson's Bay Company began to send men to find routes that led across the mountains from the Mackenzie River to the western river.

In 1831, John McLeod pushed up the Frances River to Simpson Lake, where he found a Kaska fishing camp and cache from which he took three beaver skins, leaving a knife and some other goods as payment. In 1839 John Bell went up the Peel River looking for a pass to the west, and in 1840 Robert Campbell crossed the divide from Frances Lake to the Pelly River. On a later trip, in 1842, Bell reached the Porcupine River, which flows into the Yukon. Yukon Indians still tell of the arrival of each of these traders.

The Hudson's Bay Company sponsored these explorations because it wanted to buy the Yukon furs before the local Indians sold them to someone else. If the company had its own posts in Yukon, then the Indians could trade at them instead of with other Indians or with Russians who might come upstream from the mouth of the Yukon River or up the Copper River, or over the Chilkoot or Chilkat passes. The Hudson's Bay Company wanted nobody else's trading posts in the Yukon.

By 1800 the Russians, English, and Americans had just about hunted out the sea otter along the Pacific coast, so they were eager to buy any furs that the Coast Tlingit could bring from inland Alaska, the Yukon and British Columbia. The Coast Indians realized they could sell the furs they got from their inland trading partners at a huge profit. They took them to Russian posts such as Sitka, or to the ships that came into Lynn Canal and other coastal waters. Once a year, and sometimes more often, parties of coastal Chilkat, Chilkoot, and Taku Tlingit made difficult journeys far into the Yukon to get more furs. In time, Russian traders began to think of coming inland themselves.

THE HUDSON'S BAY COMPANY TRADERS

In 1840 John Bell set up Peel River Post, later to become Fort McPherson in the Northwest Territories, and in 1847 Alexander Murray founded Fort Yukon for the Hudson's Bay Company. Murray privately thought that his post might be on Russian-claimed land, and it turned out that he was correct: Fort Yukon was in what later became Alaska. It was right in the middle of Loucheux Indian country though, and many Loucheux traded there, as did the Han Indians from around present-day Dawson and some of the Northern Tutchone from the lower Pelly and upper Yukon rivers.

The next year, in 1848, Robert Campbell set up Fort Selkirk where the Pelly River meets the Yukon. This post really was in the Yukon, in the homeland of Northern Tutchone Indians.

Campbell had already explored the Pelly River quite carefully in 1843 from his base at Pelly Banks. There in 1842, he had his assistant Francis Hoole build a small trading post. Campbell called the post Glenlyon House, after the place in Scotland where he had been born.

The Indians that Campbell met around Frances Lake and the head of Pelly River may have been Kaska, ancestors of the people who now live at Ross River, along the Pelly and Frances Rivers, and at Watson Lake and Upper Liard. Campbell called the upper Pelly River natives "Knife Indians," and the Indians at Fort Selkirk he called "Wood Indians." When they first met Campbell, some of the Knife Indians were hostile, but they later accepted him as a friend.

Both Murray and Campbell wrote in their company reports and journals about the people whom they met at their trading posts and on their journeys. Murray even kept a special sandbox in his cabin where Indians could draw maps to show him their home country and where the best furs could be found. Murray himself liked to draw pictures, and he made some wonderful sketches of Loucheux headmen, dancers, winter tents and so on.* Campbell left no pictures

* Murray's pictures were later published in England, in a popular book called *Arctic Searching Expedition*, written by Sir John Richardson. Richardson had travelled along the Arctic coast in 1847–49 looking for another explorer, John Franklin, who disappeared along with his crew in 1846. Richardson did not find Franklin, but he wrote a book about his attempt and about the country through which he had travelled. He included a good deal of information about the natural history of the Canadian North, and about the Indians. Richardson never met any Yukon Indians himself, but he collected information about them from Hudson's Bay traders like Murray.

A Loucheux dance, late 1840s, drawn by Alexander Murray

of the Indians he knew, but he was particularly impressed by two of the "leading chiefs" of the Wood Indians, whose names he wrote as "Thlin-ikik-thling" and "Hanan." Probably they were the Northern Tutchone chiefs from a village near the now abandoned site of Minto. Campbell described them as "tall, stalwart, good-looking men, clad from head to foot in dressed deer [caribou] skins, ornamented with beads and porcupine quills of all colours." They must have looked very much like Sreevyàa, one of the Fort Yukon Loucheux chiefs sketched by Murray (see page 66).

The real name of "Thlin-ikik-thling" was very likely *Tlingit tlen*, which in the Tlingit language means "big man." This chief may have acquired a Tlingit name from trading with the coastal Indians, or perhaps he was part Tlingit himself. One of his descendants is the modern Indian linguist Daniel Lhingit Tlen of Burwash.

Campbell's description of the Indians around Fort Selkirk shows that they were already great traders for white men's goods. They had a few Hudson's Bay Company guns and plenty of "Mackenzie River beads," Campbell says. He thought they got these from "Mr Bell's Indians," who were probably Peel River Loucheux, and his description goes on:

Some had belts or bands of these beads of at least 4 to 5 pounds [weight] *and of some yards long, and thrown loose around the necks and reaching to the ground as trappings to decorate their persons for their festive dances, of which those at the forks* [of the Pelly and Yukon rivers] *showed us a specimen, and pastime of which they are I believe passionately fond. . . .*

65

Murray's drawing of Sreevyàa, a Loucheux headman. His name means Sunsnare or Rainbow.

The dancers may have looked much like the Loucheux sketched by Murray at Fort Yukon. Campbell's description of other Fort Selkirk people shows that they were dressed like the Loucheux of that time:

Their dress is all leather, similar, I am told, to that worn by the Loucheux Indians, say trousers en boot [moccasins and trousers in one piece] *reaching to the band, the upper garment shirt-like but tipping to a point behind and in front and reaching down near the knees. The hair very large tied behind and reaching down near the girdle like a bushy tail and abominably mixed up and closed together with red earth. They have their noses all pierced and generally ornamented with a ring.*

The Indians were just as interested in the clothes worn by Campbell and his men as he was in theirs. They had never seen white men's clothing, although some of the upper Pelly River Indians had woolen blankets, which had probably come from the Hudson's Bay Company. The bulk of the trade goods that Campbell saw, however, came from the Russians. They had either been traded up the Yukon or Copper rivers to the Loucheux and Han Indians, who then traded them to the Fort Selkirk Tutchone, or else they had been brought in by the Coast Tlingit. The main items mentioned by Campbell were axes, knives, dentalium (a kind of sea shell from the Pacific coast, shaped like a long tooth or small tusk), buttons made from abalone shell and ivory, and — perhaps most important — guns. To his dismay, Campbell found that the Russian guns were much cheaper than those sold by his own company.

Both Murray and Campbell admired the Yukon Indians. They appreciated how well the native people had solved the problems of living well in a beautiful but difficult land, and they learned what they could from them about its topography. In 1851 Campbell floated down the Yukon through Northern Tutchone, Han and Loucheux country to visit Murray at Fort Yukon. In this way he confirmed that the river into which the Pelly flowed was indeed the Yukon — the same river on which Murray had built his post. Of course, the Indians themselves had known the path of the river for many centuries, but the whites had not. Campbell wrote that the Indians were the "great attraction" of the country. He always landed to talk to them, and whenever he met new Indians he gave them tobacco and had a smoke with them. In 1852, however, soon after Campbell had moved his buildings to a new site across the Yukon River where Fort Selkirk is today, the Coast Tlingit destroyed his post. The Tlingit were just as jealous as the Hudson's Bay Company of any other traders being in the country where they themselves bought furs.

Yukon Indians have handed down several stories about the Tlingit raid on Fort Selkirk. Rachel Dawson, who was born in Dawson, used to tell how her grandfather saved Campbell after the Tlingit had tied him up and set him adrift in a boat. As a way of thanking him, Campbell gave his own name to his Indian rescuer,

Loucheux men, women and children as Alexander Murray saw them in the late 1840s. Note the trade rifle and powder horn along with the traditional bow and arrow.

and several Indians from Fort Selkirk and the Pelly River area bear the name Campbell today.

Campbell himself did not write about being saved, unless it was in one of his journals which were later burned in Québec, but he did leave an account of a trip he made down the Pelly River in 1851. On that occasion an Indian family named their little boy for him after he rescued the child from drowning. The boy was probably a Kaska Indian, since his father had been Campbell's guide from the Frances River. Campbell also cured the sore leg of a Knife Indian from the upper Pelly River, and gained the reputation of being a powerful doctor. Older Indians from the Pelly River or Watson Lake probably know more stories about Campbell that are not in his journal.

Many of the manuscript journals of Campbell, Murray and other traders are now in the Hudson's Bay Company Archives in Winnipeg, and most are still unpublished. These early writings give a vivid, though incomplete, picture of how the Yukon and nearby Alaskan Indians were living in the mid-nineteenth century. They describe identifiable people whose descendants still live in the country. The journals also make clear how much the white traders learned from the Indians about ways to live successfully in the North and how much they depended on the Indians for meat and fish as well as furs.

When the Russians sold Alaska to the United States, in 1867, the Hudson's Bay Company had to move its operations back up the Porcupine River. Just on the Yukon side of the new border, it built the post known as Rampart House. The company refused to rebuild old Fort Selkirk after the Tlingit Indians wrecked it, even though Campbell had travelled about 3000 miles on snowshoes to ask permission to do so. Arthur Harper built the first of a series of independent trading posts at Fort Selkirk in 1889, but not until 1938 did the Hudson's Bay Company open a new store there. It was closed again in the 1950s when the Yukon River steamers ceased to run, and most of the Fort Selkirk Indians moved to Pelly Crossing on the new Klondike Highway.

THE EARLY SCIENTISTS AND JOURNALISTS

By the second half of the nineteenth century, other white men — independent traders, prospectors, explorers, geologists, missionaries, and journalists — had begun to trickle into the Yukon. At first they usually came from the Mackenzie River by way of the Peel, and often they went on to Fort Yukon via the Porcupine River. Others came up the Yukon River from its mouth. Very few whites crossed the mountain passes from the Pacific coast, because the Chilkat Tlingit and Chilkoot Tlingit of Lynn Canal controlled these passes very successfully until late in the 1880s. The Coast Indians still wanted to keep the Yukon furs for themselves.

Few of these early traders and prospectors wrote about the Indians, but some of the scientists, explorers, missionaries and journalists did. One of the earliest scientists to spend much time in the Yukon was Robert Kennicott, an American naturalist associated with

A Loucheux warrior, drawn
by Murray

Shahnahti', a Loucheux headman who traded at Fort Yukon in the late 1800s (woodcut after a drawing by William Dall, published in London in 1898)

the Smithsonian Institution in Washington, D.C. In 1860–61 the Hudson's Bay Company allowed him to travel with their fur brigades and to stay at their posts on the Mackenzie River and along the Peel River route to Fort Yukon. He made the trip from Fort McPherson (then still called Peel River Post) to Fort Yukon in September 1860 and crossed back to it the next summer. That winter he went back to La Pierre House, a small post on the upper Porcupine River, built by John Bell as a halfway house between Peel River Post and Fort Yukon.

Kennicott's journal, published in 1869, described how the Loucheux Indians living near La Pierre House hunted caribou. In the summer and fall they drove the animals into corrals, but in January and February groups of hunters surrounded or ran them down and shot them, or an individual hunter might stalk and kill a single animal. The Indians could stay on top of the snowy crust because they wore large snowshoes, but the caribou broke through it and could not easily get away. Kennicott also described with enthusiasm the large numbers of "blue" (probably coho) and other fish that the Indians and Hudson's Bay men took from Indian-style fishtraps every fall.

Kennicott liked his first stay in the North so much that in 1865 he agreed to take charge of an Overland Telegraph Company party organized to explore the best route to lay a telegraph line through Alaska. The entire line was to run from Oregon through British Columbia and the Yukon, into Alaska and across the Bering Sea to Siberia. Unfortunately, Kennicott died soon after he got to Alaska, but his place was taken by another energetic young American naturalist named William Dall, who spent many years doing scientific work in Alaska. Dall made one of his first long journeys in Alaska during the summer of 1867 when he went up the Yukon River to Fort Yukon. With him was an Englishman named Frederick Whymper who was the official artist of the expedition.

Early in the winter of 1867 Dall sent Frank Ketchum and Michel Laberge, two Canadians from his party, upriver by sled. They went as far as Fort Selkirk, and in late June they arrived back at Fort Yukon with a piece of charred wood that they said came from Campbell's ruined post. They also reported that the Indians there had made them welcome. These were probably the same Northern Tutchone people who had earlier befriended Campbell.

Both Dall and Whymper made drawings of the Loucheux and other Indians who came to Fort Yukon, and both published books about their travels. Whymper, who was a trained artist, made the better pictures, and some of his portraits are of men who had earlier been drawn by Alexander Murray. One of these was the Loucheux chief Sreevyàa.

Dall several times published systematic accounts of the names and locations of both Alaska and Yukon Indians, but what he wrote about the Yukon Indians themselves is rather vague, because he himself never actually came into the country, and he did not learn much from Laberge and Ketchum after their journey. Whymper's

Fort Yukon in June 1867 (woodcut by H.W. Elliott, after a drawing by William Dall)

book is a more personal account, but he also does not seem to have learned very much about the Indians. It would be interesting to turn the tables and to hear what the Alaskan and Yukon Indians said and thought about these early white men and others who followed.

Another early visitor was Lieutenant Frederick Schwatka, who explored the Northwest for the United States Army in 1881. Schwatka went down the Yukon River instead of up, using a raft which he built after crossing the Chilkoot Pass. Schwatka too did not understand much about the few Indians he met along the way, but he recorded the places where he saw the Tagish, Tutchone and Han camped. He also published sketches of Indian villages.

Schwatka made another trip through the Yukon in 1891, this time going up the Taku River from Juneau, across the pass to Teslin Lake, down the Teslin River to the Yukon River and on to Fort Selkirk. From there the party crossed over to the headwaters of the White River, where the Yukon and Alaskan Indians got copper. The best report of this trip is not by Schwatka, but by the geologist Charles W. Hayes, who went with him. Hayes described how he got some Indian packers at Fort Selkirk, and how the group met six families of Tutchone Indians waiting to fish salmon on the Nisling River. Later they met two other families on Kletsan Creek, which was as far as the Fort Selkirk packers would go. They said they were farther from home than they had ever been. They also told Hayes that they were related to the families fishing on the Nisling, who probably were the ancestors of present-day Indians who grew up in Aishihik or Burwash Landing.

Another expedition of geologists had been in the Yukon before Hayes took his trip with Schwatka. This was the Yukon Expedition of 1887, sponsored by the Canadian Department of the Interior. It was planned and headed by Dr George Dawson and included his associates Richard McConnell and William Ogilvie. Each of these capable men explored a different part of the Yukon, and their reports make exciting reading for anybody who knows Yukon country and Yukon Indians. Dawson wrote an overall report which was in great demand during the Gold Rush of 1898, and Ogilvie later wrote a book as well.

Dawson was employed by the Geological Survey of Canada and had worked in many parts of the Northwest. He was full of curiosity and always interested in Indians wherever he went. He usually liked them, and they liked and admired him as a tough and tireless traveller even though he was a small man with a hunched back.

Dawson always wanted to know how the Indians made their living from the land. In 1876 he sent samples of the native foods of the Indians of northern British Columbia to the International Exposition in Philadelphia as part of the Canadian exhibit. On his travels in northwestern British Columbia, the Northwest Territories and the Yukon, he collected vocabularies and all the other information he could from the different Indians he met — Kaska, Tagish, Tutchone and Han. After coming down the Pelly River to the Yukon in 1887, he realized how important Robert Campbell's early experiences had been, so he visited Campbell in Manitoba and published what the old man told him about the country and its people.

Another account of the Indians of the southern Yukon was written in 1890 and 1891 by members of an exploring party sent to Alaska by *Frank Leslie's Illustrated Newspaper* of New York. The longest and best articles were by E. J. Glave, who met and travelled with the grandparents and great grandparents of present Southern Tutchone Indians from Neskatahin, Hutshi, and Aishihik.

On his first journey into the Yukon, Glave employed Jack Dalton as his assistant. The two men visited camps and settlements at Kusawa Lake, Frederick Lake, Klukshu and Neskatahin. At Neskatahin, Glave found only Chilkat Tlingit traders. Except for the family he was travelling with, all the Southern Tutchone Indians, whose village it was, had gone to Nuqwaik (Nóogaayík), farther down the Alsek River, to fish for salmon. Glave and Dalton themselves went on to Nuqwaik and then had an exciting raft ride with Coast Tlingit guides down the Alsek River to Dry Bay on the Alaskan coast.

Glave and Dalton came back to the Yukon in 1892, this time with some horses, and travelled as far as Kluane Lake. Albert Isaac, who lived around Aishihik, Burwash Landing and Haines Junction until he died in 1970, remembered seeing Glave and Dalton when he was just a little boy. It was his father who guided them. Other oldtimers could remember them too. They have told how some of the Indian women, who had never seen horses before, thought that they were big dogs coming through the camp. They hurried to take their meat off the drying racks because they were afraid that the horses would eat it. At Neskatahin, when Glave and Dalton tried to buy some fish with silver dollars, the Indians threw the silver pieces on the ground. They did not yet know what money was.

Glave published some sketches of the Neskatahin and Hutshi Indians and of their villages. Maggie Jim, Maggie Brown, Jimmy Kane, Johnny Frazer, and other Indians who used to stay at Neskatahin knew who these people were and recognized their faces when they saw the pictures in the 1970s, almost ninety years after they had first been published by Glave.

The fur traders, explorers, scientists and journalists who visited the Yukon during the nineteenth century did not want the land of the Yukon Indians. Nor did they try to make great changes in the Indians' way of life. Indeed, the fur traders hoped very much that the natives would go on being hunters and fishermen, though they also urged them to bring in as much fur as possible. Some Indians probably began to spend more time scattered over the land in winter trapping furs than they ever had before. They also began to use more metal tools, guns and traps, and more cloth, beads, tobacco, tea and flour. Their material culture had certainly begun to change, but at this stage the Indians could still choose pretty much for themselves what they wanted to think, do and use.

THE EARLY MISSIONARIES

It was only the missionaries who openly said that they wanted to change the Indians' ways of thinking and behaving. In fact, they came to the Yukon for precisely that reason. During the nineteenth century, both the Anglican Church and the Roman Catholic Church sent missionaries across the mountains from the Mackenzie River where they already had churches at the trading stations. A few missionaries of other denominations also arrived in the Yukon before 1900, and all had as their main goal the substitution of their own beliefs for the traditional beliefs of the Yukon Indians.

The first Anglican missionary to reach the Yukon arrived in the same year as Robert Kennicott. In 1861, William West Kirkby, who was stationed at Fort Simpson, far up the Mackenzie River at the mouth of the Liard, made the long trip down to the Peel River and crossed to Fort Yukon. He stayed there for only a week, but that was long enough for him to start a mission there. He went back the next year for a short time and then sent his friend Robert McDonald, the son of a fur trader at Red River, to work there permanently. McDonald arrived in 1862, returned to Peel River Post because of illness in 1864, but was back at Fort Yukon in 1865. Four years later he reluctantly moved out for good because the United States had taken over the post. He turned over his mission work there to a Loucheux Indian catechist named William Loola. McDonald centred his own later efforts first at Rampart House on the Yukon side of the Alaskan/Canadian border and then at Fort McPherson. By this time he had been made an archdeacon.

When McDonald returned to Fort Yukon in 1865, he found many of the Loucheux Indians ill from scarlet fever, brought to the country by traders. This was one of several epidemics of illness that the

This page: Archdeacon Robert McDonald

Opposite: a page from *Thlukwinadhun Sheg Akǫ Ketchid Kwitugwatsui*, or the Tukudh Bible, Robert McDonald's translation of the Old and New Testaments into Loucheux, published at London, England, 1898

whites unintentionally brought upon the Indians. In 1838 and again in 1862 there had been terrible smallpox along the Pacific coast. Other diseases that the Indians had never known, such as measles, whooping cough, tuberculosis and polio continued to strike from time to time all through the nineteenth and twentieth centuries.

McDonald treated the sick Indians as best he could, but the work to which he devoted most of his energy was of a different sort. During his first stay at Fort Yukon, he learned to speak the local Loucheux language, which he called Tukudh, and he developed a way to write it down using the roman alphabet. With the help of many Loucheux, McDonald translated hymns, prayers, and parts of the Bible into Tukudh so the Loucheux themselves could learn to read them. In 1898 he published the Tukudh Bible that some Loucheux Indians still use today. What is more, many Loucheux learned to write as well as to read their own language, which had never been written down before. Because of McDonald's work, Loucheux Indians could kwitshịnut chikhtowhohchyah, akọ kukwadhut chohttshid Solomon zyunnohyin, ei tshinetei ha vin nikhuttriniditi thlikwinashin ttrin zit teị vuh hun yit tshi nittinilih, akọ vit ttri rsikoonchyo ttrin zit teị.

CHAPTER IV.

KWINYOOYIN, ndotinichyo, siv vettitrinidhun; kwinyooyin, ndotinichyo; nyin nde nyin nuttoutininjik kittlyọ tsinji kit tinchyo: nit tshirkhe evi notlị kit tinchyo, ei Gilead tdhah kerkhe zyuntsheltui. 2 Nyi gwo tivittrig notlị ei ketchid utchunzyuntrintyuth zyunkittinchyo, ei kunutratrhah kwut sut gininyạöth; etetkookwinyatchyo nunachyo tiyin, akọ elyet ihthlẹ kwilị kwitet kettun tidichyo. 3 Nyit teva tshih ttatsik kit tinchyo, akọ niz zhig ndotinchyo: nyit tretsị pomegranate lud kit tinchyo nyin nuttoutininjik kittlyọ. 4 Nyik kkokh David zzehyettuịë kit tinchyo vidhizzin kenjit nutrikwịntthui, kwuk kug yitvittịndui ihthlogchotyin tinillih kit chotyin kuntzechịli, tinjih chinttluthnut yitvittịndui tutthug. 5 Nyit ttokk nekthuị ttlohkugkkyi nekthuị zyunkittinchyo ei ttlohkug vutzui ttsut nunatchyo zyunnilị, ei notlhyah tet zyunuä. 6 Ttrin etsịkudh kwu tsut, akọ kwunko kethletitchiltthut, murrh tdhah kwu tsut khuttititelhtshyah, akọ rsituttatsun tuịkh kwu tsut. 7 Siv vettitrinidhun, tutthug ndotinichyo; akọ niz zit elyet koözzo kwilị.

8 Lebanon kwut sut sah, *trenjo ketchid tronjik, Lebanon kwut

* Kọ, gudhitshi.

1053

sut sah tịhah, kwinukoëkwitunạya Amana tshitig kwut sut, Shenir akọ Hermon tshitig kwut sut, leionnut un kwut sut, leopardnut tdhah kwut sut. 9 Sit ttri ooun odhịnjik, sit chyodh, su ut; sit ttri ooun odhịnjik nyin nde kwunahyin ihthlog ha, nyuk kkokh niltlya ihthlog ha. 10 Nyit chettigwinidhun ttegwanttluth ndotukoonchyo, sit chyodh, su ut! nit chettigwinidhun ttegwanttluth chugchohchoọ yendo tsut nirzị! akọ nyit ttlheh dhundui vik kwatsun tuniditshit nithlinetsi tutthug yendo tsut! 11 Su ut, nyit teva chinetsidsookkuị tahyil: chinetsidsookkuị akọ ttokk nit ttshah zug dhukkuị; akọ nyik kwutchakh kwatsun Lebanon kwatsun kit tinchyo. 12 Kwunzi tekkit kwutukulchịë sit chyodh tinchyo, su ut; kwitlit kwitugwatsuị, khuttuịluị vahthlitrigwatzi. 13 Nith thochya ketchid paradeis pomgranat zyunnilị, chug tattloth ha; *seiprus nard thochya ha, 14 Speiknard akọ saphron, kalamus akọ sinnamon, tzirsituttatsun tutchun tutthug ha; murrh akọ aloes, tuniditshit kwiyendo tsut nirzị tutthug ha. 15 Kwunzi tekkit kwunuthultrotthui khuttuịluị ịlị, choọ kwundui kwitlit, akọ Lebanon kwut sut nilluịnjik. 16 Yoti-tsuị attrui kununyạnji; akọ nun ttrintludtsuị attrui, nitchịzhit; sik kwunzitekkit kwunutthultrotthui kug nyanttrui, kwit tuniditshit chikh nutelluị. Siv vettitrinidhun tik kwunzitekkit kwunutthultrotthui kwiz zit nittevizzi, akọ tit chug tattloth vuä.

* Heb. copher-henna.

Bishop Bompas officiating at the funeral of Ellen, daughter of the headman at Forty Mile (from *An Apostle of the North: Memoirs of the Right Reverend William Carpenter Bompas,* New York, 1908)

more easily become lay readers in the Anglican Church, and several of them later became ministers. One well-known Loucheux minister was Rev. James Simon of Fort McPherson, who also spent years at Old Crow. Another was Rev. Richard Martin of Mayo and Dawson City. Sarah Simon, Reverend Simon's wife, has published a book with pictures of these ministers, their wives, their friends and relatives, and their community activities.

The white Anglican missionary who spent the longest time and travelled farthest in the Yukon in the nineteenth century was Bishop William C. Bompas. He and his missionary wife, Charlotte, both worked tirelessly to give the Indians European religion and education, and European ideas about the best ways to keep house and raise children. They built schools at several places, and Mrs Bompas often cared for young Indian girls in her home. Bishop Bompas's last school was at Carcross, where he died in 1906. (His grave is in the Carcross graveyard.) The school later became the Chooutla Indian Residential School, where many Yukon Indians were educated before it was finally closed in the 1950s.

A Roman Catholic missionary, Fr Jean Séguin, had followed Reverend Kirkby along the Peel River route to Fort Yukon in 1862, but he did not establish a church there nor in the northern Yukon. Later, however, Roman Catholic missionaries became active in the southern Yukon. One was Fr William Henry Judge, who was in Dawson during the Gold Rush of 1898. Another was Fr Marcel Bobillier, who first came to the Yukon from the school at Lower Post, B.C., in 1939. Quite a few Yukon Indians who are young adults today used to go to the Lower Post boarding school, which closed in 1975.

A small number of Yukon Indians were influenced during the nineteenth century by the Russian Orthodox Church, which had

Bishop Bompas's own funeral, Carcross, 1906. On the left is Tagish John, father of the Tagish elder Angela Sidney.

been active at Sitka since 1834. No Russian Orthodox priests visited the Yukon, but Inland Tlingit Indians from around Teslin and Atlin, who had Coast Tlingit relatives, or who themselves came from Alaska, brought knowledge of the Russian Orthodox faith into the Yukon. That is why there are Russian-style crosses on some of the graves at Teslin.

The missionaries did not understand that, like Christianity, the Indians' own religion was deeply spiritual, nor did they understand that the Indians were guided by their traditional beliefs to live good lives. The Indians' own religion taught them how to behave toward each other and toward the world in which they lived. It also taught them about the nature of power and about the spirits whose presence they sensed in the land, the water, the animals, the plants and throughout the natural world. A harmonious relationship with these spiritual forces was of great importance to people who, as hunters and fishers, derived their livelihood directly from their environment. Indian religion also taught ways of healing people who were sick. Christian sermons did not often touch on some of these topics, so while many Yukon Indians came to accept the white man's God and the gospel of Christ, they did not necessarily give up all of their earlier religious beliefs about spiritual power, the need for good relationships with animals, and how best to deal with sickness.

The whites who brought the new religious messages also built schools and hospitals, and they passed on many foreign ideas and customs. Missionaries may have changed the lives of the Yukon Indians much more than the fur traders or any other Europeans who had come into the country before them. But there were still greater changes to come — much greater than the early traders, missionaries or Indians of that time dreamed of. The agents of change this time were the prospectors for gold.

CONFIRMATION CLASS, 1931

The late Archbishop Stringer can be seen on the right and the
Rev. A. E. Longfellow, Rector of Carcross, on the left.

2. THE STAFF

THE School is managed by the following Staff: Principal, Head Matron, who is a Registered Nurse, Teacher, Boys' Supervisor, Kitchen Matron, Farm Instructor, and General Assistant. At the time of compiling this pamphlet (1935) the Head Matron is discharging the duties of Girls' Supervisor, but the Commission trust that, with the removal of part of the 15 per cent. cut in the per capita grants imposed by the Indian Department during recent years, it may be possible to appoint another Agent who will relieve her of these duties.

3. OBJECTS AND METHODS

THE School has accommodation for forty children. These are drawn from all parts of the Yukon, some from the immediate vicinity, others from the most northerly parts of the territory well within the Arctic Circle, and from many points between. The main object of this School is to send the boys and girls back to their own people not Europeanized and contemptuous of their old surroundings, but able to stand alone, living sober, well-instructed, high-principled Christian lives, and there gather others around them by the daily exhibition of a standard of truth and goodness never known before.

The Staff of the School kept this object prominently in view when drawing up the daily time table. One half of

6

Excerpt from a 1935 pamphlet about the Chooutla Indian Residential School, Carcross, published by the Indian Residential School Commission, Missionary Society of the Church of England in Canada

the day is spent in the classroom. There the children are given an ordinary common school education. During the other half of the day they are taught the things most necessary to uplift them and their friends at home to something nearer the Christian standard of cleanliness and industry. The girls learn housekeeping, sewing, cooking, etc., and the boys gardening, rough carpentering and blacksmith work, and numberless other things that will be useful in the kind of life that they will likely lead after graduation. Nor is it forgotten that mere cleverness without the Christian character will never save a man or woman. Every member of the Staff is appointed on the understanding that he or she is a missionary, and believes that the knowledge of Jesus of Nazareth, and trust in Him alone, can uplift the Indians of the Yukon and make them good and useful citizens of the greater Canada of the future.

School Prayer

(Prepared by the late Archbishop Stringer in February, 1931)

O GOD our Father in Heaven, we pray Thee to bless our School and every member of the same whether present or absent. Grant that we who are now here may grow up in Thy fear and love. Give unto us day by day Thy strength and guidance. Help us that we may continue to love and serve Thee unto our lives' end, through Jesus Christ our Lord. AMEN.

THE CHURCH BOYS' LEAGUE

7

Moosehide Village at the end of the nineteenth century (from Bishop Bompas's memoirs)

THE KLONDIKE GOLD RUSH OF 1898

Ever since Alexander Murray had built his trading post at Fort Yukon, white men had known that there was gold in the Yukon watershed. News of the Fort Yukon gold was published in 1869 by Frederick Whymper, who had learned of it from the missionary Robert McDonald. At first, Whymper's report attracted little attention, but as the gold fields in California and British Columbia gave out, white prospectors began to push farther north. Among them were Arthur Harper, Leroy "Jack" McQuesten and Albert Mayo. These three men, who came into the Yukon from the Mackenzie River, traded as well as prospected, and in 1874 they founded Fort Reliance, six miles below the mouth of the Klondike River. This trading post, and later ones that they and rival traders set up along the Yukon and its tributaries, provided supplies which made it possible for more and more whites to spend time in the Yukon looking for gold.

Like the early traders and missionaries, the first prospectors usually came up the Peel River or the Yukon River, because the Coast Tlingit still rarely permitted anyone but themselves to cross the Coast Mountains. By 1880, the Tlingit had allowed only two parties of white prospectors to cross the Chilkoot Pass. The Tlingit permitted these prospectors to take few supplies, and when they returned to the coast the Tlingit searched their packs to make sure they had not bought furs from the Yukon Indians.

In spite of the Tlingit blockade, the number of prospectors gradually increased, and in 1886 there was a gold strike at Forty Mile, forty miles downstream from Fort Reliance. Many white prospectors and Indians gathered in the vicinity. Jack McQuesten moved his store there from the mouth of the Stewart River, and Bishop Bompas arrived with his wife in 1892 to build a school and church. In 1894

Dawson Charlie, 1898, enjoying the proceeds of his gold strike (Yukon Archives)

Inspector Charles Constantine of the North West Mounted Police arrived to make a report on local conditions. A detachment of twenty police arrived the next year, and by that time there were almost a hundred cabins at Forty Mile. Mary McLeod, now of Dawson, grew up there along with quite a few other Indians, most of whom were Han-speaking.

A year later the scene shifted. In 1896, a white man named George Carmacks and three Tagish Indians — Kate Carmacks, Skookum Jim, and Dawson Charlie (often mistakenly called Tagish Charlie) — found the gold on Bonanza Creek that set off the Klondike Gold Rush of 1898. This event drew more than 40,000 white men and a few white women into a country where before there had been only a handful of whites and a few thousand Indians.

Although many of the whites left soon afterward, the Gold Rush marked the end of traditional Indian life in many parts of the Yukon. That is why the stories that Yukon Indians still remember about the earlier days are so valuable. They tell us how the people were living and how they thought about things before the Gold Rush and in the early part of this century. These stories form the basis for the last six chapters of this book, and they often contain the old people's advice about how to live a good life. Even though the ways that Yukon Indians made their living changed greatly after the Gold Rush, and the problems the native people faced were different from any they had ever known before, they managed to keep going. One reason they could do this was because they still kept many of their traditional values from the days before the Klondike Gold Rush.

5

YUKON INDIANS AND GOVERNMENT POLICIES

After thousands of years of successful living in their tundra and forest homelands with only other Indians and a few Inuvialuit as their neighbors, the Yukon Indians learned that there were white people living in the world outside. Then, soon after the Gold Rush, the Indians found that they were regarded as just part of the population of a political territory in a nation whose government was run by white people. The Indians also discovered that the white men had given the rivers, lakes and mountains of their country new names in the English language. The white visitors had also given the Indians themselves various tribal and band names, many of which the Indians had never heard and none of which they had ever used themselves.

By the early twentieth century, then, the Yukon Indians had been caught up in a network of relationships with an outside world which at first they knew very little about. By the middle of the century, they came to understand the overwhelming importance of one particular outside place known as Ottawa. The Yukon Territorial Government – which had its headquarters first at Dawson and then, after 1953, at Whitehorse – passed some laws affecting both Indians and whites, but it was the federal government in Ottawa that came to dominate the lives of the Indians. The federal government told them where they could live, how their bands should be organized, where their children should go to school, and how much monetary and other assistance they would get. This was true even though the Yukon Indians had never signed any treaties with the government of Canada.

Until World War II, even the federal government, including the Department of Indian Affairs, had rather little contact with the Yukon Indians. When the war came, though it was a long ways away from the Yukon, Ottawa suddenly began to find out quite a lot more about Yukon native people. In 1942 the Alaska Highway was hurriedly built so that military supplies could pass through the Yukon to Alaska. The highway went where there had never been roads before, and some of the Yukon Indians who knew the country helped to lay out its route. After the highway was finished, government agents found it much easier to reach many of the native bands.

It's a Long Way to Ottawa: Yukon Indians and the Government

85

When the war ended, in 1945, the federal government set up many new programs in education, health and other aid for all Canadian Indians, including those in the Yukon. Then in the late 1960s and early 1970s, Ottawa was forced to take account of the Yukon Indians in a way that it never had done before. These were the years when the Yukon natives began to take forceful political steps of their own. They formed the Yukon Indian Advancement Association (YIAA), the Yukon Native Brotherhood (YNB), the Yukon Association of Non-Status Indians (YANSI), and finally the Council for Yukon Indians (CYI). In short, they organized themselves to make claims on the federal government for title to their ancestral lands and for all the rights to go with it. They developed strong policies with respect to a proposed gas pipeline in the Yukon, and spoke up about other territorial and federal projects that might affect Indian lives.

The detailed story of how the Yukon Indians became a political force is long and complicated. Only the major events will be mentioned here, but, in order to understand what is happening now, we need to know something about the earlier relationships between Canadian Indians and the British government that once ruled Canada, as well as how the Canadian government treated the Indians after Confederation.

*Early British and Canadian Policies
toward the Canadian Indians*

In 1763 — well before Alexander Mackenzie first met the Loucheux Indians — Great Britain took over the government of northeastern America from the French. A royal proclamation for that year set out the new government's general policy towards the North American Indians. It created a large Indian reserve in what was later to be part of both the United States and Canada. It also stated that the Indians had a rightful interest in the lands where they had long been living. Thus the government recognized the Indians' "aboriginal title" or claim to their ancestral lands. Any sale or exchange of these lands to non-Indians had to be approved by the British Crown. In order to extinguish the Indians' title to the land, the Crown itself would have to buy it from the Indians.

The British government also felt responsible for other matters which it thought affected the welfare of the Indians. As early as 1755, an Indian Department or Indian Branch of the British government had been set up to regulate British fur trade with Indians, to be in charge of Indian reserve lands — since some treaties had already been signed — and to keep up other government relations with Indians.

After the Revolutionary War, which led to the independence of the United States in 1776, the British government in North America did not have to deal with Indians living in territory claimed by the USA. In Canada, however, the British went on making treaties with the Indians and buying more lands from them in order to "extinguish aboriginal title" in terms of the Proclamation of 1763.

When it became clear that Canada and the United States would become two separate nations, some Indians who considered themselves allies of the British moved from the United States into Canada. Many new white settlers from Britain and Europe also began to stream into eastern Canada, where there was already a large French population. All these immigrants to Canada began to look for new lands.

By 1830 the whites had pushed onto the prairies, where they often moved right onto Indian hunting grounds and began to farm. By this time, the British government had adopted a new policy towards the Indians. It had decided that they should be "civilized." They were to be taught to be farmers and tradesmen just like the thousands of non-Indian settlers who were crowding in on them, especially in eastern Canada and the prairies. All nomadic Indians — that is, those who were hunters or trappers and who did not live year round in the same villages — were to be put onto government reserves.

In 1860 the British Parliament formally turned over Indian affairs to the colonial government in Ottawa. At Confederation, in 1867, when Canada became a dominion instead of a colony, Section 91 of the British North America Act gave the new federal government legislative powers and responsibilities for the Indians and their reserve lands. The next year, 1868, marked the first federal Indian Act.

The new and more centralized Indian Department in Ottawa went on trying to "civilize" the Indians. The federal policy was that everybody in Canada, including Indians, should live the same way and share the same values. That meant that everybody should go to a European-style school and be a Christian.

The Indian Department also tried to do two other things at about this time. On the one hand, it tried to define as clearly as possible who was an Indian in the eyes of the law — that is, who had legal Indian status. On the other hand, it tried to encourage "enfranchisement" of as many Indians as possible. "Enfranchisement" means that a person gives up his special legal status as an Indian and takes on the legal status of a non-native Canadian citizen.* In the past an Indian might want to become enfranchised because only then could he hold a business license, send his children to a public school, vote, buy liquor or enlist in the armed forces. (Over the years, however, some of these limitations on status Indians were dropped. For example, in 1960 Indians were finally allowed to vote like other Canadian citizens.)

As part of its policy of "civilizing" the Indians, the Indian Department of the newly formed Canadian nation also imposed local governments on the Indian reserves. These included elected chiefs and councils such as most Indians had traditionally never had. In addition, the department outlawed important native rituals such as the Sun Dance of the Plains Indians and the potlatches practised by Indians on the Pacific coast and in parts of the Yukon Territory. The chief superintendent of the Department of Indian Affairs had a great deal of power. By and large, he and most of his employees wanted

* Until 1982, any Indian woman who married a man of non-Indian status automatically became "enfranchised" whether she liked it or not. She lost her Indian status, and her subsequent children were denied Indian status as well. In 1982 this law was modified so that individual band governments could decide if their female members should lose Indian status when they married non-Indians. In 1985 the law was changed again so that no person could lose native status through marriage to a non-Indian.

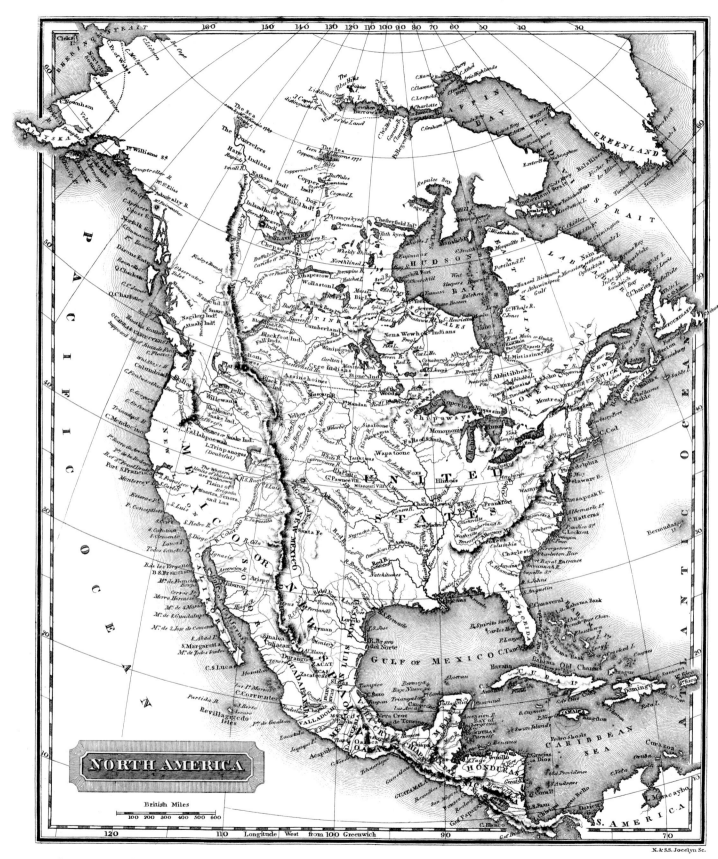

North America, as shown in the *New Universal Atlas of the World,* published by Howe & Spalding, New Haven, Connecticut, 1822. The entire Yukon region is blank.

the Indians either to "assimilate" – to become like white Canadians – or to disappear completely.

After Confederation, the government negotiated thirteen treaties with Indians all across Canada, from northern Ontario to what is now northeastern British Columbia and part of the Northwest Territories. Some treaties were signed before the western provinces and territories ever existed as they do today. Each treaty set aside reserve lands and arranged for annual payments, supplies, schooling (which was usually under missionary supervision) and other services to the Indian group that signed it.

For a long time most of this British and early Canadian governmental activity did not touch the Yukon Indians at all, because they were in such a remote part of British North America. The Royal Proclamation of 1763, which had stated the concept of "aboriginal title," covered those lands described as lying "to the Westward of the Sources of the Rivers which fall into the Sea from the West and Northwest." Just where the western and northern limits were was uncertain, but it seems that the Proclamation was, in any case, a statement of policy meant to apply to any Indians encountered in northwestern North America, no matter where they lived.

The Proclamation did not originally apply to what was known as Rupert's Land – a vast territory granted to the Hudson's Bay Company in 1670 by King Charles II. The company had complete charge over this territory until turning it over to the Dominion of Canada in 1869. When the federal government took over Rupert's Land, it extended to the natives in it the policy of the Proclamation of 1763.

Scholars still argue about the exact boundaries of Rupert's Land, but it did not include any of what is now the Yukon. From 1821 until 1859, however, the Hudson's Bay Company also had a charter from the British Crown for the exclusive right to trade in what was then known as the Northwest Territory. In return for this charter, the company agreed to be responsible for law and order in the area and to look after the Indians in certain ways. It was during just those years that John Bell, Robert Campbell, Alexander Murray and other HBC men were exploring the upper Yukon River and its branches, and building the first trading posts at Fort Yukon, Fort McPherson and Fort Selkirk. There is some question whether the company's charter was really intended to cover all of this country. It certainly did not extend to Fort Yukon, which was actually in Russian America until the United States bought the land and named it Alaska.

One reason why this history matters today is that it enters into Yukon Indian land-claim negotiations. Some legal authorities argue that the Yukon can be thought of as having been fully covered by the charter granted to the Hudson's Bay Company. This is because until 1898 the Yukon was a designated part of the Northwest Territories. Other lawyers and historians are not so sure about this point. Everybody agrees, however, that the 1821 charter never gave the HBC the kind of title to lands in the Northwest that had earlier been granted for Rupert's Land. The charter which allowed the company to operate in the Northwest gave it only the right to trade.

Elizabeth Williams and her baby at their camp on the upper Taku River, 1922 (photo by Trevor Davis)

Whether the Hudson's Bay Company's charter covered the Yukon or not, it is reasonable to think that Yukon Indians today have the same aboriginal title to their land as do other Canadian Indians who have not given up their land through a treaty or a sale approved by the government. The Yukon Indians have certainly been living in Yukon lands for a long time. Nevertheless, the legal position of the Yukon Indians seemed far from clear in the eyes of the federal and territorial governments when they finally began to consider the matter in this century.

Before 1953, Ottawa controlled most of the land in the Yukon, but since then it has turned a good deal of the land over to the jurisdiction of the territorial government. The federal government has, however, kept control of all natural resources of territorial lands except for game animals. The Yukon government has looked after game and fur animals in the Yukon since it was first created. Section 25 of the Yukon Game Ordinance of 1902 said that, except for a rule against shooting bison, Yukon Indians did not have to follow the same hunting and trapping regulations as other Yukon residents. Beginning in 1938, however, the territorial game laws were applied to Indians too. By 1950 Indians could not hunt and fish as they had done before, and they had to register their traplines.

These new rules were largely the result of pressures from outside sportsmen who could now come to the Yukon on the Alaska Highway and who wanted the Yukon game animals to be managed for trophy hunting. Many Yukon Indians, who depended on the animals for food and skins, opposed the changed regulations.

Until the 1950s, few Yukon Indians questioned the laws and policies of the federal and territorial governments. Few concerned themselves about whether they had aboriginal title to their lands, or with the legality of the rules they had to follow in hunting, fishing and trapping. Like their ancestors, they had their own ideas about their native land and how it should be used, and they still saw themselves as its caretakers. Unlike the whites, the Indians did not think of the land as something to buy and sell.

For a long time too, the Yukon Indians, like many other northern Canadian natives, paid no attention to the stated policies of the Department of Indian Affairs. In earlier days it was the missionaries who saw to whatever education young Indians got, and the Royal Canadian Mounted Police in Dawson who, in hard times, helped needy families with food or clothing as directed by the Department of Indian Affairs in Ottawa. In 1906 Rev. John Hawksley, an Anglican missionary, gave up the ministry to become the Yukon's first Indian Agent, and Harper Reed, the Indian Agent in a branch office at Telegraph Creek, B.C., also sometimes visited Yukon Indians. Generally, though, Department of Indian Affairs activity ebbed and flowed unpredictably in the Yukon, and often there was no full-time agent, especially between World Wars I and II.

After World War II, the new Alaska Highway and better air ser-

Klukshu, August 1948

Dolly Johnston, with George Johnston's 1928 Chevrolet, Teslin, 1951

vice made it easier to get around in the Yukon. When the new aid programs for Indians were announced by the federal government in 1946, Jack Meek became the resident Indian Agent in Whitehorse. At first, Meek had only one assistant, and he reported directly to Ottawa, but in 1948 the Yukon Indian Agency was placed under the control of a Department of Indian Affairs regional office in Vancouver. Soon there were several assistant agents, each responsible for just a few bands, instead of two people who had to deal with all the Yukon natives. They organized the Indians into official bands wherever these had not already been formed, and they made sure that each had an elected chief and a council. By 1952 the Yukon Indian Agency recognized sixteen legal bands of Indians including some who lived in northern British Columbia. The bands were Lower Post, Watson Lake, Upper Liard, Atlin, Teslin, Carcross, Lake Laberge, Champagne, Aishihik, Burwash Landing, Beaver Creek, Carmacks, Fort Selkirk, Mayo, Dawson, and Old Crow.

By this time, the number of non-Indians in the territory had greatly increased. The building of the Alaska Highway and the experiences of Yukon Indian soldiers in World War II also meant that many Yukon Indians now had an idea of the way of life "outside," and some of the young Indians went to school and college in large cities to the south — places like Vancouver, Victoria or Edmonton. In the Yukon itself, the education of Indians passed from church-run schools to the Yukon Department of Education. All these factors helped to make the Indians more aware of Indian Affairs policies.

Between 1920 and 1947, hunting and trapping were the major sources of income for both Indians and whites in the Yukon, but at the end of this period, some Yukon natives found it harder to stay alive. There were few jobs after the boom of highway construction was over, and the riverboats, for which many Indians had cut wood during and after the Gold Rush, were gone. A few natives had become big-game hunting guides, or had jobs in highway maintenance, or worked for the White Pass railway. Others became dependent on the Indian Agent for housing and other help. But it grew harder to live off the land, because the hunting and trapping regulations had changed, game was not as plentiful as it had been, and fur prices dropped after the 1940s.

As time went on, the federal government began to consider further changes in its Indian policy. In 1966, Prime Minister Lester Pearson created within his cabinet a new department called the Department of Indian Affairs and Northern Development (DIAND). Then in 1969 Jean Chrétien, who held this portfolio, proposed that the Indians Affairs portion of his department be abolished, that the provincial governments should become responsible for Indian affairs, and that the natives themselves should take control of their lands. Chrétien's *Statement of the Government of Canada on Indian Policy* is usually called the 1969 White Paper. (A White Paper is a federal government proposal or policy statement.) Native people all over Canada joined together to protest this White Paper, fearing that if it went into effect they would lose both their rights and their lands. They

William Peter of Ross River, setting out to hunt moose up the Canol Road, July 1965

drew so much attention to the issue that native and non-native Canadians alike became very interested in federal policy towards the Indians, Inuit (the Eskimos of the Eastern Arctic) and Inuvialuit (Eskimos of the Western Arctic).

Some of the Yukon Indians had already become very worried about what was happening to them, and what would happen to their children. Elijah Smith, a Southern Tutchone of Champagne, had served in the Canadian army during and after World War II, and had then returned to the Yukon. In 1968 he was the elected Chief of the Whitehorse Band. Here is part of a statement he made at an Indian Act consultation meeting in Whitehorse that year:

We, the Indians of the Yukon, object to . . . being treated like squatters in our own country. We accepted the white man in this country, fed him, looked after him when he was sick, showed him the way of the North, helped him to find the gold, helped him build, and respected him in his own rights. For this we have received little in return. We feel the people of the North owe us a great deal and would like the Government of Canada to see that we get a fair settlement for the use of the land. There was no treaty signed in this Country, and they tell me the land still belongs to the Indians. There were no battles fought between the whites and the Indians for this land.

Because of their concern over such issues, Elijah Smith and other Yukon natives, whether or not they had legal Indian status, began to organize themselves to speak with a single strong voice to the government. From this start in the late 1960s came the Yukon Native Brotherhood (YNB) and its pioneering document *Together Today for Our Children Tomorrow*, published in 1973. This document, which is discussed later in this chapter, had a decisive effect in convincing the federal government to begin comprehensive claims negotiations with some of the Canadian Indians. Later in 1973, Yukon Indians founded the Council for Yukon Indians (CYI) specifically in order to negotiate such claims.

Most of the suggestions in the 1969 White Paper were never carried out, but in that same year Dr Lloyd Barber was appointed Canada's first Indian Claims Commissioner. Several Indian and Inuit groups who had never made any treaties with the government were already at work trying to make sure of their land ownership and associated rights. But their cases were so different from one another, and in so many different courts, and the issues so confusing, that the government announced in 1969 that *none* of these claims could be recognized. At that point, the government even declared that there was no legitimacy to the Indians' claim to aboriginal title. Both Indians and non-Indians made such a public outcry against this position that by 1973 the government had altered it. It developed a new policy which allowed Indians who had signed no treaties to make what the government called "comprehensive claims" against it, and in 1974, the government established the Office of Native Claims (ONC) to deal with these issues.

The comprehensive claims policy means that the government will accept a variety of claims for land ownership and other social rights, based on a native group's traditional use and occupancy of the lands. The government must take into account the earlier ways of life of the people concerned and ensure that a good quality of life can be continued.

Under this new policy, the Inuit and Cree of James Bay in 1975, and the Naskapi Indians in 1978, reached final agreements about their comprehensive claims. The Committee for Original Peoples' Entitlement (COPE), which represented the Inuvialuit, also reached an agreement to settle in principle in 1978. (To settle "in principle" usually means that the native people and the government have basically agreed on an issue, but have not yet worked out final details of administering their agreement.) Because the Loucheux Indians of the northern Yukon still depend on the Porcupine caribou herd that ranges over the North Slope into both Alaska and the Northwest Territories, they are naturally interested in whether the federal government's final settlement with COPE will affect the terms of the Yukon Indians' settlement.

In January 1978 the Council for Yukon Indians presented its comprehensive claims position to the Minister of Indian Affairs, and on 19 July 1979, the negotiating team reached a first agreement in principle. The agreement concerned rights of the native people of the Yukon to harvest animals and fish. This was a start, but it was followed by a period of delays and complex negotiations between the government and the CYI representatives. However, on 23 June 1980, the CYI not only settled in principle, but persuaded the federal government to provide interim benefits for the Yukon Indian elders. After all, the CYI argued, these old people had been waiting a long time and perhaps they would not live to see the final settlement. Yukon Indians have always revered their elders and done their best to care for them. That is why the CYI put so much emphasis on getting these benefits.

On 12 December 1980, the CYI also reached agreements in principle on four more major parts of its comprehensive claims – hunting, fishing, trapping and land-use planning. Other important issues in the negotiations of the Yukon Indians remain unsettled, so the CYI is still negotiating with the federal government as of 1987.

Representatives of several neighboring native groups who did not sign treaties have also been negotiating their comprehensive claims. One of these groups is the United Tahltans. Another was the Kaska-Dené, made up of bands of Indians from nothern British Columbia that include relatives of the Kaska Indians at Watson Lake and Ross River.

How does a native group negotiate with the federal government under the comprehensive claims policy? First its representatives meet with those from the Office of Native Claims (ONC) and representatives of the provincial or territorial government involved. (In the Yukon, this of course means the Yukon Territorial Government.) When the ONC, the provincial or territorial government, and the native group have all the agreements in order, ONC sends the documents to the Minister of Indian Affairs. The Minister then responds to the claims on behalf of the government of Canada. But in 1987, because of continuing political complications resulting from changes in the federal and territorial governments as well as disagreements among the Yukon bands represented by the CYI, the final claims of the Yukon Indians still have not been settled.

Further Developments and Complications

One of the major factors affecting Yukon land-claim negotiations has been the pipeline issue. In the early 1970s, several large oil and gas companies had become interested in building a natural-gas pipeline south from the oil fields of arctic Alaska. They proposed to run the pipeline across the northern Yukon, up the Mackenzie valley and on into southern Canada and the United States. To its credit, before granting anyone a license to build such a pipeline, the federal government appointed Justice Thomas Berger to investigate the project's possible effects.

Mr Justice Berger travelled up and down the Mackenzie valley listening to what both natives and whites had to say about the pipeline proposal. He invited Yukon Indians to come to Yellowknife to express their views as well. Scientists also testified at the Berger hearings, and many of them undertook new research for this purpose. Much new information was gathered concerning the habits of caribou and other northern animals, and concerning the archaeology, languages and culture of northern native peoples.

Most of the Yukon Indians, Mackenzie valley Dené, Inuvialuit, and Northwest Territories Métis opposed the construction of the pipeline. Many feared that the pipeline, if it were built, would spoil the land and destroy the native way of life. Those who had not signed treaties particularly opposed building the pipeline before their comprehensive claims had been settled, because the pipeline would be built on the very land involved in their claims.

The complete transcripts of these hearings are part of the public record and fill thousands of pages. In 1977, Berger published his two-volume report, *Northern Frontier, Northern Homeland.* It is usually called the Report of the Berger Commission, or simply the Berger Report. It summarizes the chief findings of the inquiry and also has many pictures of the people and the country. In this report Berger recommended strongly that no pipeline be built in the Mackenzie valley for at least ten years. By 1977, of course, the comprehensive claims policy was in effect, and this ten-year delay was intended to give the Indians and Inuvialuit time to do their negotiating.

Mr Justice Berger also wrote that he agreed with the Loucheux Indians of Old Crow who said that if a pipeline went across the northern Yukon one of two things was sure to happen. Either the great Porcupine caribou herd would be destroyed forever, because the suggested routes for the pipeline cut across their calving grounds, or else Old Crow village itself would be drastically changed, because an alternate route ran very close to the village.

Berger included in his report the testimonies of several Old Crow Indians. Here, for example, is what Alice Frost said:

Do [the white people] *have a right to ask us to give up this beautiful land of ours? Do they have a right to spoil our land and destroy our wild game for their benefit? Do they have any right to ask us to change our life, that we have lived for centuries? Do they have any right . . . to decide our future? . . . We live peacefully . . . in harmony with nature, here in Old Crow. You won't find very many places left like this in the world.*

By the time the Berger report was published, both the Canadian government and the big oil companies had apparently given up the idea of building the pipeline up the Mackenzie valley and had begun to think about running it to the Pacific coast instead, through Alaska alone or through Alaska and the Yukon. Several new routes through the Yukon were suggested, but the one most favored ran along the Alaska Highway.

The government then hurried to have another series of hearings. This time Kenneth M. Lysyk, from the University of British Columbia Law School, was appointed to head a three-person Board of Inquiry, and the CYI received special government funding so its representatives could participate in the hearings. The Chairman of the CYI at that time, Daniel Tlen, stated clearly that the Yukon Indians still wanted a satisfactory comprehensive claims settlement before they would consider any pipeline routes through the Yukon. He suggested that it might take seven to ten years before an agreement could be negotiated and put into effect.

The Lysyk Board of Inquiry agreed there was much to be said for the CYI position, but suggested in its 1977 report, *Alaska Highway*

Pipeline Inquiry, that the decision should not be delayed beyond August 1981. Soon after the Lysyk Report was published, the governments of Canada and the U.S.A. agreed between themselves that the pipeline should indeed be built through the Yukon, but by 1987, only a few test sections had been built, the project had been halted, and the Yukon Indians' claim negotiations were still going on.

In 1982, another thing happened which may change government policy toward the Indians and affect the nature of the CYI comprehensive negotiations. On 17 April 1982, Canada got a new constitution. It replaced the British North America Act, previously used as a basis for the argument that Indians who never made treaties have aboriginal title to their land. Many Indians wonder if they still have the same safeguards for their welfare that they had under the earlier act. It may take many years to determine how the new constitution will be interpreted and how it will affect the Indians' position.

Indian policy is always partly at the mercy of those who are in political power. By 1982, the Yukon Indians knew a lot more about political processes, both federal and territorial, than they did in 1898, 1946 or even 1969. Soon after the CYI was formed, in 1973, its officers were on their way to Ottawa to speak face to face with Prime Minister Trudeau. In the Yukon, the Indians were also beginning to participate in territorial policies. Two Yukon Indians, Alice McGuire and Grafton Njootli, were elected to the Legislative Assembly in 1978, and David Porter, Margaret Joe and Kathy Nukon were elected in 1982. Others have followed since then, and in 1985 Sam Johnston, an Inland Tlingit of Teslin, was chosen as Speaker of the House.

YUKON INDIAN ORGANIZATIONS

YIAA, YNB, YANSI, CYI and DIAND — all these sets of letters are the initials of organizations that have something to do with Yukon Indians now or that did in the past. All but the last of these organizations were created by Yukon Indians. What were these different organizations and why did several of them finally join together to become the present-day CYI?

The Yukon Indian Advancement Association

When Chief Elijah Smith made his 1968 speech at the Indian Act consultation meeting in Whitehorse, telling DIAND officials that the Yukon Indians wanted their land and rights, he was not the first Yukon Indian to speak out to the government on this point. In fact, in 1902, right after the Klondike Gold Rush, Chief Kishwoots (Jim Boss) of the Lake Laberge Tutchone Indians had asked the federal government for a treaty to protect his people who were already suffering from the overwhelming numbers of whites who had moved into the country. Ottawa's only reply was that the Royal Canadian Mounted Police would take care of the Indians and not let them starve.

YIAA: Yukon Indian Advancement Association
YNB: Yukon Native Brotherhood
YANSI: Yukon Association for Non-Status Indians
CYI: Council for Yukon Indians

DIAND: Department of Indian Affairs and Northern Development
(Often DIAND is referred to simply as the Department of Indian Affairs, or DIA.)

99

The Yukon Indians were not satisfied with this answer, especially as times grew harder for them. They were becoming more dependent on the white economy, but were getting little benefit from it. Illnesses brought by the whites continued to cut down their numbers until almost the middle of the century. Then the Indian population began to rise rather sharply, because for the first time the government offered some health care.

Still, the Indians had not yet organized themselves to do anything about their needs. Until after World War II, it was not easy for their leaders to travel about in the territory, and until 1952, when the sixteen Yukon Indian bands were created by the Indian Act, most bands did not have elected chiefs or councils who could meet to make policy and represent their people. In the late 1950s, however, some Yukon Indians saw that their native neighbors in Alaska were pressing their land claims against the United States government, and some Yukoners who had Coast Tlingit relatives helped with the work that led to the Alaskan Tlingit and Haida land settlement in 1965.

In 1966, some of these same Yukon Indians, and others, decided to join with interested white people to found the Yukon Indian Advancement Association. The Yukon Territorial Commissioner, leaders of Yukon religious organizations, and public health officials all cooperated in setting up the YIAA and its program. Both status and non-status Indians belonged to the group, whose aim was to better the lives of Indian people, especially those living in Whitehorse. Perhaps the most important thing the YIAA did was to build Skookum Jim Memorial Hall in Whitehorse. It was named in honor of the Tagish Indian who had helped discover the Klondike gold, and it was built with funds that he had left in care of the Anglican Church.

The YIAA did not last very long. Most of its members went over to the other Indian groups that were formed in the next few years. But the hall remained an important gathering place, and in 1969 it was renamed the Yukon Indian and Métis Friendship Centre. Many Yukon Indians, as well as those from elsewhere, have spent pleasant hours there enjoying its activities and learning useful things from its many community programs.

The Yukon Native Brotherhood

The next important Yukon Indian organization to be formed was the Yukon Native Brotherhood, YNB. Its real beginning was perhaps in October 1968. At this point the federal Indian Agency recognized fourteen rather than sixteen bands. At the invitation of DIA, the chiefs of these fourteen bands from the Yukon and northern British Columbia all came to Whitehorse to discuss the Indian Act. This was the meeting at which Elijah Smith made the statement quoted earlier in this chapter. He said that the most important issue to be considered was not proposed changes to the Indian Act, but the need for the government to settle Yukon Indian land claims and rights. Chief Smith then helped to organize the YNB, and he became its first president.

Although it was not officially incorporated until February 1970, by 1969 the YNB had already begun to represent Yukon natives. Most of them were eager to support the organization because, like many other Canadians, they were angry about the White Paper issued that summer.

At first, YNB acted for both status and non-status Indians, but in 1971, after a separate group of non-status Indians formed the Yukon Association of Non-Status Indians (YANSI), membership in YNB was restricted to status Indians. In 1980, both YNB and YANSI were amalgamated with CYI, as explained later in this chapter.

From the beginning, the YNB had three goals. One was to oppose the 1969 White Paper. A second was to increase the ability of the Yukon Indian bands to manage programs that were still being run by DIA. In order to reach this second goal, the YNB argued that Whitehorse should have a DIA regional office of its own. (At that time the DIA programs for Yukon Indians were administered from Vancouver.) DIA agreed to establish a Yukon regional office, and also set up special programs to train band managers and bookkeepers. By this time the fourteen bands of 1968 had been consolidated into the current twelve: Old Crow, Dawson, Mayo, Carmacks, Fort Selkirk–Pelly Crossing, Ross River, Whitehorse (Kwänlin Dun), Kluane, Champagne-Aishihik, Carcross, Teslin, and Watson Lake–Liard.

YNB's chief goal, that of pressing comprehensive claims, seemed most difficult to pursue at first, because of insufficient funds. But in 1972, YNB obtained from the Indian Claims Commissioner, Lloyd Barber, the sum of $60,000 and a six-month contract to prepare a claim submission to the federal government. This funding enabled the YNB to write its notable document, *Together Today for Our Chidren Tomorrow: A Statement of Grievances and an Approach to Settlement by the Yukon Indian People*.

This report, published in January 1973, is a very eloquent statement about what it meant to be a Yukon Indian at that time. Every Yukon resident should read it. "The Yukon Indian people," it said, "are not a happy people," and both Indians and whites were "getting nervous because of the lack of understanding and tolerance among both groups." It tells a little about the early history of the Yukon Indians after the first whites arrived. It describes how badly off they were economically when the Alaska Highway building boom ended, for by this time many Indians had become wage earners. It explains how much the Indians needed good education and opportunities if they were to move into good jobs in the Canadian economy. It makes clear too why they needed to secure their land-use rights, because some of them wanted to follow their older hunting and trapping ways instead of becoming wage earners. It includes a position paper on education, three documents on economic development, and one other set of papers devoted to a technical issue, giving evidence that the Liard River Band had never signed Treaty Eleven.

On 14 February 1973, Elijah Smith and a delegation of Yukon chiefs presented a copy of *Together Today for Our Children Tomorrow* to

Prime Minister Trudeau in Ottawa. It was the first comprehensive claim ever to be submitted to the Canadian government by any Indian group, and the Prime Minister accepted it as a basis for negotiations.

The YNB went on to develop its own programs in five areas: community planning, economic development, social development, Indian education and band financial management. It also spoke out on several major measures at the federal and territorial levels; for example, it rejected a proposed transfer of responsibility for Indian health services from the federal to the territorial government. YNB continued all these pursuits until its 1980 amalgamation into the CYI, which now continues to be responsible for many of these same areas.

The Yukon Association for Non-Status Indians

The history of YANSI is a little different from that of the YNB. Its purpose was to represent the interests of the "forgotten people," the nearly 3000 Yukon Indians not registered as status Indians in Ottawa's records.

Like the YNB, YANSI was really operating before its official incorporation in 1971. In late 1969 and through all of 1970, Canada's Métis and non-status Indians had made a major effort to get organized. By early 1970 Butch Smitheran had founded the British Columbia Association of Non-Status Indians. Margaret Joe and Frances Woolsey, two non-status women from the Yukon, sought help from Smitheran in organizing a Yukon group. When it was first formed, the interim president was George Asp, and when an official election of officers was held in February 1971, the new executive board included Joe Jacquot, President; Margaret Joe, Vice-President; and Edna Dawson Rose, Secretary-Treasurer.

YANSI's tasks were to try to strengthen the community ties of its members, to help eligible Yukon Indians get benefits from the Tlingit-Haida settlements in British Columbia and Alaska, and to try to get better housing for non-status Indians, since they were not receiving the government aid given to status Indians by DIA.

YANSI's accomplishments are impressive. It set up an emergency housing repair program and a rent-to-purchase program, to help members buy and maintain their own houses. It helped to develop Crossroads, an alcoholism treatment centre, which was the first of its kind in the Yukon. It also set up the Yukon Trappers Association, the Yukon Native Construction Company, the Teslin Wood Products Factory, the Ye-Sa-To Communications Society, which publishes the *Yukon Indian News,* and the Outreach Project to help people gain employment. All these activities were still going when YANSI, like the YNB, amalgamated with the CYI.

Why was there a 1980 amalgamation, and what does it mean?

Neither YNB nor YANSI had much money at the beginning, and neither was set up just to negotiate comprehensive claims. Both groups decided that it would be best to create a third organization whose *only* purpose would be to negotiate the claims. This is how the Council for Yukon Indians, CYI, came to be founded on 15 November 1973. Its sole responsibility at that point was to try to get a fair settlement. The YNB and YANSI each had representatives in it, as did each Indian community. The CYI itself had no power to sign a final agreement; its duty was only to negotiate and recommend a settlement. The 6000 or so Yukon Indian people would themselves have to decide if they wanted that settlement.

In February 1980, a special Tri-General Assembly of the CYI, YNB and YANSI was called at the Yukon Indian Centre in Whitehorse. From February 4 to February 12, delegates discussed the issue of amalgamating – joining together with each other. The result of the meeting was that the three groups decided to dissolve their respective organizations. The members could then adopt a new constitution and hold elections for an amalgamated CYI.

In the new CYI, status and non-status Indians could work together as a single unit, which is very important to the Yukon Indians. Those Indians who are legally non-status have often felt that they have been unfairly treated by the territorial and federal governments. Non-status Indians usually consider themselves to be Indian in culture. Status Indians and many whites also treat them as Indians, but they have had none of the help that the government has given to status Indians, even though they have often needed it just as much, or more. Since they cannot be enrolled as Indian band members, they do not qualify for the benefits that go to band members, even though they live in the same places and in the same ways as legal members of the bands. This situation has sometimes caused bad feelings between status and non-status people. In some places it has divided the Indians among themselves.

Yukon Indian leaders, however, have argued that because no Yukon Indians ever signed a treaty, the government division between status and non-status Indians has never been legal in the Yukon. They have said that the comprehensive claims negotiations could be a good means to erase the false distinction between status and non-status Indians. The elders advising on the matter have said that such a settlement could "give us back our grandchildren," and have urged that the Yukon Indians should all be one people under the law as well as in spirit.

Claims negotiations were proceeding very slowly around 1980, and this is another reason why the Indians decided to take matters in their own hands by amalgamating all existing Indian organizations into the new CYI. Again the Yukon Indians achieved an historic first among Canadian Indians. Nowhere else in Canada are the Indian people, regardless of their status, members of one organization as they are now in the Yukon.

All of the programs formerly run by the YNB, YANSI and CYI are still maintained under four areas, each headed by a vice-chairman. These areas are Social Programs, Housing and Economic Development, Finance and Administration, and Land Claims. The chairman is the chief executive officer and the twelve band chiefs make up the board of directors.

The comprehensive claims negotiations have continued to be CYI's principal activity. Because of changes in the federal and territorial governments, these negotiations still go slowly, but as mentioned earlier in this chapter, an "Agreement With Respect to Providing Interim Benefits to Elders" was signed in June 1980, and by December the four agreements in principle on hunting, fishing, trapping and land-use planning had been reached. Finally, in August 1981, the Carcross Band signed an agreement on land selection and in the summer of 1982 began to pick out the land it wanted.

Comprehensive claims were still not settled in 1987. For a period of time all claims negotiations stopped, and federal funding of the CYI was drastically reduced, but negotiations are now again underway. The history of the CYI shows very clearly what can be done by Indian people with persistence, organization and political knowledge. Six thousand Indians in the Yukon have effectively kept the attention of what once seemed an impossibly distant, uncaring, and all-powerful federal government in far-away Ottawa as well as that of the territorial government. Furthermore, the Indians are getting from these governments some of the things that they have long needed and wanted, and they are beginning to be represented in the government itself.

6

Yukon Indian Languages

THE SEVEN INDIAN LANGUAGE GROUPINGS IN THE YUKON

If two Yukon Indians who are strangers to each other meet on the street in Whitehorse, how can each tell where the other comes from? Usually it is not possible, just from looking at someone, to be sure whether the person comes from Pelly Crossing, Old Crow, Beaver Creek, Watson Lake, Carcross or somewhere else. But if the two Indians begin to speak in their own Indian languages they can often guess where in the Yukon each was born. Before some of them began to speak English, every Yukon Indian spoke at least one of the seven native Yukon languages. Like modern ethnographers and linguists, the Yukon Indians have traditionally used language as one way to distinguish different native groups.

When the white fur traders and explorers first came into the Yukon, they too found that language was one of the best ways to tell one group of Indians from another. The traders themselves often knew only a smattering of any Indian language, but they almost always had interpreters, who were among the best paid of Hudson's Bay Company employees. Explorers tried to have interpreters too. Robert Campbell wrote that when he and the Liard River Indians with him reached the mouth of the Pelly River for the first time in 1843, "Unfortunately none of my party understood their language, except a few among them who spoke and understood a few words of the dialect to use towards that quarter." Campbell knew then that he had met a new group of Indians — the ones whom he called in English the "Wood Indians." They were different from the "Knife Indians" farther up the Pelly, who spoke another dialect.

Campbell, Murray and other traders worked out a whole set of names for the various groups of Yukon Indians. They distinguished these groups primarily by means of their languages, and secondarily by their different ways of living. Some of these groups they knew about only by hearsay from the Indians who came to their trading posts. The names used by the early traders and explorers were often kept as a basis for the later classification of Indians made by the ethnographers and usually followed by the linguists as well.

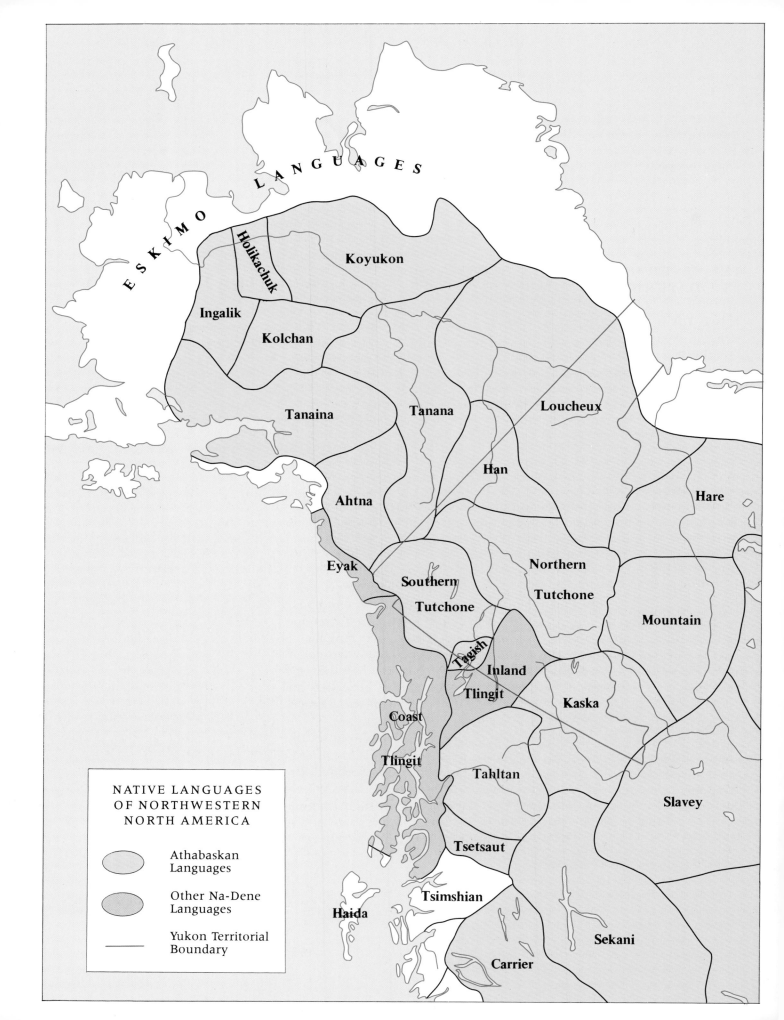

ESKIMO LANGUAGES

Holikachuk

Koyukon

Ingalik

Kolchan

Tanaina

Tanana

Loucheux

Han

Hare

Ahtna

Eyak

Southern Tutchone

Northern Tutchone

Mountain

Tagish

Inland Tlingit

Coast Tlingit

Kaska

Tlingit

Tahltan

Slavey

Tsetsaut

Tsimshian

Haida

Sekani

Carrier

NATIVE LANGUAGES
OF NORTHWESTERN
NORTH AMERICA

Athabaskan
Languages

Other Na-Dene
Languages

Yukon Territorial
Boundary

THE NA-DENE LANGUAGE SUPERFAMILY

How are the Indian languages of the Yukon related to those of Indians outside the territory? The map shows all the native languages of northwestern North America at the beginning of the twentieth century. Several of the languages spoken in the Yukon are also spoken by native people in neighboring parts of Alaska, the Northwest Territories and British Columbia. Most of these languages belong to one of three language families: Athapaskan, Tlingit and Eyak.* These three families in turn make up the Na-Dene superfamily. (The name Na-Dene comes from the Tlingit *na* and Athapaskan *dené,* both meaning people.)

The various Athapaskan languages spoken today are so different that a Loucheux speaker from Old Crow, for instance, cannot understand a Kaska speaker from Watson Lake, but the grammars and sound patterns of Loucheux and Kaska are still basically alike. Because of this, linguists are sure that both languages have come from a common source.

Long ago the ancestors of the Loucheux and the Kaska, as well as those of all other Athapaskan speakers, must once have lived together in one spot and spoken a single language. We do not know where this ancestral Athapaskan homeland was, but it may have been in the western Yukon. In any case, as time went on, some of the speakers of this language must have moved out in different directions and begun to live in other parts of the country. As the years passed, the grandchildren and great grandchildren of those who once spoke the original Athapaskan language stayed apart from one another, and little by little their speech became different. That is why today a Kaska-speaking person of Watson Lake has trouble understanding a Loucheux-speaking person who lives at Old Crow.

In Chapter Three it was mentioned that a large quantity of volcanic ash fell on the Yukon about 700 AD. Perhaps it was then that the ancestors of the Athapaskan-speaking people of the southwestern Yukon first began to split up, to travel north and south along the Cordillera and east to the Mackenzie valley and the high plains. Perhaps it was then that the Athapaskan-speaking peoples of the present began to develop their own individual languages.

Quite apart from the archaeological evidence, linguists think that only a little over a thousand years may have passed since the ancestors of present-day Athapaskan-speakers moved apart from one another. Linguists say that the split cannot be much older because Yukon and Alaskan Athapaskan Indians can still understand some of the words spoken by the Athapaskan-speaking Hupa Indians of California and by the Athapaskan-speaking Navajo and Apache Indians of the southwestern United States. Indians from all of these groups can pick up each other's languages rather easily and in a fairly short time, although they do not understand each other when they first meet.

But that is not the whole story. Many linguists think that, just as the various Athapaskan languages split off from each other and grew

*The Eyak language family is now almost extinct. According to Michael Krauss of the Alaska Native Language Center, only two fluent speakers of the language are now known (in 1987), and both of these speakers are elderly.

different, so in much earlier times the Tlingit speakers may have branched off from the Athapaskan speakers. Perhaps several thousand years ago — before the Athapaskan languages split — there was an even earlier single language from which both Tlingit and Athapaskan, as well as Eyak, all diverged. This is what it means when linguists group these three language families into the Na-Dene superfamily.

It is much harder for an Athapaskan and a Tlingit-speaker to learn to understand one another than for speakers of two different Athapaskan languages. Still, it is easier for a Tlingit-speaker to learn an Athapaskan language, or for an Athapaskan-speaker to learn Tlingit, than for a European to learn either. This is because Tlingit and the Athapaskan languages still share a common pattern, different from the patterns of any of the languages of Europe.

Indo-European is the name of the linguistic superfamily to which English, French, German and many other European languages belong. (The "Indo" refers to India, and not to North American Indians.) The grammar of all the languages in the Indo-European superfamily is very different from that of all the languages in the Na-Dene superfamily — so different that real difficulties or misunderstandings can arise when a person who speaks an Indo-European language tries to learn a Na-Dene language or the other way around.

PATTERNS OF NA-DENE GRAMMAR

Why should grammar be so important? The reason is that the grammar, or the way in which words are put together and arranged to make sense in any language, helps to order the way its speakers think about the world and the things in it. Most people never analyze their own grammar, because it just seems right and natural to them. They are not aware of its force. But a few examples will show some striking differences between the basic grammars of Na-Dene and of Indo-European languages.

A speaker of Tlingit, Northern Tutchone or any other Na-Dene tongue can easily tell whether someone speaking his language is referring to one person or to several people. He can also tell whether the speaker is referring to males or females. However, a Na-Dene speaker does not add an *s* sound to the end of a word, as an English speaker usually does, when he wants to talk about several persons. In fact, because he has learned the Na-Dene grammatical patterns, a native speaker of Tlingit or of an Athapaskan language often has a hard time knowing when to add *s* to an English word.

A person whose native language is Tlingit or Athapaskan may also not be sure when to use English "he," "she," "it" or "they," and may talk about a boy as "she," or a single girl as "they." The Indian is not stupid; he simply has a different way of expressing number and gender in his own language. Na-Dene languages do not use pronouns to give information about how many people are meant or what sex they are. Na-Dene languages give this information through their verb forms instead — and Na-Dene verbs are very different from those in Indo-European languages. This is why English or French speakers have trouble learning Tlingit and Athapaskan verbs, though they may not be stupid people either.

It is not just the changes required to indicate number and gender that baffle English and French speakers trying to learn Na-Dene languages. Other aspects of Na-Dene verbs also seem strange to them. Na-Dene verbs often classify things in ways that English verbs do not. When an English speaker says that he "picks up" something, he does not change the verb to suit the shape or quality of what he picks up. In Tlingit or Athapaskan, however, the verb for expressing the idea of "picking up" must tell the listener what kind of thing the speaker intends to pick up. A different verb for "pick up" is used depending on whether the object to be picked up is long and rigid like a pencil, or round and solid like a rock, or thin and pliable like a piece of cloth or a leaf. The verb will be different if it applies to a cup or bowl full of soup, or to a cup or bowl that is empty, or to a living baby, or to a piece of dried meat. Each time, the Na-Dene speaker has to choose exactly the right verb to show what kind of thing is being picked up. These examples reflect just a few of the far reaching differences between Na-Dene and Indo-European grammatical patterns.

MEANING IN LANGUAGE

Of course, it is not just the rules for changing forms or for putting words together — the grammar — that is important in each language. It is also the meanings of the words themselves. Some Tlingit and Athapaskan words are very hard to translate into English, just as some English words are very hard to put into Athapaskan or Tlingit.

In his preface to the *Selkirk Indian Language Dictionary*, Daniel Tlen writes about how difficult it is to explain in English how a hunter can locate game. Although this is easy to do in the Tutchone language, English has not developed the exact words needed to express the same ideas as readily. Linguists agree that no language — Tlingit, Athapaskan, French, English, or any other language in the world — is inherently better than another. But each language expresses ideas in its own way, and each develops vocabularies that are highly suited to the circumstances and interests of its speakers.

Useless misunderstandings between Indians and non-Indians have occurred in the past, and still occur, because it is so hard to make good, quick translations from one language to another. Misunderstandings can also occur when young English-speaking Indians do not fully understand the Indian languages of their parents or grandparents. The young people may scoff when the older people mix up their pronouns in English. The old people, on the other hand, may see that the young are foolish because they do not try to learn their native languages, and so they cut themselves off from the past.

WHEN SHOULD A YUKON INDIAN TALK?
LANGUAGE AND SPEECH

Language is not quite the same thing as speech. Language is really just the ground plan behind people's speech. You may know all about the rules of a language, but you still will not know just exactly what a person is going to say at a given moment. You may also know all the words a person uses when he says something, and yet not know quite what he means. Often, you will not even know whether a person is going to speak at all unless you understand the rules of that person's culture.

If you visit or live with people who have a culture and language different from your own, it may take a long time to learn the proper behavior associated with speech. In each culture people usually have very definite ideas about polite speech. There are usually rules about who should speak first when two people meet in certain situations, or if they should even speak at all. Each society too, has ways of judging who is a good speaker, or who is gifted in using speech to handle delicate social situations or to make people feel happy or sad. Sometimes the customs that go with the use of language say as much, in their own way, as the language itself. Many older Yukon Indians think, for example, that white people ask too many questions, order people about too much, and talk about things that should not be discussed. White people, on the other hand, sometimes think that Indians do not talk enough.

Traditional Yukon Indians had some very clear ideas and specific rules about when people should not speak. For example, a Kaska person who could keep silent when in pain or angry was highly valued, but women were allowed to cry out more easily than men. In a difficult situation, when someone did not know what was going to happen, it was usually thought best to say nothing. Throughout the Yukon in earlier times, certain relatives, such as a man and his mother-in-law, a grown-up brother and sister, or even an older brother and a younger brother, were either forbidden to speak to each other at all, or else they were supposed to say as little as possible, and then only when it had something to do with staying alive. These rules about not speaking did not mean that the individuals were angry with each other, as some whites thought. Rather, they were ways in which one person showed respect to another.

Among traditional Yukon Indians, certain topics were not discussed at all in public. These included witchcraft, pregnancy and sex – except when two "joking relatives," such as those described in Chapter Eight, were having fun. Someone good at "talking fun" was always liked, and an elder who could speak "high language," expressing himself or herself in age-old phrases and words, could gain much prestige. Oratory was a great Indian art in the past, and it still is today. (Have you ever heard Elijah Smith or Charlie Peter Charlie make a speech?) Yukon Indians have long known that the tongue is a powerful organ for good or bad.

Many traditional Yukon Indians "owned" special words that were believed to have great power. Their owners used the words to protect themselves from bears or from dangerous water, to ease pain, to cure a knife cut or bullet wound, to increase their ability to shoot straight, to pack heavy loads, or to have an easy trail. Sometimes the words were sung; sometimes they were just thought silently.

There is a lot more to learn about Yukon patterns of speech behavior, but these examples show how important to the Indian people their languages are, and some of the reasons why they should not be forgotten.

WRITING AND READING YUKON INDIAN LANGUAGES

A few older Yukon Indians still speak only the Indian languages they have used all their lives; others speak both their native language and English. Many younger Indians use only English. They may understand the local Indian dialect spoken by their parents and grandparents, but they themselves do not speak it. Now, however, some young Indians are taking more interest in their traditional languages, learning to speak them at home and in schools.

One reason for this new interest is that it is becoming easier both for young Indians and for other people to learn the native Yukon languages. John Ritter, a white linguist working with several Yukon Indians – Daniel Tlen, Tommy McGinty, Edwin Hager, Gertie Tom, Agnes Moose McDonald and others – and with the sponsorship of the CYI, has been developing trustworthy ways of writing these languages down. These writing systems use the roman alphabet, which is the alphabet normally used for English and other European languages. But there are many sounds in the Indian languages which are not used in speaking English or French, and these sounds are represented by using European letters and symbols in special ways.

All Na-Dene languages use some sounds that are combined with a kind of catch or pop at the back of the throat. (Modern linguists call them glottalized sounds, because the glottis is the soft part of the back of the throat where the popping sound is made.) For example, a Carmacks Indian speaking his native Northern Tutchone begins the word for "spoon" with a glottalized *ts* sound. This sound is written now in the roman alphabet with an apostrophe, like this: *ts'*. The Northern Tutchone word for "spoon" is spelled *ts'ál*.

Anybody who knows an Athapaskan language or Tlingit can think of many other sounds besides *ts'* that are glottalized and can easily say and hear the glottalized sounds. Older Indians have used these sounds from the time they first began to talk, but those who have never had such training often find glottalized sounds very difficult to say and hear.

Tone – the difference between high and low pitch – is also important in Na-Dene languages and has to be expressed somehow in the writing system. Words that sound the same to someone who

```
silver foxs ............... nos sa  tunus ta za.
foxes..................... nos sa.
red fox .................. nos sa tutulla
cross fox ................ kuk kuk
wolverine ................ ∅∅∅∅ nowah
wolf & wolves ............ cheyona. or at kui
cayote  ..................turalee
rats .....................tyoonesteya
Rabbit ...................  kkah
cooverd ..................tselle      .
mouse ....................tloona.
tree squirrel ............tuslut ta.
Ground hog ...............tet teya.
weazel ...................neba ah
chit chomoc ..............tuskossa
cattle ...................luk kui
pot in it ...............mut tut sul la
pot in sack ............. lassuk muttut suan  or  lesuk tunekus.
Rocky moutain ............khyes
Dember hill ..............tsoo khel or past or tupassa
Hill .....................tloo tsunt
River ....................tah kah.
creek ∅∅∅∅∅∅/∅∅/∅∅∅∅/∅∅∅∅ syoolaa or tyoo zoza
wilderness ............... ∅∅/∅∅/∅∅/ kosleeta
some testant .............taunna
l buy ....................oskyat
l paid ...................eskyat
l pay ....................kolla eskyat
coming ...................kweeh lud
go out ...................tantlud.
old man .................. khoo la or set chan
l fix. ...................me khee la
boat come up .............tah khosh
;  cme down ..............kah khosh
gone by ..................nakhosh
l heard come .............akhos kwet tle.
awl .....................at ses.
lots word  .............. zukke kwenes tloo.
```

```
   this  five words same  hard for me announce correctly
stone......... ... tsa.
beaver ...........tsaa.
sun  .............sah
bear ..............∅∅∅∅/ sash
dish ............ttsah.
and house  kho ah or khetty;
water  tyoo.
l want  nesun
```

and word good two way ate a or at tea some time et tea.
but only one way head man and god all same
denne tye ah. only way call god. but denne at te ah mean
good man. cheif. captain or kings all head man call denne tye ah.
and natou mean no or nothing and tou la mean same nothing. and lots
places in the grammar short word atea.the same word good.
and world nyee kuk tukwachooh. only one way earth . ground world all
nyee.

if some one kind to this Ross and pelly liard use god name same white
god. l use english that s all to them sence l came to Ross River.

lots their language hard announce right and sound more.

does not know any Tlingit or Athapaskan – and words which can even be spelled with just the same letters – may mean very different things because they are pronounced with different tones.

Look again at the Northern Tutchone word for "spoon." In the modern writing system, this is spelled in the roman alphabet like this:

ts'ál.

The mark above the *a* shows that Carmacks Indians say this word with a high pitch or tone: *á*.

The Carmacks word for "frog" is spelled with exactly the same roman letters:

ts'al.

The difference between the two words as written is that there is no accent on the *a* in the word for "frog." This is because *ts'al,* meaning frog, is pronounced with a low tone instead of a high tone.

There are many other Athapaskan languages in which tone makes a crucial difference to the meaning of words. All Yukon Indian languages are *tonal languages.* Classical Greek was a tonal language too. Many other languages still spoken in Africa and Asia are also tonal.

Yukon Indians had no writing systems at the time of contact, and the early traders, explorers and missionaries each invented their own way of writing down Indian names and other words they wanted to record. They used the roman alphabet, but they all used it in different ways. That is why the very same native words in books like the Tukudh Bible of Archdeacon McDonald, in early letters and word lists, and on various maps, are often spelled quite differently.

The new spelling systems used in the dictionaries, grammars and reading books published by the Yukon Native Language Centre can easily be read by any speaker of the Loucheux, Northern and Southern Tutchone or Tlingit languages. Soon there will be books in the Kaska and Tagish languages as well.

It is true that the dialect of every band of Yukon Indians may vary slightly from that of neighboring bands, and the dialects of individuals within the bands often differ too. However, the spelling systems have been worked out so that they serve each of the major Yukon Indian languages in the same way that a standard spelling system works for the English language. People from eastern and western Canada often speak English differently, but they can all read and understand the standard English spelling in books and newspapers, and they write English words alike. In the same way, a person who knows Loucheux, whether from Old Crow or Fort McPherson, or one who knows Northern Tutchone, whether from Pelly Crossing or Carmacks, can learn to read and write his or her own language, using the spelling systems of the Yukon Native Language Centre.

The development of systems for writing down native languages has been very important for Indian people. Archdeacon McDonald, Archdeacon Canham and native clergy trained by them taught many

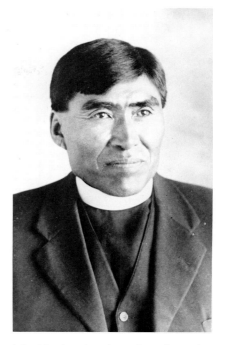

John Martin, a Loucheux from the Peel River, who worked as a missionary among the Kaska during the early 1930s, then preached at Mayo for many years. On the facing page is an excerpt from his manuscript dictionary of the Kaska language. Martin used a spelling system similar to that devised by Robert McDonald for his Tukudh Bible. This is the earliest known example of linguistic work *in written form* by a Yukon native person, but language studies and translation have always been part of life for Yukon Indians. (Archives of the Anglican Church of Canada)

A foot trail comes down from *Ttheghrá* to the junction of Big Salmon and North Fork. We went up that trail looking for sheep and groundhogs and gophers and we camped there. There was nobody around on the river, so we just pulled the boat out and tied it up there as it was. We were in the bush, so we just travelled around.

We made camp right where *Ène Chú* runs into *Gyò Cho Chú* and then we made plans to go to *Ttheghrá*. From there we started off to *Ttheghrá* but we camped before we got there. It's quite a long way up there.

We climbed up on the mountain and there were lots of gophers there. My mother and my oldest sister went out for gophers, but I was babysitting my little brother. The women went out for gophers and the men went out for sheep. My brother and I stayed at the camp while people went out hunting.

They were setting snares for gophers when it happened. My mother and my sister were setting snares close by and so were my other two sisters. My mother was cutting a spring stick for the snare. They heard rocks falling down. Ida was walking around with my mother when they hear

Ène Chú eyet *Gyò Cho Chú* uyí ìnłédlin, húyū tän húudínję hūch'i *Ttheghrá* ka huts'in. Eyet ts'ín ts'edéjael ts'ech'in mbay ke, mbay ke, denji, tsäl héech'i ke ts'ech'in. Eyet jé húyū, tl'àkú húyū łéts'adáł, kúm yóhuts'íntsin húyū nálát chūm táts'etę, eju dän húmlin yí nálát k'ē däts'intl'um ts'úmch'ō ts'ech'in né, hute hūch'i áats'edáł né.

Já húyū *Ène Chú* hédínlin eyet *Gyò Cho Chú* yí ìnłédlin húyū kúm yóhútsin k'ē tl'àkú *Ttheghrá* hunin eyet ka huts'ín ts'edujáél do ts'ech'in né. Húyū huts'ín ts'edéjael k'ē, *Ttheghrá* ka dāy ts'ín ts'edéjael k'e ddhäl ts'é'ín ts'enétro húnday chūm nìnthát.

Tl'ą́ tl'àkú ddhäl ka huts'ín táts'ejael k'ē húyū, húyū k'ē tsäl ts'ècho húmlin ne, tsäl ke dän kájáél, sän hek'e èchel yę hìde, ène èndat echo yí tsäl kéhet'rá, hék'i ejé née dän tsäl kadéjael dek'án hek'e mbay ke ładéjael. Hék'i dàkhwän k'ē èchel yí kúm yū hīki, dän hek'e tsäl kájáél k'ē.

Eyet tl'àkú tsäl yę nánéetl'ú, tsäl yę nánéetl'ú. Tsäl yę nánéetl'ú hék'i, hék'i ejé née, eyet héejé dē tsäl yę néehetl'ú ène, èndat echo yí tsäl yę néehetl'ú do héejé, eyet łákidech'i èndat hek'e déchūm ìndūm inyàkhia yū déchūm tsäl yę déehetl'ú hék'i héejé dē ène hek'e tsäl mél dänátl'ú eyet

English	Northern Tutchone		Stem & Its Meaning
I picked up the rock	tthi nedí'ę	-'ę	(compact object)
I picked up the rocks	tthi nedíle	-le	(plural objects)
I picked up the [cup of] tea	dí nedíkę	-kę	(contained object)
I picked up the [sheet of] paper	k'uk nedíchú	-chú	(fabric-like object)
I picked up the stick	dechän nedítę	-tę	(elongated object)
I picked up the dog	tlin nedíchin	-chin	(animate object)
There is a coin	dànē h'ę	-'ę	(compact object)
There are coins [or bills]	dànē hele	-le	(plural objects)
There is [a plate of] money	dànē hekę	-kę	(contained object)
There is a [single] bill	dànē hèchú	-chú	(fabric-like object)
There is [a sack of] money	dànē hètę	-tę	(sack-like object)

These are Northern Tutchone verb forms, as explained by Gertie Tom, a native speaker from the Big Salmon River area, now on the staff of the Yukon Native Language Centre. Grammatical subtleties such as these are typical of Yukon native languages.

Loucheux how to read and write. Those Indians who learned the system could write letters to each other, keep their own records and read the Bible and prayers for themselves. This helped to keep the native language strong.

Now that standard systems for writing Yukon native languages are becoming available, Yukon Indians can also write their own histories in their own languages. They can preserve stories and ideas for future generations in exactly the form they themselves think best. Over the last ten years, the Yukon Native Language Centre has concentrated its efforts in this direction by training people to read, write and speak their native tongues. The Centre, which is now a joint project of the CYI and the Government of Yukon, sponsors adult literacy classes and conversation courses in native Yukon languages. It publishes dictionaries and records of native placenames as well as collections of stories. And in 1983, at Yukon College in Whitehorse, the Centre began its first Certificate Course for Native Language Instructors. In 1986, thirteen Yukon Indians graduated from this three-year course.

In the old days, the Yukon Indians did everything they could to make sure their knowledge did not get lost. Members of each generation learned the stories of their ancestors and added new ones about their own times. Young people were trained to listen quietly and well to the older people. All over the Yukon, Indians learned the stories told by their parents, grandparents and great grandparents, and by those even farther back in time. In fact, the most valuable thing that any traditional Indian ever had was a store of knowledge inherited from his ancestors. It guided a person for all of his or her life.

What their ancestors have remembered is a priceless heritage for Yukon Indians today, whether they hear it or read it in the Indian languages or in English. This heritage has made possible the next chapters in this book. These describe how the Yukon people made their living in the late nineteenth and early twentieth centuries, what they thought about the world, and their feelings about the best ways to behave in it.

Facing page: A page from Èkeyi: Gyò Cho Chú, a book by Gertie Tom, published in 1987 by the Yukon Native Language Centre. The bilingual text (Northern Tutchone and English) records and explains many traditional placenames in the Big Salmon River area. The writing system used here for Northern Tutchone was devised by Gertie Tom in collaboration with John Ritter and others.

7

Living in the Land: Traditional Food, Shelter and Clothing

To survive in any part of the world, people must make the most of the natural habitat or environment in which they live. The natural habitat includes the mountains, hills, lakes and rivers, the climate, the plants and animals — all those things discussed in Chapter Two of this book. People are also part of the habitat. In the past, each Yukon Indian had to learn not only about the weather, the landscape and food resources, but also about other Indians with whom he or she would live, work, play, marry, trade, or perhaps fight in the course of life.

This chapter will describe how the Yukon natives used to make their living — that is, how they got their food, built shelters, clothed themselves, and moved about the country before the arrival of the whites and in the decades just after. Only a few written records remain from earlier centuries in the Yukon, but the memories of a few of the oldest people alive today can take us back to the beginning of this century, and the stories that these elders heard from their parents and grandparents take us back even earlier in time.

TRADITIONAL TECHNOLOGY

Every group of human beings has a technology. The tools, weapons, containers and other things that people need to get their food from animals and plants, and to shelter and clothe themselves, make up their basic technology. The technologies of the Yukon Indians were marvellously suited to their way of living. Because they travelled so much, the Yukon Indians did not make large items that had to be carried along to every camp and were hard to replace. What they used was light in weight or was easily made on the spot. The largest things in their technology, such as caribou fences, fish weirs and traps, log caches, boat frames and house frames, were left where they were made and used. Most of the year the people took with them just a few essential weapons and tools — bows and arrows, knives, adzes, sewing kits and perhaps some extra moccasins and clothing. Whatever else they needed they could make wherever they happened to be.

The Yukon Indians found a purpose for almost every item of their natural environment. Nothing was wasted, and most things were shared. In that way people survived in the hard times and thrived in the good times. Myra Moses, a Loucheux woman of Old Crow, recalled, for example, that when she was a child her people had no soap or towels. She kept a rabbit foot as a wash cloth, dipping it in water in order to wash her face. She tells about using this and other items that today might be thrown away as worthless:

Three months after I was born, my mother died. My grandmother brought me up. My grandmother used the skin around the caribou heart as a container for meat juice. She put a hole in the end of it and I sucked on it. I was brought up like this.

In the old days, the Yukon Indians depended on four basic kinds of materials:

1 stone
2 wood
3 bone, horn and antler
4 animal skins, sinews and organs.

In the Yukon, for thousands of years, these materials have been available almost everywhere.

Stone was used to manufacture the heads of adzes and mauls, and for arrowheads, knives, and scrapers for preparing food and skins. There is a long tradition of fine craftsmanship in stone in the Yukon, going back to the microblade makers working at Little Arm and Canyon Creek in 6000 BC. Most of the stone used was hard, like granite and obsidian, but very soft stone and earth had their uses as well. Paints and pigments were made from ochres, which are colored earths or crumbly rocks found in the mountains. (You can see the red patches of ochres high up on the mountainsides near Jakes' Corners on the Alaska Highway south of Whitehorse, at Red Paint Mountain near Haines Junction, and high in the Richardsons along the Dempster Highway in Loucheux country.)

Many stone articles needed handles or shafts of a lighter substance, so the stone was combined with the second important material on our list: wood. Wood was used to build shelters, caches, boat frames, traps, deadfalls and the frames of snowshoes, as well as the handles of tools and the shafts of arrows and spears. It was used to make big toboggans and sleds after the whites introduced them. The Indians also made plates and spoons from wood, and of course they depended on it for fuel, both to warm themselves and for cooking. They rarely cut trees for firewood, though. They looked for fallen trees and brush which they could burn without further chopping. They just kept pushing the burning ends of the larger pieces into the fire. Before steel axes were available, it was a lot of work to cut down a tree. When people had to cut one down in the old days, they used to chip around the trunk with a stone adze in much the same way that a beaver cuts a tree with his chisel-like teeth.

For some products, only the bark of trees was used. People made canoes, containers and baby carriers out of spruce bark or birchbark, depending on what was available.

Stone pestle from Klo-kut, about 17 cm long (Canadian Museum of Civilization)

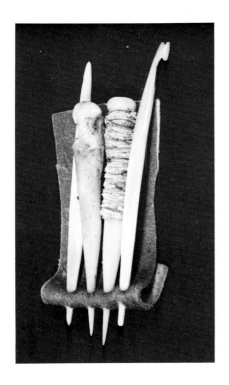

Above: Sewing kit made by Sophie Isaac of Aishihik. The kit includes a netting needle, two awls and a hook, all made of bone, in a holder of smoked moosehide. *Above right:* Babiche bag from Teslin Lake, made before 1912. The width is about 42 cm, the height about 25 cm. (Both in the Canadian Museum of Civilization)

Antler, horn and bone were very important too. Antler and horn were softened by boiling or steaming, then shaped into graceful spoons and bowls. Craftsmen carved beautiful bone and antler arrowheads, spearheads, and toggles for beaver nets. Often they cut designs into these articles, then rubbed red ochre pigments into the designs.

The fourth important class of materials is the soft parts of animals: the skin and sinews, stomachs and other organs. Clothes were made from tanned skins, and rawhide skins were used for making shelters and boats. Rawhide or semi-tanned babiche provided snares of all sizes, and lashing and netting for snowshoes. Sinews were valuable for certain kinds of lashing too – in making arrows, for example – and for snares and nets and sewing thread. The cleaned stomachs and bladders and other organs of larger animals were used as containers for grease, meat and berries. Dried beaver feet, or loons' heads and necks, were formed into pouches to hold swansdown and other treasured items. Fur, feathers and other soft animal parts were all valuable to people living off the land.

A fifth very important material for some Yukon Indians was raw copper, which could be found in the area of the upper White River. The Copper Chief, whose headquarters were near Snag, was famous for his copper knives and spearheads, and they were traded widely. Unworked copper nuggets were also traded – a pattern that evidently began with people of the Aishihik Culture, around the eighth century AD.

HUNTING

Getting enough food throughout the year depended both on an efficient technology and on keen hunting and fishing skills. Hunters had to know how to make the various weapons and traps for taking different kinds of animals and fish, and they had to know where and how to use them. They had to know the best places and times to build the caribou corrals and just how to drive the caribou into them, how to build fish traps and when and where to set them in order to get the most fish. Equally important to the oldtime Indians was a knowledge of the ritual that would ensure a successful hunt. Things had to be done properly after the hunt as well. The hunters thought that proper butchering and disposal of the carcasses was essential if the supply of game and fish was to continue. Finally, after people got the meat or fish, they had to know how to cook and preserve it.

Yukon Indians cooperated with each other in living off the land. There were only a few thousand Indians — perhaps an average of less than a single person in a hundred square kilometers — but whenever there was a lot of fish or game, such as during a salmon run or a caribou migration, people gathered together to get food for everyone. Hunting techniques were tested over and over again and passed down from generation to generation.

Caribou Hunting

The oldtime Yukon Indians liked to eat meat and fish best of all. Caribou were always important game animals because of their good meat, and they provided skins and sinew for making clothing and shelters, as well as bones and antlers for making tools. Along the major migration routes, hunters could intercept the caribou and take large numbers. For many Yukon Indians, the late fall was an especially important time for caribou hunting. This was when the big barren-ground herds returned for the winter to wooded country. A successful hunt meant that there would be a large amount of meat and top quality skins with thick fur, good for making winter clothes. Whatever the season of the year, people usually worked together to capture the animals.

The most common way to get large numbers of caribou was to build a caribou fence. There were several types of fences, with and without snare pockets or corrals, and they were often permanent constructions of great size.

Many families worked together to build and use a caribou fence. First, the hunt leaders found a good location across a valley or on the side of a mountain where the caribou were known to pass. In wooded areas, the people piled up brush about 1.5 meters high between standing trees or occasional posts. In areas lacking trees — as in the mountains near Forty Mile, or on Old Crow Flats — all the posts for the fence had to be brought from the forest and set up by hand. The fence formed either a straight or zigzag barrier, and it was often over 1.5 kilometers long. There might be up to 150 openings in

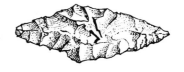

Stone points and the broken end of a decorated bone beamer (drawknife) from Klo-kut, actual size (Canadian Museum of Civilization, drawings by David Laverie)

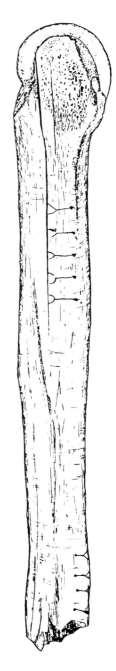

119

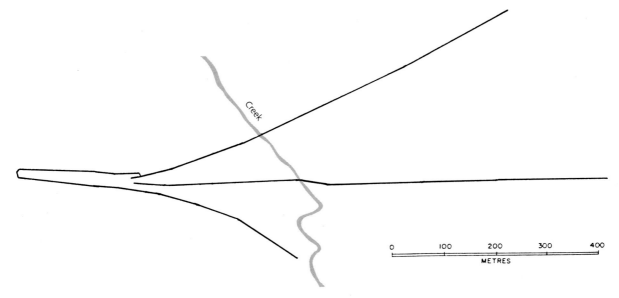

Creek

0   100   200   300   400
METRES

Caribou fence near the Driftwood River (Troo Choo Njik, a tributary of the Porcupine) in the northern Yukon. The snare pocket, at left, faces due east, and fences lead out from it toward the northeast, east and southeast. The snare pocket or corral itself is about 240 m long and about 35 m wide at the widest point. The distance from the bottom of the corral to the far end of the central fence is about 1.1 km. Caribou corrals were built facing various directions, and the length of the fences ranged up to four kilometers, but the form shown here is typical of northern Yukon snare-pocket fences. (From a survey map by Terry Alldritt)

the fence, each about 2.5 meters wide, and a snare was usually set in each opening.

The snares were made of braided babiche, and the loops of the snares were wide enough so the animal's antlers would go through them. The bottoms of the loops hung a little less than a meter off the ground. Grass and dirt were rubbed on the snares to remove the human smell from them. A long stick, called a drag pole, was tied to the end of each snare and set in the fence opening above it.

Everybody in camp cooperated to drive the caribou by howling like wolves and waving their arms. They chased the animals into the fence, where the hunters waited near the snares with bows and arrows or with spears. When a caribou entered the snare, the drag pole dropped, and the frightened animal jumped about in the heavy brush so that the pole became entangled along with the animal. The exhausted caribou then choked or was easily killed.

Straight or zigzag fences were used in both summer and winter. Fences with snare pockets or corrals were evidently used mostly in the later summer. The fences guiding animals into these corrals were sometimes four kilometers long. Two or three lines of posts formed an entrance leading caribou into the corral. The hunters hung moss on these posts to make them look like men, so that when the caribou were chased they ran straight into the corral rather than out between the posts. Once inside the corral, the animals were snared and choked or were speared to death. Those that tried to run back through the entrance were shot with bows and arrows.

The remains of several old fences can still be seen in parts of the Yukon and nearby Alaska. There is a straight brush fence near Mile 1016 on the Alaska Highway that was used to snare small bands of caribou coming off the ice of Pine Lake during the winter. You can see some of this fence in the woods today. Another such fence is near Kusawa Lake, and yet other broken-down fences are high above the Forty Mile River. Parts of them can be seen from the road between Dawson City and Eagle, Alaska. Several huge corrals still stand on the flats near Old Crow, and oldtimers know of others elsewhere in the Yukon.

A leading hunter used to direct the building of a caribou fence and act as boss of the hunt. It was sometimes said that this man "owned" the fence, but those who took part in building and using the fence all shared in what was obtained.

After guns became common in the Yukon, people made less use of caribou fences, but the old people still tell about this very effective way of getting meat. They know about it either through personal experience or through memories of their parents. Sam Peter of Mayo has described how the Northern Tutchone of McQuesten and Fort Selkirk hunted caribou:

The people sometimes chased caribou into a yard. Sometimes you saw caribou go around, and another one chased them to the people like that. Caribou came in here [into the yard or corral], and they shoot. The men behind shoot too. Go back, shoot. Back and forth like that. Sometimes they use snares in the fence for caribou. They see lots of caribou, and they got to work to put the fence around and chase them into the fence. Everybody can eat. Those people went together in the wintertime. In summertime, they scattered. Then you get meat easy, in summer. But in winter, it's cold. One man can't get game with arrows or even guns; you just can't. Sometimes the animal runs away too far. He hears you a long way in the cold. That's why they work it by building fences.

Moses Tizya described how the Loucheux of the Old Crow area captured caribou:

There was nothing but bows and arrows and snares. Every wintertime they made a fence with trees and brush and then they set lots of snares. They put them anyplace in the country, not just one place. That was just to drive the caribou in there. They got a big bunch of caribou in those snares. But the caribou fences were different altogether; there were different kinds. There's lots of them near Crow Flats. That's a different thing again. That's made of poles and most of them are still there. . . . The first one is used in wintertime. When they see a big bunch of caribou, they put a fence around. . . . They set lots of snares inside and then they chase the caribou in there. That's how they get lots of caribou that way. . . . The other kind is a summer fence. It was a big fence with poles across this way and the middle was open. Some of them, they say, had over a hundred snares in them. From the fence they made "arms." . . . They tied something on them so the wind moved the brush. And when they chased caribou they came to these and the caribou got scared and pretty soon they were in the fence. . . . That's how they got caught. . . . One caribou skin made one snare. My father had lots of them. . . . It was made out of twisted babiche, stretched with a pile of logs to make it strong. . . . After they got in the fence, if the caribou were still alive they just took a long bone

The snare pocket of the Driftwood River caribou fence. The dotted lines inside the corral are snare sets. These are from 3 to 10 m wide, and there are more than fifty of them, generally spaced between 5 and 10 m apart. The open space between the snare sets narrows from more than 15 m at the mouth of the corral to less than 3 m at the foot. (From a survey map by Terry Alldritt)

121

Remains of the Black Fox Creek caribou fence in the northern Yukon, seen from the air

spear at the end of a long stick and they poked it someplace. That's how they killed them in the snares. Then they threw them over the fence — all of them. They probably got hundreds of caribou. They threw them over the fence right away and reset the snares right away in case there was another bunch coming. And then everybody worked. The women all cut the meat up. And they had a big cache there — could be the size of this house. It was made out of logs. And they put all the meat in there. . . . They just took home what they could use and left all their meat in the cache.

A hunter might also set single snares along known caribou trails, especially when the caribou were in the woods. He had to inspect the snares every day, since the meat would spoil rapidly if it was not butchered, and a snared animal might be eaten by wolves. Very cold weather made it a hard job to visit all the snares. The hunter had to keep himself warm, especially his hands, while he took the animals out of the snares and reset them.

Sometimes hunters built blinds, or screens of brush, in which they could hide along the trails leading to salt licks. Then they shot the passing animals with bows and arrows. Another hunting method was simply to stalk the caribou and shoot them with bows and arrows. The stalkers often held up caribou antlers and tried to imitate the movement and behavior of the caribou. Because caribou are very curious, they could be lured within shooting distance. They could also be attracted by a man waving a firebrand out on a frozen lake.

In spring and summer, caribou were speared in the water as they crossed rivers or lakes. Sometimes the Indians drove them into the water, in the same way that they drove them into fences on land. Men in canoes speared as many of the swimming animals as they could. This way of hunting caribou was most common in the northern Yukon.

After the fall hunt, the foremost job was storing the meat so people could live through the long, cold winter. A meat camp was set up. Men built racks for drying the meat, and the women sliced the caribou flesh into thin pieces so it could dry in the sun. This was a lot of work, especially in the days before steel knives were available.

People had to move often in winter in search of more game, and they could not carry all of their dried meat with them. They put it in caches instead, and the young men were often given the job of getting meat from the cache and bringing it to wherever the people were staying. The caches had to be sturdy and reliable enough to protect the meat from bears and wolverines.

To build a cache, a hunter cut off the tops of four trees that grew close together. He made a log platform between the four trunks, about six meters above the ground. He placed the dried meat on this platform, covered it with hide, and then protected it further by putting logs or brush on top of the hides. He also notched a log to make a ladder to reach the cached food. Each household built one of the caches at each meat camp. When saws and axes became plentiful, in the second part of the nineteenth century, the people began to make their caches in the form of small log cabins raised on four tall posts. Sometimes they put pieces of tin or some other slippery metal around the posts so wolverines or other animals could not climb them.

Log cache at Galbraith (south of Teslin), 1949. Note the metal shields on the posts, and another, more radical innovation: the padlock on the door.

Moose Hunting

Moose cannot be captured in large numbers like caribou. A team of two or three hunters, rather than a large group of men, women and children, is most effective for hunting moose. The animals are easily excited, so extreme caution and skill are required for a successful hunt.

Moose tend to remain in the same area year around, but people do not hunt them year around. After the rutting season, in October, bull moose meat is poor. In spring, cows and calves are not killed except in times of real need. During late summer and early fall, moose are in the best condition, and this has always been the favored time for hunting them.

The Yukon Indians had several different ways to hunt moose. They sometimes made fences of brush and poles, with snares set in openings, very much like those built to capture caribou — but only one moose was caught at a time, so only a few hunters at most worked together on a moose fence. Sam Peter of Mayo explained:

They used fences to get moose. There was a hole in the fence for the snare, and the hunters drove the moose towards it. We used these especially in winter because it is too cold to hunt with arrows. One or two men could get a moose with a fence. Sometimes they make a fence up on the hill. Then they chased the moose. They made a hole like that in the fence, and the moose went in, you know. They set snares there. After they finished making the fence, they started to chase the moose. . . . That's how they got their meat in the winter-

123

Tripod cache at Ross River, 1965

time. In the cold weather they couldn't do anything with the arrows, so that's the way they worked it. Sometimes one man or two men could do that.

A more common way to get moose was to set single snares along trails where the hunters found moose signs. Moose could be snared near lakes or close to salt licks, especially in early summer before the biting insects drove them into high country. As always when hunting by this method, a hunter's first job each day would be to check his snares, so that the meat did not spoil.

Hunters also shot moose with bows and arrows, sometimes from a blind near a salt lick where they waited quietly for the moose to arrive. Stalking moose is more difficult. Since moose are very alert, a successful hunt requires a good knowledge of the land and the direction of the wind, as well as skill in tracking the animal. The hunter followed the moose trail by making wide semicircles downwind from the moose, because moose seldom travel in straight lines, and they run away if they smell human beings. If the hunter thought he had passed beyond the moose's trail, he doubled back by travelling in smaller semicircles until he located the animal. It was important to get as close as possible to ensure a good shot with the bow and arrow.

A way to get a bull moose in rutting season was to call him by rubbing a specially prepared moose shoulderblade against a tree. The blade was first dried and some of the bony ridge was sawed off. Then the hunter or the Indian doctor marked it with charcoal or ochre to give it more power. When the bull heard the blade being rubbed on the tree, he imagined another bull was rubbing its antlers, and he came ready to fight.

In late spring when the snow crusted, some Yukon Indians used hunting dogs to run down moose. Wolves hunt in the same way. The heavy moose will break through the snow crust while the dogs or

wolves can run on top of it. The moose bruises its forelegs painfully from breaking through the crust, and it soon tires. Then the dogs can drive it toward the hunters. Sometimes too, a skillful man on snowshoes could run down a moose in deep snow and get close enough to shoot it with bow and arrow.

If a man killed a moose near the camp, the women brought their skin toboggans or their pack dogs and packsacks to the kill. They helped butcher the animal at the kill site and brought the meat back to camp. If the kill was farther from camp, the hunter himself or he and his partner might butcher the animal and bring in the meat using its hide as a sled. Or the hunter might cache the meat at the site of the kill, then return to camp to report its location. People could then be sent for some of the meat, or the whole camp could move to the kill.

Men built drying racks for moose meat just as they did for caribou meat, and it was the women's job to prepare the meat for drying. They sat on the ground with the meat piled on a clean skin in front of them and split the flesh very thin with their stone or copper knives. In summer, when they hung the slices on the racks, they often kept a small fire of dry cottonwood going to keep away the flies. In winter, the meat was simply allowed to freeze.

Sheep and Goat Hunting

Mountain sheep could be hunted year round, but late summer was the period of most intensive hunting. The sheep are fat and the meat is in excellent condition at this time. Yukon Indians who were able to hunt sheep generally dried and cached the meat for use later in the winter.

Hunters made babiche snares to catch sheep, just as they did for moose and caribou. The snares were attached to drag poles or to

Barbed bone arrow points. The average length is about 22 cm.

large rocks and set in narrow places so the hunters could drive the animals toward the snares. Because sheep retreat upwards, hunters stalked them from above. If they could get close enough, they shot the sheep with bow and arrows.

Sheep hunting often led hunters into dangerous areas high in the mountains, and most Indians in earlier days believed that the actions of the hunters' wives were important to the success of the sheep hunt. A sheep hunter's wife was not supposed to move around unnecessarily nor to eat hot food nor to boil water. It was thought that if she did these things, she might cause the ice and snow in the mountains to melt or shift, starting avalanches that could endanger her husband's life.

Sheep meat was one of the favorites of Yukon Indians, and the warm fleece was used for making blankets, winter trousers and jackets. The horns were steamed and carved into spoons and dishes.

Mountain goats are less widespread and live in higher and even more dangerous places than sheep, but they were hunted in the same way as sheep. In the old days, the Indians of the southern Yukon had many special songs and rituals for goat hunters and their wives. Young goat meat, skins and horns were all highly prized.

Beaver Hunting

Caribou, moose, and sheep have for centuries been the largest game animals of the Yukon, but the Indians have always also caught many smaller animals for food. Beaver were taken for both food and fur, especially in the spring and in the fall, and the fatty tail was a favorite delicacy.

Beaver were speared or netted under the ice. The older spear points were made of antler or bone, and later ones of metal. The barbed points were about eight or nine centimeters long. When the hunter threw his spear, the point came off the end of the shaft but he never lost it, because it was tied to the shaft with a line, or in later years by a thin chain.

In the early spring, a man would chop holes in the ice five or ten meters from a beaver lodge. He put fresh poplar or willow branches in the hole as bait and then covered the hole with brush and skins. After a day or so the hunter returned to see if the beaver had been eating the food. If so, he knelt by the hole, covered himself with a blanket and waited for a beaver to come to feed. As soon as he saw one, he speared it, pulled it from the water and killed it on the ice with a club. He tried to do this as fast as he could, because it was supposed to be bad luck if the beaver urinated on the ice.

Another way of hunting beaver was to set nets of babiche or sinew in front of the entrances of the beaver lodges. Hollowed-out moose hooves were attached to the net poles, like bells. When they sounded, the hunter knew he had caught a beaver. He then pulled in the net and quickly clubbed the animal. A beaver hunter had to be strong and agile because the beavers could move so fast both in the water and on land. But no matter how they got beaver, the oldtime Indians were careful to leave an adult breeding population.

126

The spring beaver hunt was often a pleasant activity for the hunters, who had just come through a long, dark and perhaps hungry winter. They enjoyed being out in the spring sunshine. Because of the thin ice, however, there was always the danger that the hunters might drown, so the wives did not like the beaver season as much as the men.

Yukon Indians have long used the beaver pelts – particularly those of the young kits – to make winter robes, but the pelts were traded with other Indians only after the white traders east of the Rockies and on the Pacific coast began to demand them.

Ratting (Muskrat Hunting)

In some parts of the Yukon, especially at Crow Flats or around Beaver Creek (where the Alcan Highway now crosses into Alaska), spring ratting was an important way to get food. Along with beaver, muskrat helped people survive a period when bigger game was difficult to hunt because the ice was breaking up on the rivers and streams. Both men and women snared muskrats, setting spring-pole snares along muskrat trails in the grass. People also called the muskrats to them by cupping their hands over their mouths to make whining sounds like those of young muskrats. Then they shot them with bows and arrows, or in more recent times, with guns. In winter, they netted them. In some places, muskrat was also dried for winter use, and in the fall and winter, muskrats were available as an emergency food. Neil McDonald of Old Crow explained it like this:

Detail of a beaver net, with carved antler toggle and moose-hoof rattles, Teslin, 1951

A long time ago, they [the people] used to go south in the fall. After the middle of the winter when the cache with fish and meat that was dried was gone, they travelled south. If there was no game they had to rush back to Crow Flats for rats [muskrats]. And this is the way they hunted rats in the wintertime. They had a bone chisel and they went along the shore of the lake and tapped. There was a sound – that means that was a rat runway under the lake. They opened that place up and they put a net made out of roots or babiche down in the runway. So, they had a little stick in front. If the rat touched that stick, it [the net] was pulled out. They'd get quite a few rats in one night.

The nineteenth-century fur traders did not value muskrat fur highly, nor did the Indians use their pelts very much. Only after white furriers learned how to make coats of muskrat did the skins acquire commercial value.

Marmot and Gopher Hunting

Marmots – often called groundhogs, or whistlers – are another kind of small animal delicious to eat in late summer and fall, when they have grown fat. They were an important part of the diet of the Kaska, Inland Tlingit, Tagish and Southern Tutchone.

Hunters snared marmots or caught them in deadfalls made of rocks or sticks. The hunters had special songs and ritual ways of

Tosspole rabbit snare, Aishihik, 1963

treating marmots, as they did for all animals of the high mountains. They bathed ritually before the hunt, and they sang to the carcasses before gutting them and drying the meat for winter. Animals with poor fur were singed and dried; those with fine pelts were skinned before being dried, and the women sewed the skins into light, warm robes.

Ground squirrels – or gophers, as most Yukoners call them – are very good for food and skins too. Even though they hibernate, gophers lay in a supply of food for spring, so most are still fat when they emerge. They are even fatter in the late summer.

Women used to set up long lines of gopher snares around their camps. To do this, a woman set out from camp with ten or twenty snares in her belt and a bundle of willow sticks to be used as spring-poles for the snares. She also carried a stick with a hook notched in the end. The noose of the gopher snare was made from the springy midrib of an eagle feather. This was attached to a thong of moose or caribou babiche. At the top of the noose was a small wooden toggle pin. First the woman made a small hole about a meter from the side of the gopher burrow. She stuck the base of the spring-pole into this hole. Next, she used her hooked stick to make another hole in the roof of the gopher tunnel near its opening. She set the noose in the tunnel and pulled the thong through the hole in the roof. Then she bent the spring-pole over and tied the end of the thong to it. When a ground squirrel tried to run out of the burrow, it was caught in the noose. The willow rod sprang up, tightening the noose around the gopher and holding it against the burrow roof.

Sometimes a woman set a hundred or more snares in two or three days. But a snared gopher will rot in a few hours, so she had to check the snares regularly, just the way the men had to visit their game snares. Older people today remember how as children they

128

Snared rabbit, Klukshu, 1954 (photo by Frederica de Laguna)

helped their mothers by carrying the willow spring-poles, and how they went with the women to check what had been caught. There were rituals to be observed in hunting gophers too, and it was important to keep them clean as they were collected.

Rabbit Hunting

Fresh rabbit (varying hare) often made up a good part of the family diet, especially in winter when supplies of dry meat and fish were low – but people who were hungry caught them in any season. When the rabbit population peaked, there were so many that people joined together to chase them into snares, much the way they drove caribou. Men and women built long, low fences of brush that gradually came together in a V-shape, or else they lined up several straight fences, one behind the other. They put snares in openings in the fences. Then everybody shouted and beat the bushes with sticks to drive the rabbits to the snares. In summer, people could also drive rabbits to one end of an island or a point of land in a lake, where the rabbits could not escape.

A common way to get rabbits in the winter was for three or four women to cut down several jack pines or spruce in a thicket of young trees. The fallen brush attracted the hungry rabbits. After it had been there a few days, the women set snares in it. In summer the men lured rabbits by pursing their lips to imitate the sounds of baby rabbits. When the adult rabbits came close, the men shot them with bows and bunting arrows. (A bunting arrow has a blunt head of bone or antler that stuns or kills the animal, but does not break the skin.)

Rabbit skins were peeled off the bodies in long strips, washed and woven loosely into light, warm blankets and parkas. The weaving

A bundle of rabbit snares, made by Elsie Isaac, Aishihik, 1962

129

was done without a loom and was loose enough to provide air space next to the body just like modern net undergarments for cold-weather wear.

Bear Hunting

Killing a bear was a very different thing from hunting a rabbit. Because of their physical strength and size, and their great spiritual powers, grizzlies and black bears were hunted only by the bravest Indians in the old days. Sometimes, though, if a man found a bear den in winter, he secretly told his brothers-in-law or some other good friends he could trust. In the spring he and these other hunters roused the animal so that it came from its den. The hunter might then try to kill it in close combat with a spear tipped with a large point of bone, antler or copper. Or he might use a club made of moose or caribou antler which had been soaked in grease to make it heavy. Bears were also caught in strong snares or crushed in deadfalls made of big logs which fell when the bears set off the trigger mechanisms.

After a bear was killed, its head and body had to be handled in special ways to honor the animal. Slain grizzlies were treated almost as though they were guests at a potlatch. It was because they feared the spirit power of these animals that some people did not eat bear meat or grease. Women, in particular, often avoided grizzly meat, even if they ate black bear. Some link the taboo to an old story (told in Chapter Eleven) about a girl who had a grizzly bear husband. Bears were not much hunted for their skins either, until white people began to buy them as souvenirs.

Trapping Fur Bearers

The Yukon Indians have always taken some fur bearers, but they did not try to get very many until the fur trade made them profitable. Of the chief fur bearers, people usually ate only beaver, muskrat and lynx. They did not eat marten, fox or wolverine. Wolves were rarely killed, much less eaten.

The lightest and warmest furs were used to make robes and blankets, and for trimming other clothing. During the colder months, when the furs were in prime condition, hunters caught lynx, marten, fox, wolverine and sometimes wolf, either in snares or with a variety of clever deadfalls and different kinds of baits. Even after the white traders brought steel traps, many Yukon Indians continued to use snares and deadfalls to catch fur bearers. They had to know the habits of the animals very well in order to know where to set them. A few strong young men simply ran after foxes and shot them with bows and arrows, or later with guns.

Otters and mink were never trapped in the early days, because they were thought to have such dangerous spirit powers. Indeed, the bodies of all fur bearers had to be carefully treated. There were special rituals for all of them, including the beaver.

People caught grouse and ptarmigan throughout the year. Women cut down pine or spruce trees and set snares among the branches in much of the same way they did for rabbits. Hunters also snared ptarmigan and grouse in loops hung from the ends of long poles. They dropped the loops skillfully around the birds' necks as if they were fishing. The Yukon Indians may have learned how to do this from Cree Indians who came west working as hunters for the Hudson's Bay Company, or they may have figured out this technique themselves long before the traders came.

In April, when large flocks of migrating waterfowl began to arrive in the Yukon Territory, people hunted them with bows and bunting arrows, like those used for rabbits. They also set snares in the grass along trails leading to the water. Some waterfowl were eaten fresh, others hung and dried for later use.

FISHING

Almost everywhere in the Yukon, fish were an important food for much of the year. The most intense fishing took place in the summer along the Alsek and Yukon rivers and their branches when the salmon were running. During this season, many families gathered at the best fishing spots, camping at the mouths of side streams or by eddies in the big rivers, such as Fraser Falls on the Stewart River above Mayo. At dozens of places throughout the Yukon, they caught and dried salmon to fill their caches for the coming winter.

Yukon Indians used several kinds of clever fish traps. One type was a cylindrical, basket-like affair made of slender willow poles tied together with sinew or willow roots. The opening of the trap was a wide circle, but the inner section rapidly narrowed into a small cone or funnel set within the larger cylinder. Salmon that swam the whole way into the trap could not swim out again through the entrance funnel.

A second kind of cylindrical basket trap was evidently open at both ends. It was set in a kind of corral made of posts and brush in an eddy. The fish swam upstream into the corral through openings on either side of the trap and were then swept back into the mouth of the trap, which faced upstream. The downstream end of the basket was raised onto a little platform where the fish could be speared. Salmon, whitefish, grayling and inconnu were caught in this way.

The Northern Tutchone of the central Yukon used to drive a series of stakes across the salmon stream and place poles and brush between them to make a fence or weir to block the way upstream. A basket trap was then set in an opening in the weir close to the bank. When the salmon reached the weir they moved along it and eventually entered the trap. The people then harvested the fish with dip nets or spears.

The Han of the Klondike River area also used big dip nets to take fish — especially the king salmon. They did this from small birchbark

Fish traps at Klukshu, 1948. Drury Crow, Charlie Bill and Pardon Kane prepare to put a trap in the stream. In the centre photo, two salmon have entered the trap and turned around, heading back downstream, but the row of sharp stakes at the mouth of the trap prevents their escape. (Photo by Frederica de Laguna) In the upper right corner of the lower photo, this same trap can be seen from the other side. (Photo by Frederica de Laguna)

canoes which they paddled in front of the fish. The paddlers knew just where to dip for the salmon because they followed the hand directions of a man who stood on a platform built out from the shore. He watched for the ripples of the fish in the water and signaled the fishermen. The men dropped their dip nets right down to the bottom of the stream so the fish swam into them. Each man had a knife attached to a pole which he used to kill the netted fish. Some Loucheux dip-netted salmon too.

According to their old stories, the Southern Tutchone of Neskatahin and Klukshu learned from the Coast Tlingit how to build another kind of salmon trap, which they still use today. The Northern Tutchone from around Carmacks once used such traps as well. The trap consists of two parts. The first is a rectangular box of cribbing or thin pieces of wood that are set far enough apart so the water can easily flow between them, but close enough that a fish cannot get through. The boxes are about 2.5 m long, 90 to 120 cm wide, and 60 cm high. They are open on the top and at the upstream end. Each box is tied to supporting posts that are driven into the stream bed. The second part of the trap is a tongue constructed of spaced poles which are pointed at one end. This tongue slants from the stream bed into the open end of the cribbing box. Each trap is set in a V-shaped weir that prevents the salmon from continuing upstream. Instead, they swim up onto the tongue and into the box. The sharpened ends of the poles keep the salmon from swimming out again, and the water in the trap is too shallow to allow the fish to jump over the sides. People can easily gaff out the fish and club them.

Before metal tools were plentiful, building these salmon traps was a big job that took several men a number of days. The traps used to be made of spruce saplings tied together with willow roots. In recent times the sides of some traps have been made of chickenwire instead of wooden cribbing.

With several traps side by side in a narrow stream, hundreds of fish could be taken in one night. In Klukshu, Neskatahin and probably elsewhere, each salmon trap was said to be owned by one person, but a great deal of cooperation was required to set the traps properly. Though the traps were saved from year to year, they often needed repair each season. The owner of the trap asked his relatives to help him make it ready, build the weir and put the trap in the water. All the families who worked on the trap had a chance to take fish from it, and the owner might let poor people or visitors use the trap too. At Neskatahin and Klukshu the Wolf people put their traps in one stream or one part of the stream, while the Crow people had theirs in another. (The terms Crow and Wolf are explained in the next chapter.) Usually there was plenty of fish for everybody, and people gave away their fish generously.

Besides traps, spears and dip nets, people used gill nets to take salmon. At Mayo, the gill nets were made of sinew or twisted lynx skin, and they were set at Fraser Falls. One of the best places to put a net was near an eddy. The fish that swam into the net were caught by their gills and were later removed by hand.

Fish nets at Albert Isaac's camp,
Aishihik, January 1963

Inland Tlingit, Tagish, and Southern Tutchone Indians made sinew or willow-bark gill nets too. The women used to have netting parties. They all got together to prepare the sinew, rolling it in their palms and on their thighs and wetting it in their mouths to help soften and stretch it. Older women who did this remember how sore their mouths used to get when there was lots of sinew to be made.

The oldtime gill nets needed a lot of care. When not in use, they were kept moist and in the shade. They turned brittle if they were left out in the sun. And when they were in use, they could not be left too long in the water in sunlight, because they grew too soft and fell apart. They cooked, as people used to say.

Loucheux and Kaska Indians whose home territory was in the Mackenzie River watershed instead of the Yukon watershed could not get salmon. They depended heavily on whitefish and inconnu. Even people who had access to salmon usually caught quantities of other fish as well. Most freshwater fish could be taken year around.

Almost everywhere in the Yukon, people tried to stay near good fish lakes in winter so they could add to their stores of fish. Teslin, Tagish, Little Atlin, Aishihik, and Dezadeash Lakes were good locations in the southern Yukon, while Tatlmain, Ethel, Mayo, and Frances Lakes were popular fishing areas for more northerly people. The Kaska at Watson Lake had Watson Lake itself and many other lakes as well. People speared whitefish or lake trout through holes chopped in the ice with a stone or bone chisel. Usually two men worked together. They covered themselves with a blanket, skin, or brush so they could see into the water easily, and one man jigged a baited line while the other speared the fish.

Throughout the Yukon, the most common fish spear, for both salmon and freshwater fish, had a central prong and two springy, pointed side prongs. Sam Peter of Mayo says that sometimes caribou horn was used to make the prongs. Some of the fish spears had

134

horizontal sighting pieces tied across the handles near the pronged end. This made it easier to spear the fish crosswise so that it was caught by all three prongs. With every wiggle, the speared fish became more deeply impaled. This type of spear was unique to the Yukon and must have been invented by Yukon Indians.

Another way of fishing in winter was to set gill nets made of sinew or twisted willow bark under the ice. The Yukon Indians may have learned how to do this from the early fur traders or from other Indians to the east who had watched the traders or had been taught by them. Strong tools, such as metal chisels and axes, are needed to make the holes easily in order to set and retrieve the net.

In the spring and summer, people caught whitefish or grayling in funnel-shaped basket traps like these used for salmon. A favorite location for such traps was in a stream between two lakes.

Another way to fish in shallow streams between two lakes was to block up the two ends of the stream with poles and brush. Myra Kay of Old Crow explained:

Whitefish were really big — two feet in size. People blocked up the creek on two sides. People on both sides of the river poked the fish with a harpoon-like [spear] to kill them and got lots. Whoever killed the most fish cooked the fish and fed all the people. Women collected a willow-like flower while the men got the fish. They mixed this flower with fish guts and cooked it. It was greasy and they ate it with the fish.

The Yukon Indians made bone or bone-and-wood fish hooks in the last century, but we are not sure if they started to do this after they saw metal fish hooks traded from the whites, or if they had been doing so on their own for hundreds of years. A few bone fish hooks have been found in late prehistoric archaeological sites in the Yukon.

COOKING AND PRESERVING MEAT AND FISH

When the old people describe how they used to hunt and fish for food, they almost always mention the building of drying racks and caches as well. No matter how skillful they were at hunting and fishing, they and their families would not have survived if they had not also known how to preserve and store what they got. Every household had a number of caches in different places — down by the fish streams and lakes, deep in the forested foothills, up in the mountains. They always knew where to send their young men for provisions if food ran low, if the intense cold and limited daylight of winter made it difficult to hunt, or if they wanted special treats for a feast. Sometimes unexpected visitors arrived from distant places, and sometimes a family might need quantities of fish and meat for a memorial potlatch. At midwinter, the headman of each local band always tried to feast his own people too — a custom which later became a kind of Christmas party, and which depended on having well-filled food caches.

Even in good years, however, the cached food rarely lasted until

Daisy Sheldon uncovering a gill net placement and running the net, Teslin, February 1951

At right: Children setting up fish drying racks at the Hager fish camp on the Pelly River, July 1977 (photo by James Fall) *Below:* Cache and fish rack at Marsh Lake, August 1949

spring, and sometimes it was used up so quickly that people faced starvation. The Northern Tutchone from around Carmacks still tell how their grandparents once had nothing left to eat but a tiny snow-bird. Then their best hunter, who was sitting exhausted under a spruce tree, managed to shoot a moose that had come up behind him to eat a mushroom cached in the tree by a squirrel, and the people were saved.

Drying meat and fish properly was a complex task. A skilled woman could clean and cut fifty to a hundred fish in two hours, but that was only the beginning of the job. The cut fish were hung on racks, where they had to get just the right amount of sunlight and to be protected from rain and flies. A roof of brush often covered the fish rack, and some people built small smudge fires to drive off the insects. The drying fish were usually turned every day. Depending on the local weather, it usually took a week or more before they were thoroughly dry. Then the men helped to bale the fish and put them in caches for later in the year.

Much more could be written about how the people in different parts of the Yukon dried meat and fish, but the chief point to remember is that these have always been among the main foods of Yukon Indians. Any well-dried meat or fish will keep for a long time, and people can eat it raw. This makes it a good trail food when people cannot take the time to cook. It is relatively light too, and therefore easy to carry.

In winter, when extra meat and fish were usually frozen rather than dried, the food still had to be cached in some way to keep other animals from eating it. Sometimes it was just covered with a skin, over which snow and heavy logs were piled up; they froze solidly over the meat, making it almost impossible even for wolves to dig out.

Meat drying inside a cabin at Aishihik,
March 1963. The boy is Frank Smith.

In the old days, food was also preserved by mixing it with grease and storing it in containers made of birchbark, rawhide, or the stomachs and bladders of caribou and moose. Salmon heads, or whole gophers, were also sometimes buried in the ground to ferment into a kind of cheese that was a special treat.

Both men and women used to cook. In fact, some older Indians say that the men used to do more cooking than the women, and that they always did all of the cooking for the feasts, but the details of old-time Indian cooking are not well known now. Some of the foods and the ways of preparing them have changed quite a lot from earlier times.

The favorite ways of cooking in the nineteenth century were probably boiling and roasting. People seemed to like boiled meat best, because they enjoyed drinking the hot soup. After they could get tea from the traders, they began to drink that instead.

The Yukon Indians did not have pottery or metal kettles until they began to get them by trade. They made cooking pots by carving them out of birchwood, or from woven spruce roots, or folded and sewn birchbark or rawhide. They also used the paunches (stomachs) of moose or caribou. Of course, none of these containers could be put directly onto the fire, but that did not prevent the Indians from cooking in them.

One common way to cook was to hang the paunch from four stakes and fill it with meat and water or snow. Then rocks that had been heated in the fire were added to the stew. The rocks were lifted from the fire with long tongs made of two pieces of wood, then cleaned of grit and ashes, usually by dipping them into another container of water. Clean and still hot, the rocks were dropped into the container with the food that was to be cooked.

Frank Smith, a Northern Tutchone born at Selkirk, once had a race with a white man to see who could boil oatmeal the fastest. Frank cooked with hot stones dropped into a birchbark kettle, and his opponent cooked in a metal pot on a stove. Frank's oatmeal was the first to boil.

A similar way of cooking was to dig a hole and line it with a raw caribou hide, moose skin or paunch. Meat, water, and hot stones were put into the skin or paunch, and the food soon boiled. Sarah Abel of Old Crow said:

In those days, people never had any pots or anything to boil their meat in. They made wooden pots, and they cut their meat up and they put it inside this pot. They warmed up the rocks in the fire, and after it got really hot, they put them inside that pot. And that meat started boiling after they put the rocks in. And they did the same with the caribou guts. You know that bag – that long bag [caribou paunch]? *They put the meat inside it. They made a hole in the ground. They put that in there, and they do the same with it – put the rocks in, and the meat started boiling. They never threw away the meat juice.*

In Chapter Twelve, Moses Tizya of Old Crow also tells about this kind of cooking.

Moose and caribou blood soups were always favorites. The stock was made from bones, and then the blood was added to it and heated. This kind of soup was often stored in the cleaned stomachs and intestines of large animals.

People roasted fresh meat and fish by spearing pieces with willow sticks and turning them over a fire. Sometimes they laid the meat or fish on hot rocks or put it into the coals. They also buried meat and fish in the sand and built a big fire on top. When the fire burned down and the sand had cooled, the meat or fish was roasted.

Almost every part of the caribou or moose was eaten. The head and liver were roasted in the hot coals of the fire, as were the antlers of the moose when they had velvet on them. The hoofs were roasted too, and the inner parts eaten. Another important product from the moose was the grease rendered from the fat. Moose fat and water were stone-boiled in a birchbark or wooden container for a long time and then the mixture was allowed to cool so the grease hardened on the top. Then the grease was removed from the container, remelted and stored in a clean moose stomach, or it was added to dried meat and berries. The women also made various kinds of sausage from small bits of meat and berries. Sometimes they pounded dried meat, berries and fat together to make pemmican, which is a very nutritious food and easily carried.

Sheep meat was boiled, roasted or dried, as was beaver, marmot, gopher, rabbit and muskrat. The fatty tail of the beaver was usually roasted.

A good way to cook fresh gophers is to grill them. This was done by running a freshly peeled green willow stick through the necks of four or five gophers and another through their hind legs. Then the gophers were hung over the fire and turned periodically. They are small, but gophers are so fat that even a hungry man could only eat two or three at a meal. Marmots and rabbits were also often grilled individually, one to a stick.

Perhaps the most important food product made from bears was the grease, made in the same way as grease from moose and caribou. Bear grease is very rich. The old people say that a person could die from eating too much of it, especially if he drank a lot of cold water at the same time.

Both fresh and dried fish were boiled, and fresh fish were also grilled on the open fire. People liked to eat the cheeks of sockeye salmon raw, but they boiled the heads too, or buried them in the ground to make the cheese mentioned earlier. This was a favourite food in autumn.

The Yukon Indians had several good recipes for cooking fish eggs. The Han dried them and then mixed them with dried fish, stoneberries and moose fat. Mary McLeod of Dawson said people fixed the eggs this way so they would not stick in their teeth.

FOOD FROM PLANTS AND TREES

Yukon Indians also made good use of different kinds of plants and trees for food, though until the late nineteenth century they never planted any gardens. In the late summer the women picked the many kinds of berries that grow in almost every part of the Yukon — currants, cranberries, stoneberries (or bearberries), mossberries, raspberries, soapberries, blueberries, and others. They knew where each kind grew best.

The women enjoyed going out together in the bright fall days. Often they took the children with them, and everybody sang and played, but they also made sure to fill their birchbark or spruce root baskets to the tops. One reason the women made a lot of noise, both singing and shouting, was so they would not surprise a bear. Bears like to eat berries too, sweeping them off the bushes with their paws, almost the way humans do. The women knew special ways to talk to bears if they met them, so that the animals would go away without harming anybody.

The fresh fruit made a tasty addition to the diet of fish and meat in the late summer. When there was not much other food to eat, people looked for berries in the spring too. Stoneberries and rose hips keep well all winter under the snow. The berries were mixed with dried meat or fish, fish eggs and other foods, or stored in grease in the stomachs of large animals. Soapberries were dried and kept for the winter, when they were mixed with water, beaten to a froth and served as a special treat.

The women collected several kinds of roots to eat. Perhaps the best-liked were bear roots or "Indian sweet potatoes," which botanists call *Hedysarum*. This plant grows near water and has pretty pink flowers in summer. The roots were dug either in the autumn after there had been some hard frosts or in the early spring. In fall, because the roots were deep and the ground was frozen, the women needed strong digging sticks. If they could find underground caches

BOTANICAL NAMES OF SOME YUKON INDIAN FOOD PLANTS

Bear root *Hedysarum alpinum*
Blueberry *Vaccinium spp*
Currant *Ribes triste*
Lowbush cranberry *Vaccinium vitis-idaea*
Mossberry *Empetrum nigrum*
Raspberry *Rubus chamaemorus*
Soapberry *Shepherdia canadensis*
Stoneberry *Arctostaphylos uva-ursi*
Wild onion *Allium spp*
Wild rhubarb *Heracleum lanatum*

139

Brush house on the Peel River, about 1921

of "sweet potatoes" that mice had already collected, they were happy. They took most of the roots for themselves but they were sure to leave some for the mice. Otherwise, the Indians thought the hungry mice would come during the winter to raid their own food caches. In some places, people said that if Wolf people ate roots from a Crow patch of potatoes, their mouths would get sore, and the Crow people said the same thing would happen if Wolf people ate roots from Crow patches.

A few Indians gathered boletuses and other mushrooms for food. Many more gathered herbs such as wild onions and wild celery. As with bear roots, certain patches of wild celery were said to belong to Crows and others to Wolves.

In springtime, everybody liked to scrape off the inner bark of spruce and pine to get the sweet, juicy shavings of "sap." They also liked to chew the pink resinous gum from spruce and fir trees.

HOUSING

Those who live in the boreal forest need good protection from the rain, wind, snow and cold, and sometimes from mosquitoes. But most Yukon Indians of earlier days moved often, so they made only temporary shelters. Some were designed so they could be taken down easily and carried. The more common types could be built quickly on the spot. Different kinds of houses were used in different seasons.

One common type of house was the double lean-to, big enough for two to six families who might be travelling together. Each half of the dwelling consisted of a framework of poles tied together. The ridgepole was three or four meters long and about 2.5 meters high. From the ridgepole, other small poles slanted down to the back walls, which were about 1.5 meters high. Brush, moss, bark or rawhide covered the frame. Sweet-smelling spruce boughs made a soft mat

Domed skin houses as drawn by Tappan Adney in the winter of 1901

on the floor and helped keep out the cold. A good housewife brought in new brush when the old got dirty. In the centre, between the two halves of the house, there was a long fireplace over which all the families cooked their meals.

Other houses were circular. A conical frame of poles was covered with fresh brush, or poles and brush were leaned around a big tree trunk. The fireplace was near the door. These houses too were often large enough for several families.

In the central and northern Yukon, the winter house was most often a dome-shaped framework of saplings covered with caribou or moose skins. Myra Kay of Old Crow tells about this kind of house:

They cut the hairs off the caribou skin and they used it to make tents with. And in the summertime when it rained they used to use that caribou skin to cover themselves so they wouldn't get wet. In springtime they used to throw the hair away, but in the falltime they kept the caribou hair on. And they used to use this caribou skin with the hair on it to make tents too, for the winter. They used the caribou skin with the hair on it in the winter, and in summertime they put it away and used it the next year again.

Usually, two families lived in one of these skin-covered shelters. Ten to fifteen caribou skins were needed to make the cover, along with ten bent saplings for the frame. When people travelled, they carried the skins with them, and sometimes they took the frames also.

The Loucheux, the Han and probably other Yukon Indians built sturdy moss houses where they often lived from late fall until mid-winter. This was a period of deep snow when little travel was possible. Two families together usually built a new house each fall in a good hunting area. They dug a square hole 3 m on a side, and about 20 cm deep. There were four corner posts 1.5 to 2 m high. Two posts about 3 m high stood at opposite ends of the building between the

Spruce bark house on the Peel River, about 1921

corner posts and held the ridge pole. Beams were lashed in place on the corner posts and the ridgepole. Split poles were set vertically and lashed together to make walls. Finally, the builders piled large squares of moss around the sides and ends of the house and laid on a roof of brush covered with moss and earth. Willow mats covered the floor except for the fireplace in the center. Openings were left in the wall for a door and in the roof for a smokehole.

By the late nineteenth century a few Tagish, Inland Tlingit and Southern Tutchone were building quite substantial houses of split logs, which looked somewhat like the dwellings of the Coast Tlingit. There would only be two or three such houses at each place, and some of them had fancy carved and painted house posts or screens inside them. Chapter Eight tells more about these decorations.

People also made smaller, more temporary, shelters of brush and bark to sleep in when they were travelling. They put up small shelters, too, for girls who were reaching womanhood, and for women to retire to when they had their monthly periods or were giving birth.

CLOTHING

Yukon Indian women were very skillful at cutting and sewing clothing out of tanned caribou and moose hides. Women tanned skins in slightly different ways from place to place, but the same basic steps were necessary everywhere to make the beautiful soft leather.

First, the fresh skins had to be cleaned of all traces of meat and hair. Women used fleshers or punches to take off any blood, fat or meat remaining on the inside of the hide. These tools are often made today from old gun barrels or other pieces of heavy metal, but for a long time they were made of moose or caribou leg bone. (The punch had to be quite heavy and have a good edge to take off the flesh.) A bone beamer – like a long shave knife, which is a sharp blade with a grip at each end – was used to cut off the hair and the blackish layer of the skin right underneath it. The beamer was also used to even the

142

skin — to give it a uniform thickness. All of this had to be done with care so as not to cut the skin by mistake.

Ideally, the fleshing and dehairing of a large skin was done where the animal was killed, for it greatly lightened the load of a fresh hide. Some women liked to take the meat and blood off first, especially in summer, because they said it attracted flies and other insects. Others started work by shaving the hide so the loose hairs would not get all over the flesh side of the skin. In winter the women sometimes rolled the skins up tightly for several days and kept them in warm places. Then great tufts of hair could be pulled out by hand, although the black organic layer beneath would still have to be shaved off.

After defleshing and dehairing, the raw skin was washed in a stream or some other water. When it was absolutely clean, it was draped over a horizontal pole to dry. The skin stiffened and hardened as it dried, but it could be stored in that condition until the owner had time to do more work on it.

Angela Sidney of Tagish defleshing a caribou hide, Carcross, 1949

A woman who had a lot of dried, raw hides stored from the fall hunt often hung them outside in the coldest days of winter. The exposure helped to soften and whiten the skins. To complete the softening, the woman soaked the skin several times in a mixture of rotted moose or caribou brains and water. After each soaking, the brain water was wrung out and the skin was stretched smooth, then hung over a pole or laced into a frame where it could be scraped or "tanned" with a stone scraper. The process of soaking in brain water and "tanning" (scraping) was repeated several times. In many places the women gave a light smoking to the skin on both sides after each session of scraping, and everywhere, unless it was to remain white, each skin got a final smoking — inside and out — over a slow-burning fire of rotten wood, pine cones, or a mixture of both.

Women prided themselves on being good skin workers, and those in different areas or even in the same camp might do the job in somewhat different ways. They would vary the recipes for the soak water, or smoke the skins for different lengths of time or with different kinds of wood or cones, or scrape and stretch them on different kinds of poles or frames. Gertie Tom, a Northern Tutchone woman of Carmacks, has written a book called *How to Tan Hides in the Native Way* which describes how she tans skins today. Pansy Bailey taught a slightly different method which she learned from her mother, Annie Geddes, an Inland Tlingit of Teslin.

In any case, when all of the hard work was finished, the skin was soft and golden, ready to be fashioned into clothing. The pattern of the garment was then marked on the inner side of the skin with red ochre and cut out with a sharp stone or copper knife.

Most Yukon Indian women used awls to punch holes in the skin, through which they pushed their sinew thread. After the native women saw the needles brought by the fur traders, they used them too, and they made their own needles of bone or copper.

Yukon Indian women were excellent seamstresses. They sewed tight seams of several kinds, including ones that were waterproof, and they often decorated their finest clothing with real artistry.

143

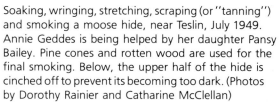

Soaking, wringing, stretching, scraping (or "tanning") and smoking a moose hide, near Teslin, July 1949. Annie Geddes is being helped by her daughter Pansy Bailey. Pine cones and rotten wood are used for the final smoking. Below, the upper half of the hide is cinched off to prevent its becoming too dark. (Photos by Dorothy Rainier and Catharine McClellan)

Mabel Johnston, Teslin, 1974 (photo by Glen Simpson)

In summer both men and women wore tailored trousers of tanned skin, tied at the waist with a drawstring. The trousers covered the feet as well, like socks. A pullover shirt, open at the neck, was worn outside the pants. It came down to the knee for men and was even longer for women. Often the front and the back of the shirt were pointed and fringed. In winter, people wore shirts of a similar style but made from skins with the hair left on. The hair side was worn against the body.

Another winter garment was the jacket of loosely woven rabbit skins or of caribou skin trimmed with fur. These jackets were usually worn with separate hoods or fur hats. Only the northern Indians wore parkas with attached hoods like those of the Inuvialuit. In very cold weather, people also wore mountain goat or sheepskin pants with the fur turned inside, and both men and women snuggled into fur robes, tied at the neck.

People kept their hands warm with mittens of caribou or moosehide, which might be trimmed with beaver or marten fur. Each mitten was usually attached to the end of a string that went around the wearer's neck, so that if a person had to take off his or her mittens for delicate work, they would not be forgotten or lost.

Yukon Indian moccasins were very well made, and there were several kinds. Some had high tops that wrapped around the ankles; others were cut lower. The Loucheux Indians often made high ones

like the mukluks of the Inuvialuit with whom they traded. Strong, soft moccasins were essential for getting around in both summer and winter. Snowshoeing was easier in soft moccasins then in hard-soled boots such as the Inuvialuit sometimes wore.

Besides using fur trim, people decorated their clothing and their footwear with beads made from berry seeds, seashells traded from the coast, porcupine quills, the spines of feathers, down, moose hair, beaver toenails, and paint. Often the clothing was very beautiful. People always put on their best clothes when they were coming into camp to visit, and for special parties and dances. After the white men's trade goods entered the country, the people began to use woolen and cotton cloth, colored glass beads, buttons, pieces of metal, feather cockades and other ornaments. They made colorful dance shirts and blankets decorated with tiny seed beads or pearl

Man's ceremonial dress from the southern Yukon, received in trade by the Chilkat Tlingit in 1900 and bought from them in 1902. Now in the Field Museum of Natural History, Chicago.

Porcupine quills in a container of trade cloth, from Aishihik (Canadian Museum of Civilization)

Above: Andy Smith in dance costume, holding a barbed metal spear point used for hunting beaver, Teslin, 1951.
Above right: A hunter visiting his wolverine trap, as drawn by Tappan Adney in 1902. Note the leashed mittens, the ornamented pouch, and the snowshoes.

buttons that flashed in the firelight as the wearers danced. Most shirts and blankets were of red and navy blue, since those were the usual colors of the trade cloth. In the southern Yukon, the designs of the shirts and blankets showed the emblems of the different clans who claimed crest animals such as the beaver, frog, crow or killer whale. These crests are discussed in the next chapter.

TRANSPORTATION

How did Yukon Indians manage to carry even their limited belongings, their food and their old or sick people and babies for the long distances they had to cover in the earlier times? They had few pack dogs and no wooden toboggans or big sleds until the arrival of white traders.

The job of packing and transporting food and other gear fell mostly to the women. In winter they pulled skin toboggans or drags made by sewing together strips of skin from the forelegs of caribou so that the hair all ran in one direction. Sometimes they used a single caribou skin shaped into the proper form by wetting it. Martha Tizya, a Loucheux woman of Old Crow, says that after a skin toboggan was piled with meat and skins, a line was tied to it and the women dragged it to the next camp while the men went ahead to break trail, and keep on the lookout for game. Only along the Peel River did some of the Loucheux have small wooden sleds with high runners. Women also pulled these.

If the loads were light enough, a young child or a very old or sick person would be warmly wrapped and also be put on the drag, or another drag might be specially made for the purpose and pulled by a younger person. Mothers carried their babies in baby packs or with

148

pack straps. Sometimes an elder had to be left behind the main group, but he or she was always provided with fuel and as much food as could be spared.

Winter and summer, people also used packsacks. These were made of tanned skins or of finely netted babiche or sinew. Again the women did most of the backpacking, even though they might also have to carry their babies. Some families had a few dogs to help. The dogs could carry thirty or forty pounds each in packs of their own.

For travel through heavy snow, the Yukon Indians and their neighbors made some of the finest snowshoes in the world. Those used for breaking trail were often as long as a person was tall, or even longer. Trail shoes, for use on a well-broken trail, were shorter. Men and women worked together to make snowshoes. The men formed the wooden frame and laced the centre with heavy babiche or rawhide netting. The women usually cut the babiche and did the finer netting of the toe and heel sections.

The Indians rarely crossed the dangerous open water of the larger Yukon lakes, and they avoided river rapids when they could, but in summer they travelled both rivers and lake margins in several kinds of watercraft. Canoes were made of birchbark where it was available. Not much birch is found in the southern Yukon, so the people there had to use the heavier bark of spruce. In the southern part of the Yukon, men also made dugout canoes from cottonwood logs. This type of canoe could carry four or five people.

Pack dog ready to go ratting, Aishihik, 1963

During the nineteenth century an Inland Tlingit headman managed to bring a Coast Tlingit dugout, made of redcedar, across the mountain pass from the Taku River to Atlin Lake. Usually, however, such canoes came no closer to the Yukon than Canoe Landing, B.C., where the Sloko and Nakina (Upper Taku) rivers meet, for this was the head of navigation on the Taku.

The birchbark canoes of the Northern Tutchone and Han Indians were particularly fine craft, graceful and well-suited to river travel. Alexander Murray, Robert Campbell, Frederick Schwatka, and Tappan Adney, an artist who lived with some Han during the Gold Rush, were all very much impressed by these canoes. They had frames of light birch or spruce, and the women sewed sheets of bark to the frame with split spruce roots. The stitches and cracks were caulked with spruce pitch which was chewed first to soften it, then melted into the bark. Some canoes were evidently flat bottomed, about three meters long and very narrow. Others were larger and heavier, about five to nine meters in length. The larger craft had high bows, usually decked with bark. In deep water, spruce paddles were used, but for upstream travel in shallow water, people liked to use a pair of slender poles.

Yukon Indians everywhere made large mooseskin boats for lake and river travel, especially after the fall hunt and spring trapping. The raw hides were sewn together over a framework of spruce or birch. The boats would hold one or two families and their belongings as well as a heavy load of meat, but the hide readily became water-logged, so the boats had to be taken out of the water after four or five

149

Two views of a boat frame, upper
Teslin Lake, July 1949

hours. They could not be allowed to dry out completely however, or the skins would split. They had to be kept out of the direct sunlight, and in hot weather they were sometimes covered with damp moss.

Often people built temporary rafts for crossing rivers and narrow lakes or to float downstream. They simply lashed three or four logs of dry wood together with rawhide lines — but a considerate traveller who made a raft was careful to girdle several green trees at the same time. Then a person who travelled that way the next year would find dead trees for another raft and have dry fuel too.

THE YEARLY ROUND

How did different Indian groups decide where to go during the course of a year? Older people, through their experience, came to know a great deal about good fishing, hunting and berrying places, where the beaver lodges were and where the waterfowl nested. They knew where supplies of medicinal plants and other useful materials could be found. As mentioned in Chapter Two, many locations were given names that indicated the kinds of resources available there, and such placenames helped to guide the people. David Moses of Stewart Crossing has explained that the Tutchone name for Ethel Lake, *Tekwǎnt'e Mǎn*, describes a way of fishing with a spear and lighted torches that was especially successful there. Another example of a descriptive placename is *Tr'ondik*, the Han name for the river which the goldseekers eventually called Klondike. The native name refers to the hammerstones used to drive stakes into the riverbed for building fish weirs.

Unless the fluctuating cycles of animals and fish caused a shortage of food, people usually went back to the same places at about the same time year after year. Each family or group of families travelled back and forth through a specific range. This area might exceed 400 square kilometers, because it had to include valleys and highlands, meadows, forests and tundra, lakes and streams. The family knew this varying terrain, within which its members ordinarily set their deadfalls and snares, stored their boat frames and fish traps, and built their caribou or moose fences, caches and camps.

Ownership of the Land

Most of the finest fishing and camping places were said to be owned, in the way that a caribou fence or fish trap was owned by the person who directed its use. This kind of ownership meant that a headman and the people who travelled with him had the first right to use the products of the local land and water, but they also had the duty of taking care of these resources. The headman and those living with him were thought of as the persons responsible for the welfare of the country. It was part of their job to see that people did not overhunt, overtrap or overfish the area, as well as to see that as far as possible everybody got enough to eat.

Ordinarily, neither the headman nor anybody else could buy or

150

Top left: Cutting babiche. *Middle left:* Annie Geddes rolling sinew. *Lower left:* Frames, made by Old Fox, drying in the rafters. *Above:* Olive Sidney, netting the shoe. *Below:* Snowshoes ready for the trail. Teslin, 1949.

sell land, although sometimes, in order to show great respect to another group, or to settle a dispute, one social unit might transfer the stewardship of an area to the care or traditional ownership of another.

In practice, individuals could hunt or fish almost anywhere they wished. Because each person in every group was part of a wide network of relatives and had partners who lived in different localities, he could always ask to use the hunting and fishing places claimed by a group other than his own. People were usually glad to share their resources. Any area that had not been used for several years was open to whoever wanted to hunt or trap there.

As is explained in the next chapter, the structure of the social groups was not exactly the same everywhere in the Yukon, but all groups had firm concepts of stewardship for the country. This feeling of responsibility for proper treatment of the land and water, and this openness in sharing it with relatives and friends, were important parts of the Yukon Indians' way of life. This combination of rootedness and mobility helped them to survive. When times were hard, people often travelled widely. If they were starving in their own country, they looked for their friends and relatives wherever there was likely to be the most food, always hoping to find other people who were having better luck than they were.

The Pattern of the Seasons

In spite of local variations and specializations, all Yukon natives followed pretty much the same sequence of activities in getting food throughout the year. Spring was often the most difficult period. All the supplies of cached meat and fish were usually gone, and the late winter caribou and moose hunts were not always successful. The rabbit meat had grown poor, and not everybody had access to ptarmigan and muskrats. By this season, families had usually scattered far from their larger settlements of midwinter. Two or three households would have been travelling together for several months, setting up their brush or hide shelters wherever they thought they had a good chance of getting fresh meat or fish and – in later days – a good fur catch. It was important for people to reach good fishing and hunting camps before spring breakup and crusting snow made travel more difficult. Until the ice went out, the men could trap beaver and muskrats with nets and snares set under the ice, or spear them through holes in the ice. Icefishing with snares and nets was also important in early spring.

After breakup, people could set up their traps for grayling, trout, inconnu and whitefish, and they could hook ling cod. At some places sucker fishing was best in spring. Where the fishing was good, a dozen or more households might stay together. Of course, some moose, caribou and sheep hunting still took place if the country was suitable, and rabbit, grouse and ptarmigan remained welcome food. In late April when the ducks, geese and swans began to come back to

the marshes and lakes, they were hunted too, as were the gophers emerging from their hibernation.

Though people could not travel far during breakup, around May, the weather was usually good. Men spent this time readying equipment to be used later in the year. They repaired fish traps, made canoes for hunting muskrats, repaired their bows and arrows and other weapons and tools, or they made new ones. Women tanned the hides that they had saved from the autumn caribou hunt, sewed clothing and made birchbark containers. They also cleaned and cooked any fish and meat brought in by the men, and they snared small animals around camp. If food was short, the women searched for berries preserved under the snow, or the men might kill a black bear or grizzly.

As the lakes and streams became clear of ice and the long sunny days of June arrived, everybody enjoyed one of the easiest times of year. In early summer, there was good fishing for grayling, whitefish, and trout in the lakes and in the eddies of streams and rivers. Because travel by boat or overland along good trails was easy at this time of the year, it was a period of visiting, feasting, and trading. In some places, the larger groups broke up again and spread out over the country in units of two to four households to hunt sheep, moose or caribou. They hoped to fill their caches with as much meat as possible.

In July and August the tempo of life also picked up along the salmon streams, where people once more gathered in numbers. The men repaired the fish-drying racks and the shelters of poles, bark and moss in which people lived at this time of the year (and in which they also often dried fish). Weirs were built and the traps were set in the streams. Until the salmon arrived, women continued to tan skins and men hunted. Once the salmon came, everyone was busy spearing or netting the fish, emptying traps, and cleaning, drying and storing the fish.

153

Where there were no salmon, families caught other kinds of river or lake fish, or began to travel to the mountains for the fall hunt. In late summer, the berries ripened, and women welcomed the chance to leave their camps for a day or so to collect the ripe fruit.

These busy times continued well into the autumn. Then, even those families that had been salmon fishing moved up to their hunting camps in the mountains, where they set to work repairing the caribou fences. Meat camps were often quite large. Many families travelled long distances to good caribou country, such as the alpine tundra on the heights of land near Forty Mile, in the Richardson, Ogilvie, and Selwyn ranges, or in the Coast Mountain passes. At these camps Yukon Indians sometimes met natives from present-day Alaska or the Northwest Territories, who also wanted caribou. When the animals arrived, everyone helped to drive them to the surrounds.

Indians in the southern Yukon, towards Teslin or Watson Lake, hunted more moose than caribou, and often they relied more on mountain sheep and goats, and on marmots and gophers, than they did on moose.

In October, families usually returned to the forested lower country where there was less wind and plenty of firewood. People often fished close to their camps after the lakes froze. They also hunted muskrats and beaver under the ice, and women and children snared rabbits and grouse. A few men might still hunt sheep in the dangerous country above timberline. This was also the time for repairing snowshoes and sewing winter clothing.

During late November and December, when the days were very short and very cold, people tried to stay together, with many households in one place. They often liked to be by a good fishing lake, and when they needed more food, they depended on the dried meat or fish stored in their caches throughout the countryside. In this season, some of the southern Yukon Indians lived in warm timber houses. Others stayed snug and warm in moss houses, domed skin houses or double lean-tos.

By late January or February, even the cached food supplies began to give out in most places, so families scattered again in search of fresh meat. The younger hunters often left the women, children and old men by good fishing lakes while they themselves looked for game, but by January the ice was usually so thick that it was difficult to take fish. In one dreadful winter, perhaps 1816, many of the shallow lakes of the central Yukon are said to have frozen right to the bottom. The starving Indians around Carmacks chopped out chunks of ice and melted them in the hopes of finding fish that had frozen in the ice.

Sometimes, if they found bands of caribou at this season, the hunters would again make a fence or use an old one to snare them. Otherwise, the men set single snares for moose, caribou, sheep, and small game. If people were very hungry, brave men who had located bear dens flushed out the bears and killed them with clubs, spears, and arrows.

154

During late winter the hunters also set deadfalls or snares for lynx, fox, wolf and wolverine. At this time of year fur bearers had prime pelts. As the fur trade with the whites grew, many Yukon Indians spent more and more of the winter months trapping for fox and other fine furs. In order to get good returns, families who might have camped together in earlier times now scattered more widely over the country.

By the mid-nineteenth century, a number of headmen had begun to make a full-time business of buying furs that other Indians had trapped. Tagish people went each winter to Little Salmon Lake and Pelly River to trade. Champagne people went to Pickhandle Lake, between Beaver Creek and Burwash Landing, to meet Indians from the Upper Tanana River in Alaska. Teslin people went to meet Frances Lake and Watson Lake Indians at Swift River and Groundhog Lake. The "banker" headmen then sold the furs they had collected to the Coast Tlingit traders who came to their Yukon headquarters every summer and sometimes in the winter too. Meanwhile the women contributed to the winter food supply by snaring rabbits, grouse and ptarmigan.

This highly mobile pattern lasted until the days again became longer and people returned to their spring fishing camps or went muskrat and beaver hunting. A new yearly round had then begun.

REGIONAL DIFFERENCES IN THE YEARLY ROUND

The Yearly Round in the Northern Yukon

The Indians of the upper Porcupine and Peel watersheds depended heavily on both fish and caribou. Ancestors of the Old Crow Loucheux caught migrating salmon from July to October, dipnetting them from open-ended fish traps set in the sidestreams of the Porcupine River, or in Crow Flats along the Crow River, north of present-day Old Crow. They also caught freshwater fish.

Since the Peel River drainage lacks salmon, the Peel River Loucheux spent most of the summer netting and trapping migrating whitefish, and spearing, hooking or trapping inconnu, herring, trout, suckers, grayling and ling cod.

Summer was also a time for trading. Crow River and Porcupine River people took caribou hides and babiche down to Fort Yukon or went to the Arctic coast to trade wolverine and mountain sheep skins with the Eskimo.

In late summer and fall, all of the northern Loucheux moved upland to meet in groups large enough to corral caribou. Upper Porcupine and Crow River people went mostly to the Old Crow Mountains and the Keele Range, while Peel River people were in the Ogilvie and western Richardson mountains. They used dog packs to help carry meat. Families then began to scatter for winter hunting and trapping. People in both areas also did some fishing under the ice of lakes and rivers.

155

Sometimes the supplies of cached fish and meat ran out by late winter and people faced starvation. "After the dry fish was gone, if they found no game," Neil McDonald recalled, the people "rushed back to Crow Flats for rats." And Sarah Abel recalled:

When people really had nothing, the only place they could get anything like fish was at Crow Flats and Crow Point. They went to these places when they really needed something to eat. They made nets of willow bark and put them across the creeks. They drank the fish juice too.

Myra Kay remember how pleasant it was during the long, sunny days of spring when people gathered again at the Flats to fish, hunt muskrats and shoot ducks with bows and arrows.

The Peel River Loucheux traditionally gathered in spring on the level left bank of the Peel at a place called *Ok Chi'* or Eddy Rock, about a hundred miles upstream from the present-day Fort McPherson. Here they danced, feasted and played games before starting down to their summer fish camps, and here John Bell of the HBC found them in 1839. Not until late in the nineteenth century did they begin to fish as far downriver as Fort McPherson, for it took long to return to the mountains for the autumn hunt.

The Yearly Round on the Stewart River

People in the Mayo area could fish all year. In April, May and June they trapped grayling, especially at Fraser Falls, near the now abandoned trading post of Lansing. Families gathered there to catch and dry fish, and to hunt muskrats and beaver.

Summer salmon fishing followed. In late July, the salmon arrived at Dawson, and a week later they reached Mayo. Traps were set on the Mayo River near the mouth of Mayo Lake and near the old village of McQuesten on the Yukon River. Salmon were also caught near Fraser Falls, in eddies in the Stewart River, and along the Hess and Beaver Rivers.

The king salmon that come in early August are fat, and they were dried for people to eat. The dog salmon that come later are usually in poor condition, and they were dried only for winter dog food.

In winter the people could still fish at Mayo Lake, Kathleen Lake, or Ethel Lake, taking grayling, trout, whitefish, and jackfish with spears or nets. They could also stay on at Fraser Falls, where they could combine hunting and trapping with fishing.

Other families moved out in the fall and winter over a wider area to hunt and snare game. In the fall they snared sheep in the Ogilvie Mountains around the Wind River or across the divide in the Mackenzie Mountains near the Arctic Red River. In winter, they built moose fences and caribou corrals in the mountains north of the Stewart River.

The Han and Northern Tutchone Indians who lived in the Yukon River watershed near present-day Dawson, and on the lower Pelly River and its tributaries, probably depended on salmon more than any other group of Yukon Indians. David Silas of Pelly Crossing remembered how the Northern Tutchone of Fort Selkirk had fish camps all along the Pelly River in the fall. These camps, he said, reached all the way up to Pelly Crossing.

Little Salmon and Carmacks Indians built fish weirs at three main places: the mouth of the Little Salmon, the mouth of the Nordenskiold, and the mouth of Tatchun Creek. They used these fish camps as bases for hunting until mid-October.

Susie Skookum, a Northern Tutchone woman, told about some salmon traps near Carmacks:

People from Carmacks went down the Dawson Road four miles to fish. They had traps there. My father made them. They were shaped like boxes. They put the trap in small creeks, such as Big Creek. Sometimes they put in three traps side by side. Sometimes they got filled up in one night. They cut the fish and dried them. Sometimes they could hear them coming.

The fall hunts of the Han and Northern Tutchone Indians were like those in many other places in the Yukon. The Forty Mile caribou herd migrated south through the mountains from north of Dawson to the Dawson Range in the southwest. Mary McLeod, who lived most of her life around Forty Mile and Dawson, said that Indians from both of those places used to gather at a long caribou fence built in the mountains near Chicken, Alaska. There they dried and cached the meat they got to supplement their stores of salmon.

Indians from the Yukon River above Dawson travelled to Nansen Hill or Treadgold Mountain where in the late summer large caribou herds used to cross the Yukon River. While the men killed the caribou, the women trapped gophers. Early in the rutting season, many moose were also killed, and the women picked blueberries, cranberries and stoneberries.

Johnny Alfred of Pelly Crossing describes how the Fort Selkirk Indians used to spend the fall and winter:

People went upriver [on the Pelly] *from Selkirk. They used to get lots of moose and caribou and sheep upriver. They used the fat of the meat to make lard. They went up the Pelly River and they got a big pile of meat, fat and skins. This was in the falltime. They left in August and came back in September. The sheep and all the animals were really fat at this time of the year. They dried the meat and had enough to eat until spring. Nobody was ever hungry. After drying the meat, in the wintertime, they went trapping for fur, such as rats, beaver, and lynx. They also ate this meat.*

In the late nineteenth and early twentieth centuries, the Tutchone Indians still farther up the Yukon did not get as many

157

caribou as the Selkirk people, because the Forty Mile herd usually did not go that far.

In the spring, Carmacks people hunted ducks, beaver and muskrats in the many lakes up the Nordenskiold River. They got whitefish, grayling and other kinds of fish in Little Salmon and Tatlmain lakes. Springtime was also when the Tagish Indian traders came to Little Salmon and when Southern Tutchone from Aishihik came to trade at Carmacks and Fort Selkirk.

Summer was devoted to fishing for the plentiful salmon, and to trade with Coast Tlingit who came down the Yukon on rafts.

The Yearly Round in the Southwestern Yukon

The Southern Tutchone who lived around Kluane, Aishihik, Dezadeash, Hutshi and Marsh lakes depended on fish in the spring. Before the ice melted, they set or speared whitefish, trout, jackfish, or grayling. Later they fished for suckers and killed muskrats, beaver and ducks. Small bands of caribou could be hunted in the mountains if people were hungry.

In June, some of the Kluane, Aishihik and Hutshi Indians travelled south to Neskatahin (Old Dalton Post) on the Alsek River. Others went northwest to the Nisling River or northeast to the Carmacks and Selkirk areas to fish for salmon with their relatives or to trade for the dry fish. They had to do this because no salmon ran in the Aishihik, Kaskawulsh or Dezadeash rivers.

Then small family groups worked their way back to their own countries hunting sheep and fishing for dogfood along the way. Two households might travel together and share the meat, but the groups were seldom larger.

Many families came together in late summer to help each other take mountain caribou, and the men hunted sheep and moose at this time too. Sam Williams of Aishihik and Haines Junction describes how Aishihik people used to hunt in different seasons:

When they went to get gophers at the timberline, everybody went. They dried and smoked gopher meat for the winter. They also got caribou and moose. They went out to get moose in September. They dried it and made a cache for it and moved on to another place to hunt more. At Isaac Creek, they dried sheep meat. This was a good place for it. Moose are poor after the rutting season in October, but in winter they could hunt cow moose for fresh meat. But they lived a lot on dry meat then. They hauled in the dry meat with dog teams from the caches in the winter. In the wintertime, maybe they'd get some rabbits for fresh meat.

The best time for gopher hunting is from the middle of August. They are fat then. Gopher is used when people have no food or have just dry meat, and they want fresh meat. They hunt them to the end of September. Then the gopher hibernate. Each woman went in her own direction. They decided ahead of time, so no places got too crowded. Each woman had her own line.

158

Ice fishing for whitefish and trout began in late October in the southwestern Yukon, but people stopped fishing in mid-November because it grew so cold and there were fewer fish. They began ice fishing again in the spring. Later in the spring, people gathered at Neskatahin with the furs they had trapped or bought during the winter so they could sell them to the Coast Tlingit. During April everyone fixed up the fish traps and drying racks so they would be ready for the season ahead. Until the salmon arrived, some Neskatahin Indians fished for whitefish, grayling, trout and other freshwater fish, but others started down the Alsek River to get early salmon near Nuqwaik, the inland settlement built by the Coast Tlingit during the nineteenth century.

By late June or July, when salmon reached Neskatahin and Klukshu, everybody was busy catching, cutting and drying salmon. This was when relatives from elsewhere might arrive, and the Tlingit traders came too. It was an exciting time of feasting, dancing, and storytelling, as well as a chance for the Yukon Indians to get European trade goods and coastal delicacies like dried clams or seaweed in exchange for their furs and other products.

In the fall, the Alsek River Tutchone moved into the mountains to hunt gopher, moose and caribou. In the coldest part of the year they returned to stay in their big winter houses at Neskatahin or Klukshu. Sometimes they were visited again by small parties of Coast Tlingit traders or they themselves snowshoed to Pickhandle Lake in the White River area to buy furs from the Indians who lived on the upper White or Tanana rivers.

In late winter and early spring, the people began to get whitefish from under the ice of Dezadeash Lake, Kusawa Lake or some other good spots; then they went back to their salmon camps.

The Yearly Round in the South-Central Yukon

The Tagish and Inland Tlingit who lived in northern British Columbia and the south-central Yukon around big lakes such as Bennett, Tagish, Marsh, Atlin and Teslin, could get freshwater fish year round. They had some salmon in the summer too, but the fish were often poor, because they had come such a long way from the Bering Sea and had little fat left. However, the Tagish had a salmon camp on the McClintock River that runs into Marsh Lake. There they built brush and bark shelters in which they lived and dried their fish, and there they traded with the Coast Tlingit who came over the Chilkoot Pass each summer.

The Inland Tlingit now centered in Teslin had salmon camps up the Nisutlin River and perhaps even on the headwaters of the Big Salmon, but they and the people in the Atlin area also used to cross the mountain passes back to the Taku River drainage where their ancestors had lived. There they could get good salmon from the Pacific, and they traded there with the Coast Tlingit, who came upriver from near present-day Juneau to dry their salmon near the old Tulsequah mine. A few Teslin and Atlin Indians went right down to the coast to trade.

As elsewhere, in late summer and fall, people left the lakes and rivers to hunt meat in the mountains. Part of the big Forty Mile herd of caribou sometimes used to winter as far south as Teslin, but more often there were only scattered bands of mountain caribou. Several families would join to build brush fences to snare caribou or moose, but they did not make big caribou corrals as often as the Indians did farther north. By the late nineteenth century, moose had become more plentiful than caribou in this area.

Mountain sheep, goats and marmots were a very important part of the winter food supply too. Sometimes the Inland Tlingit would meet bands of Kaska who were marmot hunting at the head of Rancheria River. Each family tried to fill several caches with dried meat before returning to spend the first part of the winter in one of the large winter houses.

By February families were on the move again looking for good fish lakes and fresh meat. As the fur trade grew, one or two Tagish or Inland Tlingit families might also spend part of the winter trading on the Pelly River or at Little Salmon. They took with them white men's goods which they had bought from the Coast Tlingit, and traded them for furs caught by the Indians farther inland. On the way, they would trap and hunt. Some families stayed until breakup, then returned home by boat and on foot, looking for beaver along the way. The spring beaver hunt was very important for both food and fur, and the Nisutlin River was one of the favored places.

The Yearly Round in the Southeastern Yukon

During the nineteenth century the ancestors of the Yukon Kaska seem to have lived mostly on the uppermost reaches of the Pelly River, around Frances Lake, and along the Frances and upper Liard rivers. These bands spent the spring hunting beaver. Later, the families gathered at good fish lakes to catch whitefish and trout. They fished in summer too, but since only the Pelly watershed had salmon, lake and river fishing for freshwater fish was very important.

In the fall, many families met high in the mountains to trap the marmots in both snares and deadfalls. They dried and stored great quantities of meat. Large caribou herds did not migrate through this area during most of the nineteenth century, but smaller bands of mountain caribou roamed here, and people could sometimes corral them.

One large animal available only to Indians in the southeastern Yukon was the buffalo or wood bison. These animals once came as far into the Yukon drainage as Wolf Lake and even to Atlin, British Columbia, but they were rare in the nineteenth century, even in the Liard drainage.

Those Liard River Kaska who had relatives at Dease Lake or Telegraph Creek followed much the same annual cycle except that in

160

summer most of them went to the Stikine River at Telegraph Creek to catch and dry salmon.

All these local variations on the general pattern of the yearly round were recognized by the Yukon Indians, and they took account of them in the way that they used to group and name people of different bands. Jimmy Kane, a Southern Tutchone from Neskatahin, explained that his people and others of the upper Alsek drainage who had a lot of salmon were sometimes called Fish People, to distinguish them from other Southern Tutchone bands from around Burwash Landing and Aishihik who got few salmon but ate a lot of sheep, caribou and moose meat. Those Indians were called Meat People. Albert Isaac of Aishihik, speaking in 1963, said:

We all live the same way – just the same. Some people do different ways, [but] we cut nice strip meat and smoke and dry it. And we cut dry fish and gopher and groundhog. We cut it good and dry it. They act like us – these bands of people. They have different languages, but they fix meat.

In short, Yukon Indians who lived in the same kind of natural environment and who made their living from it in about the same way felt a strong bond with each other, even if they did not speak the same languages.

NEW WAYS OF MAKING A LIVING

Yukon Indians have always been flexible enough to adjust to new circumstances. They have lived through great environmental changes, including the ending of the Ice Age and the aftermath of a great volcanic explosion, and they have lived through great social changes brought about by the fur trade and the Klondike Gold Rush. Such adaptability is essential in a world that never stays the same. The rate of change in Indian lives increased throughout the nineteenth century and has become even greater in the twentieth century, but the Yukon natives have always adapted.

When fur trapping became a major activity, setting and checking traps began to take up time that in earlier days had been spent in hunting or leisure. The Yukon Indians learned from white traders or from other Indians how to build big wooden toboggans and sleds and how to use dog teams to pull them, and this helped with the trapping, but when the family had many dogs, the men had to get more fish and meat to feed them and the women had more work cutting and drying fish and meat and preparing the skins. If food ran out, either for people or dogs, it had to be traded for or bought at the trading posts, and this meant the people needed to trap more furs.

In the nineteenth century a trapper would use his dogs to follow his traplines out in various directions, while his wife and children remained at a central camp. He brought the skins back to his wife or trapping partner who helped him prepare them for trade. In earlier times a woman would have needed just a few furs to make robes or trim clothes for her family. Now she and her husband had to fix

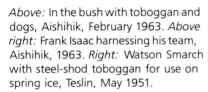

Above: In the bush with toboggan and dogs, Aishihik, February 1963. *Above right:* Frank Isaac harnessing his team, Aishihik, 1963. *Right:* Watson Smarch with steel-shod toboggan for use on spring ice, Teslin, May 1951.

many more skins and to learn new ways of doing it. The traders had fixed ideas about how skins should be prepared. They wanted beaver skins stretched into ovals; lynx skins complete with front paws, muskrat skins dried on stretchers of a certain size, and so on. Sometimes a trapper's wife made him a robe of just the ears or hind paws of lynx, or the paws of fox, because these were pieces the trader did not want. Such a blanket showed others how skillful her husband was at trapping and she at sewing.

The Hudson's Bay men also bought many tanned caribou and moose hides from the Yukon Indians. Most of these hides were exported to other HBC posts, where they were needed to make moccasins for company employees.

When the white traders finally began to build posts in the Yukon, these posts often developed into headquarters for the Indians who traded there. The people put up shelters near the posts and lived there part of the summer. Forty Mile, Fort Selkirk, Pelly Banks, Ross

Above left: Trapper in the southern Yukon, about 1930 (photo by George Johnston). *Left:* Watson Smarch stretching a beaver skin in the new style, Teslin, 1951. *Above:* Geoffrey Sheldon with stretched lynx skin, Teslin, 1951.

River, Carmacks, Champagne, Dalton Post, Tagish, Teslin, Upper Liard and Lower Post have all developed from such summer gathering places. There were almost always a few whites at these centres, but at Hutshi, Aishihik and some other places, the Indians continued to live, meet and trade among themselves with no whites involved. (How they did this is described more fully in Chapter Ten.)

Dan Lutz, a Kaska who usually lives at Lower Post, B.C., has told something of life on the upper Liard when he was a young man at the beginning of this century. Some things had not changed from earlier days; other things had:

In summertime, people come up here, take a rest in the town [Lower Post]. *Now this month* [August], *go away anywhere. They go away. Now they make dry meat, you know. In these woods they got around here, that's the time they kill some moose too. The old women cut that meat, cut that meat, cut that meat.*

Above: Eddy Isaac's wolverine deadfall, near Aishihik, March 1963. *Right:* Frozen wolverine thawing in a trapline tent, Grouse Creek, April 1951.

Watson Smarch skinning the wolverine and, above, with the stretched pelt, Teslin, April 1951

165

Watson Smarch skinning a mink, Flat Creek, 1951

Sometimes — you know those big barrels — everyone has a barrel of dry meat. Now they make a cache, and put that cache full of dry meat.

And now in the falltime, we go hunt beaver. . . .

Now it's wintertime. Cold! That's the time it's only from the cache, you see, that they get meat. They get dry meat — good to eat.

Well, February, that's the time I trapping. In the hills I trap, March month. In the hills they trap. And I got nothing — no tea, no sugar, no smoke. I go to the post. I go to the post. Well, he [the trader] *takes so much of everything.*

That's the time, March, I go in the hills again — travel, travel, travel.

Now the first of April, I quit. No more trapping. Now they go to the post. They buy as much as they can.

Now they go back again. On the sixteenth of April they go hunt beaver. The women, they stay in one place. They stay in one place, and the men go hunt beaver.

The May month is all the same as this [there is no snow] *on the ground. The first of June they come back. Now the whole bunch comes up to the post. Now the whole summer they stay in the post to sell that beaver. Now they can live the whole summer there.*

The first guns introduced by the traders were very expensive but not very reliable. Sometimes they blew up in the hunters' faces, and often they failed to fire at all. Many Indians found bows and arrows, snares and deadfalls more effective than oldstyle flintlocks. But when the Indians could get the newer repeater rifles, they began to give up some of the large-scale cooperative hunting they used to do. Individual stalking or ambushing of caribou became more common than communal drives, because the range of the rifles was far greater than that of a bow and arrow.

Left: Alice Peters and her granddaughter Mary Smarch stretching squirrel skins, Teslin, 1951. *Above:* Muskrat skins, stretched and ready for sale, Aishihik, 1963.

A more individualized hunting style was already being encouraged by the emphasis on trapping, because a large number of people cannot cooperate effectively in this activity. Most men, however, still preferred to have at least one hunting and trapping partner, and the sharing of game remained an essential part of Yukon Indian culture. It was necessary, too, because a single hunter did not always have good luck. To be sure of enough to eat, it was still a good plan to have several adult men and women and their children travelling together, sharing the risks and rewards of the winter season. On the traplines, each partner had his own line of traps, although he often ran them with the help of his growing sons or nephews, or perhaps with a son-in-law.

The introduction of metal traps, snare wire and commercial bait made trapping fur bearers very profitable if these products were properly used. Some older men continued to set up deadfalls of logs or to use babiche or sinew snares, since they did not have to buy or pack most of the materials to make these traditional devices. Even the most conservative Indians, however, usually adopted files, saws and some other metal items stocked by the traders. These tools made working with wood and bone easier than it had ever been. Old Frank Smith of Klukshu told in 1949 how when he was a boy his father showed him the stump of a tree that had been cut down with a saw. His father asked him what kind of animal had chewed it down. The puzzled boy said he did not know — maybe it was some strange beast with big, sharp teeth. He had never seen or heard of a saw, so his father explained to him about the new tool.

With the new implements, the Indians began to build log cabins and raised, cabin-style caches, fancy gravehouses and fences. Instead of the old brush shelters or moss houses, each family tried to have a log cabin or tent frame at a headquarters settlement near a trading post and perhaps one or two more cabins or tents at favorite fishing and trapping places. Canvas took the place of the skin and bark coverings used in earlier times.

As sawmill lumber became available, at the time of the Gold Rush, the people began to build with that too, though the structures were not always permanent. Such lumber was precious, so if a family shifted its headquarters from one place to another they often dismantled the house and took the boards along. Some of the old houses in Teslin today are made of boards floated down from Galbraith, a short-lived Gold Rush town at the head of the lake, or from Johnston Town (Kingfisher Fort), another lakefront settlement on the B.C. side.

Many new items were added to the Indian households. Metal pots, pans and eating utensils became more popular than bark and woven spruceroot baskets, birchwood bowls or sheephorn ladles. People no longer had to cook with hot stones; they could hang their new kettles right over the fire. After a while the Indians began to buy stoves or to make them out of sheet metal. Some curious persons burned their fingers on the stoves the first time they saw them. They could not believe it possible to have a fire inside a box. And not all of

Chief Albert Isaac sawing wood, Aishihik, February 1963

the native people liked the stoves. Many thought that flames should always be out in the open, not closed up inside a stove.

The white traders did not want the Indians to give up hunting and trapping, but in their eagerness to get furs and tanned skins for themselves and to build up their businesses, the traders encouraged the Indians to give up their traditional clothing and buy European-style clothing or cloth instead. The Yukon women found woolen cloth warm, light and attractive. They also liked the patterns and colors of the cotton cloth and the ribbons and beads that could be used for trimmings. By the turn of the century, few Indians wore skin trousers and shirts, though some continued to wear fur or netted rabbit skin parkas, skin moccasins, mukluks, mitts and fur hats. The footwear, mitts and hats were all so well suited to the country that many whites wore them too, especially if they were travelling in winter. For summer or dress-up occasions, rich Indian men often bought felt Stetson hats. A few women bought skirts or dresses, though most sewed their own clothes because they now had steel needles and scissors. Silk head scarves and shawls became popular.

The Gold Rush of 1898 brought more drastic changes in the traditional ways of living. Many younger Indians began to work part-time for wages instead of living wholly off the land. A few already

George Johnston, an Inland Tlingit, was the first native photographer to work in the Yukon. With Frank Johnston, he also ran the first store in Teslin. He is shown here in front of his store in 1951.

had experience packing goods across the mountain passes for early prospectors and other visitors. The flood of new white prospectors meant a great many more jobs of this sort. Even little children carried small packs across the Chilkoot and Chilkat Passes. Indian men also hunted for meat to sell in Dawson and Whitehorse, and they signed on as deckhands on the new river steamers. The women sewed moccasins and fancy mitts and jackets to sell to the newcomers. It was a time of great excitement and novelty for everybody. Loucheux Indians from Fort McPherson in the Northwest Territories came to Dawson to see what was going on and to make some money too. Later these ''Dawson boys'' returned to Fort McPherson to become leaders in their community. Other Mackenzie River Indians, attracted by reports of Yukon happenings, crossed the Mackenzie Mountains and travelled down the Bonnet Plume, Stewart and Pelly rivers to see for themselves what was true. Some of them settled in the Yukon near trading posts such as Lansing and Ross River.

When the steamboats began to run on the Yukon River, many Indian families in the southern and central Yukon made money by cutting wood for them in the late spring and summer. Wood was also floated down to Dawson and sold as fuel to white businessmen. Members of four or five families worked together cutting the wood to length and piling it on the river bank. When the steamers stopped at the wood camps, the Indians helped the deckhands load the wood aboard. Of course the Indians could fish and hunt locally at the same time they were cutting wood for money, so they went on making part of their living from the land just as they had done in earlier times.

Some families cut firewood during winter as well, then rafted it down to Dawson and sold it in the spring. Four men usually worked a raft to keep it from getting snagged or running aground. Johnny Tom Tom of Pelly Crossing has described the dangers and rewards of taking a large raft to Dawson. His account appears in Chapter Twelve. David Silas, also of Pelly Crossing, said that the Indian deckhands used to get paid about two dollars a day and at that time, this was "very good money." When winter came, these men could use their wages to outfit themselves with food, traps, and other supplies needed to go trapping with their families.

Working on the riverboats themselves gave the Indians not only money but a chance to learn English from the non-Indian crew. It also brought them into contact with native people from other parts of the territory and Alaska, since many boats went right down to the mouth of the Yukon River. A few Yukon Indians became pilots or captains of their own small riverboats. These summer jobs still allowed them to spend part of the year hunting, fishing and trapping.

A mixed economy in which seasonal wage labor is joined with older patterns of hunting and trapping remains important even today for many Yukon Indians. It continues in a new way the centuries-old tradition of the seasonal round and of constant adaptation to changing surroundings.

By 1910, a few Indian men and women were working full-time for wages. Some men worked on the British Yukon Navigation boats in the summer and for the White Pass Railway the rest of the year, loading and unloading freight or as section hands. But very few Indians ever worked in the mines that provided the ores carried by the boats and railroad.

Between the Klondike Gold Rush and World War II, a great many whites left the country, but those prospectors who stayed on continued to comb the country for gold or other minerals. Between 1900 and 1920 there were several small mineral stampedes that attracted whites and Indians alike. For example, between 1910 and 1915, prospectors crowded into the rugged upper White River area, drawn by the same raw copper deposits that had been a source of wealth to the Copper Chief who lived in that country earlier and whose sons became chiefs at Burwash Landing, Fort Selkirk, and Carmacks.

The prospectors clustered in tent cities such as Lynx City or Copper City in the White River watershed. Indians from both sides of the border gathered at these places too, because they could act as guides or provide meat. White traders also came to supply the miners. Most of the prospectors soon left and the "cities" disappeared, but a few of the trading posts, such as the one at Snag, continued for many years, and new Indian settlements grew up beside them. This also happened at places such as Mayo. Even if they did not work in the mines

Whitehorse, 1974

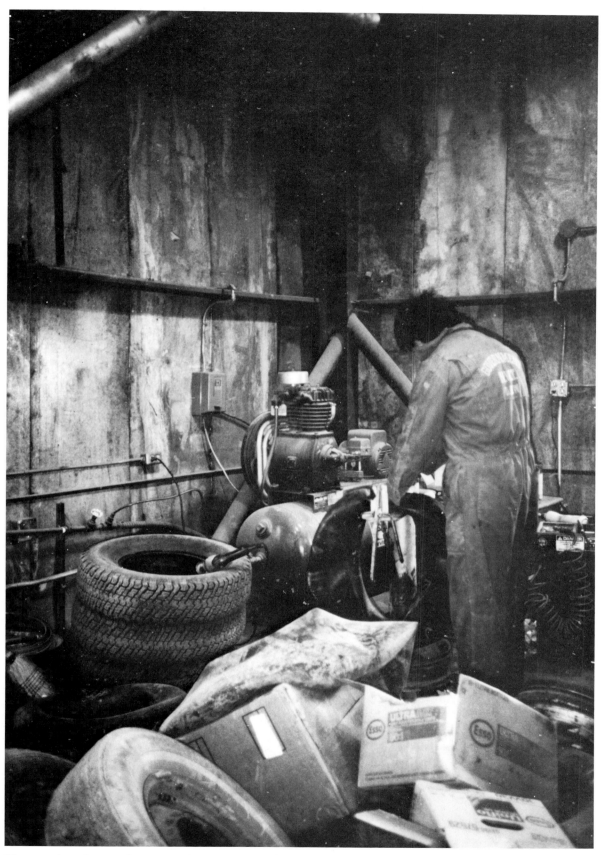

Wage work at Fort McPherson on the Dempster Highway, 1984

themselves, the Indians built homes near the mining communities so they could trade at the stores and take other jobs.

A few Indian women, in the early years of the century, also worked full-time in laundries, or became cooks or maids in hotels or private homes. But until World War II, steady wage-work was still a rarity for Indian men and women alike. Not many could find it, but not so many wanted it either.

As discussed in Chapter Four, the building of the Alaska Highway, started in 1942, gave temporary employment to many Indians. The actual building of the highway was done by troops of the United States Army, though several Yukon natives – Sam Johnston of Teslin, Johnny Johns of Tagish, George Dawson of Whitehorse, Solomon Charlie, Albert Isaac and others – acted as guides in laying out its route. Most of the employment generated by the highway was not on the road itself. Indian men worked on the boats on Dease Lake, carrying freight on the route between Telegraph Creek and the new airport at Watson Lake. They worked elsewhere transporting supplies, and they cut trees for army campsites or airfields. Indian women worked in camp laundries and as cooks, and they made and sold many moccasins and other handicrafts.

The social impact of the building of the Alaska Highway was profound, but few jobs remained for the native people once the road was in. Fur prices also dropped drastically in the late 1940s, and new laws prevented the sale of wild meat. Hard times set in for many Indian families.

By the 1950s, white missionaries and government officials had built churches and schools in many of the larger settlements. More and more Indian families began to spend at least part of the winter in these villages so their children could live at home while attending school. They liked this arrangement better than sending their children away to the church-run boarding schools at Carcross, Lower Post, and Whitehorse. After the War, because of new education programs set up by the Canadian government, Indian children stayed longer in school. Some finished high school, and a few went on to college. Others enrolled in government-sponsored courses in heavy-equipment operation, carpentry, nursing, bookkeeping, secretarial skills and other trades. Indian graduates of these programs now run private businesses of their own, publish newspapers, broadcast radio programs, or carry on the business of band offices or Indian organizations such as the CYI. In one way or another, most Yukon Indians, young and old, have adapted with success to a late twentieth-century world filled with technologies and ideologies very different from those known to their parents and grandparents. This does not necessarily mean they have rejected their Indian heritage.

8

Are You a Crow or a Wolf? Traditional Social Patterns

In the 1940s, a Peel River Loucheux who had been visiting some Southern Tutchone in the Yukon reported to his friends at Fort McPherson in the Northwest Territories, "As soon as these people meet you, they ask, *Are you a Crow or a Wolf?*"

The Peel River man was clearly surprised by the great importance of this question to the Indians of the southern Yukon. Yet asking a stranger whether he is a Crow or a Wolf seems a natural thing to many Yukon Indians even today. It is part of their traditional social pattern.

To live full lives, Yukon Indians have always needed to know far more than just how to get food and stay warm. Everyone had to be taught how to behave properly both toward the people with whom they lived and toward strangers. Someone had to help when babies were born and at other critical periods in life. Young men and women had to know who would be suitable to marry. When someone died, the family needed others to tend the corpse and to comfort them. If those who lived together became angry with each other or with foreigners, they had to have ways to settle their disputes. The sick had to be cured. People had to have ways to trade for things they did not have in their own country. Young and old liked to play games, sing, dance and tell stories – they needed excitement, pleasure and beauty in their lives.

Just as their knowledge of rivers, lakes, mountains, animals and plants guided the Yukon Indians as they moved about the country, so their rules of social behavior guided them in different social situations.

This chapter is about the various social groups of the traditional Yukon Indians and some of the behavior expected of the persons who made them up. It explains why it matters to so many Yukon elders whether one is a Crow or a Wolf.

BANDS, LOCAL GROUPS, HOUSEHOLDS AND KIN

One traditional social group is the band. Band members spoke the same language and were almost always related to each other. They never lived together year around in one spot, but the households that made up a band all shared in the use of a particular section of the country. Usually this was all or part of a single watershed, so that one band was separated from the next by a mountain divide. All the

175

Northern Tutchone families who hunted, fished, and wintered in the vicinity of Little Salmon River and Lake, for example, formed a single Little Salmon band. Other Northern Tutchone bands were centred in the Fort Selkirk area, on the lower Stewart River and elsewhere. Similarly, the Indians who lived and travelled in the mountains and valleys around Bennett, Tagish and Marsh lakes, and who spent December and January in winter houses at the junction of Tagish and Marsh Lakes, were members of the Tagish band. There was probably only one band of Tagish speakers.

Nowhere in the Yukon were the bands of traditional times as formally organized as the bands of today. They had no elected chiefs or councils, no band offices or band rolls, and even their biggest winter settlements or summer meat or fish camps were never as big as the towns in which modern Yukon Indians bands have their headquarters. During the nineteenth century there were probably twenty to thirty traditional bands in the Yukon at any one time, and only a few of them had more than twenty or thirty households. Some were much smaller.

In earlier times most bands were loosely divided into several local groups of two or three closely related households that fished, hunted and camped together continuously in given parts of the band territory. Each local group had a leader or headman. The strongest and wisest of these local headmen might act as headman for the whole band on the few occasions each year when most of the local groups came together – for example, when there was a major caribou drive, at a good fish camp, or when there was a big trading or peacemaking session with band members from some other part of the country. But a band headman could never force the band to act as a whole nor make band members do anything they did not want to do. A headman could not easily impose his will even on members of his local group, except for really poor kinsmen or slaves, who would be dependent on him for food.

The makeup of both bands and local groups easily changed to fit new circumstances. If game became scarce in an area, one or two or more households might leave to join relatives in a band or local group in another part of the country where the hunting was better.

If people did not like the headman of their band or local group, or even of their own household, rather than quarrel with him, they simply joined a different leader somewhere else. However, a headman who was a skilled hunter or who controlled a particularly good fishing place often became rich in the sense that he accumulated a lot of food and skins. If he were also wise and generous, he could attract many families and head a large local group. Still, in every band there seems always to have been a few independent households that were not strongly attached to any local group. They moved about through band territory on their own or even moved from band to band.

A household was the group of adults and children that usually stayed in the same shelter and shared all of their food, cooking it and eating it together. The people who made up a household (and the households who made up a local group) could be related to each other in various ways. In one shelter there might live the headman and his wife and young children, along with the wife's sister and her husband and children. Another household nearby might consist of the headman's brother and his wife, their married daughter and her husband, their children, and a nephew from another part of the country. In yet another shelter might be two other married daughters of the headman, their husbands and children, or perhaps a married son and his wife and the wife's parents. Any of these groupings would be good household units because each had enough grown men to work as partners in hunting, fishing or trapping, and enough grown women to take care of the meat and fish, to work the skins, bring in wood and water and care for the children.

There were many other possible combinations of people making up traditional households. The main thing was to have enough providers of both sexes to take care of the young and very old who were dependent upon them. A person living alone could not get along, and it was often difficult even for a couple. Between them, a husband and a wife might have enough knowledge and skills to manage everyday life, but if one of them fell sick or was hurt, they would have a hard time, especially if all the children were young. It was good to have at least two families together; to have three or four was even better.

Of course, the composition of households changed continually, like that of bands and local groups. Old people died, babies were born, young men and women married and left the household or brought in their new mates. People liked to live and work with close relatives, and often they could choose just which of their relatives they would stay with.

All in all, the Yukon Indians were flexible in their domestic relationships, just as they were in their relationship with the land. The local groups separated and recombined according to the seasons, the kinds of food available, and other factors. Household members likewise moved about to suit the circumstances. In the course of a lifetime a person might live in quite different parts of the country and in a number of different households. What made this possible were the real or supposed kinship ties that linked almost everybody in the Yukon together in some way.

Though every Yukon Indian was deeply attached to the country associated with the band in which he or she grew up, a person's strongest emotional ties were probably with his or her own kinship group.

A kinship group differs from a band, a local group, and a household. These last three social units are held together by the fact that the people in them are currently sharing a common section of the country, are living in the same place or are sharing a common shelter and hearth. What holds a kinship group together is that its members feel closely related to each other no matter where they may be in space or time.

In earlier times, all Yukon Indians traced their kin relationship through the mother. They had what is called matrilineal descent.*

* The word *matrilineal* comes from two Latin words: *mater*, which means mother, and *linea*, which means line or thread. The other common method of tracing descent, brought to the Yukon by white people, is called patrilineal. *Pater* is the Latin word for father, and patrilineal descent means that kin relationships are traced through the father. In other words, they are traced through the male instead of the female line.

Four generations of women at Lower Post, about 1940. From left: Hoohoo, Old Cayuse, her daughter Mrs Lotz, Mrs Lotz's daughter Mrs Piel, and Mrs Piel's two children.

Another way to say it is that the Yukon Indians traced their kinship lines only through their female ancestors. Even so, the kinship groups were not exactly the same everywhere in the Yukon.

KINSHIP GROUPS IN THE SOUTH-CENTRAL AND SOUTHWESTERN YUKON

The most complex kinship units were probably those of the southern Yukon Indians. The social organization of the Inland Tlingit, Tagish and the more southerly bands of the Southern Tutchone was much influenced by the Coast Tlingit way of doing things. Like the coastal people, the southern Yukon Indians had three kinds of formal kinship groups: matrilineages, clans and moieties. All were based on real or supposed matrilineal descent.

Matrilineages

Matrilineages are made up of persons of both sexes — males and females — even though their relationships to each other are traced only through the female line. For example, a woman and her sons and daughters, and the children of her daughters, and of her daughters' daughters would all belong to the same matrilineage. So would the woman's mother and all her mother's children, and her mother's mother, and so on, as far back as she could trace her relatives through the female line. A matrilineage can include both persons who are living and those who have died.

Among the traditional Coast Tlingit and neighboring Yukon Indians, a woman's husband, her son's children, and her husband's mother, all belonged to matrilineages different from hers. This is because of a strict rule of marriage that a husband and a wife could

Maria Johns and her descendants, at Tagish, 1949 (photo by Dorothy Rainier)

Jake Jackson wearing his Split-Beaver dance shirt, Teslin, 1951

never belong to the same matrilineage. In the old days, therefore, every family of a husband, wife and children always included persons from two different matrilineages. The children belonged to the same matrilineage as their mother, while their father belonged to a different matrilineage.

In the Tlingit social system, each local matrilineage had at least one named matrilineage house. Even though kin reckoning was through females, the head of this house was always a man. He was called the house master, and he acted as the ceremonial head of the entire matrilineage. Usually he was the oldest living man of his matrilineage. Staying with him in the house were his own wife or wives and children, as well as other males of the matrilineage — younger brothers and nephews (sisters' sons) and their wives and children. If there came to be too many people to fit comfortably into one house, the group sometimes split up and the house master's younger brothers or nephews built new houses near the old one. These brothers or nephews became new house masters.

Because a person could not marry anyone from his or her own matrilineage, the house master's wife and children, and the wives and children of any brothers or nephews who lived in the house with him, always belonged to matrilineages different from his own. A house always symbolized a single matrilineage, but persons of more than one matrilineage actually lived in it. Furthermore, those household members who did not belong to the matrilineage of the house master kept their deepest loyalties for the house masters of their own matrilineages, who of course lived in other houses.

On the coast, where there were many people and large permanent villages, matrilineage houses were usually much larger and more elaborate than in the southern Yukon, but no matter how large or small, each house had a Tlingit name — Crow House, Beaver House, Trail End House, Cellar House, Wolf House and so on. The members of the matrilineage affiliated with each house were also often called by its name — Beaver House People or Trail End House People, for example.

In addition to having a named house, or several of them, each matrilineage also had special stories and songs and a special set of personal names that referred to the history of the matrilineage. At ceremonial gatherings, the elders of each matrilineage told its history. They explained why the matrilineage members had the right to make pictures or carvings of certain animals, mountains, rivers, and other beings or things associated with the matrilineage history.

The figures in these pictures and carvings are usually called *crests* in English, because they are rather like the figures in the coats-of-arms or crests of the noble families or houses of Great Britain and Europe. The house crests of the Coast and Inland Tlingit, Tagish and Southern Tutchone were special animals with which matrilineage ancestors had developed spiritual relationships in ancient times. Eagles, bears, mountain sheep, beavers, frogs, silver salmon and killer whales were common crest animals. Superhuman beings, mountains or rivers could also be crests. Matrilineage members carved or painted their crests on the houseposts or walls of their houses, on their grave boards, boats and drums.

On the coast, crests were often carved on tall columns (totem poles) of redcedar, set outside a house to honor a dead person of the matrilineage or to mark events in its history. Yukon Indians never made totem poles in the old days, but like the coastal Indians, they painted and sewed their crests on dance shirts, blankets and banners, using beads, pearl buttons or colored cloth. Elders of the matrilineage wore these shirts and blankets when they sang and danced at potlatches, and the banners were hung on the house walls. A few important elders also had elaborate carved headdresses showing their crests, and some owned wooden dance masks. All this visual display of crests made the history and spiritual connections of the matrilineage seem very much alive.

Clans

A clan is usually a larger matrilineal descent group than a matrilineage. Most clans were made up of several closely related matrilineages. Clan structure was based on the *assumption* that all these matrilineages were descended from a single female ancestor, even though the exact links between the matrilineages often could no longer be traced. Clan histories often went so far back in time that no one could remember all the blood ties among the earlier ancestors.

Large clans with many matrilineages were represented by many houses, sometimes far apart. One clan might have member houses in two or three settlements on the Alaskan coast and more member houses in British Columbia and the Yukon. Since everybody in the clan believed that he or she was related to every other clan member, all felt a strong emotional tie to the clan as a whole, no matter where they lived. In addition to their own house crests, which varied from place to place, they had rights to a common set of clan crests and songs which were believed to go back to the beginning of clan history.

In each area, one particular matrilineage always claimed to be the oldest and most powerful house within the clan and might even give its name to the whole clan. On important social occasions, however, all the local matrilineages acted together as a single unit of the clan. A few clans consisted of only one matrilineage with one house, and in such a case, cooperation among clan members was rarely a problem. But if there were several matrilineages in the clan, and several houses representing each matrilineage, there was more chance for disagreement. Members of two houses of a matrilineage might quarrel with each other, and sometimes a whole matrilineage split off and started a new and separate clan somewhere else. The departing groups often took with them their old house and clan names and crests. Later, the members of the old clan might argue with members of the new clan over who had the rights to crests they had once shared.

A real example may make these generalities easier to understand.

Mary Anderson, Atlin, wearing her Eagle dance shirt

Some of the Tagish Indians of the Yukon belong to a local matrilineage of the Deisheetaan clan. This clan originated near Angoon, on Admiralty Island in Alaska, but several of its branches later moved to other places. According to clan history, members of one matrilineage first went to Klukwan on the coast. From there, three sisters of the matrilineage went up the Taku River. One sister married a Tahltan, one married an Inland Tlingit, and one married a Tagish man. Some Deisheetaan clan members say that a fourth sister married a Northern Tutchone of the Little Salmon area.

At the end of the nineteenth century, the Tagish matrilineage of the Deisheetaan clan built a matrilineage house at Tagish. It was called _Xaayhít_ or Warm House, and it had a large painted beaver above the door inside. The name referred to the warm winter houses built by beavers. The beaver is one of the crests shared by all Deisheetaan clan members, wherever they live.

The Tagish Deisheetaan House was also sometimes called _Deishuhít_, meaning End of the Trail House. This name recalled how the original Deisheetaan clan ancestors long ago followed a beaver until it reached the end of its trail in Angoon. The clan ancestors built a town there and named their first big matrilineage house _Deishuhít_ in honor of the beaver that had showed them such a good place to live. The name of the clan itself, Deisheetaan, is derived from the name of that house, so clan members carried the name with them when they moved to other places, and they often used it when they built a new house. The Tagish branch of the Deisheetaan clan was following this tradition.

The Inland Tlingit Deisheetaan at Teslin had two houses early in this century. Both had pyramid shaped roofs representing beaver lodges, and each was named _S'igeidí hít_ or Beaver House. The name honored a beaver with eight legs and two tails. Such a beaver, it is said, was once found by Naats, an ancestor of the Teslin Deisheetaan matrilineage. The specific beaver crest claimed by the Deisheetaan clan house at Teslin was therefore different from the beaver crest of the Deishuhít matrilineage at Tagish. Both Yukon branches of the Deisheetaan clan, however, felt that they had a right to tell about the first Angoon beaver. Both also told a story and sang a song associated with yet another beaver at Angoon.

It is easy to see why the beaver is the chief crest animal of the clan, but it is important to realize also that no Deisheetaan clan members anywhere ever thought that they themselves were descended from beavers. Nor did members of other clans claim descent from _their_ crest animals, whatever they might be. Clan stories told instead how in earlier times clan ancestors had experienced spiritual encounters with the animals or other beings that became their crests. Those who do not understand the traditional system sometimes say that clan members believed their crest animals were their actual ancestors, but this was not so. As the Indians explained it, the animals had offered themselves like gifts or had entered into special give-and-take relationships with their ancestors. For this reason, clan members were not themselves supposed to make the representations

Mary Jackson, Jake Jackson and Annie Geddes in their dance shirts, Teslin, 1951

of their own crests. A Deisheetaan man who wanted a picture of a beaver on his house wall or his drum would have to pay somebody else to paint it. For reasons explained later, this person would have to be from a clan of the opposite *side* (or moiety) to the Deisheetaan clan.

Coast Tlingit and Yukon Indians sometimes speak of their clans as *nations,* but by now it should be clear that the Tlingit clans were never political or geographical units like modern states. Basically they were matrilineal kinship groups whose members often lived in several widely separated places.

In any given place, however, the local clan house or houses did claim ownership of certain choice hunting and fishing areas. Owner-ship, as explained in the last chapter, meant that house members felt responsible for the welfare of the mountains, rivers or lakes they claimed. The house masters and other clan elders regarded them-selves as stewards of the land. It was their duty to hand down these areas to their descendants and to see that their land and waters were not abused. Sometimes the high-ranking elders gave speeches to honor particular mountains or rivers that they owned. They told how these mountains and rivers provided their families with a great deal of game, fur or fish. Then they gave gifts to the people of other clans who, by listening to the speeches, also showed their respect for such places.

For example, the local matrilineage of the Da<u>k</u>l'aweidí (or Old Yanyeidí) clan of Teslin claimed the Nisutlin River, which was a very fine place for beaver. After the spring beaver hunt, the Da<u>k</u>l'aweidí clan used to give a party at the mouth of the Nisutlin in order to give thanks and show their respect to the river. The clan elders told the guests from other clans how they tried to preserve enough beaver along its course so they would be plentiful in future years, and they gave away beaver skins as presents.

The fact that different matrilineages claimed ownership of some of the best parts of the southern Yukon did not keep others from using the land. As mentioned in Chapter Seven, anyone could hunt, trap or fish in an area claimed by a group different from his own, so long as he first asked permission. This was almost always granted, because everybody could press the right either through matrilineal descent or through marriage to a member of the clan that claimed ownership of the land.

Once in a great while a local clan matrilineage might turn over its land ownership to members of another clan. This happened once at Klukshu when a clan of the Crow moiety gave its land to a clan of the Wolf side. Such transfers of land ownership might take place either to settle a quarrel or to show honor to members of another clan. But this sort of thing did not happen very often, and selling the land for profit was always out of the question. Whoever its stewards were, it had to be kept for future generations.

Within the general territory used by a local band, any land, such as swampland or alpine tundra, that was not specifically claimed by a local clan or house was considered "free." Everybody, regardless of his or her kinship ties, felt responsible for seeing that this land too was well used and never overhunted. Nor were "free" streams or lakes overfished.

In these examples of how the Tlingit clan system worked in the Yukon, we have mentioned only the Deisheetaan and Dakl'aweidí clans by name, but at least six other clans were represented in the Yukon around the beginning of the twentieth century. A fascinating book could be written on the history of each one. Clan histories are best told by the clan members themselves, and a few have already been written and published. Others remain only in the minds of Yukon and Coast Tlingit elders.

Moieties

But what about Crows and Wolves? The Indians of the southern Yukon had a *moiety* system as well as a clan system, and it is because of this moiety system that older Indians of the southern Yukon still ask each other today, "Are you a Crow or a Wolf?"

A moiety system simply means that people divide their society into two halves and assign everybody within that society to one or the other of these two groups. *Moiety* comes from the French word *moitié,* which means *half.* Many native people call the moieties *sides.*

In the southern Yukon, every clan belonged to either the Crow or the Wolf moiety. In Tlingit, they are called *Yéil* (which means raven – or crow, as people say in the Yukon) and *Gooch* (which means wolf). The same Tlingit words are used for the bird and animal as well. Both Inland and Coast Tlingit also sometimes use Eagle (*Ch'áak'* in Tlingit) in place of Wolf as a moiety name. The Southern Tutchone often use Athapaskan rather than Tlingit names for the moieties, calling the Crow moiety *Ts'ürk'i* or *Kajìt,* and the Wolf, *Agay* or *Agunda. Ts'ürk'i* and *agay* mean raven (crow) and wolf and are the names for the animals as well; *Kajìt* and *Agunda* seem to be moiety names only.

Some small groups, such as the Tagish, had only one clan in each moiety. Indeed since they probably also had only one house or matrilineage in each clan, the matrilineage, clan and moiety appeared to be just about the same thing for the Tagish. The more numerous Inland Tlingit and some of the Southern Tutchone bands had several clans in each side.

Moiety members never lived all together in one place, nor did they ever all act together as a single social unit. There were too many people in each moiety and they were too widespread. Moreover, neither the Wolf nor the Crow moiety has a specific history or mythology of its own like the clans and matrilineages. At a potlatch or feast, all the local and visiting Crows might squawk like real crows, or the Wolves might howl like wolves, and moiety members liked to use Crow or Wolf designs on their clothing or other belongings, but these were not the same as house and clan crests. Moiety members had no stories of a common ancestor who had a special adventure with a crow or a wolf. A few clans *within* the Crow moiety did tell of ancestral encounters with the mythical Crow (Raven), and members of these clans felt they had special rights to the crow as a crest while members of other clans in the Crow moiety did not. The same thing was true of some of the clans in the Wolf moiety whose ancestors had special relationships with some kind of wolf.

All members of the Crow moiety felt that they had a right to the symbol of the crow in a more general way, and the Wolves to the symbol of the wolf, and this is why an Indian elder sometimes explains in English that he or she is a "Crow Crow" or a "Crow Beaver." In the first case, the person means that he or she belongs both to the Crow moiety and to the G̲aanax̲.ádi clan within that moiety, which has the crow as a special crest. In the second case the person means that he or she belongs both to the Crow moiety and to the Deisheetaan clan, which claims the beaver as its crest animal. In the same way, a person might say that he is a "Wolf Wolf" or a "Wolf Thunderbird," meaning that he belongs to the Wolf moiety and his clan is the Yanyeidí, which claims a special wolf crest, or that he belongs to the Wolf moiety and the Shangukeidí clan, which claims the thunderbird.

Moieties then, were neither exactly like matrilineages, in which people could actually trace close blood relationships through a common ancestor, nor like clans in which people *assumed* blood relationships even if they couldn't trace them. Moieties were much larger and more widespread social groups, and the individuals in them could not possibly all have been closely related to each other by blood.

In certain ways, however, moiety members too acted as though they were part of one big matrilineal descent group. They showed this by addressing and referring to each other by kin terms just as if they all belonged to the same matrilineage. For example, a male in the Crow moiety would call any other Crow male near his age by the native term for "older brother" or "younger brother," whichever was suitable. He would call any older Crow man by the native term for "uncle" meaning his "mother's brother." He would refer to a Crow female of his generation as "sister" and would call any older Crow woman (except his real mother) "aunty," meaning "mother's sister." He would do this whether or not these persons were members of his own matrilineage or clan. In fact, he would do it whether or not he even knew these people or had ever seen them before — so long as he knew they were members of his moiety.

Of course, the Indians could always tell their blood sisters and brothers from their clan and moiety "sisters" and "brothers," their blood uncles from their clan and moiety "uncles," and so on. However, extending matrilineal kin terms to everybody in the clan and moiety meant that no matter where a person went he would always find kin, even if the relationship were fictional. Since he also extended all the terms that he used for people of his father's matrilineage to everyone in his father's clan and moiety, he could also always find "father's brothers," "father's sisters," "brothers-in-law" and "sisters-in-law" wherever he went. Everybody in the opposite moiety was one of his "father's people," just as everybody in his own moiety was one of his "mother's people."

Why was it so important to be able to classify everyone you met as either "mother's people" or "father's people"? The answer is that in the traditional social system of the southern Yukon you always needed someone from your "father's people" (the *other* moiety) to help you through life. An oldtime Indian could not be born, grow up, marry or even die properly without the aid of "father's people." Each person belonged to his or her mother's moiety, clan and matrilineage — but that did not mean that the father's matrilineage was unimportant. "Father's people" made up the other half of every individual's social world. Both halves were needed to make a whole, and the moiety system insured that there were "mother's people" and "father's people" everywhere a person went.

One of the strictest rules of earlier times was that a Crow had to marry a Wolf and a Wolf had to marry a Crow. Elsie Isaac, a Southern Tutchone of Aishihik, tells about one of the few times this law of marriage was broken:

Two people of the Wolf side married and escaped from the village. They travelled to a mountain and built a cabin-like, dug in the side of the mountain. Here they lived for about twenty years and had a large family.

The children married each other — brother married sister. [They would all have been Wolves]. *They had a fire inside the cabin to dry meat. Finally a man hunting moose saw the smoke coming from the hill. He remembered the people who had gone. He got help, and they found a large home with thirty people sitting around the edge of the room. These people weren't killed, but were brought back to their relatives.*

Elsie added the last sentence because, long ago, if two Crows or two Wolves married they usually *were* killed.

186

In a story told by Angela Sidney of Tagish (herself a member of the Crow side), people of the same moiety are forced to marry, and it just doesn't work:

Wolf and Raven are brothers-in-law. Crow, when he made people, he made poplar tree bark and he carves it like a person. And he breathes into it, and it comes to life. And he made a Crow woman. He says, ''You're my friend, you Crow,'' he tells this woman.

And he made a Crow man too. And he made them marry each other. And here they won't talk to each other. They were shy to each other.

And he made a Wolf man and a Wolf woman. And they marry each other too. But [it was] the same. No, they don't talk to each other.

So Crow changes partners. And by gosh they start to laugh and play with each other! They're not shy any more.

''All right,'' he says, ''you people change yourselves.'' And they change themselves. That's why a Crow never marries, is not supposed to marry, Crow. It's against the law. Long time ago people don't allow that — for Crow to marry Crow.

Nowadays people marry each other. They don't care. But it doesn't matter how far Crow [how distantly related the person is] *as long as it's Crow, it's supposed to be our brother.*

In the old days, children learned at a very early age that they had to marry someone from the other moiety, but there was far more to the moiety system than just the marriage rules. Because of it, people always knew whom they could call on for help, and whom they themselves should help. In a world divided between Crows and Wolves, the Wolves aided the Crows one day, and the Crows aided the Wolves on the next.

In this system, a man and his brothers, or a woman and her sisters, are always of the same moiety — because they inherit the moiety affiliation of their mother. When you marry a person of the opposite moiety, all your brothers-in-law and sisters-in-law will therefore be of the opposite moiety as well. This relationship had special importance. In the old days, brothers-in-law were expected to be especially cooperative. Men who had married blood sisters were often partners in hunting and trapping, and as we have seen, they might live in the same household. In any case, a man was expected to give his brother-in-law generous presents of meat and fish, lend him tools or a boat, and help him in other ways. He could count on similar favors being returned. But if someone got stuck and had no real brother-in-law at hand, he could always ask for and get help from *any* man of the opposite moiety whom he addressed as "brother-in-law." (Notice how in the old stories the tricky character, Crow, tries to get special favors by calling someone "brother-in-law"!)

The coming section on the life cycle tells a little more about the daily give and take — the reciprocity — that was expected between people of opposite moieties. It also describes how the moiety system helped people in times of crisis, such as at the death of a family member. The moiety system provided guidelines for who should comfort and help the living and publicly honor the dead.

Many Indians of the southern Yukon still expect reciprocity between Crows and Wolves and believe that "Crow and Wolf" is still the law for marriage. It is only younger natives who sometimes do not know the traditional rules. Their ignorance has sometimes caused unhappiness between young people and their grandparents. The older generation thinks that the younger generation has not tried to appreciate the advantages of the old ways or realized how much they helped people to cooperate with each other.

Many of the early white fur traders, missionaries and traders did not understand the native social system either. They thought it was silly for an Indian to say that he was a "Crow" or a "Wolf" or that the beaver was his "flag." Teachers tried to make older Indian school children who were moiety "brothers" and "sisters" talk and laugh with each other, even though, as we shall see, they had been strictly trained at home never to do so. It took quite a long time before the whites and the Yukon Indians began to understand each others' kinship organization and social behavior. To some extent, they are still working on it.

KINSHIP GROUPS IN THE CENTRAL AND SOUTHEASTERN YUKON

The Southern and Northern Tutchone who lived farther north than the groups just discussed were not as much influenced by the Coast Tlingit. Like all the other Yukon Indians these people reckoned matrilineally, but they seem not to have had named houses or clans with special histories and clan crests. Everyone was, however, a member of one of two groups whose native names mean Crow and Wolf. These social units are sometimes called "clans" today, but they seem actually to have been just like the Crow and Wolf moieties of the groups nearer the coast. The difference is that they were always given Athapaskan names: *Tséhk'i* or *Handyát* for the Crow moiety, *Egay* or *Egunde* for the Wolf.

The patterns of reciprocity between members of the two groups were just like those of the moieties to the south, and the rule that a person had to marry someone from the opposite side was just as strictly enforced. The traditional Indians of Aishihik, Burwash Landing and Carmacks never tired of saying, "It's Crow and Wolf to Fort Selkirk; that's the law." They meant that the pattern of marriage and social reciprocity did not begin to change until the borders of Han country on the Yukon River below Fort Selkirk.

The Kaska people of the Upper Pelly River and the Liard drainage of the southeastern Yukon also had matrilineal moieties called Crow and Wolf in English, or *Mask'ą* and *Ch'iyōne* in their own language. In the 1940s it was said by some, however, that they had only recently learned about moieties from the Tahltan Indians of Telegraph Creek. Perhaps they learned about clans too, since the Tahltan also had Tlingit-style clans. Some Kaska said that wolverine, fox and black bear "belonged" to the Crows, and grizzly bear and lynx "belonged" to the Wolves. This sounds as though they were thinking of these animals as clan crests, but the evidence is not clear, and the Kaska do not seem to have made visual representations of these animals. Maybe some elderly Kaska can still shed light on whether their ancestors had Tlingit style houses and clans as well as moieties.

KINSHIP GROUPS IN THE NORTHERN YUKON

From Fort Selkirk north, the traditional Han and Loucheux Indians seem to have been grouped into three social units that are now often called clans in English. They were not, however, exactly like Tlingit clans, and their names were Athapaskan. Among the Loucheux and most of the Han, these groups or clans were called *Naatsaii*, *Ch'itshyàa*, and *Teenjiraatsyaa*. The Indians of today do not all agree on the translations of these names, and it is likely that the Han of the past had some additional or differently named clans.

Unfortunately, nobody alive today is sure how these clans operated in the old days. The early historic and ethnographic records are incomplete and contradictory, and the information given by living elders about the more recent past has also been variable. It was said by some Loucheux that the ancestors of the Naatsaii clan once acquired some red paint and that they also claimed the crow (raven) as their special bird. Others said that the clan had special ties with the caribou and with dark colors or black. Some Ch'itshyàa clan members felt themselves to be closely associated with the herring gull, wolf, and a special fish. They said too that they were a "bright" or "shining" people. The Teenjiraatsyaa people claimed the glaucous gull and tern as their special birds, and said that they were people "in the middle," meaning that they somehow stood in a "middle" relationship between the other two groups.

The red paint, and some of the animals, fish and birds claimed by these three groups were also claimed by the matrilineal clans of some of the neighboring Alaskan Indians — the Ahtna, Tanana, Upper Tanana, other Loucheux, and so on, but in no place were the things or animals displayed like the clan crests of the southernmost Yukon Indians and the Coast Tlingit. Clan members did not often carve or paint them or sew realistic representations of them on ceremonial dance shirts. Sometimes, however, they wore crow feathers, gull feathers, or other such symbols, and they also had special ceremonial face paintings.

The Naatsaii and the Ch'itshyàa were probably matrilineal descent groups, and the old rule was that they had to marry out of their own groups. Somebody from a different clan was also needed to help at a person's death and at other times throughout his or her life — so the patterns for social behavior between members of these two clans seem to have been rather like those expected between members of clans in opposite moieties. Yet neither group was traditionally called Crow or Wolf. The association of the Naatsaii with the crow, and the Ch'itshyàa with the wolf probably began only after the northern In-

189

dians met a lot of natives from the south at the time of the Gold Rush. At that time the Han and the Loucheux Indians may have found it very convenient to match up their clans somehow with the Crow and Wolf moieties of other Yukon Indians. In that way everybody would know who could marry whom, or which side to join at a potlatch, for the Yukon Indians were beginning to mix much more than they had in earlier days.

The role of the Teenjiraatsyaa clan in the old days is even less clear than that of the other two clans. Perhaps it was not a descent group at all, but some kind of social unit that one became a part of only after marriage. That is how Charlie Peter Charlie of Old Crow explains it. The evidence for how the entire social system of the northern Yukon Indians worked in the old days remains confusing, and sadly enough, it may now be too late to find out much more about it.

One thing, however, is certain: the Yukon Indians were always smart enough to adjust their social rules to fit the circumstances. Not only did they figure out various ways to match up their own differing clans and moieties; they could also fit Indians from other places, and white people, into their systems. They had to do this, for instance, when they met or married neighboring Ahtna, Tanana, and Upper Tanana Indians of eastern Alaska. Those Indians had matrilineal clans, which in some areas were also grouped into unnamed moieties, but the Alaska clan names and histories often differed from those of the Yukon clans. The Yukon and Alaskan Indians had to figure together how best to match their varied systems. Sometimes they seem to have switched clans from one moiety to another. At other times they created new clans or grouped into a single clan or moiety all the social units that claimed the same animals or other symbols.

The Indians from the Mackenzie watershed – the Mackenzie Loucheux, the Dogrib, Hare, Mountain, Slavey, Chipewyan and others – did not have matrilineal reckoning, nor any clans or moieties. Neither did the Inuvialuit or the whites. If such a person came to live with a Yukon Indian band, the local elders decided how best to classify the stranger. In most cases, the newcomer was apparently put into the Wolf moiety, unless, of course, he or she wanted to marry a Wolf! Even someone who just planned to stay a little while and did not want to marry would be classified, so the visitor could act properly with members of each moiety.

The Southern Tutchone probably would have had little trouble fitting into their society the Peel River Loucheux mentioned at the beginning of this chapter – the one who did not quite understand the question "Are you a Crow or a Wolf?" The Yukon Indians were just as inventive in adapting their rules of social organization to the changing scene as they were in thinking up new ways of making a living in different parts of the country as the climate and historical circumstances altered.

9

From Birth to Death: Traditional Life Cycles

BIRTH AND CHILDHOOD

When a baby was born in a Yukon Indian camp in the old days, what would its life be like? Everybody loved babies and took care of them. Of course a girl and a boy were treated somewhat differently and people did not do everything exactly the same in every place. In a general way, though, the patterns were pretty much the same in all parts of the Yukon.

Babies were usually born in a specially prepared brush shelter or, in later times, in a canvas tent that was some distance from the family house or camp. Loucheux babies, however, were often born right in the main house.

There were special helpers for the mother, and if possible, they were women from the opposite moiety or clan. A Wolf woman would have Crow helpers, a Crow woman would have Wolf helpers, and a Loucheux Naatsaii woman would have a Ch'itshyàa helper. It was thought best if these women were also close relatives in the matrilineage of the baby's father – for example, aunts who were the father's blood sisters. The baby's mother might have her own mother and grandmother there too, and women who were specialists in helping at births might be called in, no matter what their moiety or clan.

The helpers comforted the mother during labor, caught the baby, and cleaned it after birth. They straightened its arms and legs and wiped out its mouth so it would grow to be strong and healthy and speak well.

Most births were easy. Women used to drop baby rabbits or porcupines or arrows or bullets down their young daughters' dresses and perform other ritual acts, hoping that when the time came, their daughters would give birth as easily as the rabbits or porcupines, or as quickly as an arrow or bullet. Wise older women also taught young women who were expecting their first children how to bear down when the birth pains were bad.

If there was trouble, a special medicine man was called in – perhaps a man who had seen a game animal giving birth. He would usually circle the birthplace, and he might order the helpers to paint the mother in a special way. He might also sing and do other medicine, but he would not enter the birthplace. The husband stayed outside too, and the medicine man told him how to behave to make the baby

191

Babycarrier of birchbark and
moosehide, made by Elsie Isaac,
Aishihik, about 1963 (Canadian
Museum of Civilization)

come quickly. For example, he had to undo any tight strings or buttons on the clothes he wore.

The newborn baby was wrapped in a soft rabbit or gopher skin and put in a baby carrier or tanned skin lined with moss and squirrels' nests that had been rubbed fine and smoked over a fire to get rid of any fleas. This soft material was used for diapers. When it became soiled it could be thrown away, so the mother never had diapers to wash.

In many places the carrying case was fitted over a piece of stiff birchbark which kept the baby's back straight. The case was laced up in front so that it could easily be opened. When the mother had to walk somewhere, she supported the carrier on her back with a wide strap of tanned hide that went around her shoulders and tied in front. After they could get cloth, women often decorated straps with velvet and beads. The Loucheux Indians beaded particularly beautiful carrying straps, and still do so today, and some of the Kaska learned from their Slavey neighbors how to weave lovely porcupine-quill straps. Whether they were decorated or not, the straps had to be strong, for mothers often used them to help support older children who became too tired to walk, but who were no longer in baby carriers.

Some of the baby carriers of the southern Yukon Indians had two sewn-on shoulder straps. Others, made for older children, had legs and soft backs. Whatever style of strap or carrier was used, the baby could travel safely with its mother. If a mother were busy, she would often hang the carrier up near where she was working or lay it in a netted sinew or skin hammock. While she was doing other things,

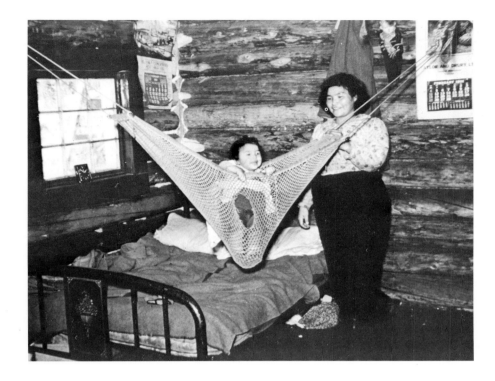

Daisy Sheldon with her child in a
babiche hammock, Teslin, 1952

she could rock the baby by pulling a long string attached to the hammock.

In the southern Yukon, the mother sewed a little skin bag which
she decorated with quills or beads. She put the baby's dried umbilical
cord in this and tied it onto the baby carrier, sometimes with a miniature bow and arrow, if she wanted her son to be a good hunter, or
with something else representing a quality she hoped her child
would develop. Later, the mother or father would leave the cord in a
symbolic place, such as a gopher hole, in the hope that their daughter would grow up to be good at snaring gophers, or a beaver dam.
Jane Smarch, an Inland Tlingit of Teslin, explained:

You could take and put it [the umbilicus] *in the beaver dam. Take the cord
and wrap it in something and you go to the beaver dam thinking to yourself,
"I wish for my child to work as good as a beaver."*

The baby had mother's milk, and then broth, fish milt, rabbit
brains and other foods. The mother chewed any hard food first to
make it soft. The baby's face was kept warm in winter and free of
mosquitoes in summer by some kind of covering, often stretched
over a frame that could be fitted onto the baby carrier. When it was
cold, the mother carried the baby snuggled on her back under her fur
robe.

Young children led happy lives. They were watched over by their
older brothers and sisters, their grandparents or some other relative
when their mother had another baby to look after. Sometimes children were scolded, but nobody ever hit them. Myra Moses, a

193

Mary Jackson with her four-day-old granddaughter, Teslin, 1951

Loucheux of Old Crow, has told how misbehaving children were warned that a large owl would take them away, or that a marten was watching them from the sky. Southern Yukon Indian children were also warned that owls would fly off with them if they were not good.

Even young children soon learned to help around the camp. Boys cut wood or fetched water. Little girls began to cook and to sew. Children helped to pick berries or to set snares, and they often did errands for older people, especially their grandparents.

Grandparents and their grandchildren were very close. Grandparents knew about family history and how people should behave towards each other. They told children how to live from the land, how to treat animals, berries and other plants. The children listened carefully and tried to remember what they were told. Sometimes a grandmother took away the children's moccasins so they could not run away and would have to stay and listen to her advice. Sometimes she snuggled down in the warm fur robes with her sleepy grandchildren and told them stories from long ago. Many old people of today recall how they did extra chores for their grandparents in the hope of hearing a story later in the evening. All children were expected to become good storytellers themselves, and they began to practise when they were still small.

As they grew older, children tried to become more useful to their grandparents and other older people. As Myra Moses explains:

Old people told their children that if they are good persons, they will live for a long time. If they look after the old people, they will live for a long time.

Dave Moses, a Northern Tutchone of Stewart Crossing, gives an example:

I had a pair of moccasins with a hole in one of them. I helped the old people with wood and water, for something to eat. I sat so that they could see the hole in my moccasins. An old lady saw the holes and repaired it quickly. I was raised to help old men. I cut wood for them and went hunting with them.

Children often imitated the actions of grownups for fun. Boys and girls played house, pretending to capture and cook game and fish. Sometimes they had make-believe potlatches. May Roberts, a Northern Tutchone woman of Carmacks, described how her husband Jimmy held a potlatch for his friends when he was a boy at Aishihik:

Mary Luke told me this story. A long time ago, Mary Luke was at Aishihik with Jimmy. All the people went way over hunting gophers and got lots. Jimmy took a bunch of kids back to the village. He said, "Let's make potlatch, like the people do." He opened up his father's cache and got out pots and lots of food for all the kids. They took out all the dry food. In those days people used to drink grease at potlatches and at this kid's potlatch they also drank grease. Afterwards, the older people were mad at them because Jimmy had given the kids all the groceries. Kids think they can just make potlatch for nothing, I think.

Children had toys both for fun and for training. With balls of mooseskin, they played games that helped them to become quick in their movements. With toy bows and arrows and other miniature tools and weapons, they practised the skills they would need when they became hunters and housewives later on.

At about the age of ten or eleven, boys and girls began to prepare seriously for their future lives. They had to spend more time watching what the adults around them were doing. Not only the family, but everybody in camp helped to teach the children. They taught them at home, in the forests, on the rivers and lakes, and in the mountains — everyplace where the children would later make their living. In that way the young became part of a long tradition that was the Yukon Indian way of life.

HOW BOYS WERE TRAINED

A young boy's most important teachers were usually his father, his mother's brother, and his grandfather (usually his father's father). When a boy went hunting with his father and these other adult men of his camp, he watched closely and tried to imitate what he saw them doing. Much of his learning came from observing and trying for himself until he learned how to do things right. Rather than just *telling* the young boys the proper way to hunt and trap, the way modern schoolteachers are likely to do, the men *showed* them what to do. Taylor McGundy, a Northern Tutchone of Carmacks, put it this way:

Young kids must watch other people and then try to [do it] *themselves. Just watch everyone and then try it out. You might even try a better way of doing something.*

Of course the boys also listened while the older men talked about their hunting experiences and how they had solved different problems in the bush.

A young boy always helped his father, because the two normally lived in the same household, but in some bands, especially among the Inland Tlingit, Tagish and Southern Tutchone, his maternal uncles (his mother's brothers) usually gave him his strictest training. They could punish the boy too, if he needed it. This was because the boy and his maternal uncle were always in the same matrilineage, clan and moiety, but his father, or an uncle who was his father's brother, would be of a matrilineage and clan of the opposite moiety. The Indians thought that these men would not be tough enough with the boy, since only the people of his own clan could discipline him. If someone from another clan tried to punish him, his own clan members would resent it and might even require some kind of payment for the offense. Sometimes a young boy moved in with his

196

mother's brother and travelled with him rather than with his father, if the two men did not already live in the same household.

Sam Williams, a Southern Tutchone man from Aishihik, explains what happened to a boy who did not behave:

If a person has a son and this son doesn't listen to his dad, he must kick him out of the house to his uncle [mother's brother]. *His uncle can discipline him. The boy won't talk back to his uncle. The uncle fed the boy too. This usually was in the same village* [camp], *and happened when the boy was about fifteen years old, old enough to get around. A boy should begin to learn when about ten years old.*

To prepare for the rigors of hunting and fighting, boys did toughening-up exercises. They got up very early in the morning and jumped into cold water, even if they had to break ice on the surface. After this cold bath, their maternal uncles beat the boys with willow branches or some form of whip. Such treatment was to make the boy strong. Old Albert Isaac of Aishihik told how he used to cover his nipples, because he was afraid they were frozen and would be knocked off by the whipping.

Lily Washpan of Carmacks has described how the Northern Tutchone boys of Little Salmon became tough:

I never saw any whipping, but a long time ago they used to do this. They hit the boys with beaver tails on the back a long time ago. They also used frozen willow sticks. They once did this to a whole family of boys. One other boy took off his shirt and went so he could be whipped too. They were learning. They did this a long time ago. This was done so they would be brave and strong in the bush. The men did the whipping while the women looked on. Some boys went in the water when everybody was sleeping so they could get strong.

In many Yukon Indian groups, all the boys of a camp left their parents' or uncles' homes when they were about sixteen and went to live together in their own shelter at the edge of the camp. They lived this way for three to five years and were under the strict supervision of their mother's brothers or other adult male relatives. They hunted and travelled for long hours, even in bad weather. They did special exercises and performed rituals which would help them to gain spiritual powers and good luck. They were careful about what they ate and drank. It was believed, for example, that if they ate young caribou, their legs would be wobbly like those of a caribou calf and they would not be good runners.

The first time a boy killed an animal, even if it was only a mouse, his parents gave a party for everybody in camp, and the guests all praised the boy. His parents might do the same thing again if he later killed a little bird or caught a small fish. They were proud of him and wanted to encourage him to be a good hunter. He was usually only five or six years old.

When he killed his first large game animal, a boy presented it to another hunter in the camp. Where there were rules of moiety reci-

197

procity, he gave it to a member of the opposite moiety; elsewhere, he at least gave it to someone from a matrilineage different from his own. The person who received the meat then distributed it to everyone in the camp. On this occasion the boy's father, especially if he were a noteworthy and wealthy man, gave presents to all those in the moiety opposite that of his wife and son. (Those who received the gifts would thus be people of the father's *own* moiety, but in this way a man honored his wife and son.) Thereafter, the boy wore a special sinew garter or some other sign of his new status as a successful hunter of big game.

It was then that the boy's most intensive training began. Everyone in camp was supposed to keep him busy packing wood and water so that he would not become lazy. Because he always had to be on his guard and ready to jump up, he sat with his feet straight out ahead of him.

If he were lucky, he might also, about this time, begin to acquire special powers from animal spirit-helpers. He might begin to dream about them, or he might have an unexpected encounter with one when he was out in the bush. Some boys, especially among the Kaska, were sent out to spend several days alone on a quest for spirit power. (A few boys got spirit power when they were still very young, but they usually did not say anything about these experiences until several years later.)

At about this time too, a young man began to do a lot of packing and trading with his elders. As he travelled about, he saw new places and met new people; he heard new stories and songs and saw new dances. He also began looking for a wife.

HOW GIRLS WERE TRAINED

When they were ten or eleven, girls too had to begin in earnest learning the skills and duties expected of them as grownups. They spent more and more time caring for their younger brothers and sisters, and helping their mothers, aunts and grandmothers with women's work. They learned to cut fish and meat, to pick berries and to dry or cook these foods, to tan skins and sew well.

Girls, like boys, learned a great deal by watching and then trying to do things themselves. A girl who did a good job was often praised in public. Her mother would tell everybody what a lot of berries her daughter had picked, or show how nicely she sewed a seam. If things did not go so well, the girl had to try again and again, and it was sometimes very discouraging.

Annie Geddes, an Inland Tlingit of Teslin, and an expert tanner, told in 1951 how when she was a little girl her mother gave her a fresh mooseskin to tan. Annie put it in a pot and boiled it on the stove, ruining the skin. She had not paid enough attention to how her mother soaked the skin in warm water with moose brains, but after that she was quick to learn.

George Billy, a Northern Tutchone of Carmacks, said that if a girl did a poor job sewing moccasins, her mother would take the stitches out and make her do it over again and again until she did a good job. Mary Charlie, a Kaska woman from Ross River, tells what it felt like to learn in this way:

Used to be no school, and these kids got taught the Indian way. They listen. Some people smart, you know. And kids [who are] smart, they can teach them fast. Me too, like that. I don't know nothing. I see people, and I copy people, and I do it. Even mooseskin too. Used to be hard for me. I try it . . . when I'm small. I copy people and then I know. . . . I don't know how to cut moccasins, but I see people and I copy and then I know. Then I do things for myself, go hunting and fishing. I talk to my kids and that's what I tell them.

Theresa Billy in a swing, Haines Junction, 1966

A very important event in every girls' life is her first menstrual period or monthly flow of blood. This marks when the girl first "turns to woman," as the old people used to say. Traditional Yukon Indians believed that how a girl behaved at this time would affect the rest of her own life and could also mean good or bad luck for all her relatives.

A mother told her daughter beforehand that the first time she started to menstruate she should stay just wherever she was. To be ready for this, girls of twelve or thirteen used to wear old clothes, and in winter a girl tried always to wear a warm parka or robe when she went outside, for she knew that if her flow began unexpectedly she might have to wait until somebody realized she was missing. Sometimes she passed many hours in the bitter cold before her mother or aunts came looking for her.

When the girl was found, her father or some other close male relative from her father's clan or moiety made a brush house for her. It was usually 300 meters or more away from the main camp — far enough away so that the girl could not hear what other people were doing. Here she lived alone for several weeks or, if her family were of high status and could maintain her there, for as long as a year or two. Only her mother and other women or young children visited her. They brought her food and supervised her throughout her seclusion. Her paternal aunts — women of the opposite moiety — usually helped her with her rituals. They taught her what she must expect in the future, what would bring good luck and what was taboo. At this period of her life the girl was believed to be in a particularly dangerous state. It was thought that the power in her menstrual blood could harm the girl herself and also other humans, as well as the spirits of game animals. So she had to learn about this new power and how to handle it. She was told that the welfare of the entire camp depended on her proper behavior.

While she was secluded in her own shelter, the girl wore a large hood or bonnet that covered most of her body and stuck out several feet in front of her, so that no one, including her visitors, could see her face.

The hood was usually prepared by a girl's mother or grandmother. The oldtime hoods were made of finely tanned hide, and some were very beautiful. Often the skin was white, decorated with fur, beads, porcupine quills and red paint. There might be a black crow feather tied to it in the hope that the girl would always have black hair. Deer hoofs, beaver toenails or danglers of copper were attached to the fringes of the hood so whenever the girl moved she made a pleasant tinkling noise. (This also gave notice of the girl's presence so hunters could avoid her.) After the traders came, hoods were made of sateen or velvet, decorated with ribbons and fancy beadwork.

The girl was never allowed to take the hood off – only to lift up some of the fringe so she could see to sew. Sometimes when it was very hot, mosquitoes got under the hood and made the girl miserable. Nevertheless, she had to try to sit very still with her legs drawn up to one side. This was hard for a young girl who had been active before. Her legs would cramp. She might be scared too, alone in the woods away from all the other people. She could have a fire in front of her lean-to, but in some groups she was not allowed to cut wood, or to cut anything else for that matter. The old people thought that she might cut her own lifeline and those of her clan relatives too. Ideally, her father's sister or some other woman of the other side cut out the things the girl sewed at the beginning of her seclusion.

People thought that the girl was becoming full of the kind of power that animal spirits do not like, so she was warned to be very careful about the kinds of food that she ate. People believed that the spirit of an animal stayed with its dead body for three or four days after it had been killed, and that it would become angry if the girl ate meat from a fresh carcass, where the spirit was still present. It would prevent the hunters from catching any more game. The same was thought to be true of fresh fish. The girl was only allowed to eat meat or fish that had been dried for at least four days.

During the first four days of her seclusion, and sometimes even during the first eight days, a southern Yukon girl was given nothing, or very little, to eat or drink. The mothers of Inland Tlingit, Tagish and Southern Tutchone girls offered them food and water, but they were supposed to throw it on the ground instead of eating or drinking it. If another woman or a child were there, the girl might give it to that person instead. She did this in the belief that when she was older she would always have plenty of food to give away.

Cold water was never supposed to touch the menstruant's teeth or lips. She had a small, straw-like drinking tube made out of the legbone or wingbone of a swan or goose, so she could drink without breaking the rule. She wore this around her neck on a fancy decorated string. Water was given to her in the shell of a duck egg, a hollowed porcupine foot or some other special kind of container made from an animal known to have its young easily. It was thought that if the girl drank from such a cup, she too would later give birth easily. She had to have all her own dishes as well, so she would not harm anyone else by eating from a common pot.

Like a boy in training, the girl had to keep busy all the time. Older women brought her piles of clothing to repair. She was given tanned hides and fur with which to make clothes, robes, and blankets. In

some places she did this sewing even though her fingers were entwined with sinew and swansdown, in the hope that this would make them light as feathers.

If the girl ran out of sewing, she picked the needles off a spruce bough. The important thing was to keep busy, in the belief that, if she did so, she would be a hard worker throughout her life. Oldtime women who had this kind of training as girls were never idle. If they had nothing else to do, they always sewed. Some elders said that they sewed so much when they were under the hood that they became "hungry to sew" ever after.

Early each morning, before the crow called, the girl did other symbolic exercises or rituals, imitating the qualities she would like to have as a woman. For example, she blew on swansdown so she would be light on her feet, or she rubbed her teeth with a white stone so they would stay strong and white when she was old. She said what she wished for when she did these things, and she could make up her own rituals for achieving a good life in the future. She had to be careful not to overdo such exercises, however, or she might have bad luck instead of the good luck that she wanted. Young people were warned never to do anything in excess. The old people told them always to be moderate in their actions.

Like the young boys, the young girls found it hard to keep all the taboos. If several girls were secluded together in the same camp during summer, as occasionally happened, they were often tempted to take off their hot bonnets and dance and play. Sometimes they did. Later, when they were grown, they felt badly about it. If their children became sick or died they often thought it was because they had broken the rules.

When her family decided it was time for a girl to come back to the main camp; her mother or some woman of her own matrilineage went to the girl's hut and took off her hood. She gave it to the girl's father's people, usually to her father's sisters, as a way of thanking them for their assistance and advice. The girl still kept part of her face covered with a scarf, but before she went back to her family, she bathed and put on new clothes. Her old ones were left hidden in the bush.

Almost every older Yukon woman who has gone through such a training period remembers it vividly. Irene Isaac, a Southern Tutchone living in Carcross, has told about her experience:

When a girl turned to a woman, they used to put a big hat on them. They did to me. That's how come you have to learn how to sew. And you are not supposed to eat anything fresh. And they get a big hat, and they leave you out in the bush where nobody can see you when you turn to be woman, when you first get your period. I didn't know too, but mom tells me. . . . Oh, right there, Mom says, ''You're a woman!'' Right there, Mom, she cut everything for me, moccasins, she just cut them up.

Daddy was out hunting. Daddy kill moose. You're not supposed to eat fresh stuff when you first turn to woman. Daddy come back, and Mom just put me away. I don't know. They had to give you everything . . . dry, you know. Not fresh meat. . . . You got to sew. Mom cut big piles of things for me. I got to sew, that's all. . . . You don't know how to sew when you are first teenager girl. When you first turn woman, that's when they do it. They teach you when you're young. After [the beginning], they let you cut it, to cut everything you have to sew after. . . .

I stayed in brush camp, stayed a couple of months. Don't have to even lift up your hat or nothing to look. You just got to be there, that's all, till they take it off you. It's pretty hard they do that to you . . . when you first a woman.

Jessie (Mrs Harry) Joe, a Southern Tutchone of Klukshu, tells how carefully the girls were watched:

Girls stay in there. . . . You sit down all the time — do all the work, that's what they do. . . . Pretty strict in the old days, really watch the girls pretty good. . . . Just like you're in jail!

Jane Smarch of Teslin remembered about the food that she ate when she was secluded at first puberty:

Just so long as it wasn't anything fresh. Just as long as it was something that was old. I could eat dry meat. I could eat old, old meat, like old boiled dry meat and stuff like that, but other than that, I had to have it fed to me by a Wolf person before I went ahead and ate anything.

(Jane's comment shows, of course, that she is a Crow.)

Jane remembered also that her grandmother sat in the room with her, giving her advice, and how, when her father returned from a

202

hunting trip, ashes had to be sprinkled on the floor before he could come into the house where she was secluded:

Oldtimers claim that when they do that, anything that would affect killing [of game] or sleep or whatever, those ashes were supposed to take it away, and everything was going to be fine. Everything was all right.

In other words, her people believed that the ashes would prevent Jane's newly acquired power from offending the spirits of the game her father had killed, or the powers of sleep and dreams.

Usually a man gave a party for his daughter when she returned to the main camp, and this signified that she was ready to marry. In some places, if the girl's parents gave away a lot of fine presents at this time to people in the moiety opposite that of the girl, it might help to make her "high-class." Most importantly, though, she was now an adult. Jane Smarch says:

It was really nice because to me it made me feel really important, having all this attention. All of a sudden you find out you're not a little ten-year-old girl anymore. You're a fourteen-year-old woman. And they use this word "woman," and you're not a girl anymore. You're a woman now, so you actually had to act like a young lady. You had to act like a woman. With people doing that, living the oldtime way, . . . it made you feel "I'm grown up now. . . . I can't go on doing foolish, dumb things anymore. I'm really going to have to live up to these things." And I think it's really, really important. . . .

After she finished her period of seclusion, and until she married, the girl stayed very quietly near her mother most of the time and kept very busy. From the time that she first put on her hood until the end of her life, she was never again supposed to speak directly to her blood brothers. Where the moiety system was in effect, this rule also applied to all her moiety brothers and all her moiety uncles. She was also forbidden to look directly into the faces of these men. Instead, she acted shy with them in order to show respect. Oldtime Indians believed that if she broke these rules, it was because she was a witch. This is one of many traditional rules that the white missionaries and schoolteachers who came to the Yukon in the nineteenth century and afterwards did not understand. These newcomers used to scold older boys and girls for not talking to each other, not realizing that they were permitted to do so only if they were of opposite sides.

All this training in practical and social skills and knowledge was to prepare the boys and girls to survive and succeed as married men and women. Without such experiences, a young person could not hope to get married, or to be a good husband, wife, father or mother in Yukon Indian society. The training period of young manhood and womanhood was critical in every individual's life.

MARRIAGE

Every Yukon Indian expected to marry. Indeed, sometimes a baby's parents made the arrangements as soon as the child was born. Marriage was important not only for the sharing of skills and labor which it involved. It also knit together the different households, clans and moieties. Socially as well as physically, nobody could live alone for very long.

Marriages never took place, though, until the participants were ready. Marriage was the last test of readiness to live in the adult world. Sam Williams, a Southern Tutchone of Aishihik, explains:

A young man thought that he was old enough to get married. He asked his dad, "Do you think it's okay if I get married?" The old man said, "I don't think so, son." The father asked his son, "Can you shoot a frozen arrow?," and the boy said, "No." He then asked, "Can you cut up the moose with a frozen knife when it's sixty below?" The boy said, "No." The father then asked, "Can you kill moose in the summer with an arrow?" And the boy said, "No." "Well son," the father said, "You've got to do better than that."

So the boy had to wait two more years before he got married. He went out to learn to do the things his father asked about. After his old man told him, he tried and he learned how. He just kept trying and watched his father. He tried to get moose with a frozen arrow, and finally he did. Then he cut it with a frozen knife. This is hard – the blade freezes, it's so cold. You must stick it into the warm meat for a while and then go on. It is hard to hold a frozen knife. Nobody helped the boy – he watched his father. This is how people learned. . . .

Marriage was never an agreement between just two persons. It was really an arrangement between two matrilineages. In the old times, certain kin were encouraged to marry each other or were even forced to do so. A young man's family might, for example, tell him to marry his father's younger sister (an aunt in the English kinship system). From the bride's point of view, she would be marrying her older brother's son (a nephew in the English system). Husband and wife would then be in matrilineages from opposite moieties, and they would be keeping up the linkage between mother's matrilineage and father's matrilineage. Some old people thought that this was very desirable.

The same kind of linkage could be kept if a man married the daughter of his mother's brother (his cousin in the English system), or a woman married the son of her father's sister (also a cousin in the English system). These "second cousins," as the Yukon Indians often call them in English, were thought to be good marriage partners because they too were always in opposite clans or moieties.

Sometimes pairs of brothers and sisters intermarried. A man's blood sister might marry his wife's brother, or two blood brothers marry two blood sisters. Such double marriages usually meant a good working relationship between close brothers-in-law and sisters-in-law, and often the pairs made up a single household.

Very often, however, the "aunts," "nephews," "second cousins," and so on who married each other were not really closely related by blood. They were clan or moiety aunts, nephews and so on — what in English are called *classificatory* relatives rather than blood relatives. Since everybody in the society was some kind of classificatory relative, even if a person had no aunt, nephew or second cousin by blood, he or she could always find a classificatory one to marry.

In some groups the elders thought that, ideally, marriages should be only with close blood relatives of the opposite side or clan. In other places they thought it better to marry more distant classificatory relatives. As usual, the oldtimers were quite flexible on the point, considering who from the opposite clan or moiety was available and judging whether it would be better for a person to marry someone from the local group or band, or whether more would be gained by linking up with a household or set of relatives from far away, with whom one had no known blood ties. So marriages actually took many forms.

Still, it was the parents and elders, rather than the young persons themselves, who usually decided just whom and where their children should marry. Young people sometimes had to marry men and women who were a great deal older than themselves, and sometimes they found this very hard. In a few cases, especially in groups influenced by the Coast Tlingit, a husband might even raise his future wife, or a future wife raise her husband, from early childhood.

A man could also inherit a wife. In fact, a man expected to marry his mother's brother's widow. She was often quite old, so if this was a first marriage for him, he hoped later to get a "second cousin" of his own age for his second wife.

If a man's wife died, he would expect to marry her blood or classificatory sister — that is, another woman of her matrilineage or clan. A widow would also expect to get her dead husband's blood or classificatory brother as a replacement for the spouse who had died. The rule was that the matrilineage or clan of a spouse that died was always responsible for giving a new husband or wife to the bereaved widow or widower. In this way the two matrilineages that had been linked through marriage kept up the reciprocity expected of them.

In the old days some men had several wives at the same time. Often they were sisters, or perhaps a woman and her sister's daughter, or a mother and her daughter by a previous husband. In the same way, a woman could be married to several brothers or to two first cousins at the same time.

An exceptionally good hunter and trapper needed more than one wife to help manage all the meat and fish and skins he got. After the fur trade began, a few men became rich from trading furs, and it was said that such men had eight or even twenty wives at a time. Families liked to give their daughters to such a man, because they benefited from his wealth and standing. He also liked to have lots of wives, because his brothers-in-law gave him some of their furs or other gifts and he became even richer. (One famous trader with many wives was Laan, a Southern Tutchone who lived near Klukshu in the nineteenth century. He got rich trading with the White River Indians, but later they became angry and killed him. More of his story is told in the next chapter.) When, on the other hand, two men shared one wife, it was often because of a shortage of women to marry, or because neither man alone could gather enough wealth to give to the bride's family.

What actually happened at the time of a marriage? Suppose a young man had seen, and even talked to, a pretty young girl he would like to marry, and that she belonged to the clan or moiety from which he was expected to take a wife. He mentioned her to his parents, and if they approved of their son's choice, they and the girl's parents began to arrange the marriage.

They discussed first of all the girl's character and her abilities to sew and put up food. If she seemed suitable, the boy's parents sent skins, furs, beads, and other wealth to the girl's mother. If she and the elders of her matrilineage thought the boy would be a good husband and provide for her daughter, the girl's mother accepted the gifts. In making this decision, she probably asked her husband's advice too, but it was up to her to accept or reject the proposal which the boy's family had made. If any of the older people in camp could prove that the young man was not a good hunter and worker, the mother could still return the presents and end the negotiations. If she approved of the boy, she often asked for more presents instead, pointing out how skilled her daughter was in skin tanning and sewing.

There were several reasons why parents asked elders of their matrilineages, clans or moieties to help them decide on the best marriage partners for their children. First of all, the old people knew how everybody was related, so they could prevent mistakes with respect to clan and moiety affiliations. In addition, the parents needed their support in the exchange of gifts between the two families. Members of the groom's matrilineage and clan or moiety helped out with the presents for the bride's mother. She, in turn, gave some of these gifts to other members of her own clan or moiety. Later — if the young husband proved satisfactory — the bride's mother's side or clan helped her with a return gift to the groom's people.

Once the parents of both young people had agreed to the marriage, the boy began to live with the girl's parents. For a young groom, reputation was not enough. He still had to prove to the bride's family that he was a good hunter and provider. During this time, which might last for a year or more, the couple sometimes did not live together, for the marriage was not final until the boy had fulfilled his obligations to his new parents-in-law.

There was no formal marriage ceremony, and couples worked out their living arrangements in various ways. Some girls were shy and afraid to go with their husbands for quite a while. Other couples who got to know each other quickly, just began to work and sleep together. In some places the bride's parents might mark this event by giving a feast or party for the camp, and the elders might make speeches advising the new husband and wife how to treat one another.

After a year or so of working for his wife's parents, the husband might take his wife to live with his own people, or he might go on staying with his wife's family. If the groom came from a different band, he could learn a lot from his father-in-law about hunting in a new country. If his father-in-law were his paternal grandfather, his mother's brother, or his own brother by blood, then the man would probably already know the country, but he might still find much to learn by helping the older man.

Where the couple lived after they were married might depend on other things too. If the wife were an only daughter, or the last daughter staying with her parents, the couple often stayed to look after the wife's parents as long as they lived. They might also stay with the wife's household if the husband had many brothers living at his own parents' camp. If his wife's family were of higher social status than his own, the husband again usually stayed with her people. In most cases, however, the husband and wife ended up in the part of the country where the husband had grown up.

No matter where the pair lived, they had a responsibility to the wife's parents. They had to be sure the wife's parents had enough to eat, wherever they were. In their old age, these parents might come from their own part of the country to join their son-in-law's household, where they would help to raise their grandchildren. This is one of the ways in which the Yukon Indians took care of everybody, whether old or young.

Husbands and wives were expected to treat each other with respect in public, even if they had openly joked a lot with each other before they got married, as "second cousins" were supposed to do in many places. They often travelled, hunted, fished and trapped together until the first baby came. After that the woman had to stay in camp most of the time unless her mother, sister, or some other female relative could look after her child.

The Yukon Indians wanted children, both for the pleasures of raising them and so the family lines could go on. Also, as we have seen, children could give quite a lot of help around the camp. In the old days, however, babies often died when times were hard, and this made the ones who lived even more precious.

Southern Tutchone parents sometimes chose one of their children to be a "favored child" and kept this child dressed in the finest clothes. (The favored child of Chief Isaac of Aishihik is said to have worn a jacket on which hundreds of dimes had been sewn.) The favored child was fed the best foods and was given other treats and gifts, and did not have to do disagreeable chores. Usually the favored child was a boy and the first or last son of a couple, but there might be other reasons for favoring another child of either sex. The custom may also have been practised in the old days by Yukon Indians other than the Southern Tutchone as well.

Very rarely – only in times of extreme starvation – a baby might be smothered as soon as it was born, because the mother did not have enough milk to feed it. If there were any chance that the baby would live, it was kept, especially if it were a boy, because he would grow up to be a hunter. In better times, couples who had no children, or only a few, often added to their families by adopting children who had lost their own parents or were from very large families. It was thought best if such children were of the same clan or moiety as the wife. If they were not, they were given new names and made members of her clan.

The oldtimers said that a woman knew she had become pregnant because she would suddenly feel a cold chill on her head. It was as if a pitcher of cold water had been thrown on her.

As soon as a woman knew she was going to have a child, she repeated many of the rituals that she had performed when she started to menstruate. She was, for example, careful with her diet. She did not eat the unborn young of any animal, nor did she look at the bodies of dead humans or at such dangerous animals as wolf, mink, lynx, otter, fox, wolverine or bear. People believed that the spirit powers of these animals might harm her unborn baby.

We described earlier how birth took place and who looked after the new mothers, but it was an important time for a new father too. During the birth and immediately after, he had to keep busy cutting and chopping wood for all the people in camp. It was just as though he were going through the young boys' exercises again. The old people thought that if both the wife and husband kept busy throughout the time of pregnancy and at the time of the birth, this would make them good parents. Right after the birth, however, the mother stayed alone for a few days in the birth hut, just as she had stayed alone during her puberty seclusion and whenever she had her monthly periods after that. But when a woman had borne many children, she and her husband did not have to be as strict about the taboos as when their first children were born.

OLD AGE

In spite of their ideal that every individual should be able to care for himself, as people got older they had to depend more on their relatives and special partners for care and comfort. All Yukon Indians respected the old people even when they could no longer contribute to the hunting or camp work. If the winter was hard, aged men or women who could not easily keep up with the others were carried or pulled on drags or toboggans. If that became too difficult and the group had to keep travelling to find food, they left the old people in a good camp – near a fishing lake if possible – and with a supply of firewood and as much food as the group could spare. The old ones left behind would try to fish and snare rabbits, grouse and ptarmigan. In the spring their families came back to find them, or if their luck changed and they killed a lot of game, they came back sooner.

Everybody tried to bring special comforts to the elderly. They were given choice food, such as the heads of game or the tender meat of young or unborn animals. They had large robes of gopher skin or other soft fur to keep them warm. Their sons or sons-in-law often brought them into their own households if they were not already living there.

Why were old people so important? It was because they were wise and experienced that they were most valued. They were the ones who knew the history of their people, and who could tell the most stories of earlier times and get them right. They knew most about the land, the weather, the humans, the animals, and the other spirit powers of the universe.

Old people, in fact, were thought to be specially close to the spirit world. It was believed that the older they were, the more spirit power they were likely to have. They knew more about curing the sick, and more about the future, than younger people did, because they knew more about the past. Some Yukon Indians used to say that as people aged they were approaching ''old peoples' mountain.'' This meant that they were getting close to beginning life over again. They were about to pass into the spirit world.

Dorothy Smith, a Northern Tutchone of Ross River, has explained:

In the olden days they always had to have respect for the elders. No matter who it was, as long as they were older they'd have to listen to them. They never talked back. That's how they learned. They didn't open their mouth. If somebody [old] told you, ''This is how it's supposed to be done,'' they'd have to do it that way.

Louis Fox, an Inland Tlingit of Teslin, said much the same thing:

Well, we used to talk to the oldest, we used to respect him. We talked to the oldest. Whatever he says, well, that's what we do. We ask him a little bit back, we talk to him good, nice.

Children were told to help their elders because they too would be old some day and would need the same help in getting food and shelter, but there were other reasons too. For one thing, helping the old people was seen as a kind of protection for the children. Some people thought that a very old person might easily become a witch and could cast a spell on a young person who seemed an unwilling helper.

Without the old people, life in the Yukon would have been far more difficult. The guidance they gave more than made up for the care they sometimes needed. Old people were the guardians of tradition and the link between the past, the present and the future.

Chief Albert Isaac, Aishihik, 1974

Angela Sidney, Tagish, 1974

Fallen gravehouse at Neskatahin, 1966

DEATH

Old people were not afraid to die. They knew that their spirits would be reborn. They felt sure that the essential part of them would go on – that they were just leaving their bodies behind, as the spirits of game animals did when the animals were killed. Often they told their families exactly when they would die – at sunrise or sunset or some other time. They might even say to whom they would be reborn and what sex they would be.

The unexpected death of a young person was usually more of a shock than the death of an elder, but any death was a crisis for the Yukon Indians just as for all other people. Not only did the survivors feel sad that someone they loved had died, but they also believed that if they did not take proper action they might be bothered by the spirit of the dead person.

When they could, the people tried to prevent a death from happening inside a family dwelling. Instead, relatives would put the dying person in a special shelter. If someone did die inside the family home, the body was taken out through a hole in the back wall, or in later times through a window. It was never carried out through the door used by living people, because it was thought that the spirits of the living might follow the spirit of the dead person to another world. If the house was a brush shelter, nobody ever used it again. If it was of logs or lumber, the family would move out for a year or

212

two — until the memorial potlatch for the dead person had been held.

In the southern Yukon, before the corpse was moved, all the close maternal and paternal relatives of the dead person gathered to sing mourning songs and make memorial speeches. Members of the clan or moiety of the dead person served food to those of the opposite side. These people ate the food symbolically, both for themselves and for their own dead ancestors. They also fed some of the dead person's favorite foods to the spirit of the corpse, either by setting it beside the body or by throwing it into the fire. In this way the spirits of the dead and the living were united, for it was believed that smoke and fire linked human beings with the spirits of other worlds. For this reason, in some places the mourners smoked as well as ate, although the Yukon Indians had no tobacco until they got it in trade.

Most southern Yukon Indians used to cremate the bodies of the dead, except for those of the Indian doctors. Members of the moiety opposite the dead person had to prepare the corpse, wrapping the body in skins or dressing it in special funeral clothes. Old people used to try to keep their funeral clothes with them, so wherever they died, they could be nicely dressed at death. Sometimes, when they felt that they were about to die, they even asked their relatives of the opposite side to dress them ahead of time. Moiety reciprocity went from birth to death and beyond.

After they had dressed the corpse, the handlers tied its limbs close

Graveyard at Teslin, 1948. In the centre is Tom Koklaw's headboard, decorated with the Crow crest. At right is a cross in the Russian Orthodox style.

213

to the body and took it to the place where it was to be burned. Goods that would be useful to a person in both the human and the spirit worlds were placed with the body. These might include such things as bows and arrows, snowshoes, sewing kits, cooking baskets or horn spoons. Valuable clan shirts or other clan items were sometimes put with a clan headman. All was gathered together on a big pile of wood, and the fire was lit by someone of the opposite moiety — perhaps a paternal uncle. The old people said that sometimes they saw a bird fly up while the body burned and that this was the dead person's spirit.

When the fire had died out, the person's ashes were collected in a skin or cloth bag and put in a bark container or wooden box. Often this was placed high in a tree near the place where the death had occurred. People were on the move so often in the old days that they did not have big graveyards. However, by the end of the nineteenth century, where the Indians gathered year after year — especially at places such as Neskatahin, Hutshi or Tagish — they had built rows of special "dead houses" or "spirit houses." These held containers of ashes. After the fur trade developed, these containers were often beautiful wooden chests from China, covered with red or blue leather, or painted, and studded with brass nails. The Yukon Indians near the coast bought them from the Coast Tlingit who got them from the Russians.

The white missionaries who came to the Yukon in the second half of the nineteenth century thought that all bodies ought to be buried, and after a while they persuaded most Yukon Indians to bury their dead. The Indians also began to put fences around the graves, as did the whites who had come to the Yukon, since this helped to keep animals away. The traders sold fancy corner posts and railings, but the Indians also often made their own. They often continued to build spirit houses as well, which they put over the burials. Sometimes they built fences around the spirit houses too.

After burial became the rule, guns, metal tools, snowshoes, toys, dishes and cooking pots for the dead person were either put in the spirit house or hung over the fence. Nobody was supposed to touch these things or take them away. It was said that the spirit of the dead person would bring bad luck to anyone who did so, and an old white trapper who took a pair of snowshoes from an Indian grave is supposed to have gone crazy because of it. When the Alaska Highway was built, the soldiers carried off most of what had been hanging on the grave fences for many years, and this was very distressing to the Yukon Indians.

Some Yukon natives say that only the people who had a lot of contact with the Coast Tlingit used to cremate the dead in the old days. In the rest of the country, they say, the Indians were more likely to put the corpse on a platform or in a tree. Neil McDonald of Old Crow has told how a coffin of logs or bark was hung on a platform resembling a cache. This way of treating the dead was also common among the Kaska in the southeastern Yukon. Yet another way of handling a corpse was to wrap it in skins, lay it on the ground and then cover it with heavy logs.

The body of an Indian doctor (medicine man) was almost always treated in some special way. Even where cremation was the rule for everybody else, the doctor's corpse was never burned. Instead, it was put on a platform or under logs or in a spirit house, far from the camp but usually in a prominent place. There is a doctor's gravehouse on a rocky point across from Teslin village, for example, and another on an island up the Nisutlin River. Unless a person wanted to become a doctor himself, he would not go close to a doctor's body. People said that all of the doctor's medicines that had been put with his corpse kept their power and could cause harm.

Because it took time to build them, the gravehouses or fences usually were not put up at the time of death — at least this seems to have been true in the southern Yukon. A small tent was often pitched over the burial place to serve as a temporary, symbolic shelter, and the house was prepared at the time of the memorial pot-latch held a year or so later.

While the members of the opposite clan or moiety were carrying out their funeral duties, the close matrilineal relatives of the dead person mourned. They blackened their faces, and had their hair cut short by someone from their "father's people" on the opposite side. In the southern Yukon, these same relatives of the dead person held a feast right after the funeral for all those of the opposite moiety who were in camp. If a Crow man had died, the Crows would invite the Wolves. At the same time, the Crows would collect food, fine skins and other wealth to give as first payments to the Wolves who had helped prepare the body and cremate it. In later times they often gave money to their opposites. This was a time when the matrilineal relatives of the dead person all had to "dig in their pockets," as Angela Sidney of Tagish put it.

However, the dead person's matrilineal relatives were not yet done with what they owed the opposite side. Right away they began saving for the memorial potlatch that would, at last, properly "finish" their kinsman's death.

THE MEMORIAL AND OTHER POTLATCHES

All over the Yukon, *potlatch* now means a feast or a party of some kind. Actually, *potlatch* is a word from the Chinook trade jargon that was used up and down the Pacific coast in the nineteenth century. The jargon was a mixture of English, French and several Indian languages, including that of the Chinook Indians of Oregon. White prospectors brought this trade language into the Yukon. In Chinook, to potlatch means to give.

The Coast Tlingit and southern Yukon Indians around the turn of the century used the word *potlatch* especially for the memorial ceremony held one or two years after someone's death. At this ceremony, the people in the moiety opposite that of a dead person

Shaman's gravehouse opposite the village of Teslin, 1951

carried out their last duties for the dead person's matrilineal relatives and then were given their final payments.

The relatives had to prepare for the memorial potlatch a long time ahead. It sometimes took several years to gather everything that was needed. Everybody in the dead person's matrilineage as well as those to whom they were married had much to do trapping furs, working skins, sewing the fine fur robes, moccasins and other clothes that would be given away as presents at the time of the potlatch. Sometimes they traded with the Coast Tlingit for precious dentalium shells, which were specially prized as gifts.

Only a very rich man could be the chief host of a large potlatch. After the fur trade began, such a host could give away, in addition to the local products, Hudson's Bay blankets, cloth, kettles, and even guns. High-class headmen usually distributed several guns at every potlatch they hosted.

The hosts also had to gather a large quantity of food — dry meat and fish, grease, and as many fresh supplies as possible — in order to feed their many guests for several days or even weeks. Late summer was the best time for potlatching, because fish, meat and berries were usually plentiful and travel was easy.

Messengers were sent to invite the guests well ahead of time. Often these messengers were young men who were close brothers-in-law of the dead person being honored. They had to memorize the names of those to be invited from different places and might have to travel for several weeks to issue the invitations. When an important person had died, his matrilineal relatives liked to invite guests from far away. People from around Fort Selkirk and Carmacks would be asked to Aishihik or Hutshi; Champagne, Lake Laberge, Whitehorse or Tagish people would go to Teslin or Atlin.

Before they entered the village or camp where the potlatch was being held, the guests dressed in their finest clothes, and whether they arrived by boat or by land, they sang as they came. The headman of the host clan made a speech of welcome, choosing the highest, most formal words he knew. Then the guests and their hosts took turns making speeches, dancing and singing for each other. Both hosts and guests told about their ancestors. They showed off their carvings, headdresses and fancy shirts bearing their clan crests, and they sang their clan songs to honor one another.

It was hard work to be a good song and dance leader, and people praised those who did it well. Some leaders took special medicines that they believed would give them the power to put on the best songs and dances. It was thought that if they made mistakes, bad luck would follow for their clan or moiety.

For several days the people danced, sang, feasted and made speeches. Even if no guests were visiting from another place, the local members of the side opposite the dead person were treated as honored guests. At every meal they wore their dance shirts and thanked their hosts by dancing and singing. Then the hosts sang and danced to give thanks in return.

Members of the host side cooked and served the food, but building the dead person's spirit house or grave fence had to be done by men of the guest moiety. The hosts just watched.

When the spirit house or grave fence was finished, everybody gathered for the most important feast. This was the time when the best food was served, especially the favorite delicacies of the person who had died. Big dishes or baskets filled with bear or moose grease were given to chosen guests, who tried to drink or eat all they were given in order to honor their hosts. A guest who was able to swallow everything often got sick and vomited, and then the hosts would give him a special gift. Johnny Alfred, a Northern Tutchone of Pelly River, said that the sicker you got, the more money you were paid. Johnny Tom Tom, a Southern Tutchone, has told how the Crow moiety at Aishihik used to have a large Crow Pot, which they got from the Coast Tlingit. They filled it with grease, Johnny said, and gave $150 to any guest who drank it dry. Usually, however, guests brought their own eating utensils.

All this while, the guests were eating and drinking symbolically for their dead ancestors. They also put food in the fire to feed the dead person or persons being honored. If they could not finish all their food on the spot, the guests took home their leftovers. Everything had to be used.

The heart of the potlach came after the feast when the closest matrilineal relations of the dead person paid the workers of the opposite side for all that they had done. First there were solemn songs and speeches by the highest ranking hosts and guests. Other important ceremonies might also be performed at this time. For instance, an elder might give a prized clan name to a young grandchild who was called out to sit on a great chest filled with blankets that would later be distributed to the guests. Or the grandchild might dance for the guests while wrapped in yards of calico, which were then also given away.

Finally, the time came for the hosts to distribute the payments. The name of each guest who was to receive a gift was called out. Important men of the guest side served as messengers, carrying the gifts from the hosts to the guests as they were named.

Every guest usually received something from the host, simply for coming to the potlatch. As the leader of the hosts announced the name of each guest, he thanked the person for coming. He also told of any particular thing each had done at the time of the death and afterwards. Those who had done a special service, such as preparing the corpse, bringing others to the funeral, or building the spirit house, received extra gifts and recognition.

It was thought that bad luck would follow if the hosts did not give away all that they had collected for the potlatch gifts, and when there were many gifts, it took a long time to distribute them. This happened especially when several matrilineages of a clan or moiety whose members had recently died joined together to host a single potlatch. Everybody from each dead person's matrilineage put something in the pile of gifts, and the highest ranking man of the host matrilineages usually acted as the chief host and spokesman.

In early times, as has been mentioned, the things to be given away were all collected beforehand. Sometimes they were hung on a fence or displayed on the walls or piled on the floor of a special house built for the occasion, so people could see and admire them before they were distributed. In the twentieth century, it became the custom just to take up a collection from the host side right at the feast itself. As the hosts were making their contributions, they announced what dead persons were being honored by them, and certain people from the host side were assigned to keep track of what was collected. Later in this century, record-keeping became easier because people began to give money instead of objects, and the amounts of their gifts could be written down. But not until after World War I did cash gifts become common. Today people often write cheques as well.

The potlatch ended with speeches of thanks, songs and dances by the guests. If all had gone well, both hosts and guests felt satisfied, and the spirit of the dead person was believed to be satisfied also.

Memorial potlatches were not managed in exactly the same way in all parts of the Yukon. Some were patterned more closely after the Coast Tlingit practice than others, but everywhere in the Yukon during the nineteenth century some form of memorial ceremony seems to have been important, and everywhere it seems to have involved social reciprocity. Potlatches still mean a great deal to the more traditional Indians of today, and it is easy to see why. Memorial potlatches drew the people together and comforted the mourners. There was solemn grieving, but both guests and hosts also had fun. From time to time, there was public joking and people had a good time singing and dancing in a light-hearted way as well as in a more formal fashion. Hosting a memorial potlatch helped those who had lost loved ones to complete their grieving. It also gave everyone a chance to remember their ancestors, and it renewed the social bonds between the dead person's matrilineage and people of the other side, who had helped at every crisis throughout that person's life from birth to death. People could be happy again.

In 1949, Kitty Henry, an Inland Tlingit of Teslin, explained how her people learned the right way to treat the dead and why they gave memorial potlatches. She told an old story about a man who had gone hunting and who had slipped down into a crevasse in a glacier. He could not get out, and he did not know what to do. He had no food with him, nor any way to make a fire. Finally he curled up and went to sleep.

Because he was wearing snowshoes and there was fresh snow on the glacier, his people were able to track him to the crevasse into which he had fallen. He was still alive when they found him, though he should have been dead. He had lived because the family had put food in the fire for him at home. The man could not be rescued, and eventually he died — but not before he had told the people how to burn the bodies of the dead, how to put things at people's graves, and how to give feasts. And he reminded them how important it was to put food into the fire so that the dead would have something to eat.

Facing Page: Potlatch given at Skagway in 1984 by Tagish Deisheetaan elder Angela Sidney. In the upper photos, Angela Sidney is shown giving a name to her great granddaughter April Baker. The bottom photo shows Ellen Johnson of Dawson (left), Angela Sidney and Angela's sister, Dora Wedge (right). (Photos by John T. Hitchcock)

In 1950 another Inland Tlingit, Frank Johnston of Teslin, who was the highest ranking man of the New Yanyeidí clan of the Wolf moiety, sang an ancient and honored clan song into a wire recording machine. He said this about it:

That's the song our ancestors gave us. We use it too, when they invite us some place. It's been used all over, down Alaska, all the way down south in Alaska. When people are inviting each other you hear that song. You know when we invited two or three hundred people, they got to get up before daybreak. That's the belief. The people we invited have got to get up before daybreak, and they sing a song [of their own clan]. You can hear it in the dark; you hear the drum — boom, boom. And then you hear it, then you hear them sing! . . .

Well, that's been going on for a long, long ways back. . . . My people invited all the Alaska people up here, up the Taku, that's 75 miles up the Taku River, upstream. Taku River is a big river, you know. Up at the head they would have a big party. They would bring up the groceries from three or four boats in loads, and they would bring back the people from here too. They are fixing up the dead body, all them people you see.

Mabel Johnston, also of Teslin, described in 1977 how her father, who was a Dakl'aweidí (Old Yanyeidí) clan member of the Wolf side, hosted a potlatch with another Dakl'aweidí clan leader:

There was one time I can remember. It was my daddy and John Jackson. My daddy was fixing up his brother's grave, the two of them were helping each other. It was Wolf, and they invited the Crows to come here and have supper with them and fix up the grave. When you are a Wolf, you don't touch your own grave. You have to invite

This page and facing page: two views
of a potlatch at Champagne, 1962

the Crows to do it for you, and the Beavers [that is, members of the
G̲aanax̲.ádi and Deisheetaan clans of the Crow moiety, who are
referred to here by their crests]. *And if the Beavers and the Crows are
fixing up their own graves, the Wolves have to do it for them. Then
they pay them for doing it. And that's what they do.*

*I remember when the Wolves invited the Crows. They came over and we
were all on the banks. The Crows were singing, and they stood up in the big
boat. They had a big boat, two boats going across and back. They were giving
their — well, how would you say it now — they were saying thank you, when
they were dancing like that, all the way across the lake in the boat. They stood
up in the boat. Looked like they were going to tip the boat sometimes. They
had two drums in the boat for the singing.*

Potlatching on a large scale probably only began in the nineteenth century. The Northern Tutchone think that Tlingit Tlen, the
big trading chief who used to live at Minto, gave the first big potlatch
in their part of the country. He did so to honor his mother, who
starved to death during a very hard winter. The time must have been
around 1820 or 1830. Tlingit Tlen may have got the idea for this kind
of potlatch from the Coast Tlingit with whom he traded, but the
Northern Tutchone and Han surely had some earlier form of
memorial ceremonials for the dead.

The Loucheux of the northern Yukon held their memorial potlatches inside special fences of brush and poles, with all the potlatch
gifts hung on the fence. At the beginning of the ceremony, the hosts
dressed in their best clothes, painted their faces, greased their hair
and wore their best ornaments. They greeted each band of visitors
with speeches. People sang special songs that they had composed for
the occasion, and there was dancing, feasting, and game playing.

Finally, the gifts were distributed. In some Loucheux groups today, every person present at a memorial potlatch receives a gift no matter what clan he or she belongs to. Things may have been done this way in the past as well, though the custom differs from that elsewhere in the Yukon, where the moiety system applied, and where either Crows or Wolves, but not both, always got presents at any one potlatch.

Whatever their specific arrangements, the traditional Yukon Indians always had some special way to honor the dead and to comfort mourners. The funeral and memorial potlatches helped the Indian people meet the crisis of death, and since every person dies, potlatching is still important today.

Besides giving the potlatches, big or small, that marked the end of every person's life, Yukon Indians also potlatched at other times in the life cycle. A man might want to have a feast to celebrate exceptionally good luck in hunting or trapping, or to mark the recovery of a dear relative from illness. A person who felt that he or she had been insulted by a member of the opposite moiety, or who felt he had made a mistake and been shamed in some way, might also hold a potlatch. Whatever the reason, a potlatch focussed public attention on the event for which it was given, and then settled the matter. The feasting and gift-giving underscored the basic rules of social behavior because those who gave the potlatch and those who came to it formally acted out their ideal social roles. After a potlatch everybody knew that a person's death had been properly "finished," that good fortune had been generously shared, that a child had a full right to his or her clan name, or that a quarrel or a shame should never again be mentioned, since the necessary payments to the right people had been made for all to see.

For a long time officials of the Canadian government did not understand potlatching, and as explained in Chapter Four, they outlawed it. They thought it unchristian, and they feared that a potlatch host would lose everything and become a public charge. They did not understand that even if the chief host of the Wolves gave away almost all of his own goods, others of his household who belonged to the Crow group would receive some of the presents. Furthermore, the chief host of one potlatch could expect to be one of the chief guests at the next potlatch. In fact, because food and gifts were distributed to many people at every potlatch, potlatching meant that people were continually sharing their food and goods with others. The potlatch made it clear that people from different matrilineages, clans, moieties, or nearby bands should always be helpful to each other. Because of the potlatch system, people were publicly reminded throughout their lives who they were and how they should behave to each other.

10

Special People, Special Events, Special Skills

CLASS AND RANK

Every Yukon Indian fortunate enough to have a long life is first a baby, then a child, a young man or woman, an adult, and finally an elder. In the old days, from the moment of birth every person was also fixed in a particular kinship group. Furthermore, every man was expected to become a hunter and father, and every woman to become a housewife and mother. But nobody – even a twin – is ever exactly like anybody else, and the Yukon Indians were just as varied in their personalities, abilities and looks as people in the rest of the world. In each band, some were good-natured, others were cranky; some were brave, others were timid; some were kind, others were mean; some were good workers, others were lazy; some were tall, others were short; some were fat, others were thin. In the small groups and close quarters in which they lived, people knew each other very well, and they sometimes called one another by telltale nicknames that called attention to particular traits – "Torn Ear," "No Hair on Top of His Head," "Big Nose," "No Brains," "Rabbit Hat," and so on.

Whatever their personal characteristics and appearance, a few individuals in every band also had special status or position because they were born into a particular kin group or learned special skills that others in their group did not. Such persons were, for example, the clan leaders, the local headmen, the doctors, midwives, healers, the professional warriors, and slaves. Those who were particularly skilled in art, song composing or storytelling had less formal status but were also well known.

In traditional Indian society, people and groups of people also varied according to their social rank or "class." Among the Coast Tlingit and those Yukon Indians influenced by them, the houses and clans in every local group were ranked as higher or lower. The ranking depended on many things: the group's current wealth; the number of potlatches it had held in the recent past and the quantity of goods given away; its history of intermarriage with high-ranking groups of the opposite side, and so on. People did not always agree on the ranking of local houses and clans, and there was continued readjustment as well as competition. Highly ranked houses and clans could drop lower, and lower ones could raise their ranking.

The same was true of the ranking of individuals. In theory, a person's rank within a local matrilineage depended on seniority within the line. First-born children had the highest rank. A man who was the youngest of a group of brothers might not be considered of noble rank for most of his life. But if his older brothers, who perhaps were house chiefs, had no close nephews to take their positions, or if one of the older brothers broke the rules for proper behavior, the younger brother might eventually find himself the highly ranked head of a house.

In the same way, a man who had been born into a poor and low-ranked family might work so hard, get so much wealth, give so many potlatches, and make such a favorable marriage that he could raise not only his own rank but that of his whole matrilineage. With his wife's help, he could even make nobles of his children — but of course, they would belong to his wife's family line. Dramatic rises in individual rank probably did not happen very often until the fur trade brought new possibilities for a man to become wealthy through trapping and trading.

Rank was never as formalized among the Tutchone and Kaska, who did not have named houses or clans, but they too often looked down on the poor as low-class. It has been reported that among the Han and Loucheux people the three clans mentioned earlier used to be ranked as high, middle and low, but the details are so hazy and the reports so contradictory that we cannot be sure this was the case. The reports may only reflect a temporary ranking of local clan segments instead of a fixed state of affairs.

LEADERS

Since the Indians did not have elected band councils and elected chiefs in the old days, who were the leaders?

Traditionally, there were several different kinds of leaders. One kind was the headman of a local group. As explained in Chapter Eight, he was almost always a good hunter and a wise man, and after the fur trade began, he had to be a smart trader as well. Usually he was a clever and forceful speaker. In the early morning he might make a speech, giving directions for the hunt. He roused the camp to get people moving and urging the young people to work hard. The headman also usually kept busy himself, setting an example for others to follow. He tried to look after all the people in his care, making sure that everybody had enough to eat. He felt responsible for his people's welfare, and he also wanted them to have fun. Modern Indians often call this kind of traditional leader a chief rather than a headman.

Sometimes a temporary headman was chosen just to direct caribou or moose hunts or the fishing. The leader of a particular hunt could be the usual headman, but it could also be another man who knew a particular stretch of country or a great deal about hunting. Such decisions often depended on the circumstances of the moment.

Even the most permanent headmen never ruled over or controlled whole bands or tribes, and their local powers were limited. A headman depended on his people for advice and for help in backing up his judgments. To be successful, the headman needed everyone's respect, and he earned this by demonstrating his own abilities. For these reasons, chiefs were rarely young men. A good headman always consulted the old people about important matters. Younger people also came to his councils, but usually they came to listen. Older women, on the other hand, often spoke freely. After everybody had had a chance to say what he thought was best, the headman announced a decision.

Among the Inland Tlingit, Tagish and some of the Southern Tutchone, each local clan had its own chief, who was usually the highest ranking man of the highest ranking house representing the clan in a given place. (Most often, he was the oldest surviving brother, or the oldest son, of the previous clan chief's oldest sister.) Because there was one chief for every local clan in each moiety — and always two moieties — every large group in the southern Yukon had at least two chiefs and sometimes more. In theory the chief of one clan could never tell the chief of another clan what to do, even when the clans were in the same moiety. But in every local group one clan was usually stronger, wealthier and more highly ranked than the other clans, so people often followed the advice of its chief, no matter what clan or moiety they belonged to.

As explained in Chapter Seven, some headmen acted as "bankers" for their people during the heyday of the fur trade. A Coast Tlingit chief would have a Yukon chief for a trading partner, or two Yukon Indian headmen would be trading partners. The Yukon chiefs would collect furs from all their followers and trade them with their Coast Tlingit or Yukon partners. Susie Skookum of Carmacks describes the arrangement:

The Coast Indians had one friend that they traded with. Lots of Yukon people paid [this] *one man, the headman, who then sold all their fur. These people* [the headmen of the Yukon Indians] *were high or rich people. They had lots of stuff. They worked hard. These headmen of the Tlingit paid others to work for them just like a job. They packed stuff. Some* [Yukon] *people had lots of fur. They dressed with nice skins. They also made their own children high people by spending* [giving away goods]. *These people told others what to do. They were headmen.*

Chiefs had to look after widows and orphans year round, and they advised the other people, particularly the unmarried young men. Persis Kendi of Mayo says this about her father, Chief Robert, of the Peel River Loucheux:

He was smart. People wanted him to do that [be chief]. *He saved starving people. He pulled meat to these people. My dad helped lots of people. He raised kids when their parents died. They got married at his house and worked for one year to get a wife. The man had to work hard, staying with his father-in-law. When these kids killed caribou, they brought it to my dad's home.*

The chiefs of the late nineteenth and early twentieth centuries who are best remembered seem to have been those who were the most generous, and who liked to feast their people and make them happy and proud. After the Indians learned about Christmas, chiefs began to give Christmas parties, and these Christmas feasts were often called potlatches, because people gave each other gifts at them just as they did at memorial and other potlatch feasts.

Old Chief Isaac of Aishihik was well known for his Christmas parties, to which people came from as far away as Selkirk. And Walter DeWolfe of Dawson has recalled how the chief of Moosehide, also called Chief Isaac in English, cared for his people:

In the old days, people were always busy and had lots to do. This is why people behaved right. . . . At Christmas time, Isaac got fur and enough food for a week or more. When they had all the food, there was dancing. Isaac told the people to work hard. He never pushed people around though. He always talked nice.

Other well-known headmen of recent times were Patsy Henderson (Kulsin) of Carcross, Jim Boss (Kishwoots) of Lake Laberge, Copper Joe or George Joe (Dultaha) of Burwash, Jimmy Wood of Moosehide, Peter Moses of Old Crow and Joe Squam of Teslin. Each cared deeply for his people and was deeply concerned with helping others. Chief Peter of Old Crow, for instance, even organized his people to send money to King George VI of England to help orphaned British children during World War II.

Yukon Indian women seem never to have become chiefs, but Robert Campbell wrote about a powerful woman who saved him and his men from starving or being killed by some Indians near Dease Lake, British Columbia, in 1839. Campbell said the woman give direct orders to her people just like a real chief, and had more courage and authority than any other Indian leader he had ever met. Unfortunately, Campbell did not record her Indian name or say what moiety or band she belonged to. He called her the "Nahany Chieftainess," but "Nahany" is not the name of any single group of Indians. It simply means strangers or foreign people. The woman might have been a Tsimshian, a Tlingit, a Tahltan or even a Kaska Indian. Maybe some old Kaska still know stories about her that are not yet written down. In any case, even if they did not become formal leaders, older Yukon Indian women had real influence in the traditional culture. They expressed their views both at home and in the council meetings, and the headmen listened to their advice.

INDIAN DOCTORS

Some people in traditional Indian society specialized in the development of spirit power and were willing to use it in public when asked. Anthropologists usually call such people *shamans**, but the Yukon Indians generally translate their native terms for such specialists by the English word *doctor*. Sometimes shamans are also called medicine men, medicine women, dream doctors or sleep doctors. A headman could be a shaman too, but not all shamans were headmen.

Indian doctors in the Yukon were usually, but not always, men, and there was usually at least one to be found in every local group. They were often asked to cure illness, and they gave many other kinds of help as well. It is said that in the old days Indian doctors could change the weather, and they could find out where the game animals were if people were starving. They could tell where to look for those who were lost and could tell whether they were alive or dead. They helped win battles, and they fought with evil doctors and witches who tried to harm people. They could do magic tricks; they could foretell the future.

How did a person become an Indian doctor?

A boy destined to become a doctor might begin to dream of animal spirits or other powers when he was only six or seven years old. These would become his special helpers or doctor powers. The boy would not say anything about his powers right away. Sometimes he was so frightened by them that he became sick. His family would ask him what the trouble was, and if they could, they sometimes got a practising doctor to take the powers on himself until the boy was strong enough to handle them. It was believed that if spirit-helpers came to someone, that person had to accept them whether he wanted to or not; otherwise he would die.

After a young man began to dream of spirit powers, he often lay around the camp for several years, sleeping and dreaming. He did not hunt or fish or carry water. It was a dangerous period in his life, because he was in contact with potent forces he could not control. He was in much the same state as a young girl just becoming a woman, or a young man acquiring spirit power to help him in his hunting — except that anyone who was becoming a doctor got far more spirit power than ordinary people did, and like any spirit power, it could backfire on him if he did not use it properly. Then he would surely die. His spirit-helpers taught their songs to the future doctor and told him what to eat and how to handle his power. When he had dreamed enough and learned enough from his spirit-helpers, he could begin to doctor in public.

A person might also become a doctor by meeting an unusually powerful animal or other being when he was out alone in the bush. This happened most frequently to someone at the limit of his endurance, when he was exhausted and hungry. The animal or being he encountered became his first spirit-helper, and he might then go out into the bush or into his dreams to look for more.

Shaman is a word that English-speaking anthropologists got from the Russians, who got it from the Tungus people of Northern Asia. It is one of the terms that the Tungus people use for their own specialists in spirit-power.

A doctor from the Taku River, about 1900 (photo by Winter & Pond, courtesy the Alaska Historical Library)

Another way of becoming a doctor was to sleep next to a doctor's corpse soon after he died. Sometimes, just before his death, an old doctor instructed his nephew to do just that. Such an instruction was dangerous to follow, but even more dangerous to refuse. The boy's relatives often went with him to keep watch at the uncle's grave. As the spirit of the dead man began to give his powers to the nephew, the relatives would hear the young man singing the old doctor's songs. Then a new song of his own would come to him, and his relatives would hear that too and learn to sing it.

Yet another way to become a doctor was to look on purpose for a powerful or dangerous animal such as a mink or otter. The Tlingit and other southern Yukon Indians said that when a person who wanted great power found a dead animal of this sort, he would slice off a piece of the tongue and put it in his dream bag. This was such strong power that sometimes the man's hands would become all knotted up, especially if he did not use the power to help out other people.

Oldtimers say that, long ago, people were hardly ever sick. For minor ailments like an upset stomach, a cut, a bruise, or rheumatism, most people had effective household remedies or went to healers who knew about them. Very serious illnesses, however, required the help of a doctor who could draw on the powers of the spirit world. When a person became really sick, it was believed that he had lost his soul or spirit, because of a terrible fright or because a powerful doctor or witch had taken the soul away — or that his spirit was troubled by something evil which a doctor had put into the sick person's body.

When a person was so ill that he needed a doctor, he often sent a relative to give the doctor a present. The doctor then decided whether he would try to help the person. It is said that he could often tell what was the matter even before he saw the patient, and could also tell in advance whether the problem was one he could cure. His spirit-helpers could find these things out for him before he took the case.

If he decided to take the case, the doctor still did not always have to go to the patient. The sick person could send him a shirt or some other piece of clothing that he or she had worn, and the doctor would sleep with the clothing. Through his dreams he would find out the cause and the cure of the patient's illness. He might send back word about certain foods the sick person should eat, or tell him to drink or eat out of a certain kind of cup or pot. If the person were sick because he had lost his soul, the doctor's own spirit or one of his spirit-helpers could travel about trying to find it. If they located it, the doctor sent it back to the patient's body, and the patient got well.

Each doctor had a medicine kit which might include things such as animal skins, bones, claws, stones from animal stomachs, and strong medicinal herbs as well as carved and painted walking sticks, painted drums and rattles. Doctors never cut their hair, and when they performed, they shook it all out loose often frightening the little children. Some doctors only wore breech cloths or fringed aprons when they were curing. Most wore necklaces of bearclaws, cedar-bark or animal bones. The doctor's equipment showed what kind of animal spirit-helpers he had.

The drum was very important. Sometimes the doctor himself drummed during the cure, but usually an assistant beat the drum while the doctor sang to call his spirit-helpers. At public performances the entire audience joined in the singing, for this helped to call the doctor's powers. Sometimes the assistant (an apprentice doctor himself) gave directions to the powers or to the audience.

When a spirit arrived, the doctor became possessed. He yelled and shouted and seemed to float several feet off the ground or pass through flames. His spirits talked through him. He might sound like a wolverine or a loon or a bear, depending on the particular spirit power that possessed him.

During this time the sick person lay by the fire under a blanket. If the patient's lost soul-spirit were found, the doctor blew on the patient's head to return his soul. Or the doctor might try to suck or pull out whatever evil thing was making the patient sick. It is said that sometimes he cut the patient open and pulled out the sickness without causing any bleeding or leaving a scar.

Joe Netro of Old Crow has told of an operation that a Loucheux doctor performed to cure a young man, and also about a doctor who cured himself.

About thirty miles upriver [from Old Crow] *a boy got sick. His father asked a medicine man to fix his son. The medicine man checked the boy and knew he needed an operation. The medicine man split a piece of dry wood straight and made a knife out of it. He put the boy to sleep and cut him open in the chest. There was lots of blood in the boy's chest. The medicine man cleaned it out and the boy got better. I saw this boy years later. He is buried by New Rampart House. He lived to be over seventy years old.*

One medicine man got hurt in the chest. He was brought inside. He told the people to shoot him with a muzzle-loading shotgun. This was the only way to make him better. Nobody wanted to do it. He told his brother to shoot him, and everyone watched. He told him to shoot him where the skin was broken. The medicine man was very clear about how to load the gun, so that the people saw him do it. His brother shot him, and he fell upside down. He lay there for a long while. The people thought he had been killed. But pretty soon he moved and got up. He then got better.

Sometimes several doctors worked together if they had a difficult illness to cure, or were trying to locate game or to help the people in some other way. They all got underneath one blanket and sang their spirit songs. They called it "going under the water." All the people had to be there to help sing, but first they tied the dogs a long way from camp. It was believed that barking dogs spoiled the power of the doctors by scaring off their spirit-helpers. The place where the doctors worked always had to be clean, and no women who were having their periods could be near the working doctor. It was also thought that doctors worked best at night, because that was the time when their spirit-helpers were most powerful. People said night was the spirits' daytime.

In times of starvation, doctors sometimes used their walking sticks to point out where game could be found and told the people just how to hunt it. If a single hunter were having bad luck, the doctor might lend him a necklace of animal teeth or claws to give him power, and the doctor would tell him exactly where to look for a moose or sheep.

Moses Tizya of Old Crow explained how the Loucheux Indian doctors used to find game.

This is what the medicine man did. If people were out of food, they got together and had something like a [church] service. The medicine people went to sleep and went someplace in their sleep and saw bands of caribou. They led the caribou to the camp. In the morning, they told the people where to go. That's how they got meat in the old days.

Neil McDonald of Old Crow and Albert Isaac of Aishihik have both told the old story of the Man in the Moon. It is about a young boy whose doctor's powers told the people where they could find caribou. In spite of the boy's help, the people were mean to him, so he left them and went up to the moon. He can still be seen there, holding out the caribou lungs, which are all he was given to eat after saving the people. (In the Yukon, nobody eats caribou lungs unless they have to.)

Several Indian doctors are said to have learned about the future when they dreamed at night. One famous Yukon doctor named Kushe'ísh, a Kaska from Pelly Banks, predicted World War II and the coming of the Alaska Highway and the Canol Road. In Chapter Twelve are more stories about the wonderful things that elders said the Indian doctors could do.

Indian doctors were valuable members of Yukon Indian society. A few of them were headmen as well as doctors, but their major role was interacting with the dangerous powerful spirit world. The traditional Indians were confident that maintaining good relations with the spirit world was necessary in order for everyone to have enough to eat and stay healthy.

MIDWIVES AND HEALERS

Though the Indian doctors of the old days were usually men, the midwives — those who helped deliver babies — were always women. They knew how to use their hands on the mother's stomach to help when the baby was in the wrong position to be born easily, and they had other invaluable skills. Other healers — both men and women — let blood, sewed up wounds, or set bones.

Everyone in the old days knew some of the common plant medicines, but certain people — usually women — made that kind of knowledge a specialty. They knew the best places to collect medicine plants as well as how to use them. Mary McLeod, a Han of Dawson, has said the women gathered these plants when they were travelling from camp to camp or when they were out picking berries or setting snares. Angela Sidney of Tagish says women sometimes brought back seeds of good medicine plants to scatter near the camps or villages.

When oldtimers gathered a strong medicine plant, such as skookum root, they left a gift where they pulled up the plant and said a kind of prayer that it would help people get well. People said if no gift were left, it would probably rain. Skookum root has other common names, such as cornlily and hellebore. Botanists call it *Veratrum viride*. Doctors all over the world use it in medicines, but it is powerful enough to kill a person if it is not properly used.

Kitty Smith, a Southern Tutchone elder from Whitehorse, has told about some other plant medicines:

You find poplar ears [bracket fungus] *growing on poplar trees or spruce trees. It looks like a thin mushroom and a bit of moss growing on them. You boil it and drink the juice. It's good for heart medicine. Groundhog roots are good for bad water in your stomach. Waterlily roots are used for heartburn and bad gases in the stomach. You slice it off like bread and chew it and swallow the juice.*

To cure a cold, Kitty says:

Use spruce gum or poplar tree sap. Get some tree gum and chew it and swallow the juice. From the poplar tree, get the sap or thin shavings off the bark and boil them in water for a few minutes and drink the juice.

Hudson's Bay tea or Labrador tea (*Ledum palustre*) was a good remedy for colds. The leaves were collected in a sack and brewed to make a tea which people drank in large quantities when they felt poorly.

Angela Sidney of Tagish tells of a wild celery medicine for rheumatism. The dry or fresh roots of this plant (*Heracleum lanatum*) were powdered, then put into a cloth and heated on hot rocks. Next, some water was poured on the bundle to make it steam and it was used as a poultice. The healer would have two or three bundles, so she could keep two hot while using the third.

Balsam fir boughs heated on a fire were used to relieve toothaches and earaches. And according to Sam Peter, a Northern Tutchone of Mayo, a poultice of warm pitch and a piece of moose skin was put on a sore back. When the pitch dried and the moose skin fell off, the back was well.

In the old days, every camp might have one or several sweat houses — small dome-shaped frames of willows covered with brush and hides. People enjoyed taking steam baths in them, and they were also used to ease the pain of rheumatism. Bessie Crow, a Southern Tutchone of Champagne, tells how the sweat house works:

You dig a big pit in the ground. Build a fire and put some rocks in the fire and heat them until red hot. And sprinkle water over the rocks. This makes steam. Then you put the person that is suffering from rheumatism in the sweat house and steam him for a couple of hours.

These are only a few of the rich store of remedies the Indians had for treating sickness, but they show what good use the old people made of the natural resources of their country.

SLAVES

The Yukon Indians had very few slaves. The Tagish, Inland Tlingit and Southern Tutchone sometimes bought slaves from the Coast Tlingit with whom they traded, but even a chief only had one or two. It is said also that in the old days a gambler might become a slave to pay off his debts, but no one seems to know of a specific case in recent times.

Other slaves were captured in raids on enemy groups. They served as war trophies and status symbols. A person who owned a slave had a lot of prestige.

Slaves lived with their owners and did heavy work around the camp. There were both men and women slaves. They carried water and collected wood but were not allowed to have weapons for hunting. Their hair was cut short to identify them, at least until their owners were sure they would not run away. It is said they were not allowed to wear moccasins but had to go barefoot or wear a kind of rawhide sandal.

Most slaves were well treated. Some even married into their owner's family. A slave woman might become the second or third wife of the man who captured her. In that case, she would be adopted into an appropriate clan or moiety, and her children would become free members of the group. Captive children were sometimes adopted by a childless couple and raised as if they were the couple's own sons or daughters. The Tlingit and other southern Yukon Indians sometimes even adopted adult slaves as members of a local matrilineage to increase its numbers. Ordinarily, however, slaves were treated as though they had no clan or moiety affiliation. They had no status in any kinship group, and this meant, of course, that they could not participate in potlatches or other social events. They had no place in the social order and were thus hardly people at all.

Men or women who became slaves through capture in war always hoped their people would rescue them or buy their freedom. If this happened, the matrilineal relatives of the slave gave a big potlatch to wipe away the shame, and nobody could ever mention the slavery again. To do so was to give a deadly insult and feuding was bound to follow.

PARTNERS

In addition to a wife or husband, every adult man or woman usually had a special friend or partner of his or her own sex; sometimes young children had them too. Ties between partners were very close. Indeed, partners often had an understanding with each other that went far beyond the kinds of support and cooperation they got even from their close kin.

Partners could be of the same or the opposite clan or moiety, but the strongest partnerships were usually between those of opposite sides. The partners might be true brothers-in-law or sisters-in-law, or they might be more distantly related. The closest male partners hunted or worked together, and they freely shared their tools, clothing and other belongings. They and their families lived together in the same local group and often in the same household.

Some men had several different hunting partners at the same time, or in different seasons, or in different years, but they would not all be equally close. Women did not so often change their partners.

A man or woman could have partners from distant bands as well as from close to home. These partners from far away places were persons with whom to trade or to visit, and they were supposed to belong to the same clans or moieties. This helped to keep everything peaceable when groups of people from different parts of the country met together, because the partners could treat each other as matrilineal kin.

The kinds of partnerships were so varied that it is hard to generalize about them, but they were a very important part of every Yukon Indian's social life. Ideally, to have a partner meant that you had a friend whom you could always trust and count on. In the stories about Crow, it is clear that one of his worst habits is tricking his partners. Crow breaks even the most cherished rules of behavior — so when people hear the stories, they are reminded how useful those rules are.

TRADING AND TRAVELLING

We do not know for sure the distances that people used to travel, but there is no question that from early times Yukon natives made long journeys to trade both among themselves and with their Indian neighbors. After the white men came into their country, of course, the Indians traded with them too. Oldtimers tell many good stories about the fur trade, but far fewer about the time when there were no European-made trade items.

Because the natural resources were not everywhere the same, the people of one place often had something that the people somewhere else wanted. For example, Loucheux of the Yukon Flats area of Alaska did not have many caribou, but they needed caribou skins to make clothes. They got them by trading with Old Crow people or other Loucheux. Sheep and goat skins, gopher skins, salmon, red paint and raw copper are other items that people exchanged within the Yukon itself.

When the Yukon Loucheux traded with the Inuit of Herschel Island and the Mackenzie delta, the Inuit wanted wolverine furs for their parka hoods, and the Yukon Indians wanted walrus ivory or lines of tough walrus skins. They also liked some of the Inuvialuit carvings and tools. Although trading sessions were usually friendly, the Loucheux sometimes had disagreements with the Inuit, especially when they thought they were not getting a fair deal.

Joe Netro of Old Crow told of these trading sessions:

Before the arrival of Hudson Bay [Company], *my father and all the other old people got muskrats at the Flats in the spring and had to go to Point Barrow to trade, a long way. They brought the skins with them to all the Eskimos there. They went with dog packs and packsacks. They also got sheep before they got to Point Barrow and sold all this to the Eskimos. They received tents and other supplies. The Eskimos went down to the Russian country to get the trade goods, I think. The Indian people didn't stay long. I don't know how long the trip took, but it was a long one. Only the men made the trip. The women stayed home and fished while the men were away.*

After 1870 the Old Crow Indians also went to Herschel Island to trade with the American whaling boats that landed there. Eliza Ben Kassi remembered how she saw white people for the first time when she went to Herschel Island:

We used to go to the [Arctic] *coast* [Herschel Island] *to get groceries. White men came in to our camp. These were the first white men I ever saw. We got groceries at the coast. When we ran out of groceries, we lived on caribou meat and other game. The first time I saw white people, I was afraid of them.*

The Loucheux of the northern Yukon also traded with other Loucheux and with Tanana River Athapaskans who brought Russian goods up the Yukon River. After 1845, some Yukon Loucheux traded at La Pierre House and Rampart House, the Hudson's Bay posts on the Porcupine River, while others went on down to Fort Yukon on the Yukon River or over to Fort McPherson on the Peel. A few even travelled to the Mackenzie River posts, where they had sometimes traded in earlier years.

The first Hudson's Bay Company men who came into Loucheux country on their way to set up Fort Yukon did not go up the Crow River. In fact, it was quite late in the nineteenth century before the whites even got into Old Crow country. Persis Kendi and Liza Malcolm, sisters who grew up in that area, both said they saw their first white men along a river at their father's camp. Perhaps these men were from the Alaska/Yukon boundary survey of 1911. The sisters said:

Six boats came, and we got blankets, grub, and clothes, and since then we have had all these things. I don't know the year, but since then we got lots of blankets. These were the first white people [we saw].

Long before the arrival of white men, the Coast Indians were bringing candlefish (or oolichan) grease, dried seaweed, dried clams, clamshells, plant medicines, cedar boxes and seashells into the southern Yukon. Seashells were said to be like jewels to Yukon Indians, and in return for these shells they offered copper, furs, tanned hides, and the lichen dyes and mountain goat hair used in making Chilkat blankets.

When the Coast Tlingit first began to trade with the Russians and other Europeans in the late 1700s, they got guns, metal knives, cloth, tobacco, and tea. At that time the Russians wanted sea otter skins most of all because they could sell their beautiful pelts to the Chinese at very high prices. But the Russians, Aleuts, and other Pacific Coast natives hunted the sea otters so hard that they had almost died out, and then the Russians had to buy the furs of land animals. The Coast Tlingit turned to their Yukon trading partners to supply these furs, and they established a trading village part way up the Alsek River at Nuqwaik. The settlement did not last long, however, because the coast people did not know how to live off the inland country year round. But the Coast Indians liked to trade every year at the same places if they could, and they often arranged to meet the Yukon Indians in summer at places where there was plenty of fish. Neskatahin, McClintock River, Aishihik and Hutshi were favorite places. There were others near Little Salmon, Minto and Dawson.

The Chilkoot and Chilkat Tlingit who crossed the passes into the Yukon each claimed to own different routes into the interior as well as the rights to trade with specific groups of Yukon Indians, but the details of these arrangements are not now fully known. The Gaanax.ádi clan of the Raven moiety and the Dakl'aweidí clan of the Eagle (Wolf) moiety at the Chilkat village of Klukwan both claimed control of the Chilkat Pass, while the Lukaax.ádi clan of the Raven (Crow) moiety of the Chilkoot said it owned the Chilkoot Pass.

When the American astronomer George Davidson went to the Chilkat village of Klukwan in 1869 to observe a full eclipse of the sun, he persuaded Koh-Klux, the chief of the Dakl'aweidí clan, to draw, with the help of his wife, a map of the route that he and his clansmen followed into the interior. This map shows the important native trading places in Yukon, including Fort Selkirk, which Koh-Klux probably helped to destroy in 1852. It gives a good idea of just how far the Chilkats used to travel and how much they knew about the Yukon.

Coast Tlingit from Dry Bay also traded with the Yukon Indians. They came up the Alsek River or else crossed to Klukwan and ascended the Chilkat and Klehini Rivers. The Lukaax.ádi clan of the Ravens and the Shangukeidí clan of the Eagle (Wolf) moiety of Dry Bay are said to have been the first ones to find a way up into the interior via the Alsek River, and today there are Yukon Indians of the Shangukeidí clan living at Haines Junction and Champagne.

The Tlingit who lived at the mouth of the Taku River and at Auk Inlet, near present-day Juneau, went up the Taku River every year, then crossed the height of land to trade at Atlin or Teslin Lakes. Often they went on to meet Pelly, Frances and Liard River Kaska Indians too.

Each Tlingit trading party was directed by a high-ranking clan member, who brought his younger relatives and slaves to pack the trade goods over the mountains. The members of the parties evidently had trading partners at several different places. Sam Williams, a Southern Tutchone of Aishihik, described how his mother's father, Chief Isaac of Aishihik, traded with the Chilkat Indians:

Grandpa traded with the Coast Indians. I don't know how the Coast Indians found the people here. I should have asked some of the old people, but now it's too late. The Coast Indians visited for a few days. They got furs and then left. My grandma told me that when no one was around [Aishihik], *the Coast Indians took food and fur from Chief Isaac's cache and paid him later. They paid with blankets, guns, powder, and shells. The first guns were flintlocks. The bow and arrow was better than those. Then came the muzzle-loading shotgun. This was before 1898.*

Whenever traders gathered together, there was always much singing, dancing, storytelling, game playing, and feasting before the trading began. Trading partners saved their best furs or goods for each other, but at first they did not bring them out. To build up suspense, they began by exchanging small presents and some of their less expensive furs or trade goods. Only at the end did they show each other their prize furs or raw copper, white men's trade goods, or whatever else valuable they had to trade.

After a man had finished trading with his regular partners, he was free to buy whatever else he wanted from whoever had it, or to sell to anybody whatever else he had left. Of course there was no money. All the trade was based on giving and receiving items which were supposed to be of roughly equal worth.

Trading was usually carried out in the Tlingit language which many Yukon Indians understood, even those who spoke Athapaskan among themselves. (It was probably because of all this trading activity that the Tagish began to speak Tlingit most of the time instead of Tagish Athapaskan, and came to have so many Coast Tlingit relatives.)

Sometimes a Coast Tlingit married a Southern Tutchone or Tagish woman who was a daughter or brother's daughter of his Yukon trading partner, but he might have a wife on the coast too. He would stay with his Yukon wife only when he came to trade, or perhaps to spend the winter trapping with his wife's family. Such an arrangement resulted in trade advantages for both partners. For the same reason, a Coast Tlingit woman would sometimes marry a Yukon Indian.

Once, however, a Chilkat Tlingit got very angry with his Yukon trading partner near Fort Selkirk. The Northern Tutchone man said

236

that he did not have many furs because his wife had been sick and he could not go trapping. The Chilkat Indian did not believe him. He thought his partner had already traded his furs to somebody else, and he felt insulted. So he kicked the Yukon man. Then the Yukon Indians themselves grew angry. They killed the Chilkat man and four relatives who were packing goods for him, and ran off into the bush. For several years after that, the Northern Tutchone were afraid to meet the Coast Tlingit traders. They thought the Chilkats would ask for an equal number of Yukon Indians to be killed in order to pay for the Tlingit deaths. When the Chilkats arrived at their regular trading place each year nobody was there.

By this time the Chilkats desperately needed furs to trade to the Russians, and they wanted to make peace. The Yukon headman agreed to start trading again if the Chilkats would accept a payment in fur for their men who had been killed instead of demanding an equal number of Yukon Indian deaths. The Chilkats agreed, and everybody was happy once more. This happened not long before Robert Campbell arrived, heralding a major shift in the pattern of Yukon trade.

The Han Indians downstream from Fort Selkirk were lucky in being able to get white trade goods from several sources — from the Mackenzie and Peel River Indians or from Fort Yukon after Alexander Murray built his post there in 1847, as well as from Chilkat traders. Some Han warriors may even have helped the Chilkats plunder Campbell's store, for like the Coast Tlingit, the Han did not want the upper Yukon and Pelly River people to get white men's goods directly from Campbell. Each Indian group wanted to be the sole supplier of white men's goods to Indians farther away.

With the tobacco, guns, knives and kettles they got from the Coast Tlingit or Han, the upper Yukon Indians often went on trading trips of their own. For example, Southern Tutchone from Neskatahin and Aishihik would go to Pickhandle Lake or the White River, where they traded for furs with Upper Tanana Indians from what is today Alaska. And when Campbell left the country, in 1852, Tagish and Inland Tlingit Indians began to take the European goods they got from the Coast Tlingit to Little Salmon or Ross River and Pelly Banks. Inland Tlingit from the upper Taku River and Atlin Lake in British Columbia and from Teslin Lake in the Yukon traded with the ancestors of the Liard and Frances River Kaska.

By the 1870s, when independent white traders like Mayo, Harper and McQuesten had begun to set up their trading posts along the upper Yukon River, the Indians saw more and more white men passing through their country, and they sometimes bought things from them whether or not they were regular traders.

After the white traders settled in the Yukon, the Indians often had big gatherings in the spring near the trading posts where they sold their fur. Ross River Indians tell how people used to come together at Ross River from all around Ross River country and even from Norman Wells on the Mackenzie River too. George Smith says of the early 1900s:

*The Canol (short for Canadian Oil) Road was built by the U.S. Army during World War II to permit the laying of a pipeline from Norman Wells to Whitehorse. The pipeline was begun in 1942, completed in 1944, shut down in 1945 and then dismantled, but the road remains. Like most roads in the Yukon, it follows a route traditionally used by the Indians.

There used to be lots of people here. Old people told me about times, not too long ago, when there would be as many as two hundred tents spread out along the shores across the river at trading time. It would be tents almost as far as you could see. Then people would split up and go south in their boats.

People would meet here in the spring because three passes meet right at Ross River; people would go down to Teslin along the Canol* route; across the Cassiar Range to Watson Lake [where the Campbell Highway now goes], *or north to Fort Norman across the Mackenzie range. But, partly because so many people would congregate here, the flu epidemic in the early thirties was really bad and caused a lot of deaths here.*

Even if they were not trading, Yukon Indians always enjoyed travelling and meeting together whenever they could. A large gathering was a special event. In the old days, when two or three families had been off by themselves hunting or trapping all winter, they were eager to get to their spring and summer fish camps. Others were happy to spend a part of the winter together with other families in a big, warm winter house.

When people had not seen each other for a long time they always had lots of news to exchange. Moses Jackson told about it this way:

When people came back from the traplines in June, my people used to have lots of fun them days. I still remember there were ball games every day. And a dance, two, three times a week. And no drinking. All the oldtimers, like my uncle George Johnston — he was a fiddler — played for the dance. And when they see that steamboat coming up, there was a lot of fun for all the people. There was always a big dance that same night. And then we got our mail. . . .

*Isaac Taylor and William Drury, two prospectors from England, met on a gold claim near Atlin in 1898. In 1899 they went into partnership as traders, setting up a tent store at Lake Bennett, and in 1900 they established a store at Whitehorse. In the following years they established stores throughout the Yukon and operated riverboats as well.

The steamboat that came was the *Thistle,* run by Taylor & Drury.*

Mabel Johnston liked the summers at Teslin, because they were a change from the winters in the bush trapping with her family, but Christmas on the trapline was a special time for her too:

I never saw Teslin in the wintertime till I was 22 years old. I never been here in the wintertime at all. We didn't stay here much, just in the summertime. Then we used to live here happy. All the women would sit down somewhere and talk, you know. Tell each other what they had done all winter and what they were going to do. They were friendly. People had lots of time for each other. Maybe somebody would fix up somebody's grave and they had a big time over that. And then in the bay over here [Nisutlin Bay], *that's where they used to go washing every Saturday. They had fires, the women, and they'd heat the water and bathe the little kids, and put up a tent for the big ones. You go inside and take a bath. Yes, every Saturday. You scrub floors! Yup — everybody busy, scrubbing floors! And the next day we dress up and go to church.*

And after us kids were all married, that's my brother and his wife, and my sister Maggie, and me, and my older sister, we lived around up there near Wolf Lake where my dad used to trap all the time. And we used to come together Christmas time, to my daddy's house. We had this record player and we danced. Christmas Eve. Nothing to drink, but we had a good time. We danced.

Yukon native people were quick to adapt to new means of transportation when these were introduced. The riverboats, the highways and airplanes enabled them to travel farther or more easily and more often, and to invite friends to come from more distant places. Now as in the past, travelling about the country is an integral part of Yukon life, and so are special gatherings. Seeing many friends and relatives is part of the fun of the Sourdough Rendezvous held in Whitehorse today by whites and Indians alike. Indian Days, the Elders' Conference, other meetings sponsored by the CYI, and curling bonspiels are other modern events where Yukon Indians meet and enjoy themselves.

FIGHTING

The Yukon Indians sometimes used to fight each other in the old days. They also sometimes fought with the Coast Indians, the Inuvialuit, the Indians of the upper White River, and with bands from the Stikine and lower Liard. But there were never any pitched battles with large armies, of course, because there were never many Indians. Usually only a few people were killed in an enemy attack. The fighting took the form of skirmishes or raids to settle feuds, rather than full-scale warfare.

No small group of people can afford to lose many adults, so people thought carefully before going off on a raid. They knew that there would probably be a counterattack. Most of the time it was more important to hunt and fish than to make war.

The land was not privately owned in the old days, so the Indians did not often fight to conquer territory. Moreover, the clan and moiety system meant that everybody had relatives almost everywhere. This helped to prevent wars, and so did the partnership system. Why then did the Indians fight?

Perhaps they did it most often in order to avenge a murder. Murders did happen in the old days, and often they involved women. Sometimes one man took another man's wife, and the deprived husband then set out to kill him.

If a man killed a member of his own clan, the clan elders talked together and tried to settle the matter without also killing the murderer. They would propose, for instance, that the murderer's close matrilineal relatives pay the victim's close relatives for his death. The amount of this payment would depend on the rank of the victim.

If the victim and his killer were from clans of the same moiety, it might still be possible, but more difficult, to arrange a payment for the death. The price would likely be higher.

If, however, the murderer and his victim were of opposite moieties, only a full-scale peace ceremony could prevent further murders for revenge. The headmen of all the clans of both moieties would discuss how to solve the matter.

239

If the murderer's clan and the victim's clan could not agree to hold a formal peace ceremony, their members would begin to feud, attacking each other by surprise whenever they could. Such feuding might continue for years until both sides were ready to make peace. If the original murderer and victim were from the same area, usually only their two clans would feud with each other. But when Indians from different places were involved, entire bands might begin to fight one another.

There were reasons for feuding other than murder. The kidnapping of women was another cause all over the Yukon. As mentioned in Chapter Eight, it was not always easy to get a wife from the right clan or moiety. A wealthy chief might have many wives, but a poor young man had difficulty finding even one. So the young men sometimes tried to capture women from other parts of the country.

Women who were particularly good workers, skilled at sewing and clever at making a living, were considered particular prizes, and warriors sometimes raided their camps specifically to try to capture them. A few of these "smart women," as they were called, became quite famous, especially among the Loucheux. Some of them were captured again and again by men of different bands of Indians or Inuvialuit. Neil McDonald of Old Crow told a story about a Loucheux and Inuvialuit war over a "smart woman":

This is why the Indians and the Eskimos fought. The Eskimos used to steal one woman, a smart woman. They captured her and she came back after running away and told the Indian people where the Eskimos were. Her people almost killed all the Eskimos. The next year, the Eskimos came up and [tried to] do the same thing. One Indian man went up the creek in a canoe. The Eskimos saw the foam and bubbles and knew someone was on the river. This man went up river and put the canoe between the brush. He counted the canoes of the Eskimos with sticks. When they passed again he moved the sticks. Finally there were two sticks left. He waited a long time and finally they passed too. He went back to his camp and told the people that the Eskimos had returned. They always fought before daybreak. The Eskimos had camped on the beach. The Indians were in the brush. From each end, two men called out like an owl, so they all knew they were ready. They rushed down and [killed] them all. This was before they had guns. They used spears and arrows.

Another Old Crow story about a "smart woman" is told by Sarah Abel in Chapter Twelve.

Matters of honor and different kinds of insults also led to hostilities. Jealousy over the fur trade was also often involved. One such fight occured in the mid-nineteenth century between the Upper Tanana Indians living near Snag and the Southern Tutchone from Neskatahin and Dezadeash. The long feuding between these two groups is sometimes called the Snag War or "the war between Alaska and the Yukon." It began when the Snag Indians heard a rumor that one of their women, who had married a Southern

Tutchone trader, was being mistreated. Then the Neskatahin headman, Laan, insulted the Snag chief when the two groups were trading at Pickhandle Lake. Laan put his foot up on the back of the Snag chief's shirt saying he wanted a patch from it to mend his moccasins. The Snag chief said nothing, except that he would see the Neskatahin people "in the spring." That March he raided them when they were getting whitefish at Dezadeash Lake and killed all but a few who hid or who were away trading at Tagish. Southern and Northern Tutchone Indians still tell stories about this war, as do some of the neighboring Ahtna and Upper Tanana Indians in Alaska. The versions are not all exactly the same, because several incidents led to the fighting, and the attacks and counterattacks continued for years.

The weapons used in war were bows and arrows, copper or bone knives that were sometimes attached to long poles to serve as spears, and antler clubs that were soaked in grease to make them heavy. These were all dangerous, but except for the bow and arrow they had to be used at close range. Because there were not many people in the Yukon, and people in different groups were related through blood and marriage, a warrior sometimes recognized someone he was about to club or stab. A fighter might spare an enemy whom he knew was a close relative or a member of his own clan.

For bodily protection, some Yukon Indians had flexible armor made of wooden slats sewed together with heavy moosehide. This worked well against arrows and spears and often saved the wearer's life.

Because a raid was such a serious matter, a council of older men usually met to discuss the action beforehand. If they agreed to dispatch a war party, each man could decide for himself whether or not he wanted to join it. No one was ever forced to fight, because the luck of the warriors depended on the spiritual readiness of everyone on the raid.

The war party had a leader — or several leaders, if men from several clans were going to fight together. Experienced fighters were chosen to plan and command the raids, so the leaders of war parties were not always the local groups' regular headmen. Sometimes a kin group that wanted revenge even hired well-known warriors from elsewhere.

Before they left their camp, warriors usually painted their faces and danced. Along the trail to the enemy's camp, they practised for battle, jumping about as if they were dodging arrows, and running. They also tested their courage by dangerous feats such as killing bears with spears. People and bears were thought to be almost the same kind of beings and were hunted with the same weapons.

Warriors also followed a special diet when they were on their way to attack. Southern Tutchone or Kaska warriors ate only raw meat before the fight. This was the kind of food that wild animals ate, and the warriors were acting like wolves or bears hunting their prey. It is said that during "the war between Alaska and the Yukon," a Snag war party, on the way to Dezadeash Lake, killed some mountain sheep. The warriors ate the sheep meat raw, but one man could not bring himself to do so — and he was the only Snag person killed in the raid.

Just as when their husbands were hunting bears, mountain goats or mountain sheep in dangerous places, the women who remained back in camp had to behave very carefully when their husbands were out on a raid. Tagish women, for example, sat very quietly until their husbands returned. People thought that if a woman moved about and accidentally hurt herself, her husband would be injured in the same spot. Once an Inland Tlingit woman hit her forehead on the fish rack while her husband was on a raid, and it is said that an arrow struck him in exactly the same place.

The Indian doctor played an important part in war. He usually stayed in camp instead of accompanying the war party, but while the women sang songs to make his powers strong, he sent out his animal spirit-helpers to confuse the enemy warriors and fight against the spirit-helpers of the enemy shamans. A doctor could send a fog to hide the attacking war party, or blind the enemy, or make a person forget to report to others in camp an accidental noise made by the raiders before the attack. It was believed that the doctor could also predict what would happen — who would win or lose and how many men would be wounded or killed, but he gave his information in a kind of riddle talk that the people did not always understand.

When people expected that their camps might be raided, they sometimes built their brush shelters with special hiding places for children in the walls, or made secret holes for them in the snowbanks. During the Snag War, one woman saved herself by crawling under a pile of skins, and she survived to become the grandmother of many of the Champagne Indians.

Fighting could be very costly for both sides. Oldtimers say they are glad that the Indians no longer fight each other. It took time that people needed for getting their food. Hunters were killed, women kidnapped, and nobody felt safe. Sooner or later those who were at war always tried to make peace.

PEACEMAKING

The Inland Tlingit, Tagish and some Southern Tutchone usually made peace through an elaborate Coast-Tlingit-style ceremony called _guwakaan_, which means _deer_. Deer are very rare in the Yukon, but the hostages taken in raids by these groups were called deer, perhaps because deer are very peaceable animals. In the peacemaking ceremony, these "deer" were given peaceful names, such as Sunshine, and special hats and clothing to symbolize peace.

A peacemaking ceremony of this type had two parts, each sometimes lasting several days. It was a tense affair, for if anything went wrong, the fighting would start again. Speechmaking, singing, dancing and feasting all took place. The chiefs and their advisors on both sides tried to equalize the losses of each group. Sometimes this required another death. If a high-ranking person from one side had been killed, then a high-ranking person from the other side would walk out where everybody could see him. His former enemies then speared him or shot him with bows and arrows. Sometimes a younger man would offer himself as a sacrifice in place of an important older brother or uncle. Such bravery earned him great praise.

If the two sides decided to settle through payments rather than additional deaths, there would be a formal exchange of goods. After the payments were agreed upon, the "deer" went to stay in the houses of their former enemies. There, they were treated as full members of the enemy clan and moiety, and special attendants were provided to take care of them. The "deer" could only use their right hands; their left hands were said to hold bad luck.

Hostages usually stayed only four days with the opposite side if the matter to be settled were a local quarrel between two clans. However, after a full-scale war between groups living in different places, the "deer" might stay with their former enemies for as long as two years. Hostages might even marry and raise children among their former enemies, and sometimes might not even want to go home, because of having to leave their new friends, wives and children.

At the closing peace ceremony, each "deer" had to dance alone while everybody watched. He composed a special song and wore the special headdress that was linked to his deer name. It was usually something meant to bring good luck, such as a miniature fishtrap or an emblem of sun. Bird down floated out of the hat while the hostage danced, to symbolize peace. If the hostage made any mistakes in his singing and dancing, this spoiled the ceremony and the people might start to fight again. After the "deer" had danced, members of the two groups making peace also danced and gave mock war cries. When they parted, the hostilities were over.

Peacemaking ceremonies were important not only for concluding feuds. Yukon Indian hunters used to treat the corpses of bears, wolverine and some other animals just as if they were making peace with them. Hunters wanted no bad feelings between themselves and the powerful spirits of these animals. Southern Tutchone from Champagne and Aishihik used to tell how a Klukshu Indian who had killed too many grizzly bears once made a peace ceremony with the leader of the bears.

GAMES

Yukon Indians did not spend all of their time looking for food, honoring the dead, trading, fighting, or making peace. Whenever people got together and living was good, the Yukon Indians had a lot of fun, and one thing they did was to play games.

Many of their games were competitive. Neil McDonald of Old Crow has told about Loucheux foot races and tugs-of-war, in which people pulled from opposite ends of a rope or tapered stick. Target shooting was also popular, both with adults and with children.

The Northern and Southern Tutchone played a game like volley-ball. The ball was made of tanned skin stuffed with animal hair, and a marten tail or some bird down was attached to it so that it streamed out behind like the tail of a kite when the ball was thrown. Men and women tried to keep the ball going in the air. In these kinds of competitive games, people from opposite clans or moieties used to line up against each other.

The Loucheux were great wrestlers. Every man in the camp wrestled in turn until a champion was determined, and his prize was sometimes a wife. The women wrestled too, to find who was best among them.

Other games tested individual skills. One was the ring and pin game. Five caribou toebones were strung on a cord with a piece of caribou skin full of holes on one end and a bone needle on the other. The player tried to pin the bones or piece of skin with the needle. Players kept score with little sticks.

Neil McDonald describes another favorite, the bouncing game:

They made the trampoline out of strong, untanned moosehide. They tied thongs to each corner of the hide and tied the thongs to trees. This piece of hide was about one foot square. A man got on top of this and jumped. People pulled on the ropes. This was to see who could go the highest. Some people were experts.

Sometimes among the Southern Tutchone everyone in camp would hold the edge of a big moose skin, using it to bounce a man up in the air to see how long he could stay upright.

Gambling was very popular, and almost any game could involve gambling. For example, in the ring and pin game, the score was kept with sticks and whoever had the most sticks at the end of the game won. People bet on wrestling matches, target shooting or skin bouncing.

Perhaps the most famous gambling game was the stick game. Many Yukon Indians agree that the Mackenzie River Indians were best at this game, but Yukon Indians played too, at Lansing, Ross River, Pelly Crossing, Little Salmon, Aishihik, Champagne, and probably many other places. Solomon Charlie said that the Southern Tutchone of Champagne had their own special gambling house in the early twentieth century, and there may have been others elsewhere.

In playing the stick game, one team of players tried to prevent the other side from guessing who was holding the stick. The team members lined up and passed the stick between themselves, always trying to fool the other side. Each team had a skilled drummer at the end of the line, and everybody sang lively gambling songs. This added to the pace and excitement of the game. The leader of the team that was watching tried to guess who on the opposite team had the stick. If he guessed correctly, the team that was hiding the stick gave him a counting stick. If he guessed wrong, the leader of the guessing team had to give up one of his own sticks. The teams played until one side had won all of the other side's sticks. The counting sticks were often of carved bone with engraved designs. Stick games could be very exciting and last a long time. Players tried to find out who had the stick by staring into the eyes of their opponents or clapping their hands quickly to surprise the opposite side into showing where the stick was.

Both men and women gambled, but men more than women. When the Indians began to work on the riverboats they almost always gambled when they were ashore. Oldtimers gambled for shells, beads, skins and other kinds of wealth. Of course in more recent times money was used. Solomon Charlie said that some people lost all their belongings by gambling and became slaves. Later they tried to win back their freedom in other gambling games.

The big stick-gambling games were like potlatches in some ways. They brought together many people from different places and involved a lot of social interaction. Often there was reciprocal feasting, singing and dancing, and those who were good performers had a chance to show their skills. People exchanged news and made new friends from other places.

SEASONAL FESTIVALS

Before the Indians learned of the white man's Christmas, they had their own kind of holidays around the time of the winter solstice, December 21. Oldtime Yukon Indians talk about this period as "Indian Christmas."

All over the Yukon people seem to have stayed in their camps during Indian Christmas and told stories to each other and perhaps asked riddles. In every household someone made a "fishing pole" — that is, a long pole with a string on one end and a big hook on the end of the string. The members of each household in turn walked about the camp, stopping outside of everyone else's house. Each person travelling with the pole whistled out a message to signify what kind of present he or she wanted, and then dropped the fishhook down the smokehole. The people inside the house had to guess what the whistles meant. Maybe an important man would want a fur or some meat or, after the fur trade, even a gun. The people inside the house had to try to give it to him. They had to keep putting presents on the hook until they guessed what it was the whistler wanted. If they guessed wrong, the person with the pole dropped whatever was on the hook back through the smokehole. When those who had been fishing got the presents they wanted, they went back home and waited for the other families to come "fish" at their house. During this week of Indian Christmas, the headman tried to give all his people fine presents and to provide a large feast.

The Kaska Indians had what they called the Biggest Cache Feast, also in December. At this event, whoever had the most groundhogs and gophers fed everybody else huge birchbark baskets full of meat and grease. Sometimes the Crow people joked with the Wolves by inviting them to a feast and then setting out only a few scraps of food. The guests called this a "wolverine party." Afterwards, the

Johnny Joe with gambling sticks, Marsh Lake, 1982

Jake Jackson with drum, Teslin, 1951

Crows would give a real feast. It was up to the best hunters to arrange these parties, for only they could provide the meat required.

We know less about other oldtime Yukon Indian festivals. It is likely that those groups who depended heavily on salmon had a special feast when the first salmon arrived each year. We know that the Southern Tutchone did this at Klukshu. People dressed in their good clothes, painted their faces, and shared a meal of salmon. There may also have been special ceremonies for everyone in camp when the first big game of each kind was killed in the new hunting season each year, but unfortunately even the oldest Yukon Indians seem to have forgotten almost everything about such festivals.

SINGING AND DANCING

The Yukon Indians were excellent song composers and singers. At every potlatch and festival there was singing and dancing, and people sang and danced at other times as well.

Composers made up songs to mark special events in the life of a single person or of the group. Songs might come to those who were lonesome, sad, or glad. A young woman who missed her lover, a mother mourning for her daughter, an old man who had talked to the wolves around his camp, a stranger who was lonely for his country, or a successful warrior might suddenly hear a new tune in his or her head. Then the person would add some words. Sometimes the tune would seem to come because a loon flew by or because the water was gurgling beside the pole where a boat was tied.

Mothers made up lullabies for their babies, and some people made joking songs for their father's people. There were songs for mourning and for war dances. Other songs were parts of clan stories and could only be sung by clan members or others who had their permission. Songs of this kind were sung at memorial potlatches.

As mentioned earlier, the Indian doctors also had special songs that came to them from their spirit powers, and they liked to have everybody join in singing these songs because it gave them more power when they were doctoring.

Some of the well-known song composers among the older Yukon Indians of recent days were Jimmy Johnson of Burwash Landing and Old Fox of Teslin. There were many others too in the past, and song composing is still an important art.

Singing was often accompanied by drumming. The drummers beat planks or skin drums when people danced and sang. These planks were generally flattened and painted with red ochre, and the beating sticks had tufts of feathers tied to the ends. Several men could beat on the plank together. Both the Loucheux and Inland Tlingit had these kinds of plank drums, and probably the other Yukon Indians did too.

Skin drums were made of untanned caribou or moose hide. A piece of wet hide was stretched over a circular wooden frame, and laced onto it with strings of babiche that crossed in the back to form a

246

Albert Isaac carving a drumstick,
Aishihik, 1963

kind of handle so the drummer could easily hold the drum. Sometimes the drumstick was carved in a fancy shape; sometimes it was a
thick stick, and sometimes a thin stick curved into a small open circle
at the end.

Some Old Crow Loucheux say that their ancestors never had
their own songs or made skin drums, but got them from either the
Inuvialuit or the Yukon River Indians. Myra Moses has told how a
Loucheux man who was giving a feast once got a drum:

*I heard that one guy made a feast. He really wanted to have fun, but he didn't
know how. Hudson's Bay Company had aluminum dishes. This man started
hitting this dish and they had a dance this way. This was the only dish he
had and when he was through hitting it, it was all warped up. The Indians
didn't have skin drums. Only the Eskimo had these. There was nothing for
this old man after he finished off this dish. It was the only dish he had.*

Perhaps the Loucheux actually did have drums in the early days
but gave up making them after the Anglican missionaries arrived and
spoke out against native songs.

There were several kinds of dances. In Tlingit-style dances, the
men and women often stood in two lines facing each other while a
leader for each line marked the rhythm by raising and lowering a

247

Old Fox, Jake Jackson, Annie Fox and Chief William Johnson at Sports Day, Teslin, 1949. Old Fox is in the foreground at left, wearing grizzly bear ears and waving swans' wings. (Photo by Dorothy Rainier)

song pole that was like a big paddle carved and painted with clan crests. The dancers lifted their feet in place and moved their outstretched arms from side to side, keeping their palms up.

Other Yukon Indian dances imitated birds or other animals. The dancers might pretend to be grouse mating or crows picking at a dead person, or warriors. A dance could tell a story, or celebrate a victory, or be a lively circle dance for both men and women. Often the leader had a short dance pole called a *gunho,* decorated with feathers and ribbons.

People were always on the lookout for a new song or dance to add to their repertoire. After the fur traders came, Yukon natives began to do square dances, jigs, and later on, polkas, waltzes and two-steps. Almost every young Indian boy learned to play the fiddle, the guitar, the mouth organ or the accordian; then he could take his turn in the orchestras that played for the village dances in the white man's style.

STORYTELLING, SPEECHMAKING AND JOKING

Storytelling and speechmaking were among the most important traditional arts in the Yukon. The collections of Yukon Indian stories that have been published in this century attest to the rich variety of stories and the great skill of the old storytellers. You can read a few of the traditional stories in Chapters Eleven and Twelve of this book but they are just a very small sample of the many good ones that have been passed down by word of mouth for many hundreds of years. Good storytellers usually change their voices to suit the characters or act out parts in a story, and this makes it more interesting and exciting to hear the stories than to read them.

Wintertime was best for storytelling, since in summer everybody was busy outside. When it was cold and dark in winter, families sat around the fires in their houses, and each person could take a turn telling a story. The highest-ranking older people began, but sometimes even the children would tell a tale. People might tell stories all night long, and for a week or more at a time.

The Yukon Indians had great respect for a good storyteller or speechmaker. The fame of such a person, who could teach all of the people important history and other knowledge, spread through the country. Well-known orators were called upon to make speeches at potlatches and peacemaking ceremonies, or when Indians were trading. They not only instructed, but also entertained their audiences and made them laugh. Young men listened very carefully to the stories and speeches they heard when they were far from home. When they returned, they could tell stories nobody else knew, and they could begin to practise the art of oratory themselves, using the high language of the speechmakers. Leaders tried to see that their smartest young nephews travelled about specifically in order to learn Indian history and wisdom from good orators. Part of a chief's power came from the way he talked to the people in the camp early each morning.

A person who could use words to persuade others to act wisely, who could calm those who were angry and raise the spirits of those who were sad, was of great value. One who could entertain people with a good story or song, and add to the fun with a good joke, was well liked. Those with a good sense of humor never got angry when their sisters-in-law, brothers-in-law, fathers-in-law or paternal "second cousins" joked with them. In the old days, those relatives were *supposed* to joke, and they did a lot of it. In the world of the traditional Yukon Indians, as elsewhere, some people were bad-tempered and some were stuck-up — but such people simply showed how important it was to be able to laugh, and how valuable to have "joking relatives."

There was much more to traditional Indian life than simply an endless round of hunting and fishing. Making a living from the land always required skill, ingenuity and unexpected adjustments, and the yearly round always included feasts or potlatches, trade and travel and seasonal festivals. Sometimes it included feuding and peacemaking ceremonies as well. There was plenty of room for the expression of individual talent and character, not only through the making of clothing, tools and weapons, but through singing and dancing, storytelling and oratory, and managing the social ceremonies that were part of the Indian world in earlier days.

11

The Old People's Worldview

How did the old people think their world was put together? What did they say about the existence and nature of other worlds? Where did they think power came from? What beings did they value and admire, and what kinds of human behavior did they cherish? What did they fear or despise?

A people's *worldview* means the picture or vision they have, not just of their immediate surroundings, but of the universe and everything in it — the sun, the moon, the stars, the mountains and rivers, plants and animals, spirits, humans, other creatures and other worlds. Worldview means a people's understanding of how the many things that exist are related to one another. It also means a people's system of values — that is, their beliefs about what is good and what is bad. So it includes their beliefs about how they should act toward one another, toward other beings, and toward themselves.

A worldview is something a person builds up slowly over a lifetime. It is hard to talk directly about such important matters, and most people express their worldview indirectly, by the way they act, by the choices they make and by the stories they tell. But a people's worldview is the very heart of their culture, because it gives order and meaning to life. It guides what people do and shapes their emotions. It is their worldview that the elders try to pass on to the young.

Each society has a unique worldview, but as times change, worldviews may also change. Historical events sometimes even bring in new ideas so fast that for some individuals the whole world seems to lose its meaning and they themselves lose their direction. In such times, the old and young find that they no longer share the same ideas about the nature of the universe and how to behave in it. Their values may differ sharply. Some people become very unhappy during such times. Some grow angry or discouraged when they see the old ways changing. Others find pleasure and excitement in trying to fit together whatever seems best of both the old and the new ideas.

The ideas described in the next pages are primarily those of the Yukon natives in the nineteenth and early twentieth centuries. Indians of today will see that some ideas and values have changed sharply since the old days, while others still stand strong. Yukon Indians reading this book in the 1980s and 1990s might well ask themselves what new ideas of good and bad have been added to native thought and the native way of life since the turn of the century.

250

Those who are are not Indians may ask themselves the same question.

So far, the Yukon Indians have been quite successful in fitting their old and new experiences together into an organized pattern of thinking and living. Unlike some peoples of the world, they have been quite willing to try out ideas and objects borrowed from others. At the same time, they have managed to retain important concepts from their traditional heritage.

The beliefs and values discussed in this chapter are only a small part of the Yukon Indian worldview. The traditional worldview is a very complex system of ideas — much larger and more sophisticated than can be explained here. It is also one that nobody will ever know completely. Though Indians all over the Yukon shared a good many ideas and values, each local group gave certain ideas special emphasis and flavor, and each group had some ideas unique to its own members. This was true of individuals also. No one Yukon native ever knew all of the beliefs held by others even in his own band, let alone those of all the Yukon Indians.

In the old days, people rarely told all that they knew in public. They understood that their knowledge was their wealth, and they felt that it had to be taken care of, not just scattered about for nothing. Some knowledge had to be kept in family lines. Other knowledge could be sold or bought by anybody. Young men used to pay older men for secret powers and songs for hunting or other kinds of good luck, just as people paid Indian doctors for help in curing someone or locating game.

The old people were also careful to protect those whom they thought might be harmed by certain kinds of knowledge. They believed, for example, that women and children were usually not strong enough to hold much spirit power. They were afraid the power might backfire on such persons and make them sick, so they seldom taught songs or words for power to women and children.

Nowadays there is a further difficulty in learning about the traditional worldview, and that is the problem of translation. The Indian people who helped to make this book often spoke of how difficult it is to translate well from their native languages to English. This is so not just for single words or for complicated ideas. The elders say it is hard just to tell their traditional stories properly when they tell them in English. Even so, many Indian stories have lasted very well in translation. They have lasted partly because of the artistry used in their retelling, but also because they have so many strong ideas and concepts embedded in them. The more the reader or listener thinks about them, the better he can understand how important and dramatic these stories are. He can learn a great deal from them about the traditional Indian worldview. The values expressed in the oldtime stories still direct the lives of many Indian people today. Each one of the stories is a treasure.

In this book there is room for only a few of the old stories. Some of the best traditional stories have been published in other books, either by Yukon Indians themselves or by non-Indians who wrote

251

them down as the natives told them. Many others have not been written down. In this chapter and the next, however, are several important oldtime stories that people wanted to tell just for this book. In addition, there are stories that some people wanted to tell about their own experiences. These accounts, just like the traditional stories, tell and show how to treat the land, the water and the animals. They emphasize desirable qualities such as cooperation, generosity, self-reliance and moderation. They tell a great deal about the traditional worldview.

The elders who contributed to this book also often remarked on how people trained themselves in the old days to remember what they heard, because it was by listening to stories and retelling them that the Indians learned and passed on much of what they knew about the world. Tom Peters, an Inland Tlingit of Teslin, said:

In the old days . . . those oldtimers were smart. They never had a pencil like you got in your hand. They never had it — just a mind, that's all. If someone is going to speak about some trouble, well, an old guy like me, we going to sit down. And the first word they are going to speak, I'm going to catch what he really is speaking about. That's how it used to be. They never take a paper and look at the paper first. Just our minds. In this country we know a lot of things, right from the beginning.

THE CREATION OF THE WORLD

Every people has its own ideas about the complexity of the universe. The traditional Yukon Indians believed that the universe contained several different worlds — worlds of the animal spirit powers, worlds of the soul-spirits of humans who had died, worlds on the other side of the horizon or in the sky, a world of living humans, and perhaps other worlds as well. And the people did not think that any of these worlds was unchanging. They said that things were very different long ago, before the universe came to be as it is now, and they told a number of stories about how the world of human beings — the world they knew best — acquired its present form. Many groups of Yukon Indians said that Crow (the same being as the Raven of the Coast Indians) had much to do with this.

In the old stories, Crow sometimes seems to look like a human, but at other times he looks and acts like a bird. Other characters with animal names also could take off their animal masks and skins — their animal clothes — or had not yet put them on.

Even today, almost every Yukon Indian knows at least one Crow story, and a few elders can still tell Crow stories for a week or more, because there are so many. Some of these Crow stories are serious and others are very funny. Often they are a mixture of both serious and comic happenings. The old people said that while Crow was fixing up the world as a suitable place to live, he often fooled people or was himself fooled by others. The stories tell the consequences of his foolishness as well as his intelligence. The stories are amusing, but also they are warnings.

Every good storyteller tells the traditional stories in his or her own way, so no story exists in only one version. Jessie Joe, a Southern Tutchone of Burwash, told this version of how Crow made the human world:

He [Crow] started. The waters flood. He can't do nothing. All the game there is gone. He don't know where to go — just fly around — to get a rest. He's going to drown himself. He flies around, he gets tired.

He sees the stars, so he flies up to the sky. He finds a star, and he puts his nose through it. He just hangs there. And from there he takes a good rest.

Then he starts to fly again. And from there, I don't know how far, he sees something bright like, in the water. So he goes to that.

He comes there. He comes close, and he sees a fire burning. A fire is burning. And he come closer, and he sees a woman sitting there in the waters, on top of just a little piece of the world. It's the same size as her. And the fire is going. Where did she get the wood from? It must be she got some sticks and made a little fire, I guess. She's got a little baby beside her, alongside of her.

Crow sees that, and he thinks, ''I'll grab that kid where he's sitting there.'' He flies. He grabs that kid like that.

''My baby!'' she says. She turns around; she tries to grab him.

''Give me my baby,'' she says.

''No, I want your baby,'' he says. ''I want to take your kid.''

He hangs on to that kid. He says, ''Where did you get this, what you are sitting on here? You sit on this land. Where did you get it from? I want you to get that same kind for me wherever you got it from''

They call that lady Sea Woman. She's in the ocean. She reaches for that kid.

''Let that kid go now, I want to go home!''

''No,'' he says, ''I want this kid.''

''That's my baby, don't take it!''

''You get a piece of it [the land] for me.''

''No, I can't do that,'' she says, ''You'll take my baby away. You won't be here when I come back.''

''No,'' he says, ''I won't do that. I'm going to stay here, and I'm going to wait for you.''

Oh, I don't know how long he's been there, maybe twenty-four hours. He's hanging on to that kid. And he told her, ''I want a piece of what you are sitting on here. . . .'' He says, ''You get this kind of ground here, this kind, for me, and you'll get your baby back.''

Finally, after I don't know how many days, he talks to her good. Finally, she says, ''Long ways to get that,'' she says. ''It takes quite a while.''

I'll be here,'' he says.

She goes in the water. She comes back again. She comes out.

''I wouldn't go away from here,'' he says, ''I'm going to be here.''

She goes in the water. She looks back again. She comes out.

''I wouldn't go away from here,'' he told her. ''I wouldn't go away from here. I'm going to be here.''

Ah, she tries again. She comes back again to check up.

''I wouldn't go away from here, I'm going to be here. Where do you think

I'm going to go? There's water all over!'' he told her. ''Well, I'm going to keep this kid here, and I'm going to be here until you bring that piece like you sit on here.''

Well, she went down. That's quite a while.

She comes back. She's got a small piece.

''Well, that's too small,'' he told her. ''I won't go away from here, I told you that,'' he says. ''You see all the water around here? I can't go away.'' He says, ''You think I'm crazy, I'm going to take this kid and put it on my back? And I get tired myself? I won't take it,'' he told her.

She believes him.

''I want a bigger piece,'' he told her. ''I want one the same size as this one here.''

Quite a while later she brings a big chunk, I don't know how big, but she got it out.

She got that baby there, and she went to the water. She goes.

And him, Crow there, he walks around that ground there. And he made the ground flat, just like a pancake [of] mud. He's doing that and doing that. He makes it bigger and bigger. He made the world that's here. He made the world. Crow made the world. That's what everybody says anyway.

In this story, as in many Yukon Indian stories, nothing happens until the fourth request or the fourth try. Many oldtime rituals and other events were also ordered in sets of four. Some Indians believed that the emphasis on the numbers four, or eight, symbolized the ideal makeup of a whole human person with two arms and two legs, each made of two large bones. Their worldview, like that of many other American Indians, stressed the number four.

The woman in Jessie's story is not given an animal name, but in some other Crow stories about the creation of the world, the keeper of the earth is said to have been a sea lion. In other versions, the one who dives for more earth is different from the being guarding the original floating piece of the world. In some versions, many animals dive and the one who succeeds may be a beaver, a muskrat or an otter.

A Loucheux from Fort McPherson told yet another version of this story to the geologist Charles Camsell in 1905. He said that Crow put his walking stick into the water so the earth could rest on it and that the walking stick never rotted, but could still be seen at the confluence of the Old Crow and Porcupine rivers.

Lucy Wren, a Tagish woman of Carcross, explained how Crow began to arrange the world for human beings. Her story tells how he got the sun, moon and daylight and also why animals look the way they do today and do not talk like people anymore.

Then Crow goes again. You know, he walks by himself, all over. He's been all over the whole world. There were lots of bad persons long time ago. Crow straightened everything out. You know, some things that eat people and some things that are hard for people, he straightens them out. That's what Crow did first time, long time ago.

254

You know at that time all the animals and everything, they talked just like us, like people. There were no people in the world hardly, just animals. So, well, he's walking, and while he's walking he hears something. It wasn't daytime then. It was dark all the time, no sun and no moon. It's dark all the time. So he doesn't know how he's going to steal it.

That bigshot that has the sun and that moon and that daylight, he's got a daughter. That man has got a daughter. So this Crow, he thinks, ''I wish I could steal it [sun, moon and daylight].*''*

So he makes himself turn to a little brush needle, one little needle.

This girl always drinks water. She comes to drink water, this girl, you know, with a little cup or something to drink water. So everytime she's going to put this water up to drink it, there's this little brush needle in there. All the time she takes it out. Then when she's going to drink it, it comes back again. Just when she's going to drink it, she can't drink that water. It keeps on like that. Pretty soon she gets tired of it, and she drinks the water with that thing in it. She drinks it down.

And that was Crow in there. And then he makes himself into a baby, and that girl gets pregnant. Crow makes a baby.

So her mom and dad ask her how she got that baby. She told her dad and her mom she doesn't know how. She has never been with anybody.

That was Crow, see?

Pretty soon, about nine months later, she started and got a little baby boy. And that's that man's little grandson. Boy, that man really loved his little grandson!

And that boy, he starts crawling around, and he grows fast too.

So that little boy, he crawls around, walks around, I guess. And he sees that moon and that sun up there. You know that man got it inside that place.

And so this baby, he sure likes that moon. He always looks at that moon, and he always cries. Everytime he cries he wants to get that moon. Oh, that little baby cries, cries, cries, cries. He can't sleep. So he wants that moon. He wants to play with it, you know.

Oh, his grandpa feels sorry for his grandson. He says, ''Take it down,'' he says. ''Let him play with it. My grandson cries too much.''

They take that moon down, and they give it to him. Boy, and he's happy! Then he plays with it, rolls it around just like the moon, just like a ball, something like this.

He plays with it, and he's happy, playing. He watches everybody; he looks at everybody. When everybody is not looking, he drops that moon, and he throws it up like that. And that moon is gone! That moon is way up there in the sky!

That man lost his moon to his grandson. That's why he didn't want anybody to touch it before. Well, he's got nothing to say. He never says anything, because he loves his grandson.

So maybe two days later the grandson sees that sun. He cries again. He wants to get that sun. He cries, cries, cries, cries! He won't eat. He won't do anything, sleep, nothing. He just cries for that sun. Oh, his grandpa feels sorry for him, so they took it down and give it to him again. He does the same thing. That sun is gone too!

So the man has got that daylight in something like a little suitcase with a cover on it. And everytime he closes it, it's dark, and there is no daytime, nothing. As soon as you start to open it a little bit, you could see it's start to getting daytime. So he keeps that so nobody touches it in there.

So this Crow he wants to get that too. He wants to get that so that he can make daytime. He doesn't like it dark all the time. So pretty soon he sees that thing there. It's just like this tape recorder, I guess. Oh, he cries, cries, cries, cries! Oh, and his grandpa feels sorry, so they give it to him so he can play with it on the ground, inside, I guess, where they staying.

But as soon as he started to shut it, it's dark again.

He keeps doing that, you know, just playing around with it. While nobody else is looking, he just drops that suitcase, and he flies through an opening. You know how Crow flies?

Now Crow's gone! He's got that thing.

Now that man has got nothing left — no sun, no moon, nothing!

So just a little ways down, just a little ways down, Crow flies and he stops. Now he's happy because he's going to have daytime. He thinks, ''I wonder what time I should open that thing, so I can get daytime, and what time I'm going to close it up and it's going to get dark again?'' So that's the way he's thinking.

Boy, he hears lots of people talking! In this meadow back there, lots of people are talking back there. They are playing ball or something. I don't know what they are doing.

All the animals, you know, they talk like us, like people. It's dark all the time then. Lots of people play that day, and he goes there. And he's got that thing. He sits down, and he watches them play out there. All the animals, they are playing out there in the meadow.

He says in the Indian way, he says, ''You guys make too much noise, I'm going to make day, and it's not going to be dark all the time! You guys make too much noise!'' He keeps on telling them that, but they don't listen to him, you know.

And pretty soon they hear him. They say, ''Who's that talking?'' they say.

''I don't know, I hear a duck or something talking.''

Crow says, ''If you guys don't smarten up, I'm going to make daytime! You folks won't have any fun playing up there!'' he says.

So they don't know who that is. They don't go check or anything.

Pretty soon now he says he's going to make day. He's going to open that thing.

Well, up there just like that, all the animals are playing. He opens that thing. He opens it right up, and then we got daytime just like this. He opens it right up, and all the animals playing up there, this one, and this one runs into the bush. Each says, ''Me, I'm going to be moose!'' ''Me, I'm going to be fox!'' ''Me, I'm going to be bear!'' ''Me, I'm going to be sheep!'' ''Squirrel'' — everything. They all run in the bush.

''Me, I'm going to be that, and that!'' And then there was no more daytime.

And those animals don't talk any more. Because it's dark all the time before, the animals talked.

That's why now it's daytime and then nighttime and then daytime. But long time ago there was no daytime. It was just dark all the time.

And then all the animals didn't talk anymore. They turned into real animals. And then they all went in the bush.

And him, Crow, he just stayed alone again. So that's how he steals daytime and the moon and everything.

The last story helps to explain why the animals are out and about while people are asleep. The nighttime of humans, the story says, is the daytime of the animals. This in turn helps to explain why the oldtimers said the animal spirits have their greatest power at night. That is why the Indian doctor used to dream or doctor in the nighttime. His animal spirit powers could come to him then and be at their strongest.

Another thing we can learn from these two Crow stories is how much mothers love their babies and how fond grandparents are of their grandchildren. However, in the story of the man who owned the light, we also find out that if a man spoils his grandson by giving him everything he wants, the man may lose his most valued possessions. And we learn from the second story that it is a good idea to pay attention to what other people are saying to you, even if you are busy playing. After his fourth warning to the animals, Crow went ahead with his plan, even though the animal people weren't listening. If you find an elder to tell you a whole set of Crow stories, you will realize that they show the consequences of many kinds of behavior, both good and bad.

Along with their Crow stories, the Kaska, Inland Tlingit, Tagish and some of the Southern Tutchone had a tradition that the first game animals were born to Animal Mother. Long ago, they say, she rocked each kind of animal on a big moosehide swing strung up between four mountain peaks and gave them the forms they have today. Before that, rabbits had antlers, but Animal Mother gave these to the moose, and she took the sharp teeth from the upper jaw of the moose and gave them to the grizzly bear. She told the animals where to live and what kinds of food to eat. According to some old people, the stony nest where Animal Mother retired to give birth to the animals was high in the Three Aces Mountains near Teslin.

Another set of stories known throughout the southern Yukon is about Beaver Doctor (also called Wise Man or Smart Man). He travelled down the Yukon River, killing all the animals that used to eat human beings, or else making them small and ordering them to eat what they eat today. Like Crow, Animal Mother and Beaver Doctor both made the world a better place for Indians to live. Marge Jackson of Haines Junction tells part of the Beaver Doctor story in Chapter Twelve.

All over the Yukon the old people also used to tell about two brothers who travelled about the world having adventures. In some versions the two brothers float away on a cake of ice with their little dog; in others only one of the brothers survives, and he travels in a canoe. According to some Southern and Northern Tutchone, Beaver Doctor himself was one of these two brothers. In any case, the adventures of the brothers are similar to those of Beaver Doctor. The heroes kill dangerous animals or monsters, and they teach people how to eat and give birth to babies as humans do today. The Loucheux tell of a hero named Ataachookaii, who had many adventures along the Mackenzie River. For a while he was married to both Light Woman and Dark Woman, and he and Light Woman had a ptarmigan baby. Then he crossed over the mountains and went down the Stewart River to the Yukon and on down the Yukon River in his canoe.

Another series of Yukon Indian stories tells about spirit powers in rocks or mountains or the sky. One widespread tale is about two girls who marry stars that look like handsome young men. When the girls get homesick they have a hard time reaching earth, but they manage through their own wits to get back to their families. Gayle Olsen of Ross River tells a version of this story in Chapter Twelve. In such stories, people who visit other worlds often find that things are different from or opposite to things in the human world. Sometimes the animals look like humans and use wet wood to make fires; and not only are night and day reversed, but what seems like four days turns out to be, in human time, four months or four years.

SPIRIT POWERS

All the traditional Yukon Indians thought there were many spirit powers in the universe, some far more powerful than the spirit powers of humans. The old stories do not make it altogether clear whether the spirit powers had worlds of their own and just came to the human world when needed, or whether some of them always stayed in some part of the human world. In any case, every Indian depended on these spirit powers for a good life. It was believed that the spirit powers could give good luck or added powers to humans, helping them in many different ways. The problem was that each Indian had to behave in the right way in order to get the spirit power's help. Then everything would go well. But if a person did the wrong things or had wrong thoughts about the spirit powers, everything would go badly.

The Indians said that almost anything could have this quality of power, because it came from spirits that could be in almost anything. It could be in a mountain, a lake, an animal, a human being, an arrow, a bow, a bullet, a knife, menstrual blood, and so on. Some spirit powers were said to be very strong, while others were weak. Spirit power was often hidden. Its presence might go undetected until someone with the proper knowledge tapped it and used it for himself or someone else.

People who could recognize and use spirit power could control their destinies better than others. Those who did not know how to tap power or protect themselves from it had bad hunting luck or got sick or died. Every person tried, therefore, to learn enough about spirit powers to be able to live in harmony with them. They knew that if they made spirit powers angry, even unintentionally, they could be destroyed by them.

258

Some signs of the presence of spirit powers were well known by all. For example, when a fire made a crackling noise, this was thought to mean that its spirit was foretelling bad luck or starvation, or to mean that the spirit of a dead person would like to be fed. So somebody would put a small piece of food or tobacco in the fire or pour a little tea in the ashes.

Certain bird calls were believed to be messages from spirit powers too. The hooting of an owl or a certain sound made by a camp robber (Canada jay) was said to mean that someone had died. People said that the cry made by the camp robber sounded like an axe chopping wood for a cremation.

Because people believed that they were in daily contact with different kinds of spirit powers, each man and woman wanted to have at least one spirit power as a personal helper. Like the doctors, people got their spirit-helpers from animals or other beings or objects. As mentioned in Chapter Nine, the Kaska sent young men out deliberately to look for power. They did not often send girls, who might spoil hunting luck by offending animal spirit powers, or who might themselves not be strong enough to manage more spirit power than they already had.

A young Kaska man seeking power went into the bush alone after his father or uncles had advised him what to do. He could not eat. He had to try to keep alert and to conquer his own fear. When he lay down at night to sleep, he wished for an animal spirit power to visit him and become his spirit-helper and power source.

When an animal spirit did come to a Yukon Indian, he or she began a relationship with that animal. The Indian's animal spirit-helper gave him a special song or special words. The spirit also often told the dreamer about certain foods to eat or to avoid, or told him of other taboos to observe as symbols of his relationship with the spirit-helper. The dreamer would put into a ''dream bag'' or special pouch some signs of his dream, like the claw of an animal, or a particular plant or stone.

Some Indians got several spirit-helpers, and each one increased the person's power. People would call on their spirit powers whenever they needed help for themselves, and sometimes they did so for others. Even if they did not want to become true Indian doctors and perform publicly, they could sometimes help members of their own households.

Not all of the Yukon Indians went on special power quests as did the young Kaska, and in all groups it was said that a person could dream about a spirit power at any time, or at any place, or at any age. Still, men were more likely acquire spirit power when out alone in the bush like the Kaska youths, and they were more likely to do so while young. Women were more likely to get strong spirit-helpers when they had passed the age of childbearing, but we know far less about how women got spirit power than about how men did. Of course, from the time they first menstruated until they finally stopped, females were believed to have a very strong power in them anyway. On the whole, women seem not to have relied on personal spirit-helpers to get along in the world nearly as much as men did. Women were expected to use their own wits and abilities when they were in tight spots. Oldtime stories and the personal experiences of the men and women who helped with this book both seem to make this clear.

Spirit Powers of Animals

Many of the strongest spirit powers were believed to be those of animals. Some Yukon Indians thought that there was a kind of powerful master spirit or headman for each kind of animal – black bears, grizzlies, wolves, salmon, whitefish, eagles, fish hawks and so on. But each individual bear or moose or other kind of animal was said to incorporate a spirit power in its own body too. This spirit power stayed in the animal's body until the animal was killed. Then, after a period of time – usually four days – it left the animal's flesh and went to where other spirit powers of that same kind of animal lived together with the master spirit of the species. After a while the spirit power of the animal that had been killed would enter the body of a new animal on earth, just as the soul or spirit of a person who had died would enter the body of a newborn baby. The new animal once again became available to the Indian for food or fur.

It was believed that the spirit powers of animals could move out of their bodies or "clothes" at any time, though they were more likely to do so at night. It was thought too that animal spirit powers always knew what the Indian people were doing and saying. They could even hear their thinking. They could also decide whether or not they would let the Indians kill the bodies they inhabited.

Hunters believed that if they had the right thoughts about animals and took care to treat their carcasses properly, the animal spirit powers would be quite willing to have their fleshly bodies killed when the Indians needed food. If they respected the animal spirit powers, therefore, the Indians would always have enough to eat. In short, it was believed that hunting luck depended on a good relationship between the hunter and the spirit powers of the hunted. That is why Tom Smith of Ross River said, "When you get luck with an animal you can catch him easy. When you have hard luck, you can't get him at all." Other elders have said that in the "long time ago," when animals talked and looked just like Indians, it was easy for people to talk with animals and to express their good intentions and respect for them. Today it is more difficult. Most humans no longer understand the animals easily, even though many animals still understand what humans think and say and are able to tell whether or not people respect them.

Oldtime Yukon hunters point out that, just as one should not say anything bad about animals, so one should never say what animal one is planning to hunt. As Timmy Stewart of Upper Liard put it:

"I'm going to kill this, this animal there. Oh, I'm going to kill moose." Don't say that! They [the animals] know that. Don't talk about it. If you want to go get something, just go get it.

260

My daddy says, ''Don't say that! You will get punished; you are going to go hungry!'' . . . I never say nothing. I hold my luck. Anytime I want more meat, I just go out and kill a moose.

One way in which the oldtimers showed respect to animal spirits was to make sure that they killed game only when people needed it. They also tried never to kill animals that were with young. Traditional Yukon Indians still do not like to kill too many animals or take too many fish in one place. Virginia Smarch of Teslin has said:

They have ways of treating an animal. They have a great belief and ways to treat an animal. Their belief is never to waste. So they never kill just for the pleasure of killing. And when they killed, they made sure they used all of it. Today when a native person has killed a moose, there's very little you'll find left there regardless of how far they have to pack it. They take it all, they don't waste it.

And Maude Smith of Teslin said this about fishing at Quiet Lake:

Used to be good fishing here till this road went through. So much trout used to be here. My dad used to be strict too. We would keep going down the line, and if we catch one, my daddy says, ''That's enough! You pull your line up.''

As Tom Peters of Teslin explains it,

They used to look after the game and the fish. We used to look after them because this is what we live on. It's a person's living. Anything we see — if we see a bunch of caribou, or if we see six moose, we tell each other, ''All right, don't bother it.'' Just get enough to use, that's all. In case maybe it spoiled [and] *we are going to waste grub.*

How did the Yukon Indians learn about animal spirit powers and the proper ways to treat animals? It is said that long ago the animals themselves taught their rules to humans, and a number of stories describe how this happened. For example, many Yukon Indians know the wonderful story about an Indian girl who married a bear. This tale explains how the Indians learned to treat the carcass of a grizzly bear properly, and also tells why many people do not like to eat its meat. Tom Peters has published this story in Tlingit and there are other published versions by Yukon Indians as well. This is the way Moses Jackson of Teslin told the story in 1977:

One woman went picking berries. It was way down in Alaska, she was one of our people, Tlingit, and this story is about that, it's known all over Alaska and the Yukon.
And when they were coming home, this woman is packing her berries that she picked that day. And she keeps falling down. She steps on grizzly bear droppings, and she starts to swear. And that bear heard it; he knows. You're not supposed to talk any old way, especially to grizzly.
Finally, the strap on her basket broke so many times that she gets tired,

and she tells the other women, "Send my husband to come and get me." And sure enough they left.

And, sure enough, that husband came.

"What you doing? It's getting late?"

"The strap on my basket kept breaking!"

That husband pack her berries then.

Nothing happened. [The strap stopped breaking.]

I don't know how many windfalls they step over. Each windfall they step over is tomorrow. [Another day has passed.] *Finally the husband said, "Let's camp here." She can't tell right away* [that the man is really a bear].

So they camp. They had supper, and then they go to bed.

And when she awoke early in the morning, she had been sleeping, but her husband made a sound and she woke up first. And when she woke up, she was sleeping with a grizzly bear.

And then they went again.

I didn't really know this story, but the best I can, I'm telling it.

Finally they came to a place where they are going to spend the winter. Her husband gets out under the trees and tells his wife to go get spruce boughs. And that woman, she's smart too. She already knows that's a grizzly bear too. And so she gets branches from high up, so her people would see. Then she brings them back to her husband.

"You brought this," he told his wife. Her husband looks at them, "You broke this from where the wind is strong."

That grizzly bear meant that they would find him by the sign. The woman broke the branches too high.

And then they go again, and they make another camp. And he told his wife, "I'll go get the brushes myself."

And so they spent the whole winter there. Well, it didn't take long and there were two young ones born. They were half human.

And that grizzly said, "Your brothers are going to come and find me."

It's a long story. . . .

So every time they got something to eat, that woman, she's got a piece of round rock. After she's finished eating, she keeps rubbing that grease on that rock. And finally the kids are growing bigger.

She's got this younger brother, that Indian woman. He's a Tlingit from Alaska. Anybody will tell you this same story.

Finally the husband said to her, "Your brothers are going to come and kill me."

When he [the bear husband] *first came into the den, he took his teeth out and hung them up on the ceiling. And that day the woman's brothers were going to come and get him, he took his teeth down and put them in his mouth.*

The grizzly reached out, and the snow is melting. And the grizzly comes out in front of the den. They usually do that when the snow is melting. And she comes out too, and she goes to her husband.

And they started to look for her, her three brothers. Her youngest brother — that's the one that found her. Because that woman had been rubbing that grease on the rock, when she hears her brother's dog start to bark, she throws that rock down outside the den. And that youngest brother picked it up and sees the grease on it.

And that grizzly told his wife, ''Your brothers are going to come and kill me.'' And he told his wife, ''Treat my body good.''

Finally he surrendered. He comes out of his den. That's when they killed him. When they kill that grizzly, that grizzly rolls right down to the bottom of the hill. And they skin it, and they treated that grizzly body just exactly the way he ordered it himself — to put that head way up in the tree. And after they skin the bear out, they barbecued some. And them young half-grizzly kids, they start to eat some of their daddy's meat. And that grease is dripping right from their elbow, and they are licking it right with their tongues.

And the woman told her brothers to treat their brother-in-law's body good.

And the brothers went back, and they told their mother, ''We found our sister.''

And when she comes back, that woman give orders just exactly the way she wants her camp, because she was just like a wild animal. People smell to her still. [She couldn't stand the smell of people because she had almost become a grizzly bear.]

Finally, after that, them boys, her brothers, they told their sister, ''Come play with us!''

That woman told her brothers, ''Leave me alone! Just by walking with you people, I almost turn into a grizzly myself at any time.''

But finally they keep after her, and they throw [her] *that grizzly bear hide and say, ''Older sister, come out and play with us.''* [They want her to pretend she is a bear; and they will pretend to hunt her].

And finally she gets tired and she puts that hide on and she starts to play with them.

In this particular telling of the story, Moses Jackson stopped here. In their versions of the same story, two Southern Tutchone men, Frank Joe of Kloo Lake and Dixon John of Pine Lake and Haines Junction, told a little more about what happened at the end. Frank Joe said:

The youngest brother, three of them, they keep on telling their mother, ''Let my sister be bear for us!''

Her mother tells them, ''Don't!'' She told them that. She said, ''She got taken away; she might change to the same way again.''

But the brothers, they keep on bothering her. They make it hard.
One time she makes up her mind she will go back in the bush.
''I'm going to do that,'' she said.

So she went back in the bush with the cubs [her half-bear children] *behind. The brothers shot at them with little straws for their arrows. They just play around.* [They hit her with a toy arrow.] *She kills them all. That's when they are gone. The bear sister and her children head over the mountain. That's the last they've been seen.*

That's why you get an oldtimer and they don't talk about a bear like that in a bad way. Because he can hear you.

Dixon John's ending went like this:

So she kills those brothers and takes off from there. Those two little boys, they follow her, their mother. They go, they're shaped like a bear now. Their mother too. See they don't have no clothes. They're shaped like a bear, and they're gone.

Moses Jackson, Frank Joe, and Dixon John all stressed that this story tells hunters how to respect the bear. Moses said:

That's what we know — that every animal is the same as according to this story. And we are not supposed to say anything bad to any animal, especially to a grizzly.

Moses went on to tell another story from his own experience:

We told this [story] to the big game hunters once when they were making fun of grizzly. . . . These two hunters were making fun of grizzly, and right away the grizzly knows it; you'd be surprised. I got a moose for my hunters, and my brother always goes back to it. There were wolves around the kill, but we got all the meat out of it already; there were just bones left.

Once late in the evening, after supper, those hunters wanted to go up there. They had gotten two wolves and they wanted some more, so they went up there again. It was late, and it was raining. I told Allison [my brother], to take my rifle. No, he'd rather take his hunter's rifle with the scope. He just put it over his shoulders, riding the horse. So they went up to the kill, and there were no wolves around.

It was raining and they started back. They didn't get very far, and sure enough those horses sure jump. The grizzly is coming right after them. And they were just making fun of it just a little while ago. Allison jumps off the horse, and Allison's hunter is over 300 pounds, his belt gets caught on that saddle horn and he just hung there. Just imagine what would happen if that grizzly comes right in!

And Allison shot just any old way twice, just to scare the grizzly away. They were lucky — that grizzly turns back and runs away. Boy, they were scared when they come back into camp, and they wouldn't even go to the washroom without a candle! . . .

Well, you see how this goes. You ask me if we handle the animal carcass special, properly. You see these two hunters can prove it to you. They were making fun of the grizzly, and the grizzly got after them.

This story about the girl who married the grizzly bear is a very dramatic one for Yukon Indians. It not only tells how the strong spirit power of the bear punished the girl who broke a taboo by saying bad things about bear droppings; it also shows the effect of breaking other important rules of behavior. Brothers-in-law, of course, were supposed to help each other as much as they could; certainly they were not supposed to harm each other. Yet in this story it is the bear's brothers-in-law who kill him. They make a kind of peace with the bear afterwards by treating its body properly, and traditional hunters still follow these rules when they kill a bear. They also sing a song that the bear's wife taught her brothers and which some elders include when they tell the story.

Other rules of social behavior are tested in the story too. A man was not supposed to marry a girl until his parents had made arrangements with her family, but in the story the bear (who looks human), just carries off the girl without asking permission, because she made the first mistake in saying bad things about bears.

The old rules were that brothers and sisters should always help and protect each other even if they were not allowed to look directly at each other or talk to each other after they grew up. They were also supposed to look after each other's children. But in this story, the brothers pester their sister and her children to put on grizzly bear skins and pretend they are bears, even though their sister has explained that wearing the skins would put her in the power of the grizzly bear spirits — and endanger her children too, because they have eaten the flesh of their own father. According to traditional rules, the brothers should not have been playing with their sister at all. In the end she kills her brothers, or kills all but the youngest one. In some versions she kills her mother too. So she has actually caused the death of the closest relatives in her matrilineage, the very ones she was supposed to love and who were supposed to watch out for her.

The story is so powerful partly because it is a story of conflicting loyalties. The girl comes to love her bear husband after staying with him, and she also loves her children by him. When his brothers-in-law come to kill the bear, she has to choose between her husband, who is of an opposite matrilineage, and her brothers, who belong to her own matrilineage. She sides with her mother's people the first time — letting her brothers kill the husband she loves — but in the end she herself is forced to kill those same brothers. Many oldtime Yukon Indians knew how hard it sometimes was to make a choice of loyalty between their matrilineage relatives and their father's people, the group to whom their husbands or wives belonged.

The girl was right to marry someone from a different matrilineage than her own — but should it have been a bear, even if the marriage had been properly arranged by the parents? Where did her children fit in, since they stayed half bear? In short, what should be the proper relationships between bears and humans? How do humans and animals fit together in the universe? Why do grizzly bear spirits seem to be stronger than those of humans?

A young person who heard this story often enough, and who really thought about its meaning, could learn a great deal about his elders' views of right and wrong, as well as about their understanding of power. He would also learn to ponder a deep philosophical problem for the Yukon Indian hunters: how to keep a balanced relationship with animals whose beauty and power they admired, but which they had to kill in order to eat, keep warm and protect themselves.

Many other old Yukon stories seem to touch on these same problems, because they too tell about how Indians had experiences with different kinds of animals, birds and fish. In each case a human who has broken a taboo learns the proper ritual for hunting an animal species and treating the bodies of those he has killed. In many of these stories, the animal first appears looking like a human. In one story a man marries a groundhog who looks like a woman. In another tale, a man lives with caribou; in another a boy is taken off by the salmon people after he says nasty things about a bit of moldy salmon. Yet another story is about a man who flies off with an eagle.

Each of these stories reveals something special about the world view of the oldtime Yukon Indians. Each reflects their ideas about the kinds of beings that animals were and about their spirit powers, as well as about the important values and powerful emotions involved in human relations with both animals and other humans.

A story told by Angela Sidney, a Tagish woman, explains how the relationship between a human and his animal spirit-helper could become a binding force for the person's entire clan. This particular story tells why the Dakl'aweidí clan of the Wolf moiety at Teslin, Carcross and Tagish has honored the wolf and used the wolf as a special clan crest.

I'm going to tell of my father's people, Dakl'aweidí. They only live because, they said, there was one man who was starving. He was starving, but he went out to hunt, anyway. I guess it's hard to get game long time ago with bow and arrow.

They say it was right here someplace in Tagish here. And he went out hunting towards Carcross. And from there, ten miles beyond this way, there's a big flood around there, and he saw caribou tracks. He follows around, and he follows around, and all of a sudden it's getting dark, and he's going to camp someplace.

And here all of a sudden he comes across this big camp in front of him. He sees a young man, a boy. He's got this nice paint on his face all over, and he's got a wolf tail tied to his cap. There's a big fire, so he goes over there.

So that man, he camps there with the young man. That young man tells him he has killed lots of caribou, lots, and they are lying all over.

And that young man tells him, he says, "You can have all these caribou I kill. They are all for you."

And he gave him his bow and arrow and his snowshoes, his roundhead snowshoes. That's where those roundhead snowshoes came from.

And he says, "Me," he says, "I'm going to go away. I'm going to kill some more caribou for you," he says. "I killed all these caribou for you, because you are my friend. You be Wolf. I'm Wolf. I want you to be Wolf." That's how come they claim Wolf.

In the evening he [the Tagish man] camps on the other side of the fire. Across the fire was the stranger.

In the morning when he woke up, here he finds himself with just no fire, no camp, nothing! He's just on top of the snow. And where the young man was camping across the fire there, there's nothing but a wolf bed there. You know wolves, they make a bed where they've been sleeping. There's nothing but a wolf bed in there. That's all. And he's gone.

266

So that man he skinned all those caribou and he came home, back here someplace around Tagish here.

And he tells his wife, "I got good luck." He says, "I come across a stranger, and he tells me he was Wolf. I know you are Wolf too, that's why I kill all these caribou for you, and I give you my snowshoes and my bow and arrow," he says. "From now on, you are going to be lucky," he tells me.

That's how come Dakl'aweidí own Wolf. My father's people, they own Wolf.

It is not surprising that Yukon Indians spent so much time thinking about how animals and humans are alike and unlike and how they interact with each other. Native hunters knew a great deal about natural history, because they have always watched very carefully how animals behave. They still do this today. For example, Frank Joe of Kloo Lake remarked:

Another thing I find out when I go out trapping there: crows. They always travel around close to the wolf. I figure that wherever the moose goes, the crow flies around there. And when the wolf gets the moose, they share the eating. I think that's the only way a person can figure it out. That's how come they are brothers-in-law.

Through such close observations of animal behavior, the Yukon Indians came to know where and how animals live throughout the year. Modern Indians can often help professional scientists by sharing with them what they know, for the knowledge represents the experiences of generations of native hunters. All this information about the natural world was passed along in the old days by word of mouth, from the elders to the younger people. It was as much a part of the Yukon Indians' worldview as were the beliefs about the spirit powers of animals.

Spirit Powers and the Weather

Knowing how to predict weather and trying to control it were also very important to oldtime Yukon Indians, because the weather had a great deal to do with their success in hunting. Everyone knew common signs of a change in the weather. For example, a ring around the sun meant either rain or snow was coming, depending on the season. Sun-dogs (vertical patches of rainbow on either side of the sun) meant very cold weather. Rainbows themselves were said to be Spider's snares or Thunderbird's snares. The Tagish used to say that many game animals lived at the end of the rainbow.

In various parts of the Yukon there are "weather mountains." One of them is a peak in the St Elias mountains northwest of Burwash Landing, which the Indians call Dry Lynx Mountain. Others are the Dawson Peaks (Three Aces), southeast of Teslin, which are called *Tléináx Tawéi,* or Lone Sheep, in Tlingit and are where Animal Mother made her nest. The local natives could tell from the direction in which the clouds were drifting off the peaks or from the patterns

Tléináx̱ Tawéi, the Three Aces,
from Teslin, 1951

of the snow cover what kind of weather to expect. They almost
never missed. Indeed, certain men made a specialty of watching the
various weather signs in the daytime. Others could predict weather
from watching the stars at night. The hunters found it very useful to
have such persons in camp.

In the southern Yukon, some people used to say that there were a
few spirit-beings who were far stronger than even the most powerful
animal spirits. Two of these were Mountain Man and Water Woman.
People said that Mountain Man was the boss of all the animals living
in the mountains – even grizzly bear – and that he also was in
charge of the weather. But people said that the spirit powers of wolverines, wolves, owls, squirrels and even lice could also affect the
weather, making it warm or cold. They also said that Thunderbird
caused storms with lightning and thunder.

Sometimes the Indians tried to make it colder or warmer to suit
their needs. For example they might want a good crust on the snow
in the spring so they could snowshoe easily. Or they might want it to
be warmer so people would not freeze, or so there would be open
water for boat travel. If an Inland Tlingit wanted it to freeze, he beat
a wolverine skin on the snow. He did this because an old story tells
how Wolverine stole the north wind. Or if he wanted a thaw, he
would put the carcass of a tree squirrel in a bucket of warm water or
tie it in a stream. He did this because tree squirrels always run
around more in warm weather than in cold, and a song that goes
with this ritual tells the squirrel to run up a tree fast! People tried to
imitate or symbolize the kinds of weather they wanted.

The traditional Yukon Indians thought too that certain kinds of
improper social behavior could cause bad weather. They said that if a
young girl looked out from under her hood when she was turning to
woman, storms would follow. Sometimes when it rained or snowed

268

or blew terribly, the people thought that a girl had broken the taboo. They pretended that they were going to burn up the girl, so that the angry spirit powers of the weather would relent.

Some other beliefs about the weather were that it would rain if a person packed fish and fresh water at the same time, and that if children played with baby birds while they were still in their nests, bad storms would follow.

When there were eclipses of the sun or moon, traditional Indians always tried to get the heavens back to normal. Tagish and Inland Tlingit women used to tie bunches of gopher snares to their walking sticks and pretend that they were going to snare the sun and pull it back into the sky. Or they might hang out all their best blankets and other valuables and sing to the sun or moon telling it to come back for all the fine presents.

The World of the Spirits of Dead Humans

As mentioned in Chapter Nine, the traditional Yukon Indians thought that when a human being died, that person's spirit would go to another world for a while and might then return in a new body. They believed in the reincarnation of both animal and human spirits. Those who were reborn could often remember events of a past life and recognize places they had once been, but as they grew older, they gradually forgot about their former lives.

It is said that just as Indians learned about the worlds of the animal spirits through visits and intermarriage, so they learned about the world of the spirits of dead humans by visiting it. Kitty Henry's story about the man who fell into the crevasse, told in Chapter Nine, is one such account. Frank Sidney, another Inland Tlingit of Teslin told a different story about a Ross River man named Magy, perhaps a Kaska. After he died, Magy went down a river to what Frank and his people believe was the ocean and then up to a place which sounds very much like the Christian heaven. There his life on earth was judged by powerful spirits who then gave him some rules for how people should behave on earth. The man's own spirit then returned to earth so he could tell people about the right ways to act:

Down this way, from the northwest, a man was nothing but skin and bones. He died. Before he died he told his wife and family, ''Don't touch me for seven days.'' That man died.

No one knew how old he was, past middle age. His name is Magy, he got that name from heaven. No white people were there that time, not one single white person was in the country then. His grave is up there in Ross River.

This medicine man died, and he claimed that his spirit [when he was dead] *was not different than when you are alive. It's not different. The only thing different, he said, is if you talk to a person, he won't answer. He's invisible. So after he died he found himself on a big log like that, a big timber, floating down the river. He was on that log, and he went downriver. He can't come close to the shore. He doesn't have any clothes on. He's naked. Pretty soon he came out on a big lake, big lake like this* [Teslin Lake].

And far across this lake he saw all these different things. And some of these things shoot water from the tops of their heads there. That's a whale, we recognize that. And then some things travel two together. All in one line they go down together and come up like that.

It's got a big fin on it. And some of them have a hole right through the fin. That's a killer whale. We recognize that.

And some of them were a funny shape. Some of them look like grizzly. That's sea lion. We recognize all of them [that Magy told about seeing].

It was right before the current caught him, and he was still going down. The whole lake is moving. It's low tide, you see. We recognize that too, because our people are from the coast.

And he died. And during the seven days he was down at the ocean. He didn't eat anything that time. And he worried about himself, how he was going to get to shore. And he sees two big animals appear near him by the timber. And he thinks to himself, ''Nothing cares about me any more!'' And he hears something way up — an eagle. So he looks, and something is coming down. He looks, and just about that far away, he sees a cage come down. He looks, and a voice speaks to him in his language. He says, ''Get in.''

He's got that cage down in front of him, and the voice tells him to get in. He can't see a man; it's invisible to him. He's all naked. He hasn't got any clothes on. He is just way out in the middle of the water.

So he thinks to himself, ''I have got no hope now.'' So he steps in. And that thing that holds the cage up, it's about as big as a train.

And then he's sitting in it. And it goes so far and then it stops on a piece of land, a big ground — beautiful, he says.

He comes beside a big building, and he sees something nice inside. And a table is set in there. For a while he sits around, and then they start asking him questions.

''Tell us the story about your life,'' they said. ''What did you do when you first come into the world, when you were born? What did you do first?''

''Well,'' he says, ''I used to go up around on four feet inside the house. [He meant that as a baby he used to crawl around.] *And I go out. Every place I come to, I go out* [to the bathroom] *right there.''*

''Yes, that's true, What else?''

''You know I lost the bow and arrow my father made for me. I kept losing them. I lost knives, pocket knives.''

And they put on the table everything he had lost. They say he's going to eat now. And they give him something that's very small, just that big.

''You put that in your mouth.''

He put that in his mouth, and he's not hungry any more.

''Well, okay,'' he says.

And they start to judge him. ''When you were big enough to kill game, what did you kill first?''

''Camp robbers,'' he says. ''I shot them with bow and arrow.'' That's all he can remember.

''One more special thing that you remember, that's what you're going to tell when it comes to your memory. You know it. It's going to come to your memory. You think hard!''

He says, ''When I crawl around the fires'' — there's no stove or anything *in this country then, just a campfire — ''I crawl around the fire and I found charcoal, I'd eat it.''*

''That's it,'' they say, ''That's the one.''

They give him clothes, and they give him paper like that, fine paper. . . . After they give him the clothes, they start to instruct him.

''You have to love each other, your fellow man. You've got to love each other. You're not to kill each other. You're going to tell that to the people down there where you come from. You're going back,'' they tell him. ''You're going back.''

He didn't know he had died. He was just like the way we are when we are living. Nothing was different, he says. . . .

They [the people who judged him] say, ''You're all right.'' They say, ''You're going to come up here later, not now. You're going back to instruct your people and tell them what to do, the way to live and not to kill each other any more, and don't burn each other!''

You know they used to burn their bodies when they died. From then on, Pelly people started burying each other.

And every Sunday and Saturday they would gather up the people, and Magy would preach to the people. He made the sign of the cross like that. Where did he know that from? . . . He could pray in any language, and they understood it up there. This was before the white people, way long before the white people. And he lived a long time.

They say he warned the people. He said this world was going to come to an end. He told the people, ''Not too long from now, the world's going to be set on fire. You're going to see a lot of things different. We're going to have shortage of food. All the moose, caribou, and all the animals that you use for food are going to die off. Fishes in the lake are going to die off, and people are going to die of starvation. That's if you are bad. But if you're good, you can eat a little bit, like that, and it will take you for a week or ten days. Just one little bit, and you will be fed for ten days!'' Well, how did he know all these things? . . .

Now these people don't believe anything, but I believe. I believe there's God. That's how he got the help, you see. There's no man on earth that's going to die for seven days and come back to life the seventh day midnight.

It is said that in the old days some southern Yukon Indian doctors had the spirits of dead persons as their spirit-helpers, but little is known about this now. People also thought that the spirits of the dead sometimes tried to take away the spirits of the living. The people were frightened when they heard noises that they believed were the noises of lost souls or human spirits wandering around a village or a graveyard at night.

As explained in Chapter Ten, a person might be without his soul if he had been badly scared or if a very strong spirit power had taken his soul away. Then an Indian doctor would send out his own spirit or one of his spirit-helpers to find the lost soul and return it to the owner's body. If he did not get it back, the person would die and his spirit would go to the land of the dead. A spirit wandering around away from its body before its owner died could frighten people, and so could a person's ghost-spirit after he had died. Charcoal marks were supposed to help keep such spirits away from the living, and many Indians put charcoal marks on their houses or their faces to scare away ghost-spirits.

When Yukon Indians saw Northern Lights that were very bright or vividly colored, they often said they were the spirits of dead warriors or other humans who had died violently. In some places their appearance was said to mean there would soon be war. Some people were afraid of the lights, and they blew into the sky telling them to go away.

SOME STRANGE OR DANGEROUS CREATURES

The Yukon natives used to say that, in addition to the human beings and animals that roamed their world, there were also a number of stranger beings. Some of them were dangerous. Those who met them told vivid stories about what happened.

One strange creature was called the bushman or brushman. There were supposed to have been lots of them in earlier times, and since the stories about them are quite varied, perhaps there were several different kinds. Young girls and women in particular were warned again and again to watch out for bushmen when they were alone in the woods.

Several older Indians have said that bushmen looked like regular people, but that they had special habits and powers. Some said they lived underground and could do anything they wanted to just by thinking about it. They could travel without anybody seeing them and without any hardships. Some said bushmen were quite small, but others claimed they were as tall as a large spruce. Many Indians thought that the bushmen really were ordinary humans – strangers from far away who were looking for women to steal as wives, or simply mean and dissatisfied or mischievous members of their own local groups. But for all their different ideas about who bushmen were, people all agreed that it could be dangerous to meet one.

Quite a few stories tell about bushmen stealing Indians from their camps. Usually they stole children, especially young girls, but they also took women and fully grown men, forcing them to become slaves. Bushmen were most active in summer. They hid in the heavy undergrowth and followed women when they went to set snares. They also sneaked up to the camps, throwing dirt at the tents, and making the dogs bark.

Jessie (Mrs Harry) Joe, a Southern Tutchone of Klukshu, told these stories about bushmen:

After hunting, right about the end of September, because snow comes down very fast after that, before the snow, all of us had to come back to camp at the same time, fast, because there were some people around they called bushmen.

We used to see something up there at camp all the time. Everybody came back at the same time because it's getting pretty late to go out. Sometimes there's heavy snowfall. So they all come back together. It was because of the bushmen. I don't know here they come from.

My mother was saying something about it one time. Mrs Joe Kane and my mother came back from berry camp. They came back, and they were supposed to hunt gopher on the other side of that big field there. That big field used to go up on a high mountain up that way. You can see that mountain. [The field] *was at Sixty-Two Mile* [on the Haines Road], *on the other side of the high mountain. That's where the Dalton Post trail goes, the summer trail. We used to come across from Dalton Post with a canoe.*

That's why they said they went back. Everybody went to Haines. They were supposed to hunt some gopher. They had some snares. They set their snares [along] *with Mrs Joe Kane.*

My oldest sister, Sadie, she was a baby. My mother packed that baby and set snares, choke snares. No traps those days. She set over 150 in one day. I remember we used to pull over those cotton trees, something like that for a choke too, bent it down like that. Way up on the mountain, where you see that brush, you had to cut it to set the snares with. So maybe they did that, my mother. That's how they set that.

That night they camped there. They had lots of grub. They didn't have a gun, so they had to have a dog to protect them. That dog barked all night. Next morning they went to see the snares. In the snare somebody put a stick in, like that. That big. This kind of a stick, a long one. They thought it was a gopher they had. [My mother] *sat down, she said, ''Oh, they must have been undone, pushed up all of them snares!''*

So that Mrs Joe Kane said, ''Something is wrong with my snares!''

My mother said the same thing. They had been undone, all the snares that they had set!

And evening time when you make a fire inside the mountain like that, you don't see smoke very much. So they made that kind of fire in that kind of place. And sure they don't go back on the trail. They had to hide their tracks all the way through. There's two big creeks at the berry camp. It's the other side of a big canyon, Second Canyon they call it. They don't go back on the trail. They had to go way down around the mouth of the creek there, they said.

So they camped way down by the steep canyon. They didn't light a fire or anything. They saw people's tracks every place where they set those snares.

So the next day, early the next morning, they got up early and they're leaving. And they see people walking on the side of the hill on the mountainside there. That's when they got scared, she said. They didn't light a fire. They hardly ate anything till they got back to Dalton Post. And nobody was in Dalton Post either. They were all out hunting, eleven miles away.

I don't know who the bush people were. They lost quite a few girls though. They wanted to get girls, those bush people, I guess. They lost quite a few girls from here, this part of the country. They'd steal girls. Some of the girls were taken when they were camping over this way. There was one that was taken, I don't remember though. Those days you didn't pay any attention to it when they told a story to you. You didn't care.

They took those girls back to their country. Not very long ago I hear they've got quite a few people over across the British Columbia boundary line. They said they used to belong to Dalton Post.

One girl, her father went out hunting. And then early in the morning they were supposed to move. You see you don't stay just one place, you got to keep on moving when you are hunting. They figure they would get a moose or something. They went on hunting. Early in the morning they were supposed to move camp. And this mother had all the kids with her and one big girl too. And when they go, they walk slow. The little kid sat on the [older people's] shoulders, so they can make it a long ways. They didn't want to make them walk. They put packs on those dogs.

And they missed that big girl. They holler and holler. Nothing. And the father went out hunting her. And he heard a song like. He heard that little girl, that girl crying. He heard it some places, and some places he didn't hear it. So he went after it. And that man, he hollered. He said, "Leave my daughter for me, and I'll give you a whole cache full of stuff inside my cache. Give me back my daughter!" He just hollered and hollered.

So at last he heard that girl holler back. One tree had grown like that on top, very high up. And that little girl had been put on top of that birch, that bushman stuck her on there, and that girl couldn't get out. So that father got that girl unstuck from out of there. But he had a hard time. So he left everything in the cache for the bushmen – everything! When he came back after two months, he didn't take anything. He left it just like that. He didn't take anything.

All those things they used to tell us long time ago. That's why we were scared of bushmen.

Apparently bushmen did not always steal, harm or annoy Indians; instead they could be helpful to them. Both Mary McLeod, a Han from Dawson, and Joe Netro, a Loucheux from Old Crow, have told of bushmen who saved people from starvation. One or two Indians are even said to have married bushmen. People said that the daughter of an Indian woman and a bushman once lived near Dawson.

A few stories about bushmen who lived underground or in mountains are like the stories about fairy people told in Scotland and Ireland. Perhaps the Yukon Indians heard such tales from Robert Campbell, Alexander Murray or other Hudson's Bay men, or from Mackenzie River Indians who had learned these traditions. They could easily have fit such stories into their own beliefs about bushmen.

The old people also used to tell of several different kinds of water monsters living in lakes and rivers throughout the Yukon. Maude Smith, an Inland Tlingit of Teslin and Quiet Lake, has told about one kind of creature said to be half fish and half Indian. She said:

I heard about this thing that happened. It was before I had any kids. John Haegstrom, the geologist, he was coming back from across the lake [Quiet Lake] late one night. He got in his boat, and he started to row. He rowed, and he rowed, and he rowed all night. He's not moving! He never got scared; he just kept on rowing.

But then he got scared. By now, he saw the trees still standing in one place! He rowed and rowed. He didn't pay attention, he just kept on rowing.

274

Then all of a sudden daylight came real good, and he heard someone laugh, just like a person. And then that boat moved. Just as soon as daylight. He kept rowing and rowing to Sandy Lake.

Long time ago, a person used to live here, one half-fish and one half-Indian person. He doesn't live here any more. Somebody saw it once when he had come all the way from Ross River. It was when there used to still be a store there, and this thing got hold of him at the foot of Quiet Lake.

The Indians also used to say there were large worms or snakes that lived under glaciers or underground and were as large as houses. Southern Tutchone elders said that if humans cooked grease near a glacier the worms would come out and cause avalanches or high water. Or if people made too much noise, they would come out of river banks or lake shores and cause big mudslides or make big holes in the ground. The oldtime Indians said that the large fossil bones, such as the mastodon bones that Robert Campbell once found near Fort Selkirk, were the remains of these big monsters.

Other fearsome creatures were the maneaters that Yukon elders used to hear about. They were said to have looked like humans but to have been very tall. Southern Tutchone Indians of Aishihik told how their ancestors once managed to kill off a whole group of these maneaters at the head of Albert Creek. There is a high bluff there, and the Indians tricked the maneaters into rushing over it so fast they fell to the bottom, where the Indians clubbed them to death. Other maneaters were said to have lived along the Kluane and Donjek rivers.

HUMAN BEINGS
AND HOW THEY SHOULD BEHAVE

Of course, the traditional worldview also included many ideas about human beings. All the old people had definite beliefs about how the Indians had come to be, even though they did not all tell the same stories. One widely shared idea was that Crow carved the first people out of poplar bark, as told by Angela Sidney in Chapter Eight.

Another Yukon story explains why individual humans do not live very long on earth. Bear and Fox once quarrelled about this. Bear heard Fox singing about how human bodies should always come back to life, just as pieces of wild rhubarb bob up when thrown into the water. Bear threw a rock into the water and said, "Why don't you say, *Die for good like this rock?*" After that, people say, the Indians all did die for good, even though their soul-spirits, like those of animals, could be reincarnated into new bodies.

Perhaps even more important to the old people than the question of how human beings came to be were the rules for acceptable human behavior. Children were constantly reminded of these rules as they listened to oldtime stories or to tales about the personal experiences of others. Some rules were very explicit, such as the rule that one should always marry a person from the opposite side. Other

275

standards of behavior were more general but stemmed from deeply held values.

The ancient Greek people had a saying or a motto that is usually translated into English as "Nothing too much" or "Nothing in excess" or "Moderation in all things." By this the Greeks meant that people should never overdo anything either in their thoughts or their behavior. They should not be too greedy, too noisy, too proud, too aggressive, too humble, too rich, and so on. Traditional Yukon Indians also had the ideal of moderation and balance in their lives. This can be seen, for example, in the way elders cautioned young people never to kill too many animals, never to take more than was needed for food or clothing. The old people scorned a person who ate too much — except at potlatches — or one who was stingy with food. It was said that someone who overate would starve later on, and that a man who killed too many bears or wolves would suffer from rheumatism or other ills in his old age. In the same vein, the oldtime Indians said that if an Indian doctor got too much spirit power, he might become evil and harm people instead of helping them. Then he would come to a bad end himself. Even a young person doing ritual exercises for his or her future welfare should never overdo them, for the qualities or powers being sought might then come in excess or backfire. A girl who performed too many symbolic acts to make herself light in her movements might, people said, end up shaking all the time.

There were many areas of life in which a person who was not careful could overdo their actions or thoughts. If others were aware of it, they would try to warn the offender, often by telling him or her a story. The Crow stories almost all tell how Crow kept getting into trouble by wanting too much food, too much sex, and so on. Such tales kept reminding the oldtime Indians that moderation was one of their most important values.

The Indians also valued harmony with the land and water, and with the animals and other nonhuman creatures who lived in the world, except for the dangerous maneaters. And they valued harmony among human beings themselves. They stressed that people should be helpful, generous and respectful to each other, sharing whatever they had in times of bad luck or illness.

Tom Peters of Teslin said:

We just try to be kind to the people, you know. And even [after] trapping grounds were individually owned, a man might ask another, "How is the chance if I go with you?"

"Sure," he would say, "Come on. . . ."

Sometimes if two, three, four, five families are together trapping, if the people see one man never gets anything — if he never gets no wolf, nothing — well, they give him all the chance. If I know anyplace, anyplace where it used to be a good place for a trap, we send him over there so he can get a little, make a little money on fur. That's the way people keep going. . . . We got to fight for our living till we got whatever we need.

And when the people go from here, out in the bush where they got a trap,

T&D [Taylor & Drury], *they got a store there. We owe money; we had a credit, $200 or $300 dollars sometimes. That lasts us pretty near half of the winter. We come back in Christmas, and we pay everything right up. I just want to let you know just the way we are, so the people can hear me when I speak. . . .*

The very first year I go to Ross River — I never been there before — I got lost that time. From Ross River I go up to Pelly Banks. I stay with a bunch over there. I started to go around. They live a different way you know. Right here we live in a different part of the country. They live different ways. . . .

Anyplace I go and sit down, they say, ''Let me give you a cup of tea.'' But one time when I first been over there, I just finished lunch. I walked over to that place just to visit the people. I sat down over there, I went inside, and we talked together.

And this man and his wife, they started to cook. ''By gosh,'' I thought to myself, ''these people haven't eaten yet, and here I come for a visit.'' So I just sit down. This man tells me they were waiting four hours for me. Then this man calls me for something to eat. Well I was just finished eating . . . but I don't want to say nothing. So I go to the table there and have something to eat anyway. It happened to me two times from there. Just anybody who comes to visit anybody, they start to cook for you right away.

Mac Peter, a Ross River Kaska, tells of some other visitors, who came during hard times:

Once people came from Pelly Lakes. They been having a hard time. They can't buy any .22 shells. [I] buy two — two cartons of everything. I give one each of everything to everyone. They can't get any credit, so I give one each to everyone.

The Yukon elders say that when white people first came into the Yukon, the Indians treated them just like other Indians who had come from far away. They often helped them like friends. This is why some old people do not understand why the whites who began to govern Canada set up rules and boundaries that seemed to separate Yukon Indians from their friends and relations in other places. Frank Sidney of Teslin explained that Indians from Alaska, British Columbia and the Northwest Territories all used to come to the Yukon:

They [Alaskan Indians] *used to come here. They used to come here too way down from the Mackenzie and all the way down to salt water. And there were no* [boundary] *lines there then. We owned the country. And white people divided us between each other — you and your brother — between B.C. and Alaska line, between B.C. and the Yukon. That one was pretty bad. And between Yukon and the Northwest Territories, Indians were also divided.*

Tom Peters of Teslin talked about these boundaries too:

Another thing, we never used to have a boundary line here at B.C. We never see a boundary line anywhere. And it's the same people living here [as]

Johnston Town [in British Columbia] *people. . . . We never called them
B.C. people. No. They are just one relation of ours. Even in Atlin, in Atlin
there are the same people as are around here.*

In 1950 the Yukon Indian Agency began to set up registered
traplines for individual Indians. This was not the old way of sharing
the country either, and many older Indians did not like the change.
Tom Peters explains:

The very first [white] *people that ever step into this Yukon, we heard about it.
These people here, they never had a war against white people. We treat them
good, as well as our own people. And another thing, they beat us on that
trapping grounds. We used to be like brothers, from Atlin, from Carcross,
sometimes from Whitehorse. That's the way we used to make free this country
here. They would come over here. When they come over here, "Well, I'm
going to try to go over there; how is that place where you people are trapping?"
   That's a big country!
   "Okay," we say, "You go over there."
   We never think about registered trapping ground. It is free for all of us.
We never make any trouble.*

Dorothy Smith of Ross River told how her people, in fact, decided
to have a common trapline rather than having individual lines, because the value of freely sharing the land was still so important to
them.

*This is the last place they still have a group trapline. All the other places have
individual traplines. Ones who still trap here, they don't care. You can go
anywhere you want, and nobody will say anything. That's why we want to
keep it that way. The game warden wanted to make it individual but we had
a meeting and we just told him no! Because if it's individual, some of the
people would probably sell out, and then the Indian people would have
nothing. . . . All the people are under the group leaders, and they trap
wherever the group line is. Whoever wants to trap can go out and trap, can
have their traps any place. . . .*

The principle of sharing and cooperation was coupled with the
principle of self-reliance, which the Indians valued greatly in both
men and women. Headmen usually just gave their opinions and advice; they were not supposed to be bossy. The old instructed the
young. A man had a right to give orders to his nephews and nieces
on his sister's side, and an older brother could tell his younger brothers what to do. Older sisters could direct their younger sisters. But,
except for the few slaves, no adult person could really be forced to
act against his or her own wishes. Of course, a person who rebelled
against public opinion might pay a terrible price for being stubborn
or different. The others could ignore him or make life so unpleasant
that he had to leave the group, but each person was respected as a
unique individual. In many situations, people could decide — and
had to decide — for themselves what was the best thing to do.

When the Department of Indian Affairs imposed the system of elected chiefs and councils on the Yukon Indians, they also tried to impose a new concept of authority. Mac Peter of Ross River said that when he was band chief in 1949, "everybody had a rough time" trying to adjust to the new band organization that the Indian Agent wanted. Mac's wife, Hazel Peter, explained:

At that time he got called out to be chief, they [the Indian Agent] *wanted him to talk to the people too much. . . . They're our own people. We don't want to boss them around. They know what they're doing.*

Hazel & Mac Peter, Ross River, 1977 (photo by Jan Sheppard)

In other words, every Yukon Indian had to be able to get along in two different ways. A person had to know how to cooperate, how to give and accept help in a friendly fashion, without being bossy, and also how to cope on his or her own.

Mac Peter also tells how he learned to make snowshoes by himself, including the parts of the task that were normally done by women:

I make snowshoes myself. Caribou skin, I make it myself. I clean it. I cut it myself. I make my own babiche. I fill up my snowshoes, and away I go! I don't wait for anybody.

My mother never ever know I could do that. We got no snowshoes when we go out to our trapline. We come back, and we go two pairs of snowshoes!
  "Where you get that babiche from?"
  "I shoot the caribou. I make the skin, I cut the babiche myself!"
  "Who teach you that? How you learn anything like that?" she tells me.
  I just got to see it first and then I do anything.

Irene Isaacs of Carmacks tells a story which shows how the idea of the relatedness of things and the principle of self-reliance work together. In this story the food comes from a store and not from the bush, but the story still shows something of the oldtime worldview.

One time I ran into a bear. One time I see a bear right in front of me. I wasn't scared. I stand right there, you know. I was going to shoot him, but I just stand there. You don't have to get scared when you meet a bear, you know. And he was looking at me, and I got my baby behind [in] my pack too. I just turn around and I just think about the Lord, I pray to the Lord, "Please, Lord, just take him away." I have got a rifle, but I didn't want to shoot him; if I miss him or wound him he's going to come after me.

That's what my dad and my mother used to tell me. They said, "Don't bother him, just talk Indian way to the animal."

The same for wolf. You know timber wolf? One time I run into that too. I run into four of them. I come down to Tagish from up at Jake's Corners [a distance of about 13 km]. I come down to get grub from Tagish. My dad was up at Jake's Corners. They were waiting for him. I was smoking then, and I ran out of tobacco too. So I left early in the morning. And daddy says, "You sure you going to make it?"

I said "Sure, I'm going to make it. I'm going to walk."

So I left about four in the morning and got back by midnight. You have to walk, you know. I got a rifle. I cut across Tagish Lake and come to what was Mr White's store. I come there. I come there by nine in the morning I guess. I got a packsack. I didn't have a dog, I just pack, and I get everything we need. They told me, "Where did you come from?"

I didn't know them. I said, "I walked." I walked, and I got all that I need. I load my packsack, and I pack. And I've got my rifle, and [I said] "I'm going back now."

They asked me, "Can we drive you back?"

I said, "No, I'll go across the lake."

Well, I did. Well, I was going back, and these wolves were there. They were sleeping in the road, you know. And I saw them, I didn't have to run. I just kept walking and I thought about God, and I just passed. I just passed. As soon as I passed them they started yelling, you know. They started crying, "Woooooooooooo!"

I looked back. I looked, and they didn't bother me, because I didn't bother them either. So I just kept walking. And I just kept going. I hit the beach, and three miles after, I go to the bush up on the road, you know. I just kept walking.

Mom and dad — I mean mom — was ready to come and look for me. Now they heard me coming back.

And I came after eight hours, just tired. I've got that packsack and I just dropped it. I couldn't say anything. I couldn't even drink tea. They had some already cooked, you know, but I say "I can't eat, I'm too tired." So I just lie down and go to sleep.

In the morning I told them. I said, "You know what? I ran into a wolf."

And mom and dad, they just were worried. They said, "How did you get out of it?"

I said, "I talked Indian way to it, because like you guys told me. . . ."

Indian way like, you say to a wolf, or the same to a bear, if a bear comes to you, you say, "I go around for something to eat, you know. I look around to make a living." That's what you tell them, and then they don't bother you. Yah, that's what you tell them and then they feel sorry.

You can tell them and they do it, that wolf. You tell them, "Kill something for me!" And then the wolf will. Then you come, and they are going to kill a moose and you're going to find it and have moose meat. They do that, the wolves. So they understand Indians. That's what my dad and my mother and my grandfather told me.

And other animals, that's what I tell my son about that too. You've got to treat animals good. You've got to talk to them Indian way.

This chapter has provided no more than an introduction to the rich and complex worldview of the old people. There is much more to learn about traditional native beliefs and values, and much of it can be learned from stories the Indians still choose to tell and memories they take care to preserve. If you are interested in hearing what they have to say, the next and final chapter of this book is a good place to begin.

12

What Yukon Indians Are Saying Today

One reason earlier Yukon Indians liked to travel around was that it gave them a chance to talk to friends they had not seen for a long time and to hear new things. This chapter is a kind of substitute for travelling around. It is made up almost entirely of the things Yukon Indian people in different places chose to say, and the stories they chose to tell, when material for this book was collected on tape in the summer of 1977. Many people are quoted here, but the chapter can only be a sampler. It tells no more than a small part of what the native people – mostly elders – had on their minds and thought important to say when we asked them to speak to you.

Some chose to explain about making and doing things in the old days; some wanted to discuss what is going on in modern times; some told traditional stories. Everybody had something of interest to say.

As you read the selections that follow, you can pretend that you are travelling about from place to place meeting old friends or making new ones. You can imagine that, at each place, you are sitting comfortably inside a house or out under the trees or perhaps on a river bank at a fish camp and the people, one by one, are talking to you, telling you what is important to them and what they think is important for you to hear.

You may also want to remember something George Smith of Ross River said to us during 1977:

Old people have lots to tell . . . but they have to think about things. Maybe it takes two hours. But you have to be patient. Lots of young people don't know, and think they are finished, and leave too soon.

Here as throughout the book, the people's words are printed in italic type, *like this,* and a word or explanation not actually given by the speaker has sometimes been added in square brackets and roman type, [like this]. In several cases, the words used are those of the translator, not of the original speaker. Some elders preferred to speak in their native languages, and translators in each village made it possible for us to put down English versions of what these elders said.

Martha Kendi

Martha Kendi's father, John Tizya, was sent to the Old Crow area from Fort McPherson by Archdeacon Robert McDonald early in this century.

My father looked after the church, and he taught all the people. And in those days, he was the first one to put up a house around here. He told us many stories, but we were just kids and we never listened to him.

A long time ago there was no [china] dishes, and they had birch for dishes. And they cleaned squirrels' heads and had them for cups. And a long time ago they never had any tea pots, and they used caribou throats [to hold hot water]. They put a stick in the caribou throat and they melted snow in it.

In those days they used some kind of round tin or black stone [steel?]. They hit rocks [flint?] with it and a spark came down and that's how fire started. At that time, my father told us to remember this if you have hard time.

At that time there was no soap. They used birch. They burned the birch first. They used the ashes. They put fat grease into the ashes. That's how they made soap.

They used to make [fish] hooks out of caribou legs and at night they put a big blanket over their heads and it was dark. They could see the fish good and they hooked fish good that way. . . .

One time a little boy cried all the time. And his father and mother asked him why he cried. He never answered. He wore marten pants. That night he told his father and mother that tomorrow morning he was going to the moon. He hung his marten pants by the door and he was gone. They knew he went to the moon.

▲ ▼ ▲

Moses Tizya

Moses Tizya is Martha Kendi's elder brother. The scarlet fever epidemic he mentions probably occurred in 1856.

My father told me that in his time there was so many people that they had to make four trails in the wintertime when they moved. And even then, he said, they moved thick. And . . . after that what they call scarlet fever came in the country. That's what killed all the people off — that's what my old man told me. Everybody died off. This was long before I was born. All these things were in 1800s, my father's time. . . .

When there was a run of caribou, [all the people] went after them [to chase them to the fence]. They couldn't get caribou every day though — not every day of the year. Just at the time that the caribou were running, like they do now [in August]. That's the time they get them. And then they'd live on that meat, probably up until New Year. And when they ran out of meat, then they started to move. That's the time they made the fence I told you about — a winter fence. They got a big bunch of caribou — three or four thousand. People have got to have a lot of meat to keep them going.

In my father's time there was lots of people. Like I told you, they made four routes when they moved from one camp to another. There were no dogs in those days. The people just [moved] straight. They had nothing at all to carry — just a little dry meat.

They used caribou skin for their camp; that's light too. And they used nothing but caribou skin clothing, that didn't weigh much. That's all they pull, caribou skin blankets, all that's light. No [metal] pots or anything. In those days they had wooden pots.

They got a big log and dug a hole [in it], *and that's how they made wooden pots. But they couldn't put it in the fire. They carried rocks and they put those rocks in the fire. They put meat and snow in there and then they put some of those rocks in there, and pretty soon that meat boiled. That's how they cooked their meat, or most of it. That's how they cooked their meat in those days.*

In the summertime they dug a hole in the ground and put caribou skins in there, and they put water in and they threw red-hot rocks in there and pretty soon they boiled their meat. That's how they boiled their meat in those days . . . The caribou skin was no good after that. they must have had a lot of skins to do that! That's what [the old people] *said.*

▲ ▼ ▲

When the people moved [to Old Crow] *from Rampart House, a minister came up. He used a man's house for services. When another minister came, they built a church. Later they built their own bigger church. The other one was too small. They did all the work themselves. . . . Moses Tizya's father* [John Tizya] *was the catechist. In the spring of 1904 the catechist from Fort Yukon, William Ruler, came to* [Fort] *McPherson. Moses Tizya's father and some young men from La Pierre House and McPherson all went to McPherson to take an examination. Seven young men took this examination; only two made it and were ordained priests. This was the year that Ruler left for Winnipeg. He told John Tizya, since he had a big family, to go build a house at the mouth of the Crow River to serve the people when they came from the Crow Flats. He was to hold services there. He built a cabin. Later Hudson's Bay Company built a store.*

There was lots of big timber at Old Crow then. When I came up in 1913 you couldn't see the mountains because of all the big timber. The people used to gather here at Old Crow and then they went to Rampart House. Downriver on a high bluff was John Tizya's fish camp. . . .

Here's another story. You heard about this Mad Trapper, Albert Johnson? Well, that time I came back from the Flats [Crow Flats], *there was a big storm while I was out at the Flats. I came home about ten o'clock at night. I was tired. The dogs were tired. And a mountie came in and said, ''Come on, we're going up to Johnson Creek to head off Albert Johnson. He passed La Pierre House.'' I said to him, ''Can't you see I just came back? I'm tired. The dogs are tired.''*

[The mountie said] *''Get everything ready tomorrow, and we'll go the next day.''*

And there was another man left [at the village]. *All the rest of them were out on the trapline. There was a man left here. I said, ''What's the matter with Elias?'' ''Oh,'' he said, ''he got sick as soon as I told him we were going up there.''*

So, the next morning after eight o'clock, this woman came in to the house. [She said,] *''This afternoon they're going to get the man. They're going to kill that man. He's going to wound a man, but the man's going to live.''*

So I told the policeman. Oh, he didn't believe it. And I didn't believe her, but I tried to make him believe that I believed it.

Neil McDonald

A son of Archdeacon Robert McDonald, Neil was born in Fort McPherson, but in 1912 he came to the Old Crow region along with the rest of his family.

"Well, by tonight we will hear over the radio that they caught Albert Johnson," [I said], *but that didn't mean that I believed what she had said.*

Around eight o'clock, he rushed in and said, "Well, they got Albert Johnson. He wounded a man, but they took him to Aklavik, and he's going to live."

"Well, that's just exactly what I told you this morning," I said.

Now, how did she know? I asked her one time how she knew these things. She hollered not to ask her that question.

▲ ▼ ▲

Myra Moses
Myra Moses of Old Crow spoke in Loucheux, and Alice Frost translated for her.

In those days some people couldn't afford to buy things. They made knives. From the time they started getting files, they made knives out of these files. I can remember the time they started getting iron. . . . They started making things, and they put a sharp [point] on the end of a stick and they used it to kill caribou from canoes while the caribou were swimming across rivers.

▲ ▼ ▲

Eliza Ben Kassi
Eliza Ben Kassi also spoke in Loucheux, with Alice Frost translating into English.

The Eskimos were good people. They used to live together, and the Indians used to like the Eskimos. They used to hunt together and they killed caribou and all that game. They used to divide it up amongst themselves. Sometimes, I heard, an Eskimo man was married to an Indian woman.

The Eskimos used to come from the coast . . . to hunt on the mountains with the Indians. . . . The Eskimo used to move towards them and they [the Indians] moved to them too. They used to hunt together.

The Indians used to dry their meat, but the Eskimo used to take the fresh meat back down to the coast. In those days they used to do that when they only lived on caribou and other game. After they started to get groceries and stuff from Herschel Island they never saw Eskimos again after that. They didn't bother with Eskimos after that.

▲ ▼ ▲

Joe Netro
Joe Netro of Old Crow has published his own book of Loucheux stories, but he told some for this book as well.

Well, I'm going to tell one from 1903. I remember stories from 1903. [In] 1903, we were down there at Herschel Island. They hunted the whales. That's where our father [and others went] to get their supplies to live on: tea, tobacco, ammunition, guns and tents.

And that winter, people had tough luck — no caribou. They pretty nearly lost their lives. Anyway, they kept on going. They had nothing to eat. And they went down to Alaska, away, and just about all [the food was gone]. They ran into a bunch of people who actually saved their lives.

Once in a while they killed one moose. They say [that was a] big bunch of people going down there together and that one moose, they got one meal out of it. They ate skin and all. And there were no dogs left. All the dogs froze to death. And the women hauled toboggans, hauling their camp supplies. And men all hunted all the time.

That winter, later on, around March I guess, they moved back around Crow Flats. That's where they lived in the summertime. They went fishing and they hunted ducks. And of course caribou and sometimes moose.

284

And that summer, 1904, Dan Cadzow [a white trader] *came up to New Rampart down near the border with the trading supplies. He travelled up from Fort Yukon. He had about eighteen men on the tow lines. He hauled about five tons with that scow. And that's where the people got their supplies from then on — right off the deck. And the people just trapped up in this country. You can't even grow potatoes here. Nothing. Somebody tried it and he couldn't make it.*

So we just live off the country — fur, fish, birds. Before that, when Hudson's Bay first came to the country, let's say 1840, these people right here went over to McPherson. And boats came from a thousand miles up the Mackenzie. Sometimes the whole boat portaged; sometimes they piled up supplies down there and they brought them to McPherson or up here, or even to the Fort Yukon Hudson's Bay post. Ammunition, tobacco and tea, that's all that they had then.

My father told me that one time he went up to Athabasca. I don't know how far that is. [He went] *up the Mackenzie and portaged around bad water. While the* [Indian men] *worked for Hudson Bay, all they ate was dry meat and tea. All summer they work as deckhands. Some of them made one kettle* [for pay]. *That must have been some kettle! They had to work for that a whole summer!*

And some of them wanted guns. They got one gun for the whole summer. In the springtime, one person wanted a gun — a double-barreled gun. The Hudson's Bay [trader] *put the gun up. Whoever wanted the gun piled the beaver* [skins] *flat. If the beaver were even with the gun, that guy got the gun.*

The Hudson's Bay shipped their fur from here. I don't know where they shipped it to. They sent it out. They had to wait three years before they got their return.

And people sold meat to Hudson's Bay. They'd save one half, and they dried it. One half they sold for 25¢ a bag . . . I don't know what the fur prices were then. I heard that marten was 50¢ in those days. That's pretty low, but I don't know what the price was outside. It might have been low out there too.

I'm going to tell you a story about this man. His name was Man Without Fire. He used to be one of the people around here [Old Crow]. *That guy, his people moved to this place by the caribou fence. I heard that they killed moose — two: one cow and one bull moose. They killed them, and he was making a feast.*

And I heard that his wife was a real Smart Woman. In those days they used skin houses, and his brother was staying across from him, with a fire in the middle. He stayed on this side and his brother stayed on the other side. He made this feast with that moose and brought people in to eat. And in those days they never had [many] *dogs and this man only had two dogs.*

These Eskimos, they came around. And these people that were eating inside the skin house, they didn't know these Eskimos had come and surrounded them. These Eskimos all went around that tent.

And Man Without Fire really made this feast, and he was feeding these people. He was hot, so he took off his coat — his skin clothes — and [there was] *fur on his coat, you know. It was so hot he took it off.*

Myra Moses, Old Crow, 1977 (photo by James Fall)

Sarah Abel

Sarah Abel, again with Alice Frost as translator, told a story well know among the Loucheux, about Kò' Ehdanh, or Man Without Fire.

285

Martha & Moses Tizya, Old Crow, 1984
(photo by John T. Hitchcock)

And these Eskimos came in around this tent. He found out, so he cut a hole through that tent on top and he jumped out. Just his brother went with him, too. The Eskimos killed all the rest of those people. Only two of them were alive.

These Eskimos knew that Man Without Fire's wife was a Smart Woman, so the Eskimos took her.

And it was in October when this happened, and there was snow on the ground. And Man Without Fire's brother's wife, she crawled under the snow. Where this woman crawled under the snow, that's where these Eskimos started kicking. These Eskimos had snowshoes on, and they had sharp rocks tied underneath their snowshoes. And the woman that was underneath the snow, they went over the top of her and they cut her ankle gristle [tendon].

This Man Without Fire only had fur pants on [because] he took his coat off. And these Eskimos, were chasing him and his brother. And among the rocks on the mountains there was just a little place. And he saw that place, and he jumped up there and hid there. And these Eskimos were following them. He made it up there and his brother started to jump up there after him, but the Eskimos got him and they killed his brother right in front of him.

Man Without Fire — lots of people had hard times — [but] he really had hard times! They killed his brother, and under him [down there] they had his wife too. And he sat up there watching all that.

And these Eskimos, they all were passing, and this last man, it was — they'd been friends before. And this last guy that was behind them was his friend [trading partner?]. And he told Man Without Fire to come back down to him, and he cried for him to do that. But he didn't want to.

This friend had a long pair of mitts that go up to your shoulders, with a string here [across the chest] and behind. His friend left that there for him, because he had no coat and this was in October. And he told his friend he didn't even have anything on, no hat, no coat. He only had his fur pants on. And he told his friend, "In December," he told him, "Don't stay home!" That's when the caribou hair gets really long, and that's why he told him not to stay home in December.

After the Eskimos all passed, Man Without Fire got down and went back to where all his friends had been killed. And he saw smoke when he was going back to that camp. And this woman that was hiding under that snow, it was her. Even though [she was wounded] she made fire for herself. When he was going back to this place, Man Without Fire was crying.

This woman was his sister-in-law, and she told him that she was alive. These two dogs that belonged to Man Without Fire, when the Eskimos came to kill these people, these dogs — they were wise dogs — they ran in the bush. But when their master was coming back, they came out of the bush. This woman that made fire, before she went under the snow she put a big piece of wood into the fire. She put ground over it and then she covered it with brush. This wood she put in was rotten wood, and there was a hole in it. They had that there, and he told his sister-in-law to put dry branches in there, once in a while and not to let the snow fall into the rotten wood.

Then he had nothing to kill anything with. He only had a good piece of hard wood. That's all he had.

He had two sisters, and he wanted [to go] there to find them. He only had those two dogs with him.

At that time they had long fur coats. The woman had a long fur coat, and she cut half of that for him and he covered himself with that. The only thing he could kill was rabbits. When he wanted rabbits, he threw the stick. And the rabbit would go under the snow by the trees [to escape]. And the rabbit was sitting under there, and he'd step on top of the snow. That's how he got that rabbit under the snow. This was in October.

And he kept walking. And by this time the winter was nearly over. He didn't have a blanket or anything. When he killed this rabbit, he cooked it in the fire and ate some of it. And he gave meat to the dogs, some of that rabbit. And when he went to sleep he put these two dogs on each side of him. And that's how he slept — they kept him warm. He made a hat for himself out of the rabbit skin and then he made himself a coat out of rabbit skin too. And then he was okay.

This rotten wood — he carried that, and he kept that fire and coals inside going, and that's how he made fire.

And when he was going along — it was January — he saw a rabbit. And he didn't set this wood up well, and it fell over in the snow, and the coals inside went out.

And about that time — about March — he got to some people. He found some people. All this time he killed rabbits. It was hard for him to eat it raw, but he took the liver out, and he just ate a little piece of that liver.

And he finally found a trail and he found an old camp. And the snow on top measured about one foot — the snow on top of that old trail, and he found an old camp where somebody had been staying for a long time. And these people had lots to eat. They had lots of meat. And he kept on following that trail, and the snow on the trail was less than when he first got to the camp.

And he got to another camp; it was real fresh. Right before he got there these people had moved from their camp. There was still fire there when he got there. He hadn't seen fire for about half of the winter.

And when he got to this fire he made a big fire, and there was lots of caribou feet around there. He put one of these under that fire to cook. And he felt like going to sleep, so he just lay down there. He put a bunch of branches under his feet, and he put his mitts on, and he just fell asleep. He slept all day.

Toward the evening he woke up. After he woke up he took this caribou feet out, and he opened that caribou foot up and between [the toes] there's a little white meat or fat and he took that out and he swallowed that.

After he had that to eat, he started walking again. He was following the trail. When he got to the camp, these hunters were out hunting. They killed lots of caribou and they were coming home. They saw smoke near their [old] camp. And these hunters saw this when Man Without Fire got to the camp. [A man] talked from the camp. In those days they had one Smart Man — not chief, but he was the boss. He used to talk loud from a long distance. And these hunters, they heard this man. These hunters saw the smoke from that camp, and he told everybody to watch real good because they were scared of enemies. And when this guy stopped talking, Man Without Fire started walking again.

Sarah Abel, Old Crow, 1984 (photo by John T. Hitchcock)

And there was a little snowhouse, and that's where an old lady stayed. And he took his snowshoes off and he went into this old lady. And he told this old lady that Eskimos had killed all his friends. Only he was alive. And he told this old lady not to call him by his own name, just to call him Man Without Fire.

And this old lady started to go out to tell the other people, but he didn't want her to. So he grabbed her back and told her, ''If there's any bone juice, give me some of that first.'' And this old lady gave him bone juice and a piece of pemmican. And he ate that and drank the bone juice with it.

And then he told this old lady, ''Now you can go out and tell the other people that Man Without Fire's friends have all been killed, and only he is alive.''

And the old lady told the people. There was about a hundred people in that camp, and they all started crying for him, and they all started running to him. He hadn't seen fire for half of the winter. He kicked his snowshoes off, and he ran away from those people. Then he stopped and he told them, ''You've got to fight [for] me.'' Those people told him they would.

And he had two sisters in that camp. And at that time people had no money. They used to have those big round beads [dentalium shells]. They were so long. And these two sisters paid these people to fight for him. With the beads; that's what they used for money.

And he worked all summer. He hunted, and he made bows and arrows. And in August those people left. He hunted all summer, and all that meat he had killed was for the women that were supposed to stay at home. These men left, and he took them to where his friends were killed and where he saw those Eskimos go. They went and followed them.

Man Without Fire's wife had two Eskimo women on both sides of her when they took her. They were watching her so she wouldn't do anything. They watched so she wouldn't make any mark on the trees.

And she had this caribou skin blanket on. She put that around her, wrapped it around her. And she had this caribou blanket wrapped around her, and even though she had two people watching her, she sometimes rubbed her arm on the bush, and even that they could trace. These people who were following the Eskimo, they [tracked them] *by that* [the caribou hair that rubbed off]. *Sometimes with her feet she broke willows too.*

They took this woman [to a place] *around the coast where all the Eskimos gathered in one place. And here they made their camp on the other side of a big lake. The Eskimos did that.*

And then these Indians followed those Eskimos. There was a mountain. On top there was snow on it. And it melted and turned to ice. And they [the Indians] *lost track of them* [Eskimos]. *This woman didn't know how to make marks any more, so she told the Eskimos that her* [moccasins] *were torn. She just did that on purpose. There was a rock* [ochre] *they used for snowshoes and that. It was just like ink. And she colored the skin with it and sewed that* [ochre] *under her foot. And that got wet, and that's how she made marks on that ice with that red ink. She sewed it under her boots.*

And the Indians that were following the Eskimos lost track; they couldn't find the tracks or any traces, so they told Man Without Fire that there was no use for them to keep going. They told him they wanted to turn back.

And there he really cried. And where these Indians were, this one man kicked out one rock, and there was shavings under it [left by the Smart

Woman]. *Soon they started* [tracking] *again. They got to the top of that mountain, and here they saw Eskimo skin tents! There was lots of them.*

Then those Indians, when they got close to that camp, they made signs to this woman, Man Without Fire's wife. And she made signs. Where it was the shortest way around the lake she threw water [in that direction]. *When they got to the camp they killed all the Eskimos. They only left Man Without Fire's friend. That's the end of the story.*

WHAT THE MAYO PEOPLE SAID

At Mayo there are Loucheux and Northern Tutchone people as well as Indians whose ancestors came from the Mackenzie River area or from the southern Yukon.

My dad used to drink and play cards and everything. But in 1925 he got ordained and he became a preacher then. So, from McPherson we walked across to Old Crow. We walked all the way. It took one week — it's not very far.

So when we landed in Old Crow, my uncle Neil McDonald took us down to Fort Yukon. From there we took the steamboat to Dawson. You know how we got up Ross River? By dog team.

We got on that stagecoach at that time — that was a long time ago. On the stagecoach we put all of our dog teams on top there, and we got to Pelly. From there we went with two or three dog teams. Then we got up to Ross River.

It was strange. Those people up at Ross River hadn't heard about the Lord. So we had to teach them, and I taught them. My daddy was a preacher there for five years, and I taught the kids there.

After that we came back on the Taylor & Drury steam boat. We came up here [to Mayo] *on the steamboat. And we landed here and ever since then we only stayed in Mayo.*

Mary Moses

Mary Moses' father was the Peel River Loucheux minister John Martin, who is mentioned in Chapter Six. She tells how her family first came to Mayo.

▲ ▼ ▲

They came down a long time ago, before me. One of them was my grandpa. My [paternal] *grandpa came from Good Hope. My other* [maternal] *grandpa came from Fort McPherson. That was a long time ago. My* [paternal] *grandpa died at Lansing Creek. He trapped all over the place — at Wind River, Bonnet Plume, Snake River, Little Arctic River, Arctic Red River — all over, trapping. I was born at Lansing. My grandpa came from Good Hope with some dog teams, my daddy's dad. All of those people are dead now.*

This was a good country; that's why they came to Lansing. There was lots of moose at that time. They came with their boats to the mountains, and came down the Stewart River. . . . They were all together all of the time. In the wintertime they trapped everyplace. In springtime they came down again and stayed at Lansing. . . .

My grandpa . . . told me everything. ''You are going to set traps. You're going to learn the right way too.'' . . . My grandpa was 70 years old then. . . . ''Do that,'' he said. He told me that all the time. My grandma told me the same too.

Lonny Johnny

Lonny Johnny, another Mayo Indian, was born at Lansing, east of Mayo. His father's father came from Fort Good Hope, on the Mackenzie River. The trading post at Lansing was established about 1898 by a white trader named Frank Braine. A number of Hare and Mountain Athapaskan Indians from the Mackenzie area came to trade there.

▲ ▼ ▲

Ellen Olin

Catherine Olin translated for Ellen Olin as she spoke of her family's arrival in the Lansing/Mayo area. The white trader she mentions was probably James Mervyn, who took over the Lansing trading post from Frank Braine and Percival Naish in 1912.

I was born at Lansing, but my dad came from Fort Good Hope. My parents came over from the Mackenzie to Lansing by trapping. They came over with a mooseskin boat. A lot of families came over together. When they moved to Lansing, they didn't want to go back. There was a big store there, a trading post. There was more animals this way too — lots. . . . There was some people from Lansing staying there before my parents came — some families.

The owner of the store was a white person from Mayo. Sometimes a few people from Mayo went up that way when they were trapping. The [Lansing Indians] fished, hunted, and the fur they got by trapping they sold to the trading post there and got food. A few families went back to the Mackenzie and never came back to Lansing. That was their country and they wanted to go back.

I learned trapping, hunting, mooseskin tanning, everything. We used to embroider with silk thread and beads and porcupine quills. They used to dye porcupine quills with dandelion flowers and they used the bark of birch trees for a brown color dye. They also used different colored roots.

▲ ▼ ▲

Edwin Hager

Edwin Hager's mother was an Indian from the Whitehorse area and his father a white man. Edwin grew up around Mayo, speaking Northern Tutchone, and was one of the main contributors to the *Mayo Indian Language Noun Dictionary*, published in 1974.

Well, we did a lot of work for ourselves all the time. I watched all those Indians, whatever they did. In the fall I'd go hunt — in September and August. We'd go hunt in September and dry meat and keep the fresh meat and cache the meat. And soon the snow came. And it froze. We all hauled it [the meat] in.

And then we'd go to Ethel Lake and set the nets through the ice and fish. We'd haul all the fish down — 400 pounds, 300 pounds — and sell it . . . That's how the people made a living in the early days — by getting all the fish from the lake and [eating] dry salmon and dry fish and fresh meat in those days.

And after that it all changed. And when the [mining] company started the camp up there, [the Indians] started to cut wood. And some Indians cut wood and made money before they went hunting and fishing. I used to work on the boats as a longshoreman and a deckhand.

In those days sometimes we bought a license for selling the meat, and we sent the meat to Whitehorse when they needed it.

Now we don't do that anymore. But we still use the fish and do the same work and do the same hunting work. We fish for grayling and hunt for duck and rats and beaver and go trapping every year.

▲ ▼ ▲

Johnson Lucas

Johnson Lucas's father came from Fort Selkirk and his mother from Moosehide, near Dawson. The family lived for a while at Fort Selkirk, then moved to McQuesten, where there was a store, and there Johnson was born. His family began to trap around Ladue and Lansing creeks and never moved back to Fort Selkirk. Johnson

I watched them. I watched how they did things, and I did the same way. I went with my dad all the time, starting when I was about eight years old. I watched them pretty good, especially when he got meat — grizzly, moose.

Indian people didn't throw anything away. They took everything. We hunted moose, grizzly, and caribou. Whatever way they went, we followed their tracks in the wintertime. . . .

I went all over the place, way up to Ethel Lake. I travelled around and trapped anyplace. My grandfather [father-in-law] Peter, my wife's dad, was my partner.

I don't know how many years we stayed at Fraser Falls. We trapped, trapped, trapped, all the time. We stayed there all winter, and then I came down the first of June [to Mayo] to work on the boats, and I went back up in August again. I went out in the bush and got ready for the trapline. I tried [to teach my grandchildren about the Indian ways] but they don't want to talk the Indian language. I talk my own language [but they don't understand]. They have had too much white man's language, and they can't understand the Indian language.

▲ ▼ ▲

People moved from Selkirk to McQuesten. I don't know what year — a long time before the Dawson strike. From Selkirk people hunted to the Wind River and up to the head of the Stewart River. They hunted for beaver there from Selkirk. They went up the McQuesten River, then they hit the Beaver River and went down the Beaver River, and then they went down to here [site of Mayo]. Then way down over to the McQuesten River there was a road [trail] that went over to Selkirk. They landed there and packed beaver skins over.

At that time Coast Indians traded with the people. They sold guns and shells and stuff like that, and clothing. So they met together at Selkirk. Some people met at Carmacks, also around there. that's the way they worked it, a long time before the white man came.

So people hunted from there to the Beaver River. That's a long way, so they moved over to McQuesten, these people. They started a store there too. . . . I don't know for how long these people traded with the Coast Indians, the Selkirk people — way before the white man came. They packed stuff from the ocean. So I understand — white people told me — they say Hudson's Bay and the Russians started stores along this [Yukon] river way down to the ocean. And then the Americans bought all the land and they split up. Hudson's Bay went to Selkirk after that. In [1848] they started a store. Before that, at that time, Coast Indians were rough. They burned down the store in [1852]. The Indians stopped it. Later, [in 1938] Hudson's Bay started running a business [at Selkirk] again. That's why the people stayed down there, for the fur, you know. . . .

Sam told another story too about the move to McQuesten:

Two brothers were hunting. One brother shot his oldest brother. He didn't do what his brother told him to do. He thought he had killed his brother. He cried so much that the people went there. And his brother died.

That oldest brother was a doctor. He touched his back, and there was no bullet hole. Just this much. Just a little bit more [and he would have been able to cure himself]. This one [wound] here [in front] was all fixed up, and his back had already started to heal. But at that time the people came, so he [couldn't finish healing himself]. He had told the people not to come. He said, "In five days, you come back."

But his brother didn't do that. The older brother was an Indian doctor. He could fix himself, you know. But his younger brother didn't obey him, so he died. So that's why the people moved over here to McQuesten from Selkirk.

married a woman from the Mackenzie River side whom he met in Mayo, and both spoke Northern Tutchone.

Sam Peter

Sam Peter, a Wolf, also contributed to the *Mayo Indian Language Noun Dictionary*. His mother and father were both from Selkirk, but his mother's mother came from Dawson, and his wife was from Dawson as well. He tells how the Northern Tutchone moved into the McQuesten area. This move began perhaps as early as 1840, with more permanent settlement in the 1880s, when there was a store at the mouth of the McQuesten River.

Edwin Hager (left) and Sam Peter, Mayo, 1975 (photo by John Ritter)

WHAT THE HAN AND NORTHERN TUTCHONE
SAID AT DAWSON

Most of the Han-speaking people who originally lived in the Dawson area died of sickness during the Gold Rush, but Indians from all over Alaska, the Yukon and the Northwest Territories also gathered there during the excitement, and some of them stayed. Thus, many of the narrators who speak in this section of the book trace their ancestry to places other than Dawson. Other Indians have come to the area even more recently.

Charlie Johnson

A Wolf, Charlie Johnson was born at Fort Selkirk and moved to Dawson in 1942. His story about a man who had eagle medicine is a tale he learned from his father. Since the man with eagle medicine also came from Selkirk, he probably spoke Northern Tutchone, but his story is told also among the Han and Loucheux, and by some Southern Tutchone as well.

This is a story about the man who the caribou took away. This is a true story. His grave is just below Three Way Channel, along the Yukon River. They buried him where he wanted to be buried. You can see his grave there on the middle of the bank — it's not too high a bank. They called him Eagle Medicine Man; Indian way, Chägaltiya. . . .

He lived with the caribou for two years, but he knew something about eagles. [He had spirit power from an eagle.] *He thought about that one, and his two* [caribou] *wives held his arms.*

"What are you thinking about? What are you worrying about?"

He said, "I'm not worrying." Pretty soon he heard something coming — a big wind, a heck of a big noise! Everything cracked. Trees fell down. Pretty soon it got close. Everybody got scared. All the caribou all ran around.

Pretty soon he jumped. He made a jump. The eagle grabbed him here, but the caribou pretty nearly pulled him back. But he made it. And the eagle took the man home.

Pretty soon they landed on the top of a mountain. He [the eagle] *said, "You take your clothes off."*

They landed there. He didn't know what he had for clothes. He had horns. He pulled everything off and he threw it away — the caribou skin, everything. He had turned into a caribou.

His [eagle] *medicine had done that* [helped him to escape from the caribou].

He was a good medicine man. He used to cure men too. When somebody got sick, he helped him out.

One time he fell. He was chasing a moose, and he fell down. He got poked with a moose horn, an old horn. It went right through and came out. He healed himself up. Nothing was wrong with him [after that]. . . .

This man's home was at Selkirk. That's where his people stayed. They all travelled around in the bush hunting meat. . . .

My dad told me this story. He saw him when he died. Everybody was there, because he got sick. He got too old, and he couldn't walk. So they all moved down there. They made a grave at Three Way Channel. You can see that grave when you go along the Yukon River. The last time I went by there, the fence was still standing.

▲ ▼ ▲

[In the old days] you could go anyplace at all along the roads. You were always welcome, as long as they had room for you. People pretty much lived on the same things — lots of fresh vegetables and moose. Stuff like that. We always had plenty. You never got stuck, regardless of where you were if you broke down or needed help. There was always help.

We lived at Halfway and we lived at Twelve Mile. It was one big family. When it came time to harvest the hay in the fall of the year, a whole bunch came down there to give us a hand. We had five horses and we had to raise a lot of hay, all by hand. It took a lot of work. So they helped. And then we went up there and did the same for them. We helped them bring in their wood for the winter and saw it up. We'd loan the horses and go up there for about a week and haul wood for them. . . .

My brother and I used to fish down at Forty Mile in the early days. When we travelled down there we could not go by this cabin on the Forty Mile River. "Come in and have a cup of tea!"

"We just had a cup of tea and piece of pie not five minutes ago!"

"Well, you've got to stop. We've got a big pot of beans going!"

You just had to stop, that's all there was to it. . . .

On the river, the whole bunch, we lived together. When one person got a moose, everybody got a chunk of that. . . .

They never killed more than they needed, and what they killed, they picked up everything. I never saw any meat left over, and I've been to a lot of places where Indian people had been hunting. They clean up everything. When we went up to Fifty Mile we used to take what we needed and no more. If we needed any more, we'd get another one. We never wasted anything.

And there's one thing I don't like to do — feed moose meat to dogs. I never give my dogs any moose meat. I gave them strong bull caribou in the fall of the year and plenty of fish. We had a big fish camp downriver. . . . It's best to save moose for people. You never know [when you might need it]. There used to be lots of old people around at that time, more than there is now — lots of them. In those days young people respected older people.

▲ ▼ ▲

I don't know where they come from. Up there someplace. These people are around Eagle. A mother was stolen with her two kids, a boy and a girl. I don't know how long she stayed with them, but . . . she brought home [another child]. And she [the third child] grew up. She's a bushman's daughter. The woman that was stolen brought her home when she was just a baby.

A long way, I suppose, in the country she was taken. they killed her little boy. They just burned the kid in the campfire. Oh, terrible! And her friend [who was a bushman] told her, "Where there's lots of smoke, there's where you stay. They're going to bring the smoke. If they see you cry, they're going to kill you too." And that was her mother. She was a small baby at that time. The mother had that one, her little girl, with her. Her boy, they killed him.

Then her friend said, "They're going to get rid of you too now. They're going to kill you, and they're going to kill your two girls. So I'm going to say,

Walter DeWolfe

Walter DeWolfe's father, Percy DeWolfe, came from Nova Scotia and carried the mail between Eagle, Alaska, and Dawson for 45 years. Walter himself worked at many jobs over the years — cutting wood, running a meat house, selling fish and carrying mail and freight by dog team.

Mary McLeod

Mary McLeod of Dawson was born near Chicken, Alaska. Her mother was from the Fairbanks area, and her father from the Han village of Eagle, Alaska. Mary tells about the bushmen mentioned in Chapter Eleven.

going to kill you, and they're going to kill your two girls. So I'm going to say, 'We're going to go look for roots or berries.' And I'm going to say, 'I'm going to look after her.' I know them pretty well. I'll make a cache for you.'' That's what he told his friend, [that woman who was stolen]. ''I'm going to say 'I'll look after you,' and you can escape. They say they are going to kill you. A long time after, I'm going to help you out,'' he told his friend.

So he told her, ''Go now. . . . When you get tired, go in a cave and block up yourself with rocks.''

She did that. While travelling around, she did that. She made a long trip. She went to where her friend had made a cache, but some animal had taken it away. So she kept on going and got to a place by a river.

In those days they had birch, and they made a little baby carrier and put the little baby inside. She put her baby inside the birch carrier, and packed that little baby.

And the current was running on the other side of the river. Some [bushmen] came already, and there was no place to hide. By a windfall, a leaning, rotten tree, she found a place to hide inside. With rotten wood, she blocked up herself. And they walked on top and didn't know she was there.

A long time after, she came out of that log and she threw that baby way over in the basket. And she thought the currents would land it on the other side. And she didn't know how to swim. She packed the oldest one, and she jumped as far as she could over the river. . . . That's how she got to the other shore.

She picked up that baby and she started again. She hid in a cave for a long time. She heard two people going back on top just where she hid.

A long time after, she came out and at the place where they had stolen her. She saw a big camp — that was her husband's. He expected her, and he [had] made a cache and left her some food. She went down to the cache. When she went down, two big grizzlies came to that cache. They got on top of the cache. Well, she talked to them. ''I've suffered enough. I've got a baby. I expect to get something. What are you guys doing there?'' She talked to the bears in their own language.

And those grizzlies looked at each other and they jumped out of the cache. On their way away, they looked back at the woman again. They looked again, and they went. See, the animals are smart sometimes, too. They understand.

So she got on top. Those bears didn't take much, just a little bit. She felt good. He had left some water there.

Her husband came along to check up on the cache. He finally brought her home.

Oh, they made a potlatch, a big potlatch! They got the woman back!

When she grew old, when she reached old age, those same people [bushmen] killed her. Down near Eagle, not very far from the village, there's a creek there. She set a snare for rabbits. She had a teapot at that creek. She made tea for herself for when she returned. Well, lots of bushmen just snatched her away. They killed her, those bushmen. They told the people what they were going to do, and they broke sticks and piled them up. They made a sign, meaning, ''This many people have been here.'' That's a sad story.

Mary McLeod told another story about bushmen that goes like this:

Mary McLeod, Dawson, 1966

Before Eagle someplace, the Indians put up lots of dry meat and fish, maybe some berries too. Lots of stuff they had. An old man and his grandson were there. People made too much noise, laughing. That old man sent his grandson, saying, ''Go down there and see what they're doing and tell me.''

He went back to his grandpa and said, ''Grandpa, they're playing with a frog. They're playing ball with it.''

''Well, go back there and try to catch hold of it and run out in the woods with it and throw it away,'' he told him. That was a stupid, foolish thing, to play with the frog like that. After that, all the food those people had, it spoiled, but that old man's food was all right.

Well, that was the time they were starving. They had no food. Nothing. One fellow went out, I suppose in March. They sent him out to look. He made some kind of arrows. Well, he was glad to see a fellow.

''Can you spare some food?'' he asked.

He went to where he had seen the man sitting down. Nobody was there. And he called out, ''We're starving. Lots of people. Women and kids. I thought I'd get something. I thought I saw a man here. Where is he?''

The man talked out from inside a mountain. ''Well, not too much. You guys have hard times. We want to make sure nobody sees us. We don't want people to see us, to know what kind of people we are. Go away someplace else and stay around there. Then come back. We are going to put food out for you to pack back to where you live and divide among your people,'' they told him. So he did it.

They put out just enough food for him to pack. I think they heard his footsteps. They asked him, ''How many in the family?'' Well, in those days, there was lots of people, you know. He told them how many families there were.

Well, every family should bring their toboggan. We're going to put out food for them.''

That man heard footsteps, lots of steps. Every toboggan was loaded with dry meat, sheep meat, all kinds mixed up. See, that's how much they helped the people!

''Well, this time we're going to help you that much. Try hard. Don't try to find out and come here to see what kind of people we are. Don't you try to sneak around and find out. We don't want to mix with people,'' they told that man.

They didn't see each other. They talked from inside the mountain.

WHAT THE NORTHERN AND SOUTHERN TUTCHONE SAID AT STEWART CROSSING, PELLY CROSSING AND CARMACKS

One time, when I was a kid, I went to a Lansing potlatch. I was a medicine man myself when I was a little kid. At that time there was one woman who had TB. She was ready to die. People were singing there, trying to save that woman.

They went inside. They put her under a blanket in the middle of the floor. Everybody sat around and watched. Two men went inside the blanket with

David Moses

David Moses of Stewart Crossing was originally from the Frances Lake area, but his father, Lucas Moses, was from Fort Selkirk, and his grandfather was Chief Tom of Mayo.

her and sucked all the pus out of her lungs. They put it in a waste pan. It was half full. And I thought about it. I was a little kid. I thought, I thought. And I could see that thing [the sickness].

And those two men knew me too. They came out there, and one said ''Something's wrong around here!'' He put up his hands and sang and danced around.

Pretty soon they came to my mother, and they stopped. Next, to my father, and they stopped. He asked my dad and he asked my mom. Me! A little kid! He picked me up and put me in the middle there. A bunch of people were watching.

He told me, ''You are thinking about something too strong. Do you think you can save this woman?''

I said, ''I don't know. She's too far gone.''

He said, ''Come with us then, and we'll try to help.''

I went inside the blanket with them. And then I could see it, that it was too late. The woman was nearly gone. The body was pretty near gone. So I ran out. I ran home. I was only a kid. I ran home and I went inside. And all the blankets we had I covered myself with. I went underneath them. And I cried.

And then I heard a shot. ''Oh, they are shooting the woman now!'' That's what I thought.

Then pretty soon I heard another shot. Finished. Then I looked. I came on top. My dad was standing there making tea. And I said, ''Dad?''

''What?''

''How come those people shot?''

''Oh,'' he said, ''they are shooting the sickness away.''

''Oh,'' I said. ''You can't shoot the sickness away. She's finished,'' I said. ''That woman is going to die tonight. You just watch.''

She died the same night.

And my dad didn't know anything about medicine men at that time, and he believed in it after that.

Yes, I flew around all over. It is just like you are sitting here, like you fly all over at nighttime. You visit people you don't know, and they don't know you. . . .

Now I quit that. I talk about it so I can get away from it, and so it will be gone.

If you're going to go out hunting, the medicine man could tell you [what you will get] *too. You sit down when you are going to go some place, and he tells you what to do. It's just like you know something. You are going to go out and shoot a moose. He could tell you what kind of moose you are going to kill and all this. I didn't like that, so I told people about it and it disappeared. It went away. If you talk about* [your medicine], *it goes away.*

▲ ▼ ▲

Dave Silas
Dave Silas moved to Pelly Crossing after spending most of his life near Fort

They used to talk about the Coast Indians. They talked about how the Coast Indians took the trade from Hudson's Bay. They burned down the store and packed all the stuff and took it out, outside. The [Hudson's Bay] *man,*

[Robert Campbell], *went down river. He was the first Hudson's Bay man, who started the business there, pretty near a hundred years ago* [1848]. . . . *They* [the Coast Indians] *burned down the store so he wouldn't start a store again. They told that man to go away. That's all, and they burned down the store.* . . . [The Selkirk] *people were out in the woods, and some were fishing* [when this happened]. *They had fish traps down at Three Way Channel. Then the Hudson's Bay man came down. He told them* [what the Coast Indians had done].

Old Matthew went up to help, but they had left already. He maybe was going to fight them, but when he got there, they all had left there already. . . . *The people were pretty mad at the Coast Indians, but they had left already. Maybe they were going to fight them.* . . . *People got pretty mad at that time, they say.*

The Indians came to sell the fur [at Fort Selkirk]. *In the springtime Pelly Indians came down and sold their fur. Some Big Lake* [Aishihik Lake] *people came down too. Beaver was worth about ten dollars at that time. They paid with money.* . . .

A long time ago, Mr Pitts [manager of the trading post at Fort Selkirk] *traded with square money. He cut up paper, something just like cardboard. He cut it and made money. He bought fur and gave the people that money.* . . . *That guy at Selkirk, he sold with paper. They couldn't use it anyplace else, just at the one store, that's all.*

▲ ▼ ▲

From Fort Selkirk, we started up [the Pelly] *River there, pulling boats too. We came back with dry meat, on a big raft, lots of fresh meat and grub. We had everything at that time. They killed a whole bunch of moose and caribou and sheep and all that. They didn't need to buy anything at the store. They used that fat out of the moose and caribou meat, whatever they can get a hold of. They used that for lard. They used to have a pile as big as this house here when they came back with dry meat.*

This was in the falltime; they left in August. We went up [the Pelly] *River. In wintertime, we came back. As soon as it got cold, we let it go. We didn't shoot anything anymore.*

They went in the mountains. There were bull moose in the mountains in August time. They went up high. Did you ever see the dog packs they use? I had six dogs. They could pack anything. They could pack a moose all the way down here! My father-in-law had six dogs too. We packed one moose, fat and skin too.

We didn't let anything go, if we got anything. Sheep — they got fat sheep in the falltime. We dried meat, and we dried meat. We got enough until springtime, everything.

Nobody was hungry. . . . *We helped all the time one another too. We trapped for fur. We trapped lynx. It tastes as good as turkey! We ate beaver meat and muskrats. We trap, we trap, and we got lots of fur too when we trap.*

▲ ▼ ▲

Selkirk. He often worked on the riverboats, starting in 1918. Here he tells an old story about the destruction of Robert Campbell's Fort Selkirk store, and about the later store run by Arthur Harper. These later events probably occurred about 1890, since a man named Pitts was keeping the store for Harper at that time.

Johnny Alfred

Johnny Alfred, a Wolf from Pelly Crossing, speaks here with the help of Rachel Tom Tom, a Crow. Johnny used to hunt and trap with Rachel Tom Tom's father.

Ellen Silverfox

Ellen Silverfox, of Pelly Crossing, was also born at Fort Selkirk.

A long time ago people had hard times, you know. They stayed out in the bush camp, with no tent, no stove. Now we have all kinds of things — spoons, plates to eat on.

A long time ago Indians used birch, you know. They used that kind of plate — birch. They used sticks for spoons. They had a little knife to hollow it out with. . . . You know copper, that kind? They use that kind to make knives and adzes. It was very sharp.

My old man used that copper for nets — with that big copper rock, it sunk down. It was heavy [the net sinkers]. *He could see it. It was a green rock. They got this rock down the Pelly River at Moose Skin Rock. . . .*

They made birch pots. They packed rocks in the wintertime. They just made a fire and threw the rocks in. They put meat in. Then they drank soup. No tea long time ago! That's what our old dad told us. That's why we know the stories. . . .

I wish I had some birch. You know, it's easy to make baskets. . . . We cut a stick, a little bit sharp [to pry the birchbark off the tree] *around this time of the year* [late July]. *Right now is a good time. You wet the bark to use it. And from any tree, they got roots. They split them and used them to sew baskets together.*

▲ ▼ ▲

Johnny Tom Tom

Johnny Tom Tom's parents were from Champagne and Aishihik, so he grew up speaking Southern Tutchone. He cut and rafted wood, worked on steamboats and ferries, on the Klondike Highway and as a carpenter, prospector, hunter and trapper. Here he tells about rafting wood on the Yukon River.

I brought lots of wood down in my day to Dawson City. I sold wood. I cut it in the winter and rafted it down in the summertime. For twelve years I worked for myself. I didn't work for wages. I made a lot of money. I cut sixty cords of dry wood and rafted it down to Dawson City. Lots of people in Whitehorse and Dawson at that time. They had no oil stoves.

We took the wood by big rafts, seven sections long. Four men worked altogether on the raft. I took maybe two or three rafts every summer to Dawson. I had a boat with a six-cylinder motor. I beat the steamboat up all the time. I passed it all the time.

We stayed in Dawson three or four days and we hauled that wood out. I sold the wood, the raft of wood, while it was in the water. I sold it in the water. And then we hauled it out on the beach.

I worked three summers for Taylor & Drury on the steamboat. Taylor & Drury paid $2.50 a day. I worked as a deckhand for the White Pass steamboat for two years. I put away all the money I made in the bank when I worked on the steamboats. . . . I used that money when I started to cut the wood. That way I worked for myself. I didn't work for anybody. Twelve years is a long time.

The rafts were of dry wood, 16-foot lengths, 32 feet wide. They were pretty well loaded.

This is a story about one of the biggest rafts I took down to Dawson City, from White Pass. Two men came up to see me. They made a deal with me. They had no wood for the steamboat at Dawson City. So they told me, ''We'll transfer all your crew back. The boat, everything.''

''Okay.''

So we made a deal. They agreed to pay me $14 a cord on the water. Okay. Seven sections long. Oh, boy, talk about a big raft! And that raft drew 2.5 feet in the water, down in the water. And I had an inboard motorboat. Some *places, where there were two or three channels, I kept pushing with the boat on the sides and pushed ahead. In three nights I went down to Dawson City from the wood camp. And I tied my raft right across from Sweet Creek, by Big Eddy. I pushed with my boat. Every place we tied the raft with two snapping lines — heavy. I helped with the boat too.*

Somebody who was taking a raft down, Little Sam, told me, ''That raft is too big. You're going to lose the wood. You're going to hit that bar. It's too big.''

Well, I had a boat and that boat helped me. So, I landed it okay. Big Slough, from there I went down to Dawson, and I went right up to White Pass office. ''I've got the raft up there now on the slough.''

''Good!'' he said. ''We're going to get it now,'' he told me.

They had a big boat, a White Pass boat. I wanted three boats to push the raft. Tom Gwynn, the man knew how to land the raft. I wanted him. We landed that raft right where they wanted it. We tied it up with two lines.

And they put lots of crew to work there. They took some of my crew too, and they tore up the raft, and put it up on the bank. They used horses — four horses. They had two long skids, with two horses each. They pulled one cord at a time from the water. In two days and a half they finished. All the wood was on the bank.

I got hold of the guy there. ''Come down and measure the wood.'' He measured the wood. You know how much I brought on one raft? 156 cords, in one raft! Just think of that. I got lots of money.

I went to the bank and they made up a cheque for me. I got a big pile of money, and I put it inside a big envelope. And I paid the boys. I put all the tools in the boat, and I took it down to the White Pass dock.

''Okay'' he said. ''Put your boat in the scow.''

This was in September. So the next day the boat left. And all the crew got a free ride — bed, meals, everything. They hauled the boat too. They took the boat home to Fort Selkirk. And I went back too.

Ellen Silverfox at the Hager fish camp on the Pelly River, 1977 (photo by James Fall)

You know, that frog there talked all the time in the lake. You know the way they talk every morning?

Then the headman [of the Indians] said, ''Why's that frog talking down there all the time? Bring him here. I want to talk to him.'' He said this to his people.

They went down there, and they brought back the frog. Then the headman said, ''Why do you talk all the time in the morning? We can't get to sleep good. And you talk every morning!'' He told this to the frog.

And the frog answered, ''Why do you people never wash? You've got to wash your hands and your knees. Wash them, and your feet, after you eat. That's what I talk about.'' Then he went back. They put him back down there.

Then those people talked about it. ''Oh, we'll try to talk to him alongside the lake. We will tell him we're going to make a potlatch. Then he will come.''

Then they went to the lake. They stood there. They talked to that frog

Susie Skookum

Susie Skookum of Carmacks tells about a frog's potlach.

alongside the lake. ''We're going to make potlatch. You come now, all you [frog] people,'' they told him. And they went back.

Pretty soon they came. All the frogs came. Then, they ate like the people. They sat down and ate. All the frogs did that.

Then the people took down all that food to the lake. The frogs went back without the food that was inside the plates. The people couldn't take the food to the frogs. ''How are we going to do this?'' they said, those people.

They put the plates alongside that lake. They left them with food inside there — all, everything that they wanted to give to those frogs.

Then, the people came back. Nothing was left inside of those plates. The frogs had taken it all. Then, after, the people sat down. Then pretty soon one [frog person] came. He called those people. ''We are going to make potlatch too. You come,'' he said. ''All you people come.''

''Oh, we will try to go. those people came here. We've got to do the same,'' they said.

Then, they went alongside the lake. They went in under the lake water. It was all just like a big potlatch there, just like people give. They went in. Then they ate there. They took their food.

Then they came back there. One man went ahead. They all came out of the water. Then they took home all that food that the frogs had given them. After, they put back the plates in the same place. Then, all the plates were gone. That's how it ended.

▲ ▼ ▲

May Roberts

May Roberts, Susie Skookum's half-sister, was also born at Carmacks. Her husband, Jimmy Roberts, was born at Aishihik. (People from the Aishihik and Carmacks areas often intermarried, and those with family ties in both places usually grew up speaking both Northern and Southern Tutchone.) Here May Roberts tells a story about a girl who turned into an owl.

One girl had two husbands, and her own mother just loved her son-in-law. She wanted to get rid of her daughter and marry her son-in-law.

And at that time that girl stayed with these two men. Her husbands went out hunting. And her mom told them, ''I'm going to stay back at camp again. I want to finish this skin,'' she said. So her mom's husband went ahead too, to make camp. . . .

''We'll stay at this camp again,'' the mother said to her daughter. And she knew, you know, that her daughter was just like an Indian doctor. She made medicine with an owl, I think. The mother knew that her daughter was like that.

And the girl's mother saw an owl's big nest. It had young ones in it. And she told her daughter, ''Go climb up to that owl there. I want a feather for a snare. For a gopher snare.''

''Mom, please, no. I'm going to turn into an owl [if I go up there]!'' the girl said.

The mother got mad. ''Go up there and get it!''

So she climbed up there, and pretty soon she reached the owl. Her body just fell down, and she turned into an owl. Her body was just dead there. And her mom was glad that the girl died.

And she [followed] those men that her daughter stayed with. She dressed up with the clothes her daughter had. She tried to take off her [daughter's] skin and put it on herself. She got there [to the camp] and her old husband found out about it some way. He killed his own wife. He got mad. ''Where did you put my daughter?'' he said. That woman went after her own son-in-law. That's all.

That's all I know. That's an oldtime story, I think. An old story.

300

WHAT THE SOUTHERN TUTCHONE SAID
AT BURWASH LANDING, HAINES JUNCTION
AND KRAK-R-KRIK

Copper Lily: *We have no sugar. We come this way, that time. Long time* [ago]. *Long ways.*

Mary Jacquot: *We don't know anything that time. We are coming down there. I don't know how old I am that time.* [They] *tell us, ''Just like lots of sheep coming in there.* [There were so many prospectors they seemed like sheep.] *You going to go to Big Lake.'' Mom* [and us], *we come over across here.* [It's the] *first time I see Kluane Lake. We come this way.*

Copper Lily: *You see that mountain there, other side?* [That was the direction from which the family came. I was] *that big when mama died. Jessie* [was] *just a little baby.*

Mary Jacquot: *My daddy, he had a hard time with her. My uncle and lots of people were cutting wood down there for the boats. Taylor and Drury, two men, they go down the Yukon. So those Indians there, they cut lots of wood for them, for their boat. So we went down there. We go down Copper Creek. Nisling over there, that's the place we were born, at Nisling River. We go right down there to Copper Creek, way down.*

My grandpa is Copper Chief. He lives down there by White River. He's got a house there. Copper Chief is a big man. I know my grandpa. He is a big man. He makes a lance just like that of copper. No arrow, no file, nothing. He puts it on a long stick like that, you know. He ties the end with string. Women, they are scared of that thing. They got just like a big gun. He has got a copper knife. If a bear comes in there, well, just he kills it right there! . . . Arrows too, he pounds them in there. Gee, my dad and my mom, they make that arrow for my cousin, my uncle's brother. [He has a] *big bow, just like that. He goes after that moose up there with a bow. It doesn't matter that he's got no gun. He kills those moose.*

Young people now, these boys, they don't know nothing. On snowshoes they run after those moose [long time ago]. *That's my cousin, Copper Peter, he killed all kinds of moose only with bow and arrow. My mom, she makes a big bag like that for his dad too. My dad was Copper Joe. His dad's name is George, George Copper. And Copper Jack, that's my Uncle.*

Copper Chief had five boys; he lost all the girls; I don't know [why]. *Five boys. Copper Charlie and Copper Jim at Carmacks. Right here my dad Copper Joe, Copper George. Copper Jack down in Snag.*

Not one aunt, only those five boys, that's all we know, we lose all the sisters.

▲ ▼ ▲

My daddy went to Champagne. My sister [Mary] *was down there. When I was old enough, about three years old, my dad takes me and my brother too. And after that we stay down in Champagne, about around a year, I guess. Then we come up this way. That's how far I can know. . . .*

Well, my daddy stay with us, cause in the wintertime he can't take us out in the bush, I guess. [It is a] *warm place. We stay in the house. Summertime, I know, we go out someplace. We stay in the bush, kill a moose, I guess, sometimes, like that.*

Copper Lily & Mary Jacquot

Copper Lily and Mary Jacquot are sisters, members of the Crow side, living at Burwash Landing. Here they tell something of their family and how they got to Kluane Lake from the Nisling River when they were both small children. Their grandfather, the Copper Chief of the White River, probably spoke Northern Tutchone and Upper Tanana, but Copper Lily and Mary Jacquot speak a dialect of Southern Tutchone close to that used at Haines Junction and Champagne.

Mary Jacquot at the Elders' Conference, Champagne, 1977 (photo by Janice Sheppard)

Jessie Joe

Jessie Joe of Burwash Landing is also a sister of Copper Lily and Mary Jacquot.

Copper Lily, Burwash Landing, 1968

Then after that, and Mary too she stays with somebody else. My other sister, Copper Lily, she stays with somebody up here this way. I didn't know her. My dad told me about her, but I didn't know who he meant. He told me I got a sister up here. I and my brother, Jimmy Joe, were with my Dad. He [my brother] *was small too.*

All the Champagne people come up. Moose John and everybody come up here. They come over by the lake. Somebody comes with a horse there. . . . They go down below from up here, where the airfield is. That's what Mary told me.

My dad take us down. We all move. Everybody moves camp. . . . We take the cut-off that way. We get down there. Hey! Lots of people! Lots of different houses. [It was] *all covered up with willows, you know.* [There was] *lots of timber. . . .*

And we come there, and my daddy made a fire. And we start to make tea. I play around there, and I hear somebody call me. I see a tent there in the bush. Somebody calls me, so I turn around. She says, "Come on!" She says, "You come on here." She says, "Your food. You eat here!" She tells me.

So I run over there. It was Copper Lily. She had her first baby that time. . . . She [the baby] *died in 1942 or 1941, just a year before the highway.*

I started to eat. She cooked gopher there. "Who did you come with?" she said. "You and your brother, who did you come with, my dad?" she asked me. "Did you come with my mother?" she asked me.

I says, "No, we don't come with your father, we come with my father, I tell you! We come with my father, not your father!"

She started to laugh. "That's my father!" she says. "You're my sister!" I don't know.

So she says, "You take this gopher to my dad," she tells me. "You come back here after you eat."

So we come back and eat. I take that gopher to my dad. I told him, "That lady over there, she told me, 'He's my dad,' she told me. How come she told me [that]?"

Dad told me, "You, you got a sister up here," he told me then. "That's her," he told me. "There's Kitty and Mary and her. There's five girls. One girl died. . . ."

▲ ▼ ▲

Dixon John & Frank Joe

Dixon John, a G̲aanax̲teidí Crow, and Frank Joe, a Wolf, were recorded at Haines Junction. Dixon's father was from Lake Laberge. His mother's father, from Dalton Post, spoke Tlingit, and Dixon himself understood both Southern Tutchone and Tlingit. He lived most of his life around Pine Lake. Frank Joe's mother was a Northern Tutchone from Selkirk, but after her marriage she lived first at Aishihik and later at Kloo Lake and Haines Junction. Frank spent much of his life at Kloo Lake. He and

Frank Joe: He's an A-1 singer. He's the one. Wait till I explain. . . . He used to come here before. One time they were going to hang him down in Dawson City. He flew out of there as a crow. He's past the time [set for the hanging] *then,* [so] *they wouldn't hang him. That's the song he's going to sing: "When his time* [is] *coming, he* [is] *past it now."*

They couldn't do anything, those Mounted Police. [When] *they tied a rope around there, he sure started to sing that song. People listened to that song. He flew out of there. They call him by an Indian name, Sakwaye. His dad was Sakwaye, but they call him Sakwaye though,* [like his dad].

Dixon John: His dad [was] *outside Indian* [a Coast Tlingit]. *You know what he did? He killed somebody. They take him to Dawson. They hang them there, anybody who kills somebody. So that time he says, "Well, give me chance! I did a little singing before. Let me sing!"*

The policeman look at him. "Go ahead, sing!" they tell him.

Pretty soon he sings. The judges all forget that they were going to hang him. He sings [until after] *half past two. Now he gets past over his time* [when he was supposed to be hanged]. *He makes it!*

Frank Joe: *He flew out of there as a crow, I think.*

Dixon John: *Well he sings all right! Well I'm going to sing again.* [Dixon then spoke in Tlingit]. *I talk Tlingit pretty good myself you see.* [Then Dixon sang the song.] ·

He flies! That's right, he flies! I don't know what he does [to be able to fly]. *He make money that way though.*

You know they are going to hang him to the pole. They have got a rope pretty well placed around his neck, you see. So that time he says that, you know, that song. But he means, "My time's not now to hang until I'm dead."

So he says that, "If anybody cries for me, all my aunties," he says. See, that's what I said. [Dixon sings again.]

That time I tell you true. That's the time he sings again. We don't understand much. I'm going to explain to you right, so you understand me good, but you don't understand me quite enough, you. I haven't been to school myself. [Dixon sings again.]

Joe Singer is a good singer. They call him Joe Singer. I am going to sing [that song] *again.* [Dixon sings again.]

[He was] *just an Indian like me. He climbs up top of that tree, but he is just, you know, like somebody has wings on. He makes it there.*

Frank Joe: [He was] *just like a crow, or raven — something like that.*

Dixon John: *Crow. So he said — he's talking too — he said, "It's a good thing you made me too late!" he said.*

So they tell the judge, "No more hanging. You are too late now. It is over time. It's pretty near half past two now." . . .

That judge said, "Joe, you are a good man. You passed your time," he tells him. "You were going to hang. About ten minutes ago we were going to have you hung." So he passes them there, you see. You see, he thinks he'll make them crazy. That fellow has got a good head, you know, so he make it this time. That's the time he sings, you see.

Dixon John tell here about an Indian who escaped being hung at Dawson. A song goes with the story, and many oldtimers all over the Yukon still sing it.

▲ ▼ ▲

This valley [Shakwak Valley], *up this way, used to be quite a bit of water too. It flooded with water, that other side. Grandma's mother* [was alive] *when the water flooded down here that time. Somebody, they stayed there, up that way. They make lots of gopher then* [snare and dry them]. *Now this time, just after two nights, they go up to the store if they run out of food or something. It's hard to get a moose too. Some people, they don't know how to hunt fur. Some people, they don't get stuck. You see, uncle* [Albert Isaac of Aishihik], *when he traps for lynx, or he sets snares, he gets them. Now nobody is like that now. Not much fur now this winter. Nobody hunts anyway.*

We stay a different place now. Where we used to stay, we used to get fur, at our place. It's hard for us now, up this way where we stay. Now I move

Annie Nicholas

Annie Nicholas, a Crow, was born at Aishihik and lived there much of her life before moving to Haines Junction.

back a little. I do what I like. I set fish net anyway. I pull them out once in a while when I need fish. Then I set it again; it's okay. . . .

Now some people, they got a bunch of dogs, but this time they stay in one place anyway. My son too. he doesn't use his dogs now for four years. He uses a skidoo now. Since spring now he went with the hunters. He doesn't go in the bush now.

▲ ▼ ▲

Jessie Joe

Jessie (Mrs Harry) Joe is a Wolf from a family that has lived for a long time around Dalton Post, Klukshu, Dezadeash and Champagne. The story she tells here shows how strict oldtimers were about the rules for marriage partners. She also refers to the war between Alaska and the Yukon, mentioned in Chapter Ten.

A long time ago they pack their babies so the baby wouldn't get hurt. Every day they pack it and pack it. Never any chance at all to put their baby down. A long time ago those people didn't have their babies till they are grown up to good size, but this time here, I don't know. [Girls have babies when they are too young to care for them.] Everything really changed this time. A long time ago they were never married for quite a long time. But they don't know their ages, that's the trouble; they don't know how old they are.

You did lots of things before you got married. Not like today when you just walk up to a man and just go around with him. In those days it was not like that. In those days if your mother and father wants a woman [for their son], which girl they want, you have to take. . . . [A boy's] mother has to make choice, and his father. You have to get a good wife, smart; that's how it goes.

Crow and Crow are not supposed to marry to each other; Wolf and Wolf are not supposed to. All those things. Now Crow and Wolf, two Crows, marry to each other, two Wolves, all things like that now! Quite a change! Those days you can't even talk to your own friends [people of the opposite sex in your own moiety]. You're shy with them. It's no good if you talk to your brother. Son-in-law; you never used to talk to him too [if you were a woman]. You only used to talk to your sister-in-law and brother-in-law and things like that.

The boy is the one supposed to buy her. . . . If your mother is here, you are not supposed to go about with anybody. They lock [a girl who is not yet married] in. . . . [She doesn't] see anybody till she's married. It's just like you're in jail! Nobody has babies before they're married long time ago. This time here, so many people [do have babies before they are married]. They are the ones that are welfare children.

Girls [used to] stay in until they are married, till they are fourteen or about twelve years old. You couldn't do anything you want to do all the time. You sit down all the time, do sewing and things like that, you do all the work. That's what they do. [Now girls don't] even know how to tan a skin. That's an easy thing to do. See how the girls are all turning out. They all really lost everything, really lost it all what we have been doing [before].

Pretty strict in the old days. They really watched the girls pretty good. . . .

A long time ago we used to live Dalton Post. My dad made the house down there at Dezadeash Lake 1914. He just kind of dreamed that house when he made it. So we moved from Dalton Post to close to Champagne. . . . We used to go Haines [Junction] before — first, before we moved to Champagne. then we moved to Dezadeash Lake.

When we moved there, my mother didn't like to move to Dezadeash because people got killed there from Dalton Post. I don't know how many, maybe 150 altogether, from the war and so on. So nobody used to stay there. When they stayed there at Dezadeash, they had to go across the lake, from the other side. The war was with Snag people. Only one woman was saved out of there. That was Mrs Pringle's grandmother. Only one was saved. Some people used to live in the bay too, way down below. Six Mile Lake too. See, that [group was] *all saved too. Only one* [person was saved] *in that Dezadeash there.*

All the people used to come up here from Dalton Post to the other end of Dezadeash. That's where the fish always started. They come out past here in the springtime — whitefish, jackfish. That's why they used to move to here from Dalton Post spring of the year.

Then when the leaves start to grow, they had to go down Dalton Post [Alsek] *River. I don't know what they call that, way down**. . . . [From] *all over this Yukon, they go down there. . . . They have to go down as far as they could to meet that fish. When they meet the fish, well they stay there maybe about a week, then they start to follow fish back to Dalton Post.*

▲ ▼ ▲

That Smart Man, he goes to a lot of places. He goes to any place in the world. Crow, he's the one; he went there too. . . .

They were singing away, singing away. He [Smart Man] *went out. Somebody was there though, tanning skin. This old lady was tanning skin. They know about it though. That woman was tanning skin all the time, human skin. So she tanned it. And it was Mink Woman.*

And he [Smart Man] *found out. That guy there, that Smart Man, thought it did not look like a moose skin what she was tanning. It was a human skin, because it had long arms, where she was tanning. The way a moose skin is shaped, that's a different shape, that one. That's the way he found out.*

After he found out, he know it was a human skin. He knew it was human skin. After, he goes back; he wants to do something to her. And after, that man thinks what he is going to do. . . . He knows it was Mink. And he kills her, that man.

After he kills her, she turns to mink then. That's how he know she was one. He found out she was mink after he kills her.

After he gets rid of that one, he heard about people [who] *were going one way all the time someplace. So they don't come back. That same man, after people don't know what way to do, after nobody knows which way the others go, he goes there, that man. Smart Man goes to see it.*

After he walked where the people had been going to, he just goes over there. He was just tracking people which way they go to. Snow, I guess. He sees where people were sliding down, where they were sliding down. So he sees it. He sees that thing there, hard like this. It was a sharp thing, maybe iron I guess. It was kind of hard, maybe hard horn, I guess, not iron. It was horn, I guess. It sticks out there, and people just slide right into it. It just goes right into them, and afterwards they're dead.

Wolverine, it was Wolverine [who had put up the sharp stakes], *eating people. He talks just like a human too. That's the way he speaks, they say.*

After Smart Man saw that one there, he hid himself. And he makes himself a mooseskin [pouch]. . . . *He puts it inside his clothes. And he has*

* The people probably went downriver as far as Nuqwaik, where E. J. Glave sketched their fish camps in 1890 (see Chapter Four).

Marge Jackson

Marge Jackson is a Southern Tutchone Wolf from Haines Junction and Klukshu. Her mother, Maggie Jim, grew up in a traditional matrilineage house at Neskatahin, and she remembered the first visits there of Glave and Dalton. Here, Marge tells two episodes from the story of Smart Man (Beaver Doctor), mentioned in Chapter Eleven.

Marge Jackson, 1977

got that thing there, and it makes blood. [Smart Man pretends to get stuck on the stake, but he really runs the stake through a pouch filled with moose blood.]

So Wolverine comes back. That Wolverine Man, he is coming. He sees Smart Man. He says, Indian way, ''Someone is there again! Someone is there again!'' he says.

After, Wolverine Man goes over, and he picks him up. His [Wolverine's] *wife is with him too, I think; he is not alone.*

He goes back home. He packs him. He packs him, I guess. That Smart Man [pretends] *just like he's dead like.*

So that man [Smart Man] *gets a little loose* [the pack straps come loose] *and things like that, I guess. So that man* [Wolverine], *he pulls like this, he pulls like that, I guess. And he just gets mad after. Funny story, I just got to say it. They just say it's true.*

So Wolverine Man just keeps going. And after, he comes back to where his wife and kids are there. He comes back.

''Daddy brings back something again! Something to eat!''

So he looks, that Smart Man. He [Wolverine] *says to himself, ''I want that knife.'' And after they come back, Smart Man opens his eye like this to look for a stick. He wants to club those people, you know. He looks for a club. After, he* [Wolverine] *thinks to himself he wants one knife. It's lost like, you know. He can't find it. So that man, he just thinks that way.* [Smart Man, by his spirit power, prevents Wolverine from finding his knife.]

Finally they go to sleep. Smart Man opens his eye on one side, just one eye.

''Daddy,'' he [one of the children] *says. ''Look at that man. He opens his eye.''*

''Do you think you are going to open your eye when you got that thing in your body, that iron?'' (I don't know what that was, maybe horn, or something like that.)

So that Smart Man, he spots that hot burning stick. It is like a long pole, you know. It is a stick like for the campfires. Smart Man is going to grab that one.

So finally he grabs that one. He grabs that stick, and he just clubs them, you know. He clubs Wolverine's wife. He clubs that man's wife, and Wolverine too, both of them. He clubs [the] *kids too.*

Then after, that Wolverine's wife has got little ones inside ready to be born. They just come out from inside there. They just all come out and go right up a tree.

So that man builds a fire to burn that tree down. He can't burn it. As soon as he starts to burn that tree, the little wolverines just start in peeing. The fire goes out again. Smart Man can't do nothing. He starts to chop the tree down. These wolverines think to themselves, they say, ''I hope it just grows together again, just like healing, just like it comes back again same way again.'' And after he cuts it, the tree comes [back together] *the same way again. Smart Man keeps on doing that. He just keeps on, I don't know how long he tries that. He puts a fire on, and the same way again. They pee on it, put it out. Finally Smart Man gives up. He tells them, ''You are going to be the same size you are; only don't eat humans. Just live on somebody's cache.''*

▲ ▼ ▲

Well I'm going to tell you [about] *my oldest people, you know, that I used to know. In Champagne was a fellow named old John Jake. He was in old age when he died. He had flu in 1919, that one. The other fellow here, at Canyon you see his grave there. That's an old man, Wolverine John. There were pretty old man too around this country. They must have been 90 or 100 years old when they died.* [In the] *next village, Kloo Lake, two old man there. One was named Moose John, the other one named Lynx John.*

In Burwash, you know, that old Copper Joe was there. Jimmy Johnson was there. They're good people, never did any wrong, never tell anything on anybody. Not bad friends to a guy, those people.

Those days there now, they let you stay in the country and do what you like. And if you are travelling along there in their own country with a pack, you know, they let you trap there and stay there all you want. They don't say anything. Now today, well even if I stay here, they can't let me trap here. I got to have my own trapline. I build my house here, I stay here. My mother used to stay here before.

We had one good village down here [about] *35 miles from here, in a place named Hutshi. There were lots of people. It was the biggest village there before. All the people died off there. Only me, Harry Joe, and Moose Jackson* [are left]. *Oh, quite a few kids you know, Bessie Crow, all come out of there. All come out of Aishihik. We are all the same people, you know. . . .*

We stayed here now. Well, we make our own living here. Our people make their own living. They don't work [for wages]. *They trap here in the winter, everywhere around here. They make their own living. The government didn't help people in those days. You got your dog team. You got your own saddle horse. No car in those days. Not very long ago car comes around. All the cars started to come out around 1927. In Whitehorse, there used to be one or two old* [Model] *T Fords that come here first. The rest was horse teams, everything in Whitehorse. You know, when the train was coming in, there were those teams of horses. Two people have got teams of horses there. One was named Bob Low, and the other one was George Ryder. That's an oldtimer. And Tony Sears. They* [would] *give you job, cutting wood, sawmill wood. The government wouldn't give you job those days. Not even on the road. No, if you* [were] *Indian, no work. They sometimes give you job as woodcutters. But White Pass would give you a job too. No government jobs those days. In 1929, still* [just] *White Pass. Government won't give you a job till just now, not very long ago. Those days, nothing.*

So lot of people from Champagne go down to Whitehorse. [They] *go down to cut wood. They got their own team, the Indians from Whitehorse. Then about this time they always take off in the bush. I stay down there at Carmacks till winter. In fall, about October month, they come up to Champagne. They get groceries, stuff like that, for winter. Shells. Us, we don't see no white man. . . .*

Lots of people here don't work, you know, never been anywhere, never see the country because they stay in the bush all the time. But me, I got away from my people. When I was 15 years old, I was down at work already. . . . One time in one year, 1919, April maybe, I had two days' school. Fellow come from outside to the old log school and church in Champagne. They still stay yet. So I pick up a little bit. I know A, B, C, things like that. . . .

Solomon Charlie

Solomon Charlie, a Crow, grew up in the Champagne area and has worked all over the southern Yukon. He now has a house at Krak-R-Krik, where his mother and father lived earlier. Hutshi, which he mentions, is a place where no one lives now.

Solomon Charlie, Krak-R-Krik, 1986, with a model of a traditional Yukon Indian fish spear

WHAT THE KASKA SAID
AT UPPER LIARD, ROSS RIVER
AND ALONG THE CAMPBELL HIGHWAY

Timmy Stewart

Timmy Stewart, a Kaska, was born in 1904 at Liard Crossing and lives now at Upper Liard. He tells of the arrival of the first whites at Frances Lake.

The Hudson Bay people, the first ones, they come up from way down. . . . They come up the river there and walk right up to Frances Lake . . . and they make a little boat. They cross, go on the lake, and they found the island. They land there. Something on that tree. [They find a cache in a tree.]

Those people [the Indians at Frances Lake], *they never see no white people that time . . . and they* [the HBC men] *found this cache.*

Well, one guy, he climb up in that tree there, to look at it. He see nothing but that . . . snare there, you know, that sinew. They make a snare for rabbits [out of sinew], *and that axe made out of the rock, cached up in that tree, and mooseskin tent.*

Well, this Hudson Bay people don't know what to think about it. He think it was Indian do that. So he put everything in a pack and, same way again, he hung it up the same way there [with] *tea, some sugar, you see, tobacco . . . , axe or something, knife. . . .*

Oh yeah, they built a house. That's right, they built a house.

That Indian come back. By God, they look at those things. They see it. They don't know what it is. They don't know nothing about that what they got there. . . . They smell 'em . . . but they don't know what it is — tea. And pretty soon those Indians, they heard someone cutting over there. Someone, those white people, was cutting the logs, you know, build up the house.

Now they go out. They good people, I guess, so from long ways they watch 'em. They sneak in there, and everybody scared.

One old man, he say, ''Let me walk in, see what kind of people.'' And he look and watch. . . .

''That's the one. He cache everything for us,'' one guy says.

''Alright. Okay.''

One old man, he want to walk over.

''Well . . . could be an animal,'' he says.

And what's there, he don't know. He never see people there. He say, ''What kind of animal, this one here?'' . . .

Everybody, some of them, they hide people away, and then some of them go over there . . . and those white people, they laugh, oh they laugh and they say, ''Come on, come on.''

They don't understand what they talk about, you see. ''Come on! Come on!'' . . . And those Indians, they don't know what kind of people this.

. . . Finally they show them a gun. They don't want to take it. Maybe they get better, you know, but they can't understand them [at first]. *Can't even hear one word, you see. . . . So one guy, he show them.*

Bang!

The boys run away, see. One Hudson Bay guy, you know — the Indians just look at that man.

Bang!

''Go ahead. You try it.''

He put the shell in there again. . . . Never see that gun, you know. . . . Just hold this way. . . . That gun wouldn't go off!

308

And that store man, he tell them, ''Okay, hammer back, go ahead, your powder. . . . Pull 'em!''

They don't know. . . . But just one guy, I guess he pull the trigger. It take a long time to find out. They were used to arrows, those days. They don't know white people. . . .

Tobacco . . ,they think it's some kind of medicine, something, I guess. Just smell 'em, good enough. And pipe, they don't know what it's good for. Pipe and tobacco — they get it anyway, just look at it. they don't know what is that for.

They said it takes a long time before they learn something else to use, axe and some knife. They show that knife, and they cut something with it, and them Indian guys were watching. Well, they know how to use it now. The old knife, that knife, they forgot about it now; this one, they get it.

▲ ▼ ▲

If you don't know nothing, and you go in the bush long way, you going to starve. You've got to know how to catch anything before you go in the bush long ways. And then when you're in the bush, and you starve. And then you got to try everything. And then you're not going to starve. . . .

I tried lots of times. Nobody teach me. Just I see somebody do like this, when I'm young. I see people what they do. I copy, and then I do good. Anything. I set any kind of snare, gopher snares, rabbit snares, beaver snares, set fish net under the ice. I see people what they do, you know, the oldest ones — Big Bob and them — they do it. I see them, and then I do it. Lots of people, that's what they do. You know, they do things, and then I copy people. That's good, you know, that way. Some people, some kids, they don't do it. That's why they don't know anything. I see people cut meat, make dry meat, long time ago. I'm a kid that time. And then I copy the people. My cousin, that's what they do — they make dry meat. Some oldest one I see, they make it dry, and they go a long ways, you know. They go someplace sometime, and they got nothing to eat. And they get something and they make dry meat, and they made mooseskin. And sometime they catch rabbit. They dry it on their way. And gopher, beaver. In the springtime they hunt beaver, and they make beaver meat. Anything like that, I copy people. That's good that way. . . .

Long time ago people used to listen, but these white people, they bring that drink. Kids are no good now this time. People steal. It used to be they talked to the kids and they listen. Even past twenty, they listen. Now this time, nothing. They don't care about building houses, cutting wood, going hunting. They keep on thinking about drinking.

Around Pelly Banks people used to go hunting, go fishing, go trapping in wintertime. They come back when falltime is coming and make dry meat for wintertime. They get ready for trapping, make dry meat, fish, get everything ready for wintertime. Lots of kids, they stay one place wintertime, and go trapping in cold weather. Nothing bothers people. . . .

It used to be good, long time ago. All the people stayed where they had got traplines. Long time ago everybody went to where they had traplines. They think about trapping. That's all. They think about where they are going to go

Mary Charlie

Mary Charlie grew up along the upper Pelly River and in Watson Lake but now lives in Ross River. Her daughter, Dorothy Smith, translated from Kaska into English for her.

309

hunt, good places for moose, caribou. . . . That's what they do long time ago. But now this time, when we try to teach these kids, they just keep on drinking. . . . It used to be good. People could live. They make a little money; they buy things — shells — things like that — traps, fish nets, all the things they need. That was good.

The oldest people are the only ones who still do like that. They should teach those kids like that, take them in the bush and teach them how to set trap for beaver under the ice, set fish nets. That would be good that way.

▲ ▼ ▲

Dorothy Smith

Dorothy Smith, Mary Charlie's daughter, speaks of the problems at Ross River caused by the arrival of new ways and new people, and of the gulf between the old and the young.

Little kids don't hear stories so much. Just a few people still tell old stories. My little kids hardly understand the language. This is why people around here feel that they should teach it in the schools, because soon they won't understand at all.

The mine [at Faro] opened in 1966. It was really good before. In 1966 they opened the bar, and that's when all the trouble started. This is why [the Indians] don't want the pipeline, because it will be something like that again. When they first opened the mine, the men would be out of Ross during the summer doing work for the mining exploration. And then when the [white] men had days off they would come down here and just be all over in the village, get women drunk and stuff like that. But then one Indian guy was home, and he scared them off. And they stopped coming to the village then.

My mother remembers the way it was before when they put that [Canol] pipeline through. The army would chase Indian kids; it was bad.

I'd like my kids to know a bit of everything about the old ways, and I want for them to go to school. But I don't want them to learn all white ways of life. Because I think white ways of life make the Indians feel so small, as people to be looked down upon. This is one of the things I don't like my kids to learn. I'd like them to know and be proud of the ways my mother and our people lived because I think there is a lot that they could learn. How to make their own living and still be proud to be Indian.

▲ ▼ ▲

Tom & Tilly Smith

Tom and Tilly Smith were recorded at their woodcutting camp at Bruce Creek, on the Campbell Highway. One of Tom's grandfathers was from Fort Norman, but Tom himself was raised around Ross River. Tilly's parents were from Pelly Banks. Doris Bob translated the Smiths' Kaska into English and also took part in the discussion.

Tom: *Long time ago it is tough. We starve. We go hunt. Sometimes three days nothing to eat. I go hunt till I get moose. I snare rabbits. 1946, before that. I was fourteen years old, I learn to trap that time.*

A hundred miles from Pelly Banks, there was trading post. Long time ago. We hardly know [about it]. There were no moose too. No caribou — not very many. Rabbits can get smart too, because we starve. We set lots of snare for rabbits but they can't get snared.

Tilly: *The kids are hungry. They cry. The little kids. We get two rabbits. We cook it like that. They just drink it like that, my kids. Just cheap like that, they drink it like that, rabbit soup.*

We set fish nets. We can't catch fish too. Nothing.

Tom: *Every night we camp. Three days. We camp three days. Nothing. It's only in camp two fish, maybe three or four. People starve. Everything is hard to get.*

Tilly: *We were a long way from store too. Nothing to eat, just like that*

*now. My old man, he goes to the store. The kids are hungry. In one night he
just walks up there. In one night he comes back. We have nothing. Nothing.
Nothing to eat for the kids!*

Tom: *The store is maybe a hundred miles away, maybe ninety miles. In
summertime it is alright, but wintertime* [is hard]. *Summertime is good, see?
When the bears are growing up. Gopher and rabbits are easy to get,
groundhogs.*

Doris Bob: *But in wintertime it's hard for them to break a trail, to get
some meat. They get tired. They have no food.*

Tom: *We can get anything in summertime, fish.* [But in] *wintertime,
have to chop ice. It's hard, to set the net. Maybe deep ice, too deep.*

▲ ▼ ▲

*There were two girls sleeping. And they see two pretty, just like blue and red,
stars.*

"That's mine."

"That one's mine!"

After they keep on saying it, they go to sleep. And they come to sky.

They get up and look around and see the sky. [They married two men
there, who were really the blue and red stars. The men hunted and
brought back moose.]

"Look at grandma's moose skin," they say.

*They cut it up to little pieces. The ends, they tie. It just goes like that. And
then they put it down.* [The girls tied together strips of moosehide so
they could drop it down out of the sky to the earth.]

And they crawled down. They say, "Who is going to be first?" they say.

*"I am," the youngest girl says. And then the other girl crawls down. And
they get to that tree. They landed in a big tree* [and could not get down.]

*They say, "Look! Those guys walking around." Different animals were
passing under the tree. "That last guy* [walking around below the tree] *is
really crazy."*

Those girls say, "Go!" Something like that. They try to call him.

*That man, he just goes alongside of the tree. He looks up. He never saw
anybody* [before] *just crawling around a tree. He never goes* [away like the
others]. *He climbs up to those girls. He takes them down one by one. They
marry him. He has two funny stupid wives.*

They say, "Go kill moose!" He brings back rotten wood.

They say, "Let's run away!" After, they run away.

*After, they see that kind of bird that has got long skinny legs for their
bridge.* [They see a bird like a crane and cross the stream, using its legs
as a bridge.] *The* [girls] *then put those kind of things just like socks,
something* [like that], *around his legs.* [They tie garters on the bird's
legs.] *And they say* [to the bird], *"If that guy comes, say 'My leg hurts!'
After he says, 'Let me pass,' put out your other leg. If he is going across,
when he is right in the middle* [of the stream], *bend your knees so he falls
in!"*

The bird says, "Okay!"

The two sisters go. They [want to] *meet their mother.*

They were standing [there], *hiding away, watching what he does.*

Gayle Olsen

Bernice Tom and Gayle Olsen, both
from Ross River, were nine years old in
the summer of 1977, and both told
stories to the recording team. One of
Gayle's stories — a story many Yukon
girls used to learn — is about two girls
who married stars. Though Gayle did
not say so, in most versions of this story
the "crazy man" is a wolverine.

311

That crazy man comes. He says, ''What's that thing around your leg?''
[The bird] says, ''Those two girls give it to me, because my leg hurts.''
[The crazy man] says, ''Put the other leg across. I want to go across.''
Okay, he puts it across. And when the man is in the middle, you know,
he bends it. And the crazy man falls in the water. And he dies. The bird
doesn't even care. The man is just in the canyon. He dies there.

And then those two girls were free. And they go back to their mother. They
find her.

That's the end. I don't know the other part.

WHAT THE TAGISH SAID AT CARCROSS

Lucy Wren

Lucy Wren is a Dakl'aweidí woman of the Wolf moiety. She grew up speaking the Tagish language and learned Tlingit as well. Her first husband was an Inland Tlingit from Atlin. She now teaches Tlingit in the Yukon school language program.

Lucy Wren, at a performance with her students in the Tlingit Language Program, Carcross, 1984

You know, long time ago there was no water in the world, no water to drink.
And so this Crow is the one who steals water. He gets water. He wants to
make water in the world. There was just dry land, you know, no water.
There is only just one person that's got water — in the cellar. He's Loon. He's
got water in the cellar. He doesn't want anybody to touch it. It's just for
himself, that's all. So that Crow wants to steal that water so he can make
water in the world, so everybody can have water.

So he comes to this Loon. This Loon, he sits on top of his cellar, you know.
He sleeps on top, and he sits on top. And then nobody can touch it.

So this Crow, he comes to him. He just wants to look which way he's
going to steal that water. ''Okay,'' he said, ''I'll call that Loon my brother-
in-law.''

''I'm going to tell you a story, brother-in-law. I'll tell you good story!''
''Okay,'' Loon said. ''Okay.''

So Crow, he tells a story, tells a story, tells a story. For about two days or
three days, I guess, steady, he tells stories, you know. He doesn't give that
guy a chance to sleep.

So that guy is getting sleepy, you know. He didn't sleep while Crow was
telling stories. [Finally] he falls asleep on top of that cellar, and that Crow is
still telling him stories, stories.

And that Crow knows what to do. So he runs outside. And he's got dog's
poop out there. I don't know how he puts it on. He puts it on that guy there,
where he sleeps on his bed, you know.

He tells him, ''Brother-in-law, brother-in-law, get up! Get up! You dirty
yourself. You did too much!''

Oh, that Loon, he gets up, and he puts his hand. Then he knows. He gets
up, and he takes his blanket and all, and then he goes outside, you know, to
get clean.

As soon as that guy went outside, that Crow, he just jumps in that cellar.
He drinks the water. He drinks it and drinks it and drinks it. He drinks the
whole cellar dry!

By this time that Loon thought about his cellar of water, so he goes back in
the room. And the Crow has all that water already.

Just as soon as that Loon comes back in, the Crow just flies up and flies
away.

So that's how he steals water from that old man.

So he flies over the whole world, the whole world, you know. He just
drips one [drop of water] down. And every drip he makes, it turns to a lake,

the water. Some of them he spits fish in. That's why there are fish in the lakes.

That last one, he flies around for about two days you know. He gets all the water in the world. That last one, the water is getting sour in his mouth, you know. That one, he spit it out good. That one is salt water, they say. That's the one [that is] salt water. And that's how people got water. Before, there is no water, nothing, in the whole world. And Crow, he steals water.

▲ ▼ ▲

Okay, my dad, my dad Shakoon, he tells us this story when we are kids like my little boy there — teenagers.

So this Crow came down to salt water. This Crow, he goes around. And this Crow comes to an old lady who was staying by the salt water. She gets fish, you know. Saltwater fish, salmon, things like that, you know.

And this Crow comes. Gee, he was hungry! He can't get any fish, you know. That Crow can't get any salmon.

So he comes to this old lady staying there. He tears her blouse off, you know, and he scratches her back.

"You're going to give me some salmon!"

He tells her to holler at the salt water, "Tide go down!"

"Say, 'Tide go down!'"

Oh, that old lady there, she just hollers. She says, "Tide go down!" And the tide goes down, and he sees the fish. And Crow goes down there.

Poor old lady, she just suffers when Crow scratches on her back! He gets all the fish. And Crow goes "Caw!" and flies away.

Oh boy, I tell [my] daddy, "You are a Wolf. What does the wolf say when the crow flies away?" I say, "The wolf cries." I say, "A wolf can't fly, but Crow does!" . . .

It's okay if you are a Crow and your husband is Wolf. You get married. . . . Two Crows, they can't get married. They are [first] cousins or something [and] they can't be brothers-in-law. . . . But these days, young girls, you don't know, they just go. They don't know if [they are] Crow or Wolf these days.

WHAT THE INLAND TLINGIT SAID AT TESLIN

In the old days, the white people, oldtimers like us, they use very, very easy words, not the hard words like you people got. This time, when the whites start to speak, there is a lot of words I can't understand now. It is too hard for us. And therefore when they make a meeting, they use hard words, and we can't understand them. If we understand them, some of us, we will stand up and start to speak what we think is right to talk about. But we can't understand it. . . .

I'm going to tell you a story about Porcupine and Beaver. They used to be best of friends [partners]. Porcupine and Beaver, they used to be best friends. In the Indian language we call our best friends ax shaaw. And finally they started to talk to each other, about how they take this, how they are going to make out.

Irene Isaac

Irene Isaac is a G̲aanax̲teidí Crow. Her mother spoke Southern Tutchone, and her father, from Marsh Lake, spoke Tlingit, but Irene was born in Carcross, which is a Tagish settlement, and the story she tells here is well known to all older Tagish people.

Tom Peters

Tom Peters was a long-time Teslin resident, though he often used to go up to the Pelly River with his family. His father's people were from Dawson, which is where he was raised, but he was a Tlingit speaker, and in 1977 he was head of the Deisheetaan clan of the Crow moiety at Teslin. Here he tells a story about Porcupine and Beaver. Although Tom did not mention it, many oldtimers who tell the story say that, because Beaver and Porcupine

313

became such bad friends, the Yukon Indians never used to cook beaver and porcupine meat together nor say any of the Indian names for beaver where a porcupine could hear them, or for porcupine where a beaver could hear them. There is a song with the story, and oldtimers sing it to bring on cold weather.

And Beaver asked Porcupine, ''How many months do you think there are going to be?''

''Well, you see my tail,'' Beaver says. ''How many marks are on it? How many marks are on it?''

There must be pretty near 200 marks on his tail.

''One year, there are going to be this many months,'' says Beaver.

''Ha, ha, ha'' says Porcupine. ''Ah, a<u>x</u> *shaaw, I feel you made a mistake! I ask you for [just] one year's months!''*

I don't know how many toes he used to have, Porcupine, but he put up [his foot] *like this. ''There's going to be too many'' he says. ''I'm going to cut this one off.'' He throws off this, and he throws off this. Porcupine threw a toe off of each of his front feet.* [Now Porcupine has only four toes on his front feet. He meant that winter should be only four months long.]

''Twelve months in the year!'' Porcupine says. ''Look there, look at that timberline,'' he says.

Beaver looks at it.

[Porcupine says,] *''Oh yes, that's food too, up at that timberline. I don't mind if* [winter is] *a hundred months a year, I'm going to live. But look at you. The outfit you got in there, that little house building. You can't stay out in the wintertime, in the open. I'm sorry for you.''*

''A<u>x</u> *shaaw, now* [you] *give me a mind to think about it, I think twelve months is the best,''* [says Beaver].

And then they talk so much to each other. [They argue over how many months long the seasons should be.]

And finally there's an island, I don't know how far, and Beaver says he wants to go to his house. . . .

''A<u>x</u> *shaaw,'' he says, ''let's try to go to that house.''*

''Ah, it's too far'' Porcupine says.

''No'' Beaver says, ''I'm going to pack you.''

Beaver swims over there. Beaver tells Porcupine, ''You get on my back.''

And so Porcupine, he get on Beaver's back. And they swim straight, a long way out. They are pretty near shore. That Beaver, he tries to get the best of his partner. He packs that Porcupine over there at that time. He has got some trees and some willows.

''I'm going to leave you here. I'm going to go back to the shore.''

I guess that Porcupine, he knows what Beaver is thinking about. He never says anything.

Beaver just gets in the water, and he starts to swim back.

And that Porcupine, he says he doesn't know how long he will stay there. He started to eat all those trees, the bark. He cleans everything up. And then he starts on the willows, the bark. He never eats like a moose, you know. He just eats the bark [not twigs and leaves].

And finally, they say, he has nothing to eat.

It's the middle of the summer. ''Well, how am I going to make out?'' he thinks, the Porcupine. ''It's a long way to swim. I'm not going to make it,'' he is thinking, ''if I ever try to swim over there.''

His friend there, he never comes back to get him.

Finally that Porcupine, he figures he's going to try to make medicine for himself. He's going to try to make medicine for cold weather.

And then this Porcupine started singing. [Tom sings and hits the drum]. *That's his song, Porcupine's. The same night a northern wind started blowing. He was singing about a north wind. Oh, I don't know how many degrees below that time, might be sixty! In the morning when he wakes up, he starts to go around. All the way around and across that lake is frozen. He puts up his tail, and he starts to go across to the mainland.*

He meets his friend Beaver. Beaver says, ''Ah, ha ha, a<u>x</u> shaaw, you came, eh?''

''Yes.''

''How did you make out?'' Beaver asks.

''Oh, not bad,'' he says.

Finally the Porcupine tells him, ''A<u>x</u> shaaw, let's go up in the tree,'' he says. ''A big tree.''

''No,'' Beaver says, ''I don't know how to climb a tree,'' he says.

''Oh, it's all right,'' Porcupine says, ''get on my back I'll take you up the tree!''

Yah, Beaver gets on the Porcupine's back there. He puts his hand around him like that. He starts to go up. They come right to the point [of the tree].

''You sit down in there for a while,'' Porcupine tells Beaver.

There are some limbs in there, two limbs like that. Beaver, he starts to sit down in there.

''I'm hungry, a<u>x</u> shaaw. I'm going to eat,'' says Porcupine.

Porcupine left the Beaver way up at the point of that tree. And then the Porcupine starts to chew that bark, off all these trees. Finally, it comes like this. the tree looks like a straight pole. He chews all of those limbs that stick out, he chew them out. And that tree sticks up like this, like a flagpole.

Beaver tried to look down. ''Hey, don't go away!''

Porcupine evens up with his friend, for what he did it to him, taking him way out on the island and just leaving him there.

They never ask help from each other either.

Porcupine never asks Beaver to help, to give him a little hand.

Well, he's got him on his mind, I think, that Beaver. He stays up there. He decides to go down, and finally he tries, I think. I don't know how many days he stayed up there.

And then that Beaver, he tried to go down. He tried the whole day. He tried to hold that tree like that I think, and then he starts to slip down. Before he goes half way, they say, he falls off, right to the ground. Well, Porcupine evens things up.

Another old story that Tom Peters told concerns a wolf who married an Indian girl. The story is somewhat like that about the girl who married a bear.

One time here, there was a wolf, you know, a wolf. It's something like a person in the old days.

Well one time, they say — that is, in the old, old days — they say there is a girl whose daddy has forgot his knife someplace. No guns that time, just the arrow. And you can't waste the meat that much in those days. You have to save everything.

Tom Peters, Teslin, 1966. (The treasured Deisheetaan Beaver shirt worn here by Tom Peters was worn fifteen years earlier by Jake Jackson. See the photo on page 183.)

And the man sends his daughter back. They got a camp there too [where the father left the knife].

And she runs back, and she comes to the place where they used to kill the moose. They had left some meat there. And she looks for it, and she gets the knife. I don't know where she found the knife.

And then she starts to go home, that girl. She doesn't go very far, they say. It's just a little ways till home. And she sees a very bush-looking boy. He was naked and pretty young. You see, it didn't look any different than a person, a regular person.

And he asks this girl to stay with him.

"No," she says.

He keeps on asking her.

"No, I can't do it."

"Okay," he says.

And finally she got beat. She got beat, I think, and finally that girl tells him, "Let's go and see my dad and my mother before I go with you."

"Oh, that's okay. We are going to go back," he says.

"Well, we have meat." That girl has meat.

But this wolf, he never changes. He never looks any different than a person. She likes him too, I think. Yah, he's a nice looking boy!

They started to go. They say they just go a little ways, they say. And they step over a windfall, about two, three different places. She thought it was a windfall, that girl, but it was a mountain. Just that quick they go over the mountain three places. But she still did remember where she had her home, that girl, but the wolf can't let her go.

And finally they come to a big camp. There's a lot of people with them. They come over there. She looks around at those people there. She doesn't know what people they are. But anyway, there are some people.

"Well, son," they say. "You bring somebody, a stranger here."

"Yes."

"Are you going to keep her?" they say.

"Yes."

And they give them a good place, just like this house we got here. I don't think they have any rooms in them days, just an open place, but the people sleep right around that building with a great big fire in the middle.

And then after they came there, oh, they go around. They go hunting sometimes.

And the brothers and the sisters of that wolf, the one the girl stays with, his sisters go around with the girl all the time up in the mountains. They snare gophers, things like that. That's the way the people used to do it.

And finally they come back. They come home. They say they had a trail, like we got a trail around here. They follow the trail, they say, those girls, that husband's sisters, the ones who go around with her. And they say they see her all the time when they go. They come through there.

And she sees somebody is staying over there. It's an old lady, just by herself. And they tell her, these girls tell her, "You see this person who lives over there?"

She tells them, "Yes."

"Don't go close to her, and don't talk to her," they tell her.

Well, I don't know how long she was out. She was there pretty nearly two years. Finally she had a little kid.

Finally they go out to hunt gophers again, and they come back. And this girl was just thinking about how when they come by there, she was always there, that old lady. She looks out all the time, just wherever the girl is walking, the lady looks at her all the time when she goes by. I don't know how many times she did it.

They come around. Finally they start to go. She tells those girls, ''Say, you girls, you follow me too much all the time when we are setting snares. I'm going to go by myself,'' she says.

And they tell her, ''Okay.''

She has got her on her mind, that old lady that lives on the trail there. And so she went. She just goes up that way, but she makes a circle around. She comes to that old lady. By gosh, as soon as she goes in there, that old lady starts to speak to her. ''Why have you come here? Where's your daddy and your mother?'' she asked her. That's her auntie, that girl's auntie, and they have been missing her for pretty near four or five years. She goes the same place where that girl walked. They say it's not a person, they say, she stays with. A mouse is with her.

[The old lady] says, ''That's the wolf people. It's the same thing. They [the mouse people] take me away,'' she says. ''But I can't do anything for myself now,'' she says. ''But you are only a young girl.'' (I think she's got a kid already, that girl.)

And so the lady tells her, ''You go back home. You try to go to the place where you live.''

And that girl thinks, ''I don't know how I'm going to make it!'' The lady gives her a piece of meat, about that much, gopher meat. And she gave her feathers, about that long.

''You know the place where you stay when you sleep? You take off [from there]. Don't you sleep. They are not going to let you go. It's a different kind of thing, that wolf. They have something like they know where you walk.'' She gives her feathers.

''When you sleep,'' she says, ''You put the feathers under your pillow, across this way. And where is your home,'' she says, ''it's going to point that [way] over there [to your home]. And you are going to go the same way! And that gopher . . .''

She [the girl] has got two gophers. She [the old lady] puts them on their sides. The lady tells her, ''Don't eat them up! . . . Take the heads of those gophers. Put them on their sides, and that food will come out of it. When you start to get short of it, you are going to have another one. And something else I'll give it to you.''

And the lady gave her moccasins, and the moccasins never get worn out.

''Try to go as far as you can,'' she tells her.

Finally the old lady says, ''Eh, no more! And tell your husband, 'I'm going to run my snares as far as I can. I'm going to go around the mountain. I'm going to set some more snares.' That's not a camp you stay in. You stay right in the wolf den,'' she says.

The girl sleeps on that wolfskin robe. That fur is just a wolf skin, that's the one the girl sleeps on there. They cover themselves.

[The auntie says,] "*In the morning as soon as daylight breaks you try to pull that thing* [that wolf skin] *out and put it around yourself, and then you going to see it, when you look around yourself.*"

And so the girl did. She pulled the skin down a little bit and started to look around. Wolves just covered around whole place! That one that is her husband is just about that far away. She closed her eyes again.

In the morning she starts to take off. She goes by her . . .auntie, and she tells her she's going now. Then [her auntie gives her something with water inside].

For three days the girl goes. Then she hears this wolf. He's coming out there. Don't you ever think they don't go a long ways. They can't give up, if they go after you, those wolves!

[The girl's auntie had told her,] "*If that wolf gets right close to you, you take this thing that I got with this water inside. Throw it behind you, and start to go. And that wolf will get just this close to you.*"

And the girl threw that water behind her, and this great big lake came right over the land. She doesn't go very far when the wolf comes up, and she sees him at the end of that lake, that way — I don't know how far. That kid sure goes long ways!

One time, they say, it started to snow. It was falltime. Well she doesn't have any more things to use if that wolf catches up.

Finally, she does not know how far she goes, when that wolf goes right around the lake and gets on her track, and starts to track her. Then he is behind again. The girl climbs up on the tree. She is shaking way up there. All those wolves come up, under that big tree there. Lots!

They say she stays up that tree about three days. The wolves try to get up it, they say, but they can't make it. Finally they start to go back. Those wolves, they give up.

The girl starts to holler, starts to holler. Finally she comes down. Snow about that deep. She didn't know it, you see, but she comes pretty close to that place where her daddy used to live in the falltime. It looks like she comes pretty close, but she doesn't have anything to eat, and she's got that little boy too.

And the father, he comes to the place where there is a real big tree. The snow was deep for two weeks anyway. The father doesn't know where she is.

She comes right up and she sees the tracks; she just comes right up there and starts to look out for them. That man is her brother. That's her father's family.

"Who are you?" her brother asks her.

She says, "That's me! You used to see me. You see I have that little baby too. You tell my mother," she says, "to come and meet me."

He went and told her.

"I don't know what I see over there. It looks like it's my sister," he tells his mother. "You try to go over there to see too."

She doesn't believe him, but she starts to pack up. She started, the girl's mother. Sure enough! She sees that's her daughter.

And that kid there, that kid [the girl's baby], *they say that he grows fast. Finally he's big. When he's a little bigger he starts to hunt. He starts to go hunting. He goes just a little ways and he kills game.*

That's why the wolves, you're not supposed to make fun out of them. A wolf is something like a person, they say. They hate somebody talking about them. Well, there is no song for that one, though. It's just a story. Well, I tell you, and I'm finished.

▲ ▼ ▲

The war broke out, September 10th. And then the army comes in and starts building the highway, the roads.

That time I don't have a job; there [are] no jobs anyway. I start working on the road, cutting timbers. They had a sawmill, cutting lumber for houses and mining camps. Quite a thing to see, that time, when the first army was coming through Carcross. You know that airport in Carcross? There were tents all over there, army tents, and hundreds of people!

I went to work for White Pass in 1941 or 1942. That time you only get $70 a month. But that was good money then. Everything was cheap then. A can of corned beef cost 35¢. Now [it costs] $1.90. One pound of tea 50¢, coffee 75¢, Twenty pounds of sugar was $2.

My parents were getting $20 a month from the government — rations, you know. That was enough. They had everything. A dollar would buy a big bag of dried fruit this full.

Fur wasn't so high then. . . . Mink was $12, a real good price. Lynx that time was $15 to $25 — $25 for big pelt, like that.

▲ ▼ ▲

And there was another way to settle the troubles between the Indian people, you know. If one of my people kills a man from another tribe [clan], some of my people have to be killed, or settle it somehow. That's what we call the peace dance.

When they going to settle that trouble between two tribes, they have songs. Something like this it goes. ''When you have a rock, and you drop it in a deep place in the lake, you never see that rock again.''

Well, that's the way this song goes. The trouble, it's settled once and for all, and nobody has to mention it again. It's got to be forgotten.

That's the way they used to settle the trouble, no more to remember it. If I kill your brother, your people have to kill my brother too. But sometimes they settle it a peaceful way. They pay hundreds and hundreds of dollars for the damage they made. That's the way they used to work it.

▲ ▼ ▲

In 1965 I went to Vancouver vocational school to learn carpentry. Once we came back, George Sidney and I start building houses. Before we go to Vancouver we don't know anything about carpentering. After we came back it sure makes a lot of difference. When we going to cut rafters we don't have to climb up there to do the measuring up there. We just pick up the carpenter rafters and plane it square and read the numbers. We'd cut the rafters on the ground, and nail them together and hand it to them guys up there. And it sure fits, no mistake. We sure would like to see a lot of younger people take up training in any course they want. Because I know, I learn quite a lot from vocational school. . . .

Geoffrey Sheldon

Geoffrey Sheldon is a Wolf. His father's people were from the coast, and he lived in several different places in the Inland Tlingit country — at Hundred Mile on the Teslin River, Squanga Lake, Carcross and elsewhere — before settling in Teslin. He tells about prices, jobs and wages in the 1940s, when the money economy was still a relatively new thing in the Yukon.

Frank Sidney

Frank Sidney is headman of the Teslin Dakl'aweidí. He has worked as a big game outfitter and has served as elected chief of Teslin. His father, a Gaanax.ádi man of the Crow moiety, came to the Yukon from Juneau about the time of the 1898 Gold Rush. He speaks here of a peace dance of the kind mentioned in Chapter Ten.

Moses Jackson

Moses Jackson is the son of a Tlingit couple who moved to the Yukon from the Alaska coast before the Gold Rush of 1898 and stayed in the country. He belongs to the New Yanyeidí clan of the Wolf side. His father was headman of the Kóokhittaan clan of the Crows.

I sure would like to see the kids that are growing up right now [get training in hunting and trapping too]. *When you take them out in the bush, they are just greenhorns. Some of them, they don't even know how to make fire. I remember I took some out hunting, and they talked and laughed. They don't even know how to hunt. Well in the old days that's where I learned from the old people. See, the way you could look at it now — they learn* [only] *so much, and then some never even finish their education, and they drop out. So they are just in between. They aren't good enough to go get a decent job. . . .*

Well, myself, I learn trapping and hunting from the old people. I teach my kids what I know, and they are pretty good. I teach my Jane how to set snares for gophers. She uses anything with strength. She catches it. When I first start catching gophers, and we singe them over the fire, it looks funny to those kids, I think. The gophers look like pups. They tell us, ''Mom and dad, you eat gophers first!''

▲ ▼ ▲

George Sidney

George Sidney was a Dakl'aweidí man of the Wolf side. His grandfather Jim Sidney taught him to hunt and trap in the 1920s.

Many years ago when we live, [when] *our grandpas* [live] *. . . by this July, towards the end of July, we used to go back trapping from Teslin. I had only a month and a half of going to school. That's all the education I got, we don't need much education those days. We all go back trapping. Trapping, that's the main part in 1932, '28.*

The first time I start trapping was with my grandpa. The first I remember was 1924 when I was going out trapping. It was a beaver hunt, special.

Come summer, we come down here and I go to school. After a month, a month and a half, we have to go back trapping. Already [we have to start] *to the trapline, overland. That's the only way we get our supplies to where we trap. The dogs pack — twelve dogs, fourteen dogs, sometimes. They pack forty, fifty pounds to a pack. Flour, cereal, some dry stuff, and especially* [a] *can of malt for grandpa. Those days I don't drink, me.*

My grandpa, he shows me how to hunt, how to get some meat for the winter, and how to fish. My grandpa put the nets in the water where we trap. He puts nets across the river. And they used to use a canvas boat and gets lots of fish. They dried it for a winter, for the dog team. That way grandpa doesn't have to hunt for fresh meat. They dry up all the dog feed. [They get] *meat, moose meat, grease.*

And in 1928 fox is a good price. Cross fox was worth over $600 or $400. In 1930 prices come up more. That time outside there was a depression. I never know anything about it.

After that I went to start building the road, the highway. In 1930 my grandpa died. They bring him all the way from Wolf Lake, his body, and bury him right here.

During the war, 1940, 1939, I work in the airport, for 75¢ an hour, ten hours a day. After, when I had been working there for six months, planes landed.

After that we start to slow down on trapping, I work odd jobs. My first job was as prospector. Then in 1947, I go for horse wrangler. [The pay] *was $7 a day. But in those days it's high, good wages!*

320

1948 I start to guide for the big game outfitter, Johnny Johns. 1949 I come to be a chief guide for Mike Nolan. Ever since, I start to get good pay. $10 a day for chief guide was good in 1949.

From there I stay going for chief guide, but only three months [of the year], and I get odd jobs in between. I cut wood for $5 a cord. . . . I cut the wood, and in between times, I do snowshoes in the winter when I have spare time. When we have shorter days and longer nights, I get lonesome sitting around, so I work on snowshoes.

▲ ▼ ▲

So, olden days people used to be good people. Used to have really respect for each other. Used to get along good, just like they were one sister and one brother. In olden days, before the white people came, we didn't try to go against each other wherever we met each other, even on our trapgrounds. We used to get along good. And we didn't try to own just one place you know. But this time we try to be against each other, even with our food.

We used to be ready for winter, and that way we could get our food. We looked after it really good. We didn't waste things. This time white people can fish, and they waste it. They kill things, just for nothing sometimes. But we don't look after things like that, us Indians. We still hold up our traditions. We try to carry them on as much as we can, us oldtimers. There are just a few around here now. But the younger people, they don't care.

Us, my old man and I, we still go out in the bush. We get our food for winter. We trap — and my son, he still carries on in the oldtimers' way having fun. He dances with oldtimer clothes from way back from our people, from my side. He still carries it on. . . .

▲ ▼ ▲

There was a hunter went out with his guide one time. This was back thirty years ago. And this hunter wanted this grizzly. They saw it on the sidehill, and it was quite a ways over from them — straight across.

So this guide — he was kind of an elderly person — he says, ''Well let's go up straight across here to get that grizzly bear.'' And the hunter argued with him, ''Why do we have to go straight across?'' Then this guide asked him, ''Do you see that big rock across there?''

Knowing exactly where that bear [was], where that animal was going to pass through, he took him to that big rock where that bear was supposed to come through. They went over there, and they waited. And sure enough, just like it had been led, the bear went right below that place, right exactly where that guide said it was going to go. And they killed that grizzly bear right there.

That hunter was amazed, because there were lots of other places it could have gone. It could have even turned back, but that guide knew exactly where that bear would go, even the time. He said, ''By 3:30 that bear will have crossed beyond that big rock, because,'' he says, ''that's the time they go down to bed down.'' And he knew where that bear would bed down.

There's so many things that the native person knows — exactly where an

Rosie Johnston
Rosie Johnston is a Deisheetaan Crow, and her husband David is headman of the New Yanyeidí Wolves at Teslin. Their ancestors came up the Taku River from Alaska.

Virginia Smarch
Virginia Smarch, a Dakl'aweidí Wolf, gave this book its title.

Virginia Smarch, Teslin, 1978

animal should be at a certain time of the day, or where they might be at feeding time, or different things like that.

That's why I don't hesitate to say an old native person is part of the land, part of the water, because when they used to go around in this country they didn't stay in one place long enough to make such a mess. And they're always saving. I've seen places where they've had winter cabins with a dry tree maybe standing right outside the doorway. Just because it was handy, they didn't chop it down. When they left that tree standing there, it was for when they really needed it. They were always people that were saving. They never thought, ''Well, there's an animal. I'm going to kill it.'' They had to have a need for that animal before they killed it. They never killed anything just for the sport of killing, because in their ways that was wasteful. And they believed strictly in that — that they had to treat their animal spirits right, or else they would go without.

There were lots of things like that that I learned growing up in the environment I was in. And the different signs they used to go by was really something. But you don't hear too much about it today. Like my kids, I'll tell them, ''Well, it's no good to do this.'' They want to know why.

In my times, we didn't ask the reasons why. We just did as we were told. We never asked what were the reasons or anything.

But today, these kids, they want to know the reason why. It was never explained to us, so there was no way we could explain something either. So that's the way they learned — by doing, not by asking what's wrong with it if they didn't do it.

And a lot of them worked by signs. . . . I don't know what they call them, the scientists nowadays. But those older people [read the signs]. *I think ''signs'' is the closest I can come to it, because I've tried. . . .*

A great many people have helped to make this book a reality. I have tried to list here and on the title page the major contributors to this book, but many others have helped too, and I give my deepest thanks to each one of them. I hope that all who have been involved with this volume in any way will feel rewarded in part by finally having it in hand.

James Fall wrote a preliminary version of the material in Chapters Two and Seven and parts of Chapters Eight and Nine. Janice Sheppard wrote an early version of what is now Chapters Ten and Eleven. From their notes and the tapes, Fall and Sheppard selected most of the texts making up Chapter Twelve. As explained in the preface, Lucy Birckel and Carol McCarthy worked with Fall and Sheppard in making the tapes. In 1977, Jeffrey Hunston and Steven Walsh, both then with the Council for Yukon Indians, provided substantial data for use in Chapters Three and Five, and Walsh wrote a preliminary version of the last incident in Chapter One. John Ritter of the Yukon Native Language Centre gave much helpful advice for Chapter Six and assisted with the spelling and identification of many terms and names used elsewhere in the book. Marlyn Horsdal gave early editorial advice. Funding was provided by the Yukon Department of Education and the Council for Yukon Indians.

Here is a list of people in the various parts of the Yukon who gave texts or in other ways offered their help and hospitality to members of the teams taping material for the book in 1977. There was not enough space to print texts from all these contributors, but all did contribute to the book.

Burwash Landing: Grace Chambers, Copper Lily, Mary Easterson, Louis Jacquot, Mary Jacquot, Jessie Joe, Rita Joe, George John, Agnes Johnson, Grace Johnson, Lena Johnson, Jessie Johnson, Sam Johnson, Sandy Johnson, Smokey Sheldon.

Carcross and Tagish: John Atlin, Irene Isaac, Stanley James, Johnny Johns, Agnes Johns, Peter Johns, Peter Johns Jr., Dan Johnson, Vic Johnson, Darla Lindstrom, Angela Sidney, Daisy Smith, Jimmy Tizya, Ann Wally, Evelyn White, Lucy Wren.

Carmacks: Lorraine Allen, Eva Billy, George Billy, Jessie Jonathan, Mary Luke, Taylor McGundy, May Roberts, Evelyn Skookum, Happy Skookum, Susie Skookum, Clarence Smith, Lily Washpan.

Dawson: Edgar Russel, Mary McLeod, Stanley Roberts, Joe Susie Joseph Walter DeWolfe, Joe Henry, Elsie and Charlie Johnson.

Acknow-ledgements

Haines Junction, Klukshu and Champagne: Bessie Allen, Jack Allen, Bessie Crow, Mary Daguerre, Barbara Hume, Elsie Isaac, Sophie Isaac, Marge Jackson, Maggie Jim, Frank Joe, Harry Joe, Jessie Joe, Francis Joe, Kiddie Joe, Dixon John, Bessie Kane, Lily Kane, Parton Kane, Annie Sam Nicholas, Lena Smith, Mary Smith, Sam Williams, Vera Williams.

Krak-R-Krik: Annie Charlie, Solomon Charlie.

Mayo: Edwin Hager, Mary Hager, Lonny Johnny, Persis Kendi, Cal Lindstrom, Shirley Lindstrom, Johnson Lucas, Liza Malcom (Eagle, Alaska), Mary Moses, Norman Moses, Catherine Olin, Ellen Olin, Lucy Peter, Sam Peter, Edwin Simon (Elsa), Jennie Simon, Margaret Simon (Elsa), Roy Wilson (Pelly Crossing).

Old Crow: Albert Abel, Sarah Chitze Abel, Robert Bruce Jr., Alice Frost, Clara Frost, Eliza Ben Kassi, Myra Kyikavichek [Myra Kay], Martha Kendi, Peter Lord, Gordon Marsh, Neil McDonald, Myra Moses, Hannah Netro, Joe Netro, Dick Nukon, Martha Tizya, Moses Tizya, Len Vickars.

Pelly Crossing: Jennie Alfred, Jessie Alfred, Johnny Alfred, Julius Hager, Lizzie Hager, Lois Joe, Victor Mitander, David Silas, Clara Silverfox, Ellen Silverfox, Johnny Tom Tom, Rachel Tom Tom.

Ross River: Doris Bob, Mac Bob, Pam Lee Bob, Doreen Charlie, Mary Charlie, Paul Charlie, Frank Dick, Margaret Dick, Joe Dick, Mary Dick, Allan Dickson, Liza Dickson, Helen Etzel, Couscon Glada, Tsetl'elé' Glada, David Glada, Julia Glada, Clifford McLeod, Rosie Ollie, Gayle Olsen, Hazel Peter, Mac Peter, Alex Shorty, Elsie Shorty, Dorothy Smith, Ceda Smith, Jim Smith, Tilly Smith, Tom Smith, Betty Souza, Margaret Thompson, Bernice Tom, Grady Tom.

Stewart Crossing: Dave Moses, Bob Martin (Mayo), Tommy Harper.

Teslin: Terry Dickson, Lillian Fox, Louis Fox, Allison Jackson, Maggie Jackson, Moses Jackson, Robert Jackson, Cheryl Jackson, Robert Lee Jackson, Mary Joe, Mabel Johnston, David Johnston, Rosie Johnston, Frank Morris, Frank Peters, Tom Peters, Geoffrey Sheldon, Frank Sidney, George Sidney, Lena Sidney, Georgina Sidney, Florence Smarch, Jack Smarch, Jane Smarch, Virginia Smarch, Watson Smarch, Bouson Smith, Lucky Smith, Maude Smith.

Watson Lake and Upper Liard: Lila Brown, Lorna Carlick, David Dick, Mary Dick, John Dickson, Julia Dickson, Clara Donnessey, Carol Edzerza, Lizzie Edzerza, Arnold Frank, Thomas Frank, Little Jimmy, Johnson Jules, Helen Kirk, Dan Lutz, Dixon Lutz, George Miller, Marilyn Moon, Charlie Porter, Lucy Porter.

Whitehorse and Lake Laberge: Ronald Bill, Rosie Bill, George Dawson, Violet George, Frankie Jim, Celia Jim, Drury McGundy, Helen McGundy, Mazie McLeod, John Shorty, Scurvy Shorty, Kitty Smith.

I also wish to thank Terry Alldritt, Harry Allen, Gloria Barsnese, Paul Birckel, Donald W. Clark, Julie Cruikshank, Bill Ferguson, Maralyn Horsdal, Linda Johnson, Jack Meek, Anne Tayler, Dietmar Tramm and Tish Woodley for their help in bringing the book to fruition.

Of the many published sources consulted, only a few of the most important are listed here:

Campbell, Robert. *Two Journals of Robert Campbell (Chief Factor, Hudson's Bay Company), 1808–1853*. John W. Todd, ed. Seattle. 1958

Coates, Kenneth. "Best Left as Indians": Government-Native Relations in the Yukon Territory, 1894–1950. *Canadian Journal of Native Studies*. Fall 1984.

Cruikshank, Julie. *The Stolen Women: Female Journeys in Tagish and Tutchone Narrative*. Ottawa. 1983

Cumming, Peter A., & Neil H. Mickenberg. *Native Rights in Canada*. 2nd ed. Toronto. 1972

Greer, Sheila C., & R. J. Leblanc. Yukon Culture History: An Update. *The Musk-Ox* 33. 1983

Helm, June, ed. *Handbook of North American Indians*, vol 6: *Subarctic*. Washington, D.C. 1981

Honigmann, John J. *The Kaska Indians: An Ethnographic Reconstruction*. New Haven, Conn. 1954

Karamanski, Theodore J. *Fur Trade and Exploration: Opening the Far Northwest, 1821–1852*. Norman, Okla. 1983

McCandless, Robert G. *Yukon Wildlife: A Social History*. Edmonton. 1985

Morlan, Richard E. *The Later Prehistory of the Middle Porcupine Drainage, Northern Yukon Territory*. Ottawa. 1973

Osgood, Cornelius. *Contributions to the Ethnography of the Kutchin*. New Haven, Conn. 1936. Reprinted 1970

Osgood, Cornelius. *The Han Indians: A Compilation of Ethnographic and Historical Data on the Alaska-Yukon Boundary Area*. New Haven, Conn. 1971

Slobodin, Richard. *Band Organization of the Peel River Kutchin*. Ottawa. 1962

Tanner, Adrian. *Trappers, Hunters and Fishermen*. Ottawa. 1966

Workman, William B. *Prehistory of the Aishihik-Kluane Area, Southwest Yukon Territory*. Ottawa. 1978

Wright, Allen A. *Prelude to Bonanza: The Discovery and Exploration of the Yukon*. Sidney, B.C. 1976

Many further sources are listed in Volume Six of the *Handbook of North American Indians,* edited by June Helm (cited above) and in the Yukon Bibliography Updates, published since 1973 by the Boreal Institute for Northern Studies, University of Alberta, Edmonton.

C. McC.

Index

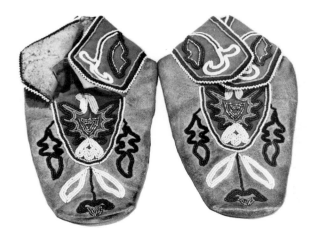